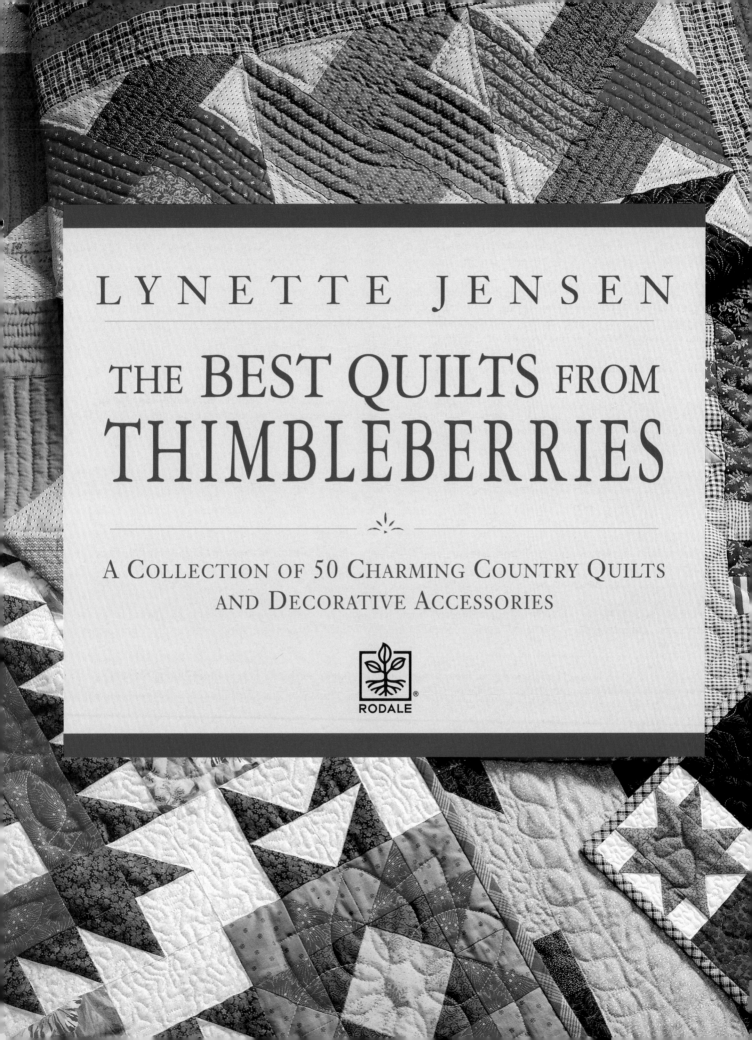

LYNETTE JENSEN

THE BEST QUILTS FROM THIMBLEBERRIES

❧

A COLLECTION OF 50 CHARMING COUNTRY QUILTS
AND DECORATIVE ACCESSORIES

RODALE

Printed in the United States of America
Rodale Inc. makes every effort to use acid-free (∞), recycled paper (♺).

Cover Designer: Christopher Rhoads
Cover and Interior Photographer: Mitch Mandel
Interior Book Designer: Sandy Freeman
Interior Photo Stylists: Mary Ellen Fanelli, Lynette Jensen, Marianne Grape Laubach, Mary Newton, and Jody Olcott
Illustrator: Jack Crane
Pastel Artist: Emilie Snyder

Photo locations: Photos not taken at Lynette Jensen's home were shot at Max and Carol Sempowski's Light Farm Bed and Breakfast, Kintnersville, PA; Maple Hill Farm, Kennett Square, PA; and the Georgetown Manor, Ethan Allen Home Interiors, Allentown, PA.

Stencils from the following companies were incorporated in the design of this book: American Traditional Stencils, American Home Stencils, Inc., The Stencil Shoppe, Inc., and Liberty Design Co.

ISBN 1-57954-735-4 hardcover

2   4   6   8   10   9   7   5   3   1   hardcover

The Thimbleberries
Book of Quilts

Quilts of All Sizes
Plus Decorative Accessories
for Your Home

LYNETTE JENSEN

Rodale Press, Emmaus, Pennsylvania

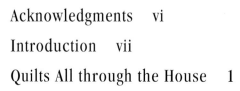

CONTENTS

CONTENTS

ACKNOWLEDGMENTS

All my life I have been surrounded by talented, energetic, and creative people.

My mother and grandmother could do everything, making wonderful things from almost nothing. I lived just one house away from my grandmother as I was growing up. I spent many hours at her side soaking up an attitude about "busy hands." I first learned to sew at her treadle machine, stitching rag strips together for rugs she would weave on her loom. I always felt encouraged about my efforts through the unconditional love, acceptance, and approval that only a grandparent can give. I am still surrounded by things that she made or that belonged to her.

My mother is amazing. She is an exceptional seamstress, a great cook, a master gardener, and the best mother and grandmother ever. I have been fortunate to have her as an ever-present role model. She always maintained "a job worth doing is a job worth doing well." From her I learned how important it is to take pride in doing quality work and to enjoy the whole process of a project, not just the end result.

I think my father has always felt a quiet kind of pride in my efforts. He never fails to ask about my most recent endeavors and mostly just shakes his head and smiles. When I was growing up he would always inquire, "What are you doing now? Cutting and pasting?" I guess that was my response to his question at a very young age. I seem to be still cutting and pasting.

Thank you, Mom and Dad, and Grandma, too.

For the past 25 years my husband, Neil, has patiently put up with tons of quilt projects, countless pins hidden in the carpet, excursions for antique treasures, a garage full of items waiting to become wonderful, and renovating old homes. He is a dear and has always been so very encouraging and excited about my business and my accomplishments. From him I have learned to put family first, to be happy, to be proud of my work, and to "take a chance." Thank you, Neil.

I want to thank our children, Matthew and Kerry, for helping us keep all things in perspective. They are bright, beautiful young people, and I hope they, too, take pride in their mom's efforts.

Thank you to everyone connected with Thimbleberries as designers, office staff, seamstresses, or quilters: Marilyn Ginsburg, Jean Lepper, Sherry Husske, Peggy Christianson, Kathy Lobeck, Dale Ann Foster, Julie Borg, Leone Rusch, Esther Grischkowsky, Julie Jergens, and Tracy Schrantz. A special thank you to Sue Bahr and Lisa Kirchoff for all their wonderful technical skills that helped create this book. We have such a good time together . . . I think of them as family and hold them dear to my heart. I know Thimbleberries would not exist as it is without them.

A special thank-you to Rodale Press, Suzanne Nelson, and her staff for giving me this exceptional opportunity to put the Thimbleberries collection in one big, beautiful book. It has truly been a wonderful experience.

INTRODUCTION

Quiltmaking became a big part of my life 19 years ago when I attended an antique quilt show.

That's when I fell in love with everything about quilts. They seemed to speak to me—the colors, the designs, the fabrics, the thousands and thousands of stitches. Mostly I was captivated by what they represented—artistic expressions and a desire to make a home more comfortable and more beautiful.

With my background in home economics (I have a Home Economics Education degree from the University of Minnesota), the world of quiltmaking seemed to pull all of the elements of my life together in a very unexpected manner. My love for the needle arts, antiques, fabrics, color, and design and my years of teaching led me to create Thimbleberries, a company that produces patterns for quilts and creative home accessories. Thimbleberries is the result of my love of color and quest for maintaining a connection to the past. It flourishes because there are people who value a handcrafted approach to accessorizing their home.

(Before I go any further, let me answer the question I know you're asking. A *thimbleberry* is a native

American wild raspberry that grows in the northern Great Lakes area and southwest to New Mexico. The fruits are red, very tiny, and shaped like a thimble. When I first came across the word years ago in a magazine article, I tucked it away, saving it for a time when I would be doing exactly what I am doing now. To me, the word represents the "fruit of the thimble" or "the fruits of the labor of the thimble" and seems a fitting name for a company that revolves around stitching.)

Thimbleberries is located in Hutchinson, Minnesota (population 11,486). We have been in business since 1989. There are six employees in addition to myself, and I use other community people who have their own sewing and quilting businesses.

My business is my passion! Given a choice about what to do with my time, I would choose to do what I am already doing! I am constantly surrounded by things that excite me and give me joy, but most important, I am surrounded by people that I love. My coworkers are now good, loyal friends. They are hardworking, motivated, positive, and supportive.

At Thimbleberries, our families are the number one priority. Throughout the day we duck out to attend baseball games, tennis matches, basketball and hockey games, swim meets, skating lessons, community volunteer work, and other responsibilities. Our flexible (if sometimes crazy) schedules

allow us to blend home life with work we love. Somehow, the work always gets done!

I began teaching quilting classes 18 years ago. More recently, however, I teach just occasionally. Designing and running a business demands most of my time, but I appreciate the time spent with others who love what I love to do. I have met so many dear people who enjoy the world of quiltmaking and all it involves: planning, selecting designs, gathering fabric, piecing, and quilting.

My particular style is a unique mix of simple, graphic images that reflect an antique flavor. I like designs that are straightforward and uncomplicated. I want people to feel that they can relate to the designs and that they can be successful when they choose a project. Throughout the book I have included tip boxes called "Hints & Helps." These are tips and bits of information that we find helpful here at our studio and that I pass on when teaching classes and seminars. Before you begin any of the projects, I recommend that you read "Thimbleberries Guide to Quiltmaking," starting on page 232, to get an overview of the basic techniques we use.

When designing Thimbleberries patterns we try to offer a mix of techniques as well as a mix of skill levels. The quilts in this book are not difficult. Some are projects that can be done quickly, and others require more of a commitment. We try to help you achieve a quality project without requiring too many expensive or hard-to-find tools. However, we do assume that the rotary cutter has become a standard tool for the majority of quiltmakers.

Most of our designs have a strong traditional approach. We like to combine techniques and special touches to create a product that will endure the test of time to become a family heirloom.

A few of the projects in the book were designed by Marilyn Ginsburg, a dear friend of mine who designs for Thimbleberries from time to time. Her designs have been interspersed throughout our line of patterns over the years. In this book, the following designs are Marilyn's: Baby Rosebud, Dresden Square, Star Patch, Tabletop Tree Skirt, Holiday Hearts, Holly Tree Skirt, and Winter Posies.

Over the years, quilts have become a big part of every aspect of

my life, including my home. I love the feel of quilts tucked into the nooks and crannies of every room in my house—draped over a chair, spread casually across a bed, or flowing from baskets and crocks. I enjoy combining the softness of the fabrics with antique furniture or layering quilt upon quilt. In the special section that follows, "Quilts All through the House," you'll get a glimpse of how I use quilts to decorate. The intent is to inspire you to come up with even more creative ways to display the wonderful quilts that you create.

I hope you enjoy the designs and projects in this book as much as we have enjoyed putting them together for you.

Lynette Jensen and the staff at Thimbleberries

Quilts add just the right touch of handmade and heartfelt warmth to any room in the house. Come take a tour of my home and see what I've done with my quilts. Don't be afraid to dress up your dining room with quilts. I display a smaller-than-bed-size version of *Cottage Flower* on the table. *Sunflower Field* spills over the edge of the buffet, proving that wall quilts don't always have to end up on a wall. Try tucking a small quilt like *Mountain Flower* into a basket and have portions of it tumble out, as seen on the left of the buffet. A pottery crock filled with rolled *Twilight Village* place mats completes the display. The antique high chair in the corner is the perfect place to drape a large quilt like *Midnight Sky.*

On my son's bed, you'll see a good example of what I call the "layered look" in decorating with quilts. I've covered his bed with *Midnight Sky* and on top of that have draped a smaller quilt, *Harbor Town.* These two quilts have compatible colors, and the soothing repeat design of the bed quilt creates the perfect background for the more active design of *Harbor Town.* Next to the bed I've draped *Pine Grove* over a simple pine bookcase, which serves nicely as a quilt rack. I made the pillow shams on the bed from some of my favorite plaid and checked fabrics, using a regular pillow case as a pattern.

Don't let the size of small quilts fool you—I've found that they are big in creative decorating options. *Small Pines* can make a wonderful table topper for a painted or rustic-looking coffee table. The *Tabletop Tree Skirt* can be used year-round, not just at Christmastime, if you put it under decorative crocks or baskets, like the apple-filled one shown here. Miniature *Baby Rosebud* adds bold color to the antique child's wagon and creates an unusual tabletop display. Look around your home for similar child-scale items or small boxes or baskets that could showcase a miniature quilt.

My mellowed pine table is the perfect setting for a *Twilight Village* table runner. For an attractive and handy way to store the companion place mats, roll them when they're not in use and store them in a crock. I treat my place mats with a Scotchgard spray and wipe off any light spots with a damp cloth. When they need a better cleaning, I put them in the washer, then lay them flat to dry, blocking them into shape, if necessary. For items like the table runner or wall quilts that don't really get dirty, only dusty, I "dry clean" by putting them in the dryer for a couple of minutes on the heatless cycle.

I like to make Christmas morning breakfast extra festive by using *Christmas Game Board* as a table topper over the regular tablecloth and dressing up the chair backs with *Holiday Hearts. Jingle Socks* filled with candies and tiny gifts and hung over chair spindles are a delightful breakfast surprise. Or consider filling them with small stuffed animals and antique toys and hanging them on the chairs as part of your holiday decorating. On the chair seat I've nestled a small quilt, *My Friend's House,* inside a wooden basket as a way to present a special gift.

I like to be surrounded by quilts wherever I am, including my living room. One of my favorite places to hang a quilt is over the back of a couch, where you see *Birds and Blooms.* Slide one side of the quilt behind the loose cushions and let the other drape over the back. I folded *My Friend's House* and let that hang off the mantel, anchored by a flower arrangement. An open bookshelf door displays *Paddlewheels and Pinwheels.* Small quilts are also nice to scatter around: *Tabletop Tree Skirt* sits under a basket on the coffee table, and *Small Pines* peeks over the radiator. *Pine Grove* pillows nestle in a chair, while the *Star Patch* table runner drapes over a chair back. The framed quilt above the fireplace is not a project in the book but does give you another display idea.

This cozy view of a corner in my living room is a perfect example of the warm and comfortable feeling quilts add to a room. This chair, piled with a plump pair of *Pine Grove* pillows, looks like an almost irresistible place to sit down, kick off your shoes, and settle in with a good book. Behind the chair, I've opened one of the glass doors of our bookshelves, which becomes the perfect place to drape a lap-size quilt like *Paddlewheels and Pinwheels.* Look around your home for doors like this, in out-of-the-way corners, where you can display your quilts. Don't overlook room doors; a folded quilt draped over the top of a door can add a welcoming touch. Next to the chair, I've draped *Heart Blossom* over a trunk for an extra dash of color and texture.

Decorating for Christmas means changing the quilt accessories. In this corner by the fireplace, I've draped *Fireside Cozy* on an armchair next to a trunk that is artfully covered by the *Holly Tree Skirt.* The door of the bookcase holds a casually draped *Holly Ribbons* quilt, and the mantel showcases a lineup of *Jingle Socks* (amid a garland I made from cranberries and star-shaped cookies). A folded quilt pops out of the corner of an antique produce crate for a little bit of color on the mantel top. On the shelf below the window, you'll see a framed quilt block from *My Friend's House,* which makes a nice holiday or hostess gift.

One of my decorating tricks is to think of unexpected places to put quilts. In this corner of my bedroom, I've taken a full-size bed quilt, *Apple Bars,* and displayed it on a hall, or clothes, tree. I folded the quilt like a fan and then draped it over one of the arms of the hall tree, arranging it so that one end hangs down a little lower than the other. This sort of arrangement gives you a way to display large quilts other than just spreading them out on a bed. By draping them vertically, you can add a pleasing touch of color and texture to an empty or unexciting corner of a room. As with any quilt you keep out, be sure to protect it from strong sunlight and rearrange the folds at least once a month. To keep it fresh and get rid of the dust, put it in the dryer on air fluff for several minutes.

If you're a prolific quiltmaker, the layered look gives you an opportunity to show off your work when you've run out of beds! On my daughter's bed, I've fanned out *Dresden Square* over *Baby Rosebud.* Miniature *Baby Rosebud* drapes over a footstool, which makes a perfect-size quilt rack. The wall cupboard holds *Birdhouse Row,* while the radiator serves as a handy quilt rack for *Heart Blossom* and *Birds and Blooms.* The radiator is for summer display only—I never keep quilts there when the heat is on.

Here's the spot where you're most likely to find me in the evening, working on a quilt. I love the way *Around Town* fills the space on the wall. My trick for hanging quilts like this one is to use 1 × ⅜-inch flat molding instead of a dowel or curtain rod; you won't end up with a lump along the top of the quilt. Baskets and quilts make perfect companions. Here I've paired *Peppermint Swirl* with a basket from my collection. When you display a quilt in a basket, play around with the folds and draping until you have a gentle cascade of fabric that shows off an interesting part of the design. *Winter Posies* quilt casually tumbles over the side of the wing chair, a nice look for chairs that aren't used often. The matching pillow serves as an anchor.

This display of quilts and accessories in our bedroom is a good example of how you can decorate with quilts without creating a look that's too feminine. *Cottage Flower* on the bed serves as a good backdrop for a green wicker basket in which I've arranged *Apple Bars.* A quilt rack by the door holds both sizes of *Birdhouse Row.* Creative draping shows off both quilts. The square pillows on the bed were made from the same large-scale floral I used in *Cottage Flower.* To tone down the frilly and feminine feel of the fabric, I added plaid ruffles.

I sat in this high chair when I was a baby and kept it around to use for both of my children. Now that they're grown and it's no longer needed, I still can't bear to put it away. I decided it made the perfect quilt rack to display a large quilt like *Midnight Sky*. I gently folded and scrunched the quilt and draped it over the back and through the seat until I had an arrangement I was pleased with. Take a look at your family heirlooms and think about how you might be able to use them to display your quilts.

An antique hat rack mounted on the wall in my son's room was the inspiration for this arrangement. I took *Starbound* and folded it like a fan, then pushed one end through the wires on the rack. The lower portion of the quilt fanned itself out in a graceful way that gives a nice sense of dimension and fills this corner of the room. Bed quilts can make especially dramatic displays when you take them off the bed! An antique wooden basket below the window holds other quilts folded neatly into bundles.

HOMEGROWN QUILTS

Pick a bouquet of your favorite flowers and let them be your inspiration to make one of the captivating quilts in this section. These projects take you down a garden path or into fields, meadows, and mountains. You'll capture the spirit and bold, bright colors of the flowers to enjoy all year long.

Quilt Diagram

Mountain Flower reminds me of the bold flowers that push through the snow early each spring near our family's lakeside cabin. The flowers on this quilt couldn't be easier to appliqué. Fusible webbing keeps them in place while a simple buttonhole stitch enhances their centers and outside edges. The twisted ribbon effect in the inner border adds a striking final touch to the quilt, which works wonderfully in an entranceway to welcome guests to your home—or mountain cabin!

SIZE

Wall quilt: 41 inches square (unquilted)

Finished block: 6 inches square

FABRICS AND SUPPLIES

Yardage is based on 44-inch-wide fabric.

1¼ yards of dark green print fabric for leaves, nine patch, and outer border

1 yard of cream print fabric for background

1¼ yards of red print fabric for flowers, narrow border, binding, and corner blocks

¾ yard of black print fabric for flower centers, nine patch, and pieced middle border

1¼ yards of fabric for quilt backing

1 yard of 16-inch-wide, paper-backed fusible webbing for appliqué (sewable)

Batting, at least 45 inches square

1 skein of black embroidery floss *or* 1 spool of #8 black pearl cotton

1 skein of gold embroidery floss *or* 1 spool of #8 gold pearl cotton

Rotary cutter, mat, and see-through ruler

Template plastic

FABRIC KEY

 DARK GREEN PRINT

 CREAM PRINT

 RED PRINT

 BLACK PRINT

GETTING READY

- Read instructions thoroughly before you begin.
- Prewash and press fabric.
- Use ¼-inch seam allowances unless directions specify otherwise.
- Seam allowances are included in the cutting sizes given.
- Press seam allowance in the direction that will create the least bulk and, whenever possible, toward the darker fabric.
- Trace the **Flower** and **Flower Center Templates** (page 18) onto template plastic and cut out.
- Cutting directions for each section of the quilt are given in the areas following the row of scissors. If you like to cut as you go, simply follow the directions as you get to them. If you'd rather cut all your pieces at once, skip ahead and look for the scissors to do all the cutting before you begin to sew.
- Instructions are given for quick cutting and piecing the blocks. Note that for some of the pieces, the quick-cutting method will result in leftover fabric.

MOUNTAIN FLOWER BLOCKS
(Make 13)

Cutting for Leaves

From the green fabric:
- Cut three 1⅞ × 44-inch strips

From the cream fabric:
- Cut three 1⅞ × 44-inch strips
- Cut one 2½ × 44-inch strip. From this strip, cut twenty-six 1½ × 2½-inch pieces.

Piecing the Leaves

Step 1. Layer a 1⅞ × 44-inch green and a 1⅞ × 44-inch cream strip, right sides together, and press. Layer the remaining strips in pairs of green and cream strips. Press together, but do not stitch.

Step 2. Cut the layered strips into fifty-two 1⅞-inch squares, being careful not to shift the layers as you cut.

Step 3. Cut the layered squares in half diagonally. See **Diagram 1.** Stitch ¼ inch from the diagonal edges, then press seam allowances toward the green fabric to make 1½-inch triangle-pieced squares.

Diagram 1

Step 4. Referring to **Diagram 2** for color placement, sew the triangle-pieced squares together two at a time. Then sew the top leaf to the bottom leaf for each leaf section, as shown in the diagram.

Top leaf
Bottom leaf

Diagram 2

Step 5. Sew two leaf sections together, as shown in **Diagram 3,** to make a leaf unit. Repeat to make 13 leaf units.

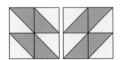

Diagram 3

Step 6. Stitch a 1½ × 2½-inch cream piece to the left and right sides of all 13 leaf units. See **Diagram 4.**

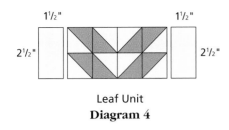

1½"   1½"

2½"   2½"

Leaf Unit
Diagram 4

Cutting for Flower Blocks

From the cream fabric:
• Cut two 6½ × 44-inch strips. From these strips, cut thirteen 4½ × 6½-inch pieces for the background.

From the red fabric:
• Cut one 4 × 44-inch strip for the flowers
• Cut one 4 × 12-inch strip for the flowers

From the black fabric:
• Cut one 1½ × 23-inch strip for the flower centers

Assembling the Flower Blocks

Step 1. Sew a 4½ × 6½-inch cream background piece to the top of each leaf unit. See **Diagram 5.**

Step 2. Fuse the webbing onto the wrong side of the red and black strips, following the manufacturer's instructions.

Step 3. Place the template patterns on the paper side of the prepared fabrics and trace. You will need 13

6½"

4½"

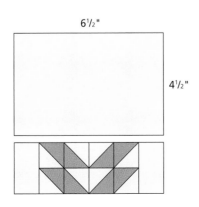

Diagram 5

Tips and Tricks for Machine Appliqué

If you'd rather use machine appliqué, follow the same procedures given in Steps 1 through 4 under "Assembling the Flower Blocks" below.

❖ Lay a piece of typing paper on the back side of the block to stabilize the fabric and prevent puckering when you machine stitch.

❖ Adjust your machine's tension to the buttonhole setting so that the top stitches are pulled slightly to the bobbin side, producing a nice smooth stitch on the flower's edge. Using matching thread, satin stitch the flower's edges with a medium-width stitch.

❖ If your machine has the capability to do a buttonhole stitch, follow Steps 1 through 4 under "Assembling the Flower Blocks," then do the decorative buttonhole stitch by machine instead of by hand.

flowers and 13 flower centers. Cut out the shapes and peel off the paper backing.

Step 4. Position the flower shape on the cream background fabric so that the bottom petals are just above the leaves. See **Diagram 6.** Press in place, following the manufacturer's directions. Position the center on the flower. Press in place. Repeat to complete all 13 blocks.

Diagram 6

APPLIQUÉING THE FLOWERS

Step 1. Although the fusible webbing will hold the flowers securely to the blocks, it is nice to add a decorative stitch along the outside edges. Use three strands of black embroidery floss or one strand

of pearl cotton to appliqué the flowers onto the block. Use the buttonhole stitch, as shown in **Diagram 7.**

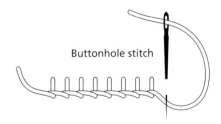

Buttonhole stitch

Diagram 7

Step 2. With three strands of gold embroidery floss or one strand of pearl cotton, appliqué the centers onto the flowers using the buttonhole stitch.

HINTS & HELPS

If you're trying to decide between using the pearl cotton and the embroidery floss, consider this: Pearl cotton is a bit thicker and has more sheen than embroidery floss. Your buttonhole stitches will be more noticeable with the pearl cotton.

NINE PATCH BLOCKS
(Make 12)

Cutting for Nine Patch Blocks

Each Nine Patch block is made up of two different strip sets. To minimize cutting and piecing, the fabrics are first cut into strips. These strips are then sewn together and cut into segments for the block assembly.

From the green fabric:
• Cut five $2\frac{1}{2} \times 44$-inch strips

From the black fabric:
• Cut four $2\frac{1}{2} \times 44$-inch strips

Piecing the Nine Patch Blocks

Step 1. For Strip Set 1, sew a green strip to each 44-inch side of a black strip. See **Diagram 8**. Press seam allowances toward the black fabric. Make two of Strip Set 1.

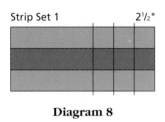

Strip Set 1 $2\frac{1}{2}$"

Diagram 8

Step 2. For Strip Set 2, sew a black strip to each 44-inch side of a green strip. See **Diagram 9**. Press seam allowances toward the black fabric. Make one Strip Set 2.

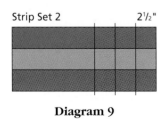

Strip Set 2 $2\frac{1}{2}$"

Diagram 9

Step 3. With the right side of the fabric facing up, lay Strip Set 1 on the cutting mat. Using a see-through ruler and rotary cutter, cut the strip set into $2\frac{1}{2}$-inch segments. Refer to cutting lines in **Diagram 8**. Cut 24 segments from Strip Set 1.

HINTS & HELPS

After a few cuts you may need to straighten the cut edge of the strip set with the ruler to ensure that each of your segments is exactly $2\frac{1}{2}$ inches wide.

Step 4. Repeat Step 3 to cut 12 segments from Strip Set 2. These segments should also be $2\frac{1}{2}$ inches.

Step 5. Sew a Strip Set 1 segment to the top and bottom of a Strip Set 2 segment, as shown in **Diagram 10**. Press seam allowances toward Strip Set 2. Repeat to make 12 Nine Patch blocks.

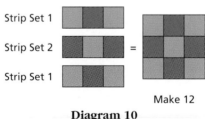

Strip Set 1

Strip Set 2   =

Strip Set 1

Make 12

Diagram 10

QUILT CENTER

The Mountain Flower Quilt is assembled in five horizontal rows of five blocks each. See the **Quilt Diagram** on page 13 for the order of block placement.

Step 1. Sew the blocks into rows, alternating Flower blocks and Nine Patch blocks, as shown in **Diagram 11**. Make three rows with Flower blocks at each end and two rows with Nine Patch blocks at each end. Press seam allowances toward the Nine Patch blocks.

Step 2. Join rows so the Flower blocks and the Nine Patch blocks alternate, referring to the **Quilt Diagram**.

Step 3. A star stitch was used at the block intersections. See the **Quilt Diagram** on page 13 for placement and **Diagram 12** for stitch detail. Use three strands of gold embroidery floss or one strand of pearl cotton. The long stitches are $\frac{3}{4}$ inch long, and the short stitches are $\frac{1}{2}$ inch long.

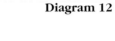

Diagram 12

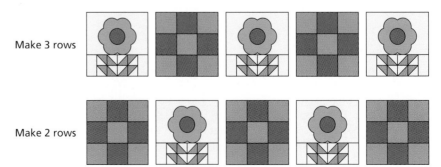

Make 3 rows

Make 2 rows

Diagram 11

BORDERS

The yardage given allows for the border pieces to be cut cross-grain.

Cutting for Borders

From the red fabric:
• Cut four $1\frac{1}{2} \times 44$-inch strips for the inner borders
• Cut one $1\frac{1}{2} \times 10$-inch strip. From this strip, cut four $1\frac{1}{2}$-inch corner squares.

From *each* of the black and cream fabrics:
• Cut three $1\frac{7}{8} \times 44$-inch strips for the pieced border

From the green fabric:
• Cut four 4×44-inch strips for the outer border

Assembling the Pieced Border

Step 1. With right sides together, layer a $1\frac{7}{8} \times 44$-inch black strip and a $1\frac{7}{8} \times 44$-inch cream strip together. Layer the remaining strips into black and cream pairs. Press.

Step 2. Cut these layered strips into sixty-four $1\frac{7}{8}$-inch squares.

Step 3. Cut the layered squares in half diagonally. Stitch $\frac{1}{4}$ inch from the diagonal edge. Press seam allowances toward the black fabric to make a $1\frac{1}{2}$-inch triangle-pieced square.

Step 4. The pieced border consists of two different sections. See Section A and Section B in **Diagram 13**. Then, referring to **Diagram 14** for color placement, sew the $1\frac{1}{2}$-inch triangle-pieced squares together to make 32 Section A and 32 Section B units.

Step 5. For each side of the quilt you will need eight Section A and eight Section B units. Sew the sections together alternating Section

Section Section
←—A—→ ←—B—→
Diagram 13

Section A   Section B
Make 32   Make 32
Diagram 14

Make 4
Diagram 15

Diagram 16

A and Section B, as shown in **Diagram 15**. Start with a Section A and end with a Section B. Repeat to make a total of four pieced border strips.

Attaching the Borders

Step 1. Measure the quilt from left to right through the middle to determine the length of the top and bottom borders. Cut the red inner border strips to the necessary length and sew to the top and bottom of the quilt.

Step 2. Measure the quilt from top to bottom through the middle including the borders you just added to determine the length of the side borders. Cut the red inner border strips to the necessary length and sew to the sides of the quilt.

Step 3. Attach a pieced border strip to the top and bottom of the quilt, as shown in the **Quilt Diagram** on page 13. Press seam allowances toward the red inner border. If the pieced border does not fit your quilt exactly, you must adjust the seam allowances by taking in or letting out a little bit at several seams.

Step 4. Add the $1\frac{1}{2}$-inch red squares to the ends of the two remaining pieced borders. Press

seam allowances toward the red squares. See **Diagram 16**.

Step 5. Stitch these pieced borders to the sides of the quilt, referring to the **Quilt Diagram.** Press seam allowances toward the red border.

Step 6. Measure the quilt as you did in Step 1 for the inner border. Cut the green outer border strips to the necessary length and sew to the top and bottom of the quilt.

Step 7. Measure the quilt as you did in Step 2 for the inner border. Cut the green outer border strips to the necessary length and sew to the sides of the quilt.

QUILTING

Step 1. Prepare the quilt backing by trimming the selvages.

Step 2. Trim the backing and batting so they are 4 inches larger than the quilt top dimensions.

Step 3. Mark the quilt top for quilting.

Step 4. Layer the backing, batting, and quilt top. Baste these layers together and quilt by hand or machine.

QUILTING IDEAS

▨ Quilt all of the Nine Patch squares in the ditch on the side of the seam line that does not have the seam allowance.

▨ Outline quilt the flowers, leaves, and pieced borders in the ditch so that they puff out a little.

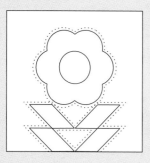

▨ The quilting in the outer border is a feathered quilt design from a quilting stencil.

BINDING

The 2¾-inch strips will make a ⅜- to ½-inch-wide binding. If you want a wider or narrower binding, adjust the width of the strips you cut. (See page 247 for pointers on how to experiment with binding width.) See "Making and Attaching the Binding" on page 245 to complete your quilt.

Cutting for Cross-Grain Binding

From the red fabric:
• Cut five 2¾ × 44-inch strips

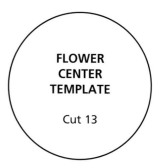

FLOWER CENTER TEMPLATE

Cut 13

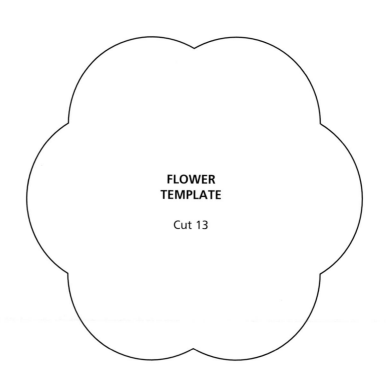

FLOWER TEMPLATE

Cut 13

SIZE

Wall quilt: 46 inches square (unquilted)

Finished block: 10 inches square

FABRICS AND SUPPLIES

Yardage is based on 44-inch-wide fabric.

1/4 yard of red print fabric for hearts

1/8 yard of gold fabric for blossoms

1 1/4 yards of cream fabric for background, lattice posts, and side and corner triangles

1/4 yard of dark green fabric for leaves

1/2 yard of medium green fabric for leaves and inner border

1 1/2 yards of small red check fabric for lattice strips, outer border, and binding

3 yards of fabric for quilt backing

Quilt batting, at least 50 inches square

Rotary cutter, mat, and see-through ruler

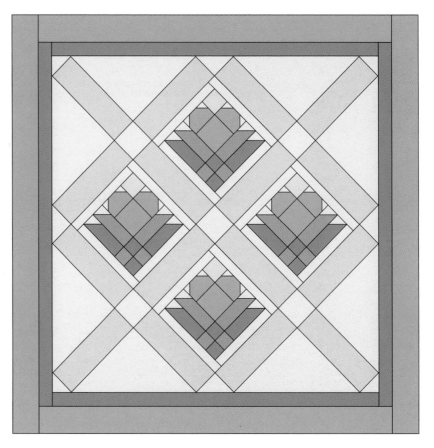

Quilt Diagram

When I was designing this quilt, I gave myself a challenge: Using only four very simple, identical blocks, could I create a quilt that looked interesting and had a lot of drama? I wanted the central design of the block to fill the entire space and look as if the blossom had emerged from the leaf base. My solution was the bold, graphic element of the Heart Blossom blocks framed with a lattice and an unusual diagonal setting. The result is a nice clean, crisp design that's quick and easy to make.

GETTING READY

- Read instructions thoroughly before you begin.
- Prewash and press fabric.
- Use ¼-inch seam allowances throughout unless directions specify otherwise.
- Seam allowances are included in the cutting sizes given.
- Press seam allowance in the direction that will create the least bulk and, whenever possible, toward the darker fabric.
- Cutting directions for each section of the quilt are given in the areas following the row of scissors. If you like to cut as you go, simply follow the directions as you get to them. If you'd rather cut all your pieces at once, skip ahead and look for the scissors to do all the cutting before you begin to sew.

FABRIC KEY

- RED
- CREAM
- GOLD
- DARK GREEN
- MEDIUM GREEN
- RED CHECK

HEART BLOSSOM BLOCKS
(Make 4)

Cutting for Heart Blossom Squares

From the red print fabric:
- Cut one 3½ × 16-inch strip. From this strip, cut four 3½-inch squares.
- Cut one 2½ × 30-inch strip. From this strip, cut eight 2½ × 3½-inch pieces.

From the gold fabric:
- Cut one 2½ × 12-inch strip. From this strip, cut four 2½-inch squares.

From the cream fabric:
- Cut one 1¼ × 24-inch strip. From this strip, cut sixteen 1¼-inch squares.

Heart Blossom Assembly

Step 1. With right sides together, lay a 1¼-inch cream square in *each* of the two upper corners of the 2½ × 3½-inch red print rectangles. See **Diagram 1**. Stitch diagonally

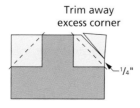

Trim away
excess corner

—¼"

Diagram 1

from corner to corner. Trim away excess corner fabric, leaving a ¼-inch seam allowance. Press seam allowances toward the red print fabric. Repeat to make eight of these units—two for each block.

Step 2. Add a 2½-inch gold square to the left side of four of the units from Step 1. See **Diagram 2**. Press seam allowances toward the gold fabric.

Diagram 2

Step 3. Stitch a 3½-inch red print square along the long red edge of the remaining four units from Step 1, as shown in **Diagram 3.**

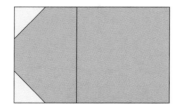

Diagram 3

Step 4. Sew the units from Steps 2 and 3 together to make four heart blossom squares. See **Diagram 4** on page 22. Press seam allowances toward the center square.

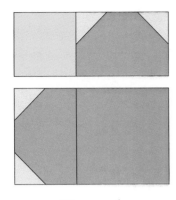

Diagram 4

Cutting for Leaf Four Patch Squares

From *each* of the dark green and medium green fabrics:
• Cut one 2 × 18-inch strip. From *each* of these strips, cut eight 2-inch squares.

Four Patch Square Assembly

Step 1. With right sides together, stitch the dark green squares to the medium green squares, as shown in **Diagram 5.** Press seams toward the dark green fabric.

Diagram 5

Step 2. Join two of these assembled units into a four patch square, positioning the units, as shown in **Diagram 6.** Press. Repeat to make four of the four patch squares.

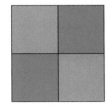

Diagram 6

HINTS & HELPS

You will be making one right leaf unit and one left leaf unit for each Heart Blossom block. Use labels to keep your pieces and units organized.

Cutting for Leaf Units

From *each* of the dark green and medium green fabrics:
• Cut one 2 × 44-inch strip. From *each* of these strips, cut eight 2 × 5½-inch rectangles.

From the cream fabric:
• Cut one 2 × 34-inch strip. From this strip, cut sixteen 2-inch squares.

Assembling the Leaf Strips

The leaf unit is made up of two right leaf strips and two left leaf strips.

RIGHT LEAF STRIPS

Step 1. With right sides together, lay a 2-inch cream square on the right-hand corner of a dark green rectangle. See **Diagram 7.** Stitch the two layers together diagonally from corner to corner, with the cream fabric on top. Trim away excess corner fabric, leaving a ¼-inch seam allowance. Press seam allowances toward the green fabric.

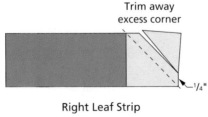

Trim away
excess corner

¼"

Right Leaf Strip
Diagram 7

Step 2. Repeat to make a total of four dark green and four medium green leaf strips for the *right* side.

LEFT LEAF STRIPS

Step 1. With right sides together, lay a 2-inch cream square on the left-hand corner of a dark green rectangle. See **Diagram 8.**

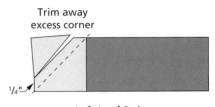

Trim away
excess corner

¼"

Left Leaf Strip
Diagram 8

Step 2. Stitch the two layers together diagonally as for the right leaf strip. Trim away excess corner fabric, and press seams toward the green fabric.

Step 3. Repeat to make four dark green and four medium green leaf strips for the *left* side.

Assembling the Leaf Units

Step 1. Stitch a *right* dark green leaf to the bottom of a *right* medium green leaf strip along the long edge, as shown in **Diagram 9.** Press seam allowance toward the medium green fabric.

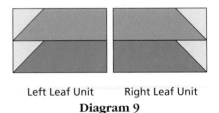

Left Leaf Unit   Right Leaf Unit
Diagram 9

Step 2. Stitch a *left* dark green to the bottom of a *left* medium green leaf strip along the long edge, referring to **Diagram 9.** Press seam allowance toward the medium green fabric.

Step 3. Repeat this process to make four right leaf units and four left leaf units.

Adding the Four Patch Squares

Step 1. Add a four patch square to the left side of a *right* leaf unit, as shown in **Diagram 10**. Press seam allowance toward the leaf unit.

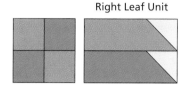

Right Leaf Unit

Diagram 10

Step 2. Stitch a *left* leaf unit to the bottom of a heart blossom square. See **Diagram 11**. Press seam allowance toward the leaf unit.

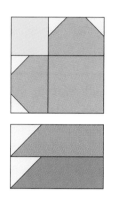

Diagram 11

Step 3. Add the four patch leaf unit made in Step 1 to the heart blossom leaf unit made in Step 2. See **Diagram 12**. Press seam allowance toward the leaf unit. Repeat to make a total of four Heart Blossom blocks.

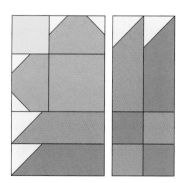

Diagram 12

Cutting for Block Border

From the cream fabric:
• Cut four 1½ × 44-inch strips

Adding the Block Border

You will be stitching the cream border to the Heart Blossom block in a Log Cabin fashion. One 44-inch strip will complete the four borders for one block. Do not cut the strips into sections before sewing them to the block. You will stitch the strips clockwise onto the Heart Blossom block, as shown in **Diagram 13**.

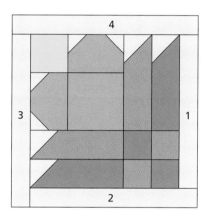

Make 4
Diagram 13

Step 1. For the first border, stitch a cream strip to the block, right sides together. See **Diagram 14**.

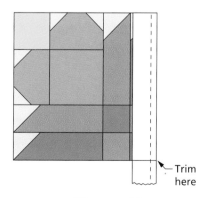

Trim here

Diagram 14

Step 2. Press the seam allowance toward the block and trim the border strip even with the length of the block.

Step 3. Stitch the second, third, and fourth borders onto the block in the same fashion, trimming the excess fabric from each consecutive strip. See **Diagram 15**. When you've completed all four borders, your block should measure 10½ inches square. Repeat Steps 1 through 3 to attach borders to all four blocks.

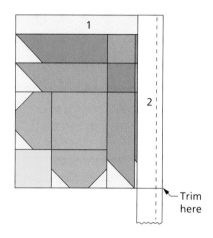

Trim here

Diagram 15

QUILT CENTER

Cutting for Lattice Pieces and Side and Corner Triangles

From the red check fabric:
• Cut four 3½ × 44-inch strips. From these strips, cut sixteen 3½ × 10½-inch lattice strips.

From the cream fabric:
• Cut one 3½ × 20-inch strip. From this strip, cut five 3½-inch square lattice posts.
• Cut one 6½-inch square. Cut this square diagonally into quarters to make four small side triangle As.
• Cut two 4½-inch squares. Cut these squares in half diagonally to make four corner triangle Bs.
• Cut two 16-inch squares. Cut these squares diagonally into

quarters to make eight outside triangle Cs.

Note: The A, B, and C triangles will be larger than necessary and will be trimmed before the border is attached.

Assembling the Quilt Center

Step 1. Referring to the lower right portion of **Diagram 16,** join two lattice strips with a lattice post in the center. Sew a triangle A to each end of the strip, as shown in the diagram, to complete the lattice strip. Make one more lattice strip in this same fashion; this is used in the upper left portion of the quilt.

Step 2. To make the long lattice strip that will run through the center of your quilt, join four lattice strips separated by three lattice posts, referring to the diagram. Do not sew triangles to the ends of the long lattice strip yet.

Step 3. Lay out the quilt blocks and lattice strips in diagonal rows, adding lattice posts between the blocks in the rows and at the ends of the blocks. Stitch the $3\frac{1}{2} \times 10\frac{1}{2}$-inch lattice pieces and blocks together into rows, referring to **Diagram 16.**

Step 4. Add a large triangle C to each end of the diagonal block rows. Add a large triangle C to the long sides of the two remaining lattice strips.

Step 5. Stitch the rows of blocks and lattice strips together to form the quilt center. Add a corner triangle B to each of the four quilt corners.

Step 6. Trim off excess fabric from the side and corner triangles, allowing $\frac{1}{4}$-inch seam allowances beyond block corners. Before you trim, be sure to see "Trimming Side and Corner Triangles" on page 236 to be certain you make these cuts

QUILTING IDEAS

☑ The quilt design in the large side triangles is made from half of an $8\frac{1}{2}$-inch quilting stencil. Find one that you like and hold it up to the quilt to see how half of the design looks in the space. (A triangular quilting design isn't necessary.)

☑ To outline the heart blossom unit, leaves, four patch square, and lattice pieces, quilt in the ditch along the edge of the seam line on the side where there is no seam allowance.

☑ Quilt each of the four patch squares $\frac{1}{4}$ inch inside of the seams. The leaf units and the shapes of the heart and blossom are also quilted $\frac{1}{4}$ inch in from the seams.

☑ In the lattice posts, quilt a four-petaled flower template design. Sections of that same motif are used in the small side triangles as shown.

☑ Quilt a 1-inch cross-hatch pattern in the lattice strips and both of the borders. See "Cross-Hatching Tips" on page 243.

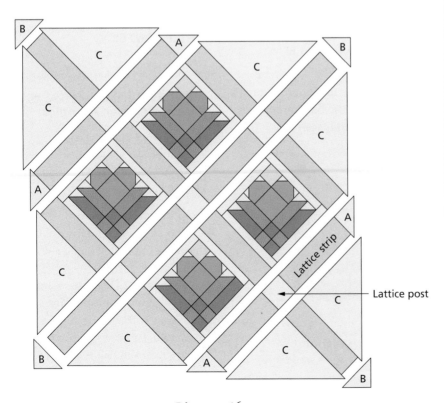

Diagram 16

accurately. Make sure the corners are accurate 90 degree angles.

BORDERS

Cutting for Borders

From the medium green fabric:
• Cut four 2 × 44-inch strips for the inner borders

From the red check fabric:
• Cut five 3½ × 44-inch strips for the outer borders

Attaching the Borders

Step 1. Measure the quilt from left to right through the middle to determine the length of the top and bottom green inner borders. Attach the top and bottom inner borders.

Step 2. Measure the quilt from top to bottom through the middle, including the borders you just added, to determine the length of the side green inner borders. Attach the side inner borders.

Step 3. Measure the quilt in the same manner as you did for the inner border. Attach the top and bottom red check outer borders. For the side outer borders, piece three red check strips with diagonal seams. Then cut two pieces to the necessary length and sew them to the sides of the quilt.

QUILTING

Step 1. To prepare the backing for the quilt, cut 3 yards of backing fabric in half crosswise to make two 1½-yard lengths. Remove the selvages and sew the two pieces together lengthwise.

Step 2. Trim the backing and batting so they measure approximately 4 inches larger than your quilt top.

Step 3. Mark the quilt top for quilting.

Step 4. Layer the backing, batting, and quilt top. Baste or pin these layers together and quilt by hand or machine.

BINDING

The 2¾-inch binding strips will produce a ⅜-inch-wide binding. If you want a wider or narrower binding, adjust the width of the strips you cut. (See page 247 for pointers on how to experiment with binding width.) See "Making and Attaching the Binding" on page 245 to complete your quilt.

Cutting for Cross-Grain Binding

From the red check fabric:
• Cut five 2¾ × 44-inch strips

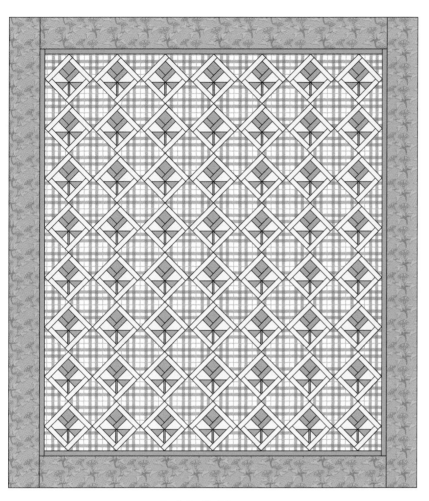

Bed Quilt Diagram

BABY ROSEBUD BED QUILT

SIZE
Bed quilt: 92 × 102 inches (unquilted)
Finished block: 7 inches square

FABRICS AND SUPPLIES
Yardage is based on 44-inch-wide fabric.

1 yard of rose print fabric for rosebuds and inner border

2¼ yards of green solid fabric for bud base, leaves, stems, and binding

3 yards of beige fabric for background

3½ yards of blue check fabric for alternate blocks and side and corner triangles

3¾ yards of floral fabric for outer border

8 yards of fabric for quilt backing

Quilt batting, at least 96 × 106 inches

Rotary cutter, mat, and see-through ruler

The simple and sweet flower bud motif and easy piecing techniques used in Baby Rosebud result in a bed quilt full of old-fashioned charm. At home, this quilt covers my daughter Kerry's bed, where it gives a restful, inviting feeling to her room. I've found that this quilt makes a perfect backdrop for layering other quilts on the bed. And the adorable miniature version is just right for a doll's cradle.

FABRIC KEY

 ROSE PRINT

 GREEN

 BEIGE

 BLUE CHECK

FLORAL

G E T T I N G   R E A D Y

- Read instructions thoroughly before you begin.
- Prewash and press fabric.
- Use ¼-inch seam allowances throughout unless directions specify otherwise.
- Seam allowances are included in the cutting sizes given.
- Press seam allowances in the direction that will create the least bulk and, whenever possible, toward the darker fabric.
- Cutting directions for each section of the quilt are given in the areas following the row of scissors. If you like to cut as you go, simply follow the directions as you get to them. If you'd rather cut all your pieces at once, skip ahead and look for the scissors to do all the cutting before you begin to sew.
- Instructions are given for quick cutting and piecing the blocks and borders. Note that for some of the pieces, the quick-cutting methods will result in leftover fabric.

ROSEBUD BLOCKS
(Make 56)

Cutting for Rosebud Blocks

From the rose fabric:
- Cut four 2½ × 44-inch strips. From these strips, cut fifty-six 2½-inch squares.

From the green fabric:
- Cut nine 1½ × 44-inch strips. From these strips, cut fifty-six 1½ × 2½-inch pieces and fifty-six 1½ × 3½-inch pieces.
- Cut seven 2½ × 44-inch strips. From these strips, cut one hundred twelve 2½-inch squares
- Cut six 1 × 44-inch strips. From these strips, cut fifty-six 1 × 4-inch pieces

From the beige fabric:
- Cut ten 2½ × 44-inch strips. From these strips, cut one hundred twelve 2½ × 3½-inch pieces.
- Cut four 2⅝ × 44-inch strips. From these strips, cut fifty-six 2⅝-inch squares.
- Cut thirty-five 1½ × 44-inch strips. From these strips, cut fifty-six 1½ × 5½-inch pieces, one hundred twelve 1½ × 6½-inch pieces, and fifty-six 1½ × 7½-inch pieces.

Piecing the Rosebud Blocks

Step 1. Sew a 1½ × 2½-inch green strip to a 2½-inch rose square. Press. Sew a 1½ × 3½-inch green strip to this bud unit, as shown in **Diagram 1.** Press seam allowances toward the green fabric.

Diagram 1

Step 2. With right sides together, place a 2½-inch green square on a 2½ × 3½-inch beige rectangle. See **Diagram 2.** Draw a diagonal line from corner to corner on the green square as shown. Do not stitch on top of the line drawn. Stitch just a hair (approximately $\frac{1}{32}$ inch) to the outside edge of the line. Trim away corners leaving a scant $\frac{1}{4}$-inch seam allowance. Press seam allowance toward the green fabric to make a leaf unit. The leaf unit should measure $2\frac{1}{2} \times 3\frac{1}{2}$ inches. Make 56 leaf units for the left side. To make 56 leaves for the right side, draw a diagonal line from corner to corner in the opposite direction. Stitch, trim, and press as you did for the left side.

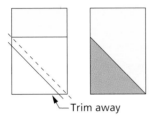

Left Leaf Unit
Diagram 2

Step 3. Cut the $2\frac{5}{8}$-inch beige squares in half diagonally. Sew a 1 × 4-inch green strip between these triangles. See **Diagram 3.** The green ends will extend beyond the beige triangles. Press seams toward the green stem. This stem unit must measure $2\frac{1}{2}$ inches square. If it does not, adjust the seam allowances. Trim the green stems off as shown and trim the square to $2\frac{1}{2}$ inches if needed. Make 56 stem units.

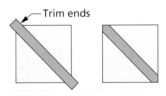

Diagram 3

Step 4. Sew a stem unit to a left leaf unit. See **Diagram 4.** Sew a rosebud unit to a right leaf unit, as shown in **Diagram 5.** Sew these two units together, as shown in **Diagram 6.**

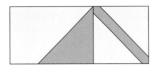

Left Leaf Unit   Stem Unit
Diagram 4

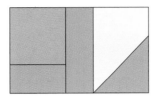

Bud Unit   Right Leaf Unit
Diagram 5

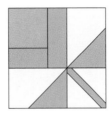

Diagram 6

Step 5. Sew a $1\frac{1}{2} \times 5\frac{1}{2}$-inch beige strip to the bottom left side of a Rosebud block, as shown in **Diagram 7.** Continue adding beige strips to the block, moving in a counterclockwise direction around the block. Add a $6\frac{1}{2}$-inch strip to the bottom right side, another $6\frac{1}{2}$-inch strip to the top right side, and end with a $7\frac{1}{2}$-inch strip on the top left side.

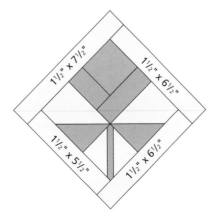

Make 56
Diagram 7

QUILT CENTER

Cutting Alternate Blocks and Side and Corner Triangles

From the blue fabric:
• Cut nine $7\frac{1}{2} \times 44$-inch strips. From these strips, cut forty-two $7\frac{1}{2}$-inch squares.
• Cut three 12×44-inch strips. From these strips, cut seven 12-inch squares. Cut these squares diagonally into quarters to make 28 side triangles. (You will have two extra triangles.)
• Cut two 9-inch squares. Cut these squares in half to make four corner triangles.

Note: The side triangles and corner triangles will be larger than necessary and will be trimmed after they have been added to the pieced blocks.

Assembling the Quilt Center

Step 1. The quilt is assembled in diagonal rows. Join the Rosebud block units and the $7\frac{1}{2}$-inch blue alternate blocks, as shown in **Diagram 8.** Begin and end with the side triangles as needed. Do not attach the corner triangles yet. While making the diagonal rows, press the seam allowances for each row in the opposite direction of the one before for easy matching and sewing of block intersections.

Step 2. Join the diagonal rows, pinning the block intersections for accuracy. Press these seam allowances all in one direction.

Step 3. Sew the corner triangles to the quilt top. Trim off excess fabric from the side and corner triangles. Before you trim, be sure to see "Trimming Side and Corner Triangles" on page 236 to be certain you make these cuts accurately. Use a ruler, cutting mat, and rotary

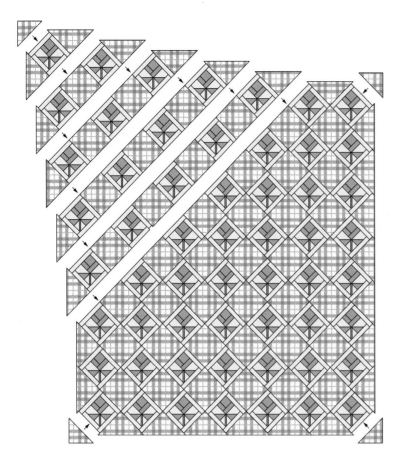

Diagram 8

cutter, leaving ¼-inch seam allowances beyond block corners. Make sure the corners are accurate 90 degree angles.

BORDERS

Cutting for Borders

The yardage given allows for border pieces to be cut cross-grain.

From the rose fabric:
• Cut nine 2 × 44-inch strips for the inner border

From the floral fabric:
• Cut thirteen 10 × 44-inch strips for the outer border

Attaching the Borders

Step 1. Stitch two rose inner border strips together with diagonal seams for each side of the quilt.

Step 2. Measure the quilt from left to right through the middle to determine the length of the top and bottom borders. Cut two of the pieced rose inner border strips to the necessary length and sew to the top and bottom of the quilt. Press all seams toward the borders.

Step 3. Measure the quilt from top to bottom through the middle, including the borders you just added, to determine the length of the side borders. Cut the remaining two rose inner border strips to the necessary length and sew to the sides of the quilt.

Step 4. Piece the floral outer border strips together with diagonal seams. You will need to piece two strips for the top border, two strips for the bottom border, and five strips for the side borders. Cut the long strip for the side borders in half crosswise.

Step 5. Measure the quilt as you did for the inner border in Step 2. Cut the top and bottom floral outer border strips to the necessary length and sew to the quilt.

Step 6. Measure the quilt as you did in Step 3. Cut the remaining floral outer border strips to the necessary length and sew to the sides of the quilt.

QUILTING

Step 1. Prepare the backing for the quilt by cutting the 8-yard length of backing fabric into three 2⅔-yard lengths. Remove the selvages and sew the three lengths together along the long edges. Press the seam allowances open.

Step 2. Trim the backing and batting so they are 4 inches larger than the quilt top.

Step 3. Mark the quilt top.

Step 4. Layer the backing, batting, and quilt top. Baste these layers together and quilt by hand or machine.

BINDING

The 2¾-inch strips will produce a ⅜- to ½-inch-wide binding. If you want a wider or narrower binding, adjust the width of the strips you cut. (See page 247 for pointers on how to experiment with binding width.) See "Making and Attaching the Binding" on page 245 to complete your quilt.

Cutting for Cross-Grain Binding

From the green fabric:
• Cut eleven 2¾ × 44-inch strips

QUILTING IDEAS

◢ My quilt was machine quilted with a flower design in the alternate blocks and a feather design in the outer border.

◢ You can do meander quilting around the pieced rosebud and the quilted flower and feather designs. See the diagram here and "Meander and Stipple Quilting" on page 246 for details of this technique.

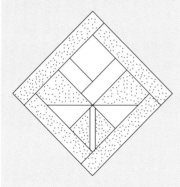

◢ To hand quilt, stitch in the ditch along the rosebuds and inner border so they puff out a little.

◢ Add a floral design in the alternate blocks.

◢ A hand-quilted large feather design would be nice in the outer border.

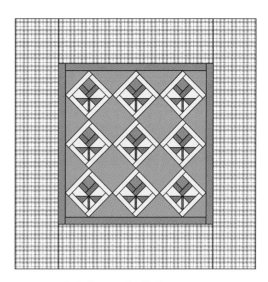

Miniature Quilt Diagram

BABY ROSEBUD MINIATURE QUILT

SIZE

Miniature quilt: 25 inches square (unquilted)

Finished block: 3½ inches square

FABRIC AND SUPPLIES

Yardage is based on 44-inch-wide fabric.

¾ yard of red solid fabric for rosebuds, inner border, and binding

¼ yard of dark green print fabric for bud base, leaves, and stems

⅜ yard of beige print fabric for background

¼ yard of medium green print fabric for alternate blocks and side and corner triangles

⅔ yard of green plaid fabric for outer border

¾ yard of fabric for quilt backing

Quilt batting, at least 29 inches square

Rotary cutter, mat, and see-through ruler

FABRIC KEY

 RED

 DARK GREEN PRINT

 BEIGE PRINT

 MEDIUM GREEN PRINT

 GREEN PLAID

ROSEBUD BLOCKS
(Make 9)

Be sure to read "Getting Ready" for the Bed Quilt on page 28 before you begin.

Cutting for Rosebud Blocks

From the red fabric:
• Cut one 1½ × 15-inch strip. From this strip, cut nine 1½-inch squares.

From the dark green fabric:
• Cut one 1 × 44-inch strip. From this strip, cut nine 1 × 1½-inch pieces and nine 1 × 2-inch pieces.
• Cut one 1½ × 28-inch strip. From this strip, cut eighteen 1½-inch squares.
• Cut one ¾ × 24-inch strip. From this strip, cut nine ¾ × 2½-inch pieces.

From the beige fabric:
• Cut one 1½ × 37-inch strip. From this strip, cut eighteen 1½ × 2-inch pieces.
• Cut one 1⅝ × 18-inch strip. From this strip, cut nine 1⅝-inch squares.
• Cut one 1 × 29-inch strip. From this strip, cut nine 1 × 3-inch pieces.
• Cut three 1 × 44-inch strips. From these strips, cut eighteen 1 × 3½-inch pieces and nine 1 × 4-inch pieces.

Piecing the Rosebud Blocks

Step 1. Sew a 1 × 1½-inch dark green strip to a 1½-inch red square. Press seam allowances to the dark green fabric. Sew a 1 × 2-inch green strip to this unit. Press. See **Diagram 1** on page 28. Repeat to make 9 units.

Step 2. With right sides together, place a 1½-inch dark green square on a 1½ × 2-inch beige leaf strip. See **Diagram 2** on page 29. Draw a diagonal line from corner to corner on the green square. Do not stitch

on top of the line. Stitch just a hair (approximately ¹⁄₃₂ inch) to the outside edge of the line. Trim corners leaving a scant ¼-inch seam allowance. Press seam allowances toward the green fabric. The leaf unit should measure 1½ × 2 inches. Make nine leaf units for the left side and nine for the right side. To make leaf units for the right side, draw a diagonal line from corner to corner in the opposite direction. Stitch, trim, and press as you did for the left side.

Step 3. Cut the 1⅝-inch beige squares in half diagonally. Sew a ¾ × 2½-inch dark green stem strip between these triangles using a ¼-inch seam allowance. See **Diagram 3** on page 29. The green ends will extend beyond the triangles. Press seams toward the stem. This stem unit must measure 1½ inches square. If it does not, adjust seam allowances. Trim the square to 1½ inches if needed. Make nine stem units.

Step 4. Sew a stem unit to a left leaf unit, as shown in **Diagram 4** on page 29. Sew a rosebud to the right leaf unit. See **Diagram 5** on page 29. Sew these two units together. See **Diagram 6** on page 29. Repeat to make nine Rosebud blocks.

Step 5. Sew a 1 × 3-inch beige strip to the bottom left side of a Rosebud block, as shown in **Diagram 9.**

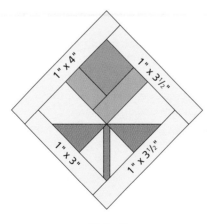

Make 9
Diagram 9

Continue sewing beige strips to the edges of the block, moving around the block in a counterclockwise direction. Add a 3½-inch strip to the bottom right side, another 3½-inch strip to the top right side, and end with a 4-inch strip on the top left side. Repeat this step for all of the Rosebud blocks.

QUILT CENTER

Cutting for Alternate Blocks and Side and Corner Triangles

From the medium green print fabric:
• Cut four 4-inch squares
• Cut two 7-inch squares. Cut these squares in quarters diagonally to make eight side triangles.
• Cut two 5½-inch squares. Cut these squares in half diagonally to make four corner triangles.

Note: The side and corner triangles will be larger than necessary and will be trimmed after they have been added to the pieced blocks.

Assembling the Quilt Center

Step 1. This quilt is assembled in diagonal rows. Join the Rosebud blocks and the 4-inch medium green alternate blocks, as shown in **Diagram 10.** Add the side triangles as necessary. Press the seam allowances for each row in the opposite direction of the previous row to allow for ease in matching and sewing block intersections.

Step 2. Join the diagonal rows, pinning at the block intersections for accuracy. Press all these seam allowances in one direction.

Step 3. Sew the corner triangles to the quilt top. Trim off excess fabric from the side and corner triangles. Before you trim, be sure to see "Trimming Side and Corner Triangles" on

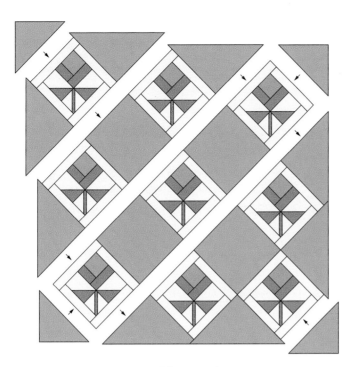

Diagram 10

page 236 to be certain you make these cuts accurately. Using a ruler, cutting mat, and rotary cutter, leave ¼-inch seam allowances beyond block corners. Make sure the corners are accurate 90 degree angles.

BORDERS

Cutting for Borders

The yardage given allows for border pieces to be cut cross-grain.

From the red fabric:
• Cut two 1¼ × 44-inch strips for the inner border

From the green plaid fabric:
• Cut four 5 × 44-inch strips for the outer border

Attaching the Borders

Step 1. Measure the quilt from left to right through the middle to determine the length of the top and bottom inner borders. Cut one of the red inner border strips to the necessary lengths and sew to the top and bottom of the quilt.

Step 2. Measure the quilt from top to bottom through middle, including the borders you just added, to determine the length of the side borders. Cut the other red inner border strip to the necessary lengths and sew to the sides of the quilt. Press seams toward the borders.

Step 3. Attach the green plaid outer borders to your quilt. Measure as you did for the inner border, adding the top and bottom borders first, followed by the side borders.

QUILTING

Step 1. Trim the backing and batting so they are 4 inches larger than the quilt top.

Step 2. Mark the quilt top.

Step 3. Layer the backing, batting, and quilt top. Baste these layers together and quilt.

BINDING

The 2¾-inch binding strips will produce a ⅜- to ½-inch-wide binding. If you want a wider or narrower binding, adjust the width

QUILTING IDEAS

◪ The rosebud pieces, as well as the inner border, have in-the-ditch quilting.

◪ Divide the alternate blocks diagonally into quarters and quilt with straight lines. See the diagram.

◪ The side triangles have two Vs quilted an equal distance apart, while the corner triangles have two parallel quilting lines.

◪ The plaid border contains a twisted rope quilting pattern taken from a quilting stencil.

of the strips you cut. (See page 247 for pointers on how to experiment with binding width.) See "Making and Attaching the Binding" on page 245 to complete your quilt.

Cutting for Cross-Grain Binding

From the red fabric:
• Cut four 2¾ × 44-inch strips

Quilt Diagram

SIZE

Bed quilt: 84 × 108 inches
(unquilted)

Finished block: 12 inches square

FABRICS AND SUPPLIES

Yardage is based on 44-inch-wide fabric.

⅓ yard of gold print fabric for flower centers

½ yard of blue print fabric for flower centers

1¼ yards of red print fabric for flowers and inner border

1¼ yards of medium green print fabric for flowers

2 yards of dark green print fabric for leaves and sawtooth border

3 yards of beige solid fabric for background, alternate blocks, and sawtooth border

3¼ yards of large floral print for alternate blocks and outer border

1½ yards of fabric for bias binding

7½ yards of fabric for quilt backing

Quilt batting, at least 88 × 112 inches

Rotary cutter, mat, and see-through ruler

Cottage Flower brings to mind long summer days, white wicker furniture on the porch, and cabbage roses in a country garden. It also gave me a way to use one of those delightful, large-scale floral prints many of us fall in love with but then never know how to use in a quilt. In this design, the floral print appears in the pieced alternate blocks and outer border, where you can appreciate it without being overwhelmed. One suggestion for selecting fabrics is to start with this large-scale print, then pick the other fabrics to coordinate with the colors in the print.

FABRIC KEY

- GOLD PRINT
- BLUE PRINT
- RED PRINT
- MEDIUM GREEN PRINT
- DARK GREEN PRINT
- BEIGE SOLID
- LARGE FLORAL PRINT

GETTING READY

- Read instructions thoroughly before you begin.
- Prewash and press fabric.
- Use $\frac{1}{4}$-inch seam allowances throughout unless directions specify otherwise.
- Seam allowances are included in the cutting sizes given.
- Press seam allowance in the direction that will create the least bulk and, whenever possible, toward the darker fabric.
- Cutting directions for each section of the quilt are given in the areas following the row of scissors. If you like to cut as you go, simply follow the directions as you get them. If you'd rather cut all your pieces at once, skip ahead and look for the scissors to do all the cutting before you begin to sew.
- Instructions are given for quick cutting and piecing the blocks. Note that for some of the pieces, the quick-cutting method will result in leftover fabric.

COTTAGE FLOWER BLOCKS

(Make 18)

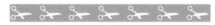

Cutting for Flowers

Note: You will be cutting pieces to make 18 Flower blocks. You will also have some leftover pieces that will be used later to make 4 partial Flower blocks for the quilt corners.

From the gold fabric:
- Cut two $3\frac{3}{8} \times 44$-inch strips.

From these strips, cut twenty-two $3\frac{3}{8}$-inch squares.

From the blue fabric:
- Cut four $2\frac{7}{8} \times 44$-inch strips.

From these strips, cut forty-four $2\frac{7}{8}$-inch squares. Cut the squares in half diagonally to make 88 triangles.

From the red fabric:
- Cut six $2\frac{7}{8} \times 44$-inch strips

From the medium green fabric:
- Cut six $2\frac{7}{8} \times 44$-inch strips
- Cut six $2\frac{1}{2} \times 44$-inch strips.

From these strips, cut eighty-eight $2\frac{1}{2}$-inch squares.

Piecing the Flowers

Step 1. Lay a blue triangle along one edge of a gold square with right sides together, then stitch. See **Diagram 1.** Repeat this step for the opposite side of the square, and press seam allowances toward the blue fabric. Sew a blue triangle to each of the two remaining sides of the gold square. Press seam allowances toward the blue fabric. Repeat to make 22 flower centers.

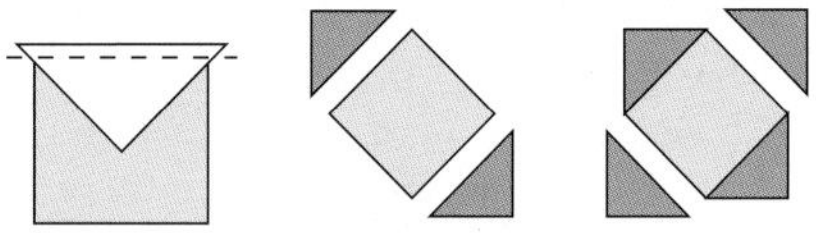

Diagram 1

Step 2. With right sides together, layer a $2\frac{7}{8} \times 44$-inch red strip and a $2\frac{7}{8} \times 44$-inch medium green strip together. Layer the remaining $2\frac{7}{8}$-inch strips into pairs of red and green strips. Press together, but do not stitch.

Step 3. With your rotary cutter, cut the layered strips into eighty-eight $2\frac{7}{8}$-inch squares. See **Diagram 2.**

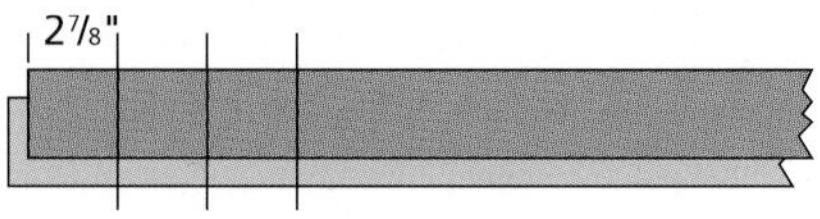

Diagram 2

Step 4. Keeping edges even, cut the layered squares in half diagonally, as shown in **Diagram 3.** Stitch $\frac{1}{4}$ inch

from the diagonal edge, being careful not to stretch the fabric, since you will be sewing on the bias edge. Press seam allowance toward the red fabric to make a 2½-inch triangle-pieced square. Repeat for the remaining layered squares.

Diagram 3

Step 5. Sew two triangle-pieced squares together, referring to **Diagram 4** for color placement. Make 88 of these petal units. Press. Sew a petal unit to the top and bottom of each flower center. See **Diagram 5**. Press seam allowances toward the petal units.

Diagram 4

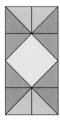

Diagram 5

Step 6. Sew a 2½-inch medium green square to each end of the 44 remaining petal units. See **Diagram 6**. Sew these units to the remaining sides of the flower centers, as shown in **Diagram 7**. Press seam allowances toward the petal units. At this point, your block should measure 8½ inches square. Set aside four of these flowers to be used in the corner blocks.

Diagram 6

8½"

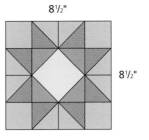

8½"

Diagram 7

Cutting for Leaves

From the dark green fabric:
• Cut seven 2⅞ × 44-inch strips
• Cut ten 2½ × 44-inch strips.
From these strips, cut one hundred forty-eight 2½-inch squares.

From the beige fabric:
• Cut seven 2⅞ × 44-inch strips
• Cut five 2½ × 44-inch strips.
From these strips, cut seventy-six 2½-inch squares.

Piecing the Leaves

Step 1. With right sides together, layer a 2⅞ × 44-inch dark green strip and a 2⅞ × 44-inch beige strip. Layer the remaining 2⅞-inch strips into dark green and beige pairs. Press strip pairs together, but do not stitch.

Step 2. Cut the layered strips into 92 squares, each 2⅞ inches. Cut layered squares in half diagonally as in **Diagram 3**. Stitch ¼ inch from the diagonal edge.

Step 3. Press seam allowance toward the dark green fabric to make a 2½-inch triangle-pieced square. Repeat for the remaining layered squares to make 184 triangle-pieced squares.

Step 4. Set aside eight triangle-pieced squares to be used in the corner blocks. Sew the remainder of the triangle-pieced squares together in pairs, as shown in **Diagram 8.** Press seams open. Make 88 of these leaf units. Set aside 16 of these leaf

units to be used in the corner blocks. Sew a 2½-inch dark green square to each end of the 72 remaining leaf units, as shown in **Diagram 9.** You will have four extra dark green squares that will be used in the corner blocks.

Diagram 8

Diagram 9

Step 5. Sew a leaf unit to the top and bottom of each of the Flower blocks to be used in the quilt center. See **Diagram 10.** Press seam allowances toward leaf units.

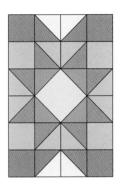

Diagram 10

Step 6. Sew a 2½-inch beige square to each end of the 36 leaf units, as shown in **Diagram 11.** Press the seam allowances toward the beige fabric. (You will have four extra beige squares that will be used in the corner blocks.) Sew the leaf units to the sides of each of the Flower blocks. See **Diagram 12** on page 38. Press the seam allowances toward the leaf units. The blocks should measure 12½ inches square. Adjust seam allowances if necessary.

Diagram 11

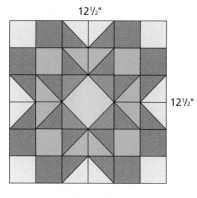

12½"

12½"

Make 18
Diagram 12

ALTERNATE BLOCKS
(Make 17)

Cutting for Alternate Blocks

From *each* of the beige and large floral print fabrics:
• Cut three $13\frac{3}{8} \times 44$-inch strips. From these strips, cut nine $13\frac{3}{8}$-inch squares of each fabric. Cut the squares diagonally into quarters, forming 36 triangles. (You will use only 34 of the triangles in the quilt.)

Assembling the Alternate Blocks

Step 1. With right sides together, layer a floral triangle on a beige triangle. Sew a $\frac{1}{4}$-inch seam along one of the bias edges, being careful not to stretch your triangles. Also, make sure you sew along the same bias edge for each triangle set so your pieced triangles will all have the floral fabric on the same side. See **Diagram 13.** Press the seam allowance toward the floral fabric. Make 34 of these units.

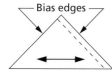

Bias edges

Diagram 13

Step 2. Sew two of these units together to make an alternate block measuring 12½ inches square, as shown in **Diagram 14.**

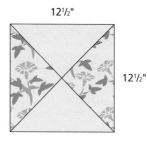

12½"

12½"

Make 17
Diagram 14

QUILT CENTER

The Cottage Flower Quilt is assembled in seven horizontal rows of five blocks each. See the **Quilt Diagram** on page 35 for the order of block placement.

Step 1. Sew the blocks into rows, alternating Flower blocks and alternate blocks. Press seam allowances toward the alternate blocks.

Step 2. Join the seven horizontal rows to make the quilt center. Your quilt top should measure $60\frac{1}{2} \times 84\frac{1}{2}$ inches at this time. If it doesn't, adjust seam allowances so borders will fit.

BORDERS

Cutting for Borders

The yardage given allows for border pieces to be cut cross-grain. The inner, sawtooth, and outer borders will be sewn together as one border unit, which will then be attached to the quilt.

From the red fabric:
• Cut eight $2\frac{1}{2} \times 44$-inch strips for the inner border

From the beige fabric:
• Cut six $2\frac{7}{8} \times 44$-inch strips for the sawtooth border
• Cut two $2\frac{1}{2} \times 44$-inch strips. From these strips, cut sixteen $4\frac{1}{2}$-inch lengths for the corner blocks.

From the dark green fabric:
• Cut six $2\frac{7}{8} \times 44$-inch strips for the sawtooth border

From the floral fabric:
• Cut eight $8\frac{1}{2} \times 44$-inch strips for the outer border

Piecing the Inner Border

Step 1. Piece three red inner border strips using a diagonal seam to make one long border strip. See **Diagram 15.** From this strip cut two inner border strips $60\frac{1}{2}$ inches long.

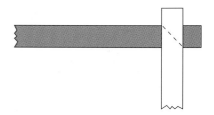

Diagram 15

Step 2. Piece five red inner border strips together diagonally as you did for the top and bottom borders. From this strip, cut two inner border strips $84\frac{1}{2}$ inches long.

Piecing the Sawtooth Border

Step 1. With right sides together, layer a $2\frac{7}{8} \times 44$-inch dark green strip and a $2\frac{7}{8} \times 44$-inch beige strip. Layer the remaining dark green and beige strips into pairs. Press the pairs, but do not stitch.

Step 2. Cut these layered strips into seventy-two $2\frac{7}{8}$-inch squares. Cut the layered squares in half diagonally, as shown in **Diagram 3** on page 37. Stitch $\frac{1}{4}$ inch from the diagonal edge.

HINTS & HELPS

The sawtooth border requires very accurate cutting and stitching. Because so many seams are involved, half of which are bias, there is always an opportunity for a sawtooth border to be "off" a bit. Measure often as you stitch the triangles together. If the completed sawtooth border is too long or too short, adjust seams in many places rather than trying to make up the difference in just a few places.

In making adjustments, you must match the center of the border to the center of the quilt and adjust the seams going in either direction. This is especially critical in borders with a center point such as this one.

Step 3. Press seam allowances toward the dark green fabric to make 144 triangle-pieced squares.

Step 4. Sew 30 of the triangle-pieced squares together for each of the top and bottom sawtooth borders, as shown in **Diagram 16.** Notice how the sawtooth border changes direction from the center out. Sew 42 triangle-pieced squares together for each side sawtooth border. The sawtooth borders should be the same length as your inner border strips. Adjust seam allowances if necessary to achieve the same measurements.

Center

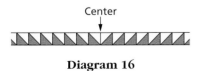

Diagram 16

Piecing the Outer Border

Step 1. Piece three floral outer border strips together diagonally, as shown in **Diagram 15.** From this strip cut two 60½-inch border strips, which should be the measurement of your quilt top and bottom.

Step 2. Piece five floral outer border strips together with diagonal seams. From this strip cut two 84½-inch side border strips, which should be the measurement of your quilt sides.

Assembling the Borders

Step 1. Referring to **Diagram 17,** arrange the inner, sawtooth, and outer borders in the correct order for the top, bottom, and sides.

Step 2. Sew the red inner borders to the sawtooth borders. Press seam allowances toward the inner borders.

Step 3. Sew the floral outer borders to the other side of the sawtooth borders. Press seam allowances toward the outer borders.

Diagram 17

Step 4. Attach the top and bottom border units to the quilt. Press seam allowances toward the inner borders. Set aside the units for the side borders.

Making the Corner Blocks

You will be using four Flower blocks, eight 2½-inch triangle-pieced squares, sixteen leaf units, four 2½-inch dark green squares, and four 2½-inch beige squares to make the four corner blocks.

Step 1. To make a double leaf unit, sew together two of the leaf units that you set aside earlier. See **Diagram 18.** Repeat to make eight double leaf units. Sew a 2½ × 4½-inch beige rectangle to each side of a double leaf unit, as shown in **Diagram 19.** Repeat for each of the remaining double leaf units. Sew a double leaf unit to the top of each of the remaining Flower blocks. See **Diagram 20.** Press seam allowances toward the Flower blocks.

Diagram 18

Diagram 19

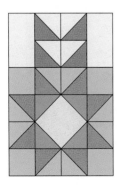

Diagram 20

Step 2. Sew four 2½-inch dark green squares to four 2½-inch triangle-pieced squares, as shown in **Diagram 21.** Sew four 2½-inch beige squares to four 2½-inch triangle-pieced squares, referring to **Diagram 21** for color placement. Sew these units together, as shown in the diagram. Make four units.

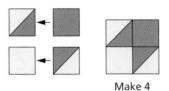

Make 4

Diagram 21

Step 3. Sew these corner units to the remaining four double leaf units, as shown in **Diagram 22.** Sew these units to the flower/leaf units from Step 1 to complete the corner blocks. See **Diagram 23.**

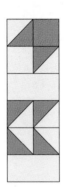

Diagram 22

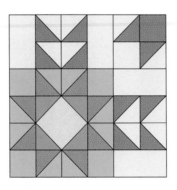

Diagram 23

Step 4. Sew the four corner blocks to the ends of the side border units, referring to **Diagram 24** for directional placement of each corner block. Attach the side border units to the quilt. Press seam allowances toward the inner borders.

QUILTING

Step 1. To prepare the backing for the quilt, cut the backing fabric crosswise into three 2½-yard lengths. Remove the selvages and sew the lengths together along the long edges. Press seam allowances open.

Step 2. Trim the backing and batting so they are approximately 4 inches larger than the quilt top.

Step 3. Mark the quilt top for quilting.

Step 4. Layer the backing, batting, and quilt top. Baste these layers together and quilt.

BINDING

The 2½-inch binding strip will produce a ¼-inch-wide binding. If you want a wider or narrower binding, adjust the width of the strip you cut. (See page 247 for pointers on how to experiment with the binding width.) Refer to "Making and Attaching the Binding" on page 245 to complete your quilt.

Cutting for Bias Binding

From the binding fabric:
• Cut enough 2½-inch wide bias strips to make a 400-inch strip

Diagram 24

QUILTING IDEAS

▨ My quilt was machine quilted.

▨ The Flower blocks are quilted with an allover flower design. For a different look, outline quilt the small pieces in the Flower blocks.

▨ Quilt each triangle of the alternate blocks with half of the flower design used in the Flower blocks.

▨ You can do machine stipple quilting around the half flower in the beige triangles to fill in the rest of the beige background area. See "Meander and Stipple Quilting" on page 246.

▨ Quilt a simple chain in the inner border.

▨ Outline quilt the sawtooth border and do machine stipple quilting in the beige triangles.

▨ The outer border could be quilted with a large chain or feather design.

Quilt Diagram

Birds and Blooms is one of my favorite quilts because it has a little bit of everything I love about quilting. Its old-fashioned colors, folk-art appliqué shapes, and hand quilting give it the appearance of an antique scrap quilt. It's easy to make the many components of this quilt work together when you choose colors with a similar value (lightness or darkness). Here's a chance to use some of your scraps, or check out the wonderful fat quarters (18 × 22-inch pieces) many quilt shops carry so that you can work with a wide variety of colors and fabrics.

SIZE

Wall quilt: 44 inches square (unquilted)

Finished block: 6 inches square

FABRICS AND SUPPLIES

Yardage is based on 44-inch-wide fabric.

½ yard of unbleached muslin for pieced blocks and pieced border

1 yard of medium beige print fabric for alternate blocks, side and corner triangles, and inner border

¼ yard *each* of nine different medium to dark print fabrics for pieced blocks and pieced border

½ yard of green print fabric for stems and leaves

½ yard of scraps for flower and bird appliqués

1½ yards of dark red print fabric for outer border and binding

2¾ yards of fabric for quilt backing

Quilt batting, at least 48 inches square

Rotary cutter, mat, and see-through ruler

Template plastic

Freezer paper

FABRIC KEY

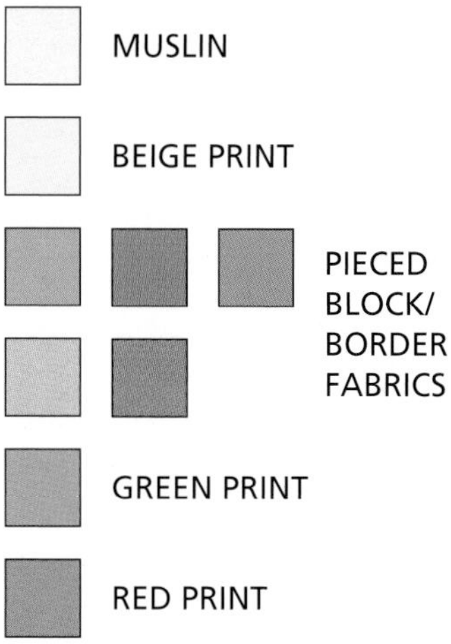

MUSLIN

BEIGE PRINT

PIECED BLOCK/ BORDER FABRICS

GREEN PRINT

RED PRINT

- Read instructions thoroughly before you begin.
- Prewash and press fabric.
- Use ¼-inch seam allowances throughout unless directions specify otherwise.
- Seam allowances are included in the cutting sizes given.
- Press seam allowance in the direction that will create the least bulk and, whenever possible, toward the darker fabric.
- Trace templates (pages 48–49) for appliqué patterns onto template plastic and cut out.
- Cutting directions for each section of the quilt are given in the areas following the row of scissors. If you like to cut as you go, simply follow the directions as you get to them. If you'd rather cut all your pieces at once, skip ahead and look for the scissors to do all the cutting before you begin to sew.

BIRDS IN THE AIR BLOCKS
(Make 9)

Cutting for Pieced Blocks

From the muslin:
- Cut three 2⅜ × 44-inch strips. From these strips, cut thirty-six 2⅜-inch squares.

From *each* of the nine medium to dark print fabrics:
- Cut one 5-inch square
- Cut four 2⅜-inch squares

Assembling the Pieced Blocks

Step 1. With right sides together, layer a 2⅜-inch muslin square and a 2⅜-inch colored square from the pieced block fabric. Cut the layered square in half diagonally, as shown in **Diagram 1.** Stitch ¼-inch from the diagonal edge. Press open to form a 2-inch triangle-pieced square. Repeat to make seven triangle-pieced squares from *each* of your nine colors for the pieced blocks.

Diagram 1

You will have one extra triangle-pieced square of each color.

Step 2. Referring to **Diagram 2** for color placement, stitch three triangle-pieced squares together. Make sure your squares are all of the same color fabric. Make another unit with four same-color triangle-pieced squares as in **Diagram 2.** Repeat for all nine blocks.

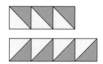

Diagram 2

Step 3. Stitch the unit of three triangle-pieced squares to the top of the coordinating 5-inch colored block. Press seam toward the colored block. Now add the unit of four triangle-pieced squares to the right side of the colored block, as shown in **Diagram 3.** Repeat for all nine blocks.

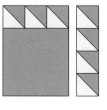

Make 9
Diagram 3

QUILT CENTER

Cutting Side and Corner Triangles and Alternate Blocks

From the beige fabric:
• Cut two 10½-inch squares. Cut these into quarters diagonally to make eight side triangles.
• Cut two 7½-inch squares. Cut these in half diagonally to make four corner triangles.
• Cut one 6½ × 44-inch strip. From this strip, cut four 6½-inch squares.
Note: The side triangles and corner triangles will be larger than necessary and will be trimmed after they have been added to the pieced blocks.

Assembling the Quilt Center

The quilt is assembled in diagonal rows, as shown in **Diagram 4**. The pieced blocks change direction in alternating *vertical* rows. In the first

and last row, the triangle-pieced squares point downward. In the center row, they point upward. When sewing the blocks into rows, press the seam allowances for each row in the opposite direction of the row before. This allows for easy matching and sewing block intersections.

Step 1. Sew the pieced blocks and alternate blocks, as shown in **Diagram 4,** beginning and ending with side triangles as needed. Do not attach the corner triangles yet.

Step 2. Join the diagonal rows, pinning the block intersections for accuracy. Press the seam allowances in one direction.

Step 3. Sew the triangles to the corners of the quilt top, as shown in **Diagram 4.**

Step 4. Trim off excess side and corner triangles allowing a ¼-inch seam allowance *beyond* the block

corners. Before you trim, be sure to see "Trimming Side and Corner Triangles" on page 236 to be certain you make these cuts accurately.

BORDERS

The yardage given allows for border pieces to be cut cross-grain.

Cutting for Inner Border

From the beige fabric cut:
• Four 4½ × 44-inch strips

Attaching the Inner Border

Step 1. Measure the quilt from left to right through the middle to determine the length of the top and bottom borders. Cut the beige inner border strips to the necessary length. Sew the inner border strips to the top and bottom.

Step 2. Measure the quilt from top to bottom through the middle, including the borders you just added, to determine the length of the side borders. Cut the beige inner border strips to the necessary length and sew to the sides of the quilt.

Step 3. Stay stitch ⅛ inch from the raw edges of the inner border to stabilize them for the appliqué process.

Appliquéing the Border

The designs can be hand appliquéd with a blind stitch or machine appliquéd with a satin stitch. I used the freezer paper method of hand appliqué. All the appliqué should be done using thread that matches the appliqué fabric. For *hand appliqué*, add ⅛- to ¼-inch seam allowances to each appliqué piece. For *machine appliqué,* cut out the appliqué pieces with *no* seam allowance added. See "Hand Appliqué" on page 238 or "Machine Appliqué" on page 239.

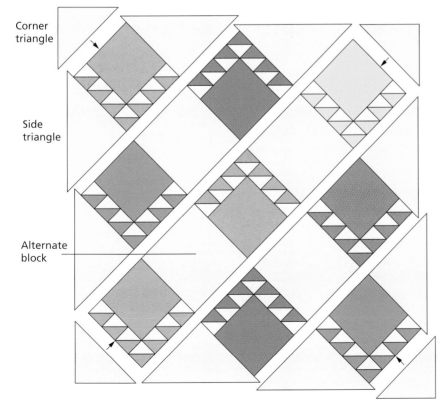

Corner triangle

Side triangle

Alternate block

Diagram 4

FREEZER PAPER APPLIQUÉ

Step 1. Trace the appliqué shapes onto the dull side of the freezer paper. Cut out the shapes. **Note:** You will need to reverse the bird pattern when you trace it so that it will be facing the right direction when you cut it out of the fabric.

Step 2. Press the shiny side of the freezer paper to the wrong side of the fabrics chosen for appliqué. Make sure to space the shapes at least ½ inch apart so you will have enough fabric for seam allowances.

Step 3. Cut the fabric ⅛ to ¼ inch outside of the freezer paper shapes to allow for seam allowances. Finger press seam allowances over the paper edge.

Cutting for Appliqué

From your appliqué fabrics:
- Cut 1 bird
- Cut 2 bird legs
- Cut 4 eggs
- Cut 1 outside nest
- Cut 1 inside nest
- Cut 4 round flowers
- Cut 1 oval flower
- Cut 1 oval flower center
- Cut 2 flower tops
- Cut 2 flower bases
- Cut 6 flower centers
- Cut 15 berries
- Cut 15 large leaves
- Cut 7 small leaves
- Cut enough 1⅜-inch-wide green bias strips to make a 90-inch strip. From this, cut one 9½-inch-long strip, two 8½-inch-long strips, two 7½-inch-long strips, three 5½-inch-long strips, two 4-inch-long strips, and one 3½-inch-long strip. (See "Making Bias Binding" on page 246 for tips on cutting bias strips.)

Making and Attaching Stems and Branches

❖ Fold each 1⅜-inch stem strip in half lengthwise with wrong sides together and press.

❖ Draw a very light placement line on the background fabric.

❖ Place the raw edges of the folded strip along the placement line. Use a matching green thread to stitch the strip to the background with a small running stitch ¼ inch from the raw edge as shown.

❖ Bring the folded edge over to cover the raw edges and pin in place. Tuck the ends under if they will not be covered by other appliqué pieces.

❖ Appliqué the folded edge and ends in place.

Bring fold over raw edges

Stitch ¼" from raw edge

Fold

Raw edges

Step 4. Refer to the **Appliqué Guide** on page 48 for placement of the appliqué pieces. See "Making and Attaching Stems and Branches" for details on the bias stems and branches. Pin the appliqué shapes to the quilt top. Hand appliqué the shapes in place, layering in order, as numbered in the **Appliqué Guide** for each portion of the quilt. Leave openings where stems and leaves

HINTS & HELPS

I do not cut away fabric behind appliqués unless there are a great many layers and it's obviously bulky and difficult to quilt through. It just adds another step that's not necessary. Plus, there's always the danger of cutting straight through your appliqué. My more primitive and chunky appliqué designs don't really warrant the cutting, and it does weaken the quilt top somewhat.

need to be inserted. When you have about ½ inch left to appliqué, remove the freezer paper. Then finish stitching.

Cutting for Pieced Border

From the nine medium and dark print fabrics and appliqué scraps:
- Cut forty-four 2⅜-inch squares. (Use fabrics from both blocks and appliqués to get a good variety of colors.)
- Cut four 2-inch squares for corner blocks

From the muslin:
- Cut three 2⅜-inch × 44-inch strips. From these strips, cut forty-four 2⅜-inch squares.

Assembling the Pieced Border

Step 1. With right sides together, layer a colored square and a muslin square. Cut in half diagonally. See **Diagram 1** on page 44. Stitch ¼ inch from the diagonal edge of each triangle set. Press seams

Diagram 5

Diagram 6

Diagram 7

toward the darker fabric to make 2-inch triangle-pieced squares. Repeat with the remaining squares to make 88 triangle-pieced squares.

Step 2. Sew two triangle-pieced squares of the same colored fabric together, as shown in **Diagram 5,** to form points. You will have 44 of these units.

Step 3. Join 11 of the units from Step 2 together to make each border strip. Make sure all the points are facing in the same direction. See **Diagram 6.**

Step 4. Sew a pieced border strip to the top and bottom of the quilt, with the colored points pointing toward the quilt center. Make seam allowance adjustments if necessary to make the border fit.

Step 5. Sew the 2-inch corner blocks to the ends of the remaining two pieced border strips, as shown in **Diagram 7.** Sew these strips to the quilt sides.

Cutting for Outer Border

From the red fabric:
• Cut five 4½ × 44-inch strips

Attaching the Outer Border

Step 1. Measure the quilt from left to right through the middle to determine the length of the top and bottom borders. Attach the top and bottom red outer borders to the quilt.

Step 2. Measure the quilt from top to bottom through the middle, including the borders you just added to determine the length of the side borders.

Step 3. Piece the three remaining border strips together with diagonal seams to form one long strip, then cut two pieces to the length needed for your side borders. Sew the red outer border strips to the sides of the quilt.

QUILTING

Step 1. Prepare the backing for the quilt by cutting the 2¾-yard length of backing fabric in half crosswise to make two 1⅜-yard lengths. Remove the selvages.

Step 2. Sew the two lengths of backing fabric together with one center seam. Press the seam allowance open. Trim the backing and batting so they are approximately 4 inches larger than the quilt top.

Step 3. Mark the quilt top for quilting.

Step 4. Layer the backing, batting, and quilt top. Baste these layers together and quilt.

BINDING

The 2¾-inch binding strip will produce a ⅜- to ½-inch-wide binding. If you want a wider or narrower binding, adjust the width of the strips you cut. (See page 247 for pointers on how to experiment with binding width.) Refer to "Making and Attaching the Binding" on page 245 to complete your quilt.

Cutting for Cross-Grain Binding

From the red fabric:
• Cut five 2¾ × 44-inch strips

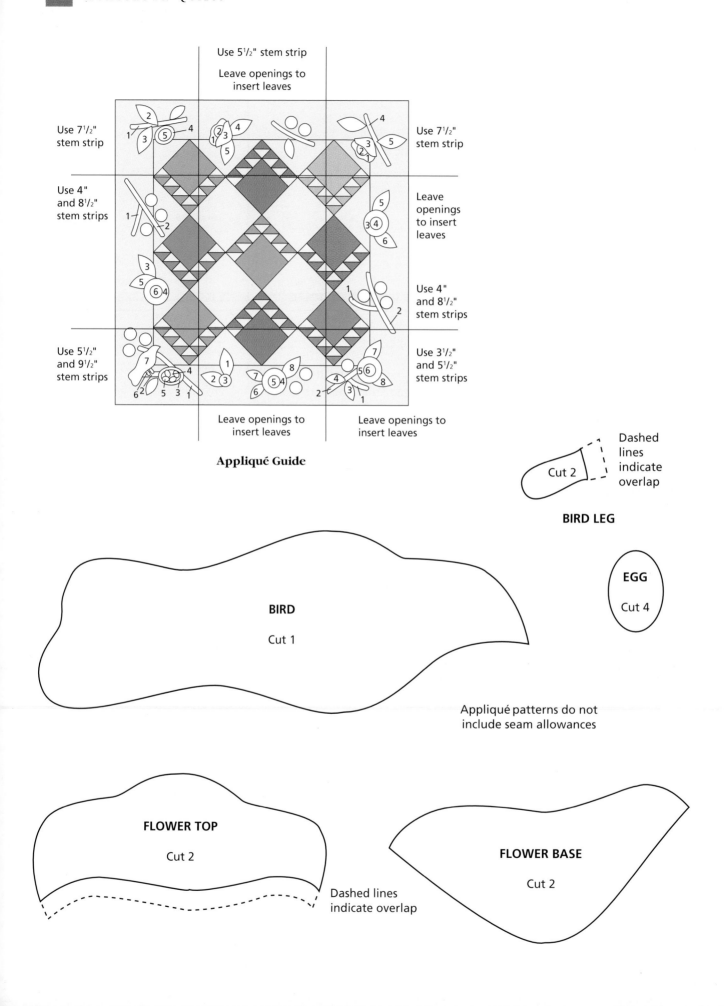

Use 5½" stem strip

Leave openings to insert leaves

Use 7½" stem strip

Use 7½" stem strip

Use 4" and 8½" stem strips

Leave openings to insert leaves

Use 4" and 8½" stem strips

Use 5½" and 9½" stem strips

Use 3½" and 5½" stem strips

Leave openings to insert leaves

Leave openings to insert leaves

Appliqué Guide

Cut 2

Dashed lines indicate overlap

BIRD LEG

BIRD

Cut 1

EGG

Cut 4

Appliqué patterns do not include seam allowances

FLOWER TOP

Cut 2

Dashed lines indicate overlap

FLOWER BASE

Cut 2

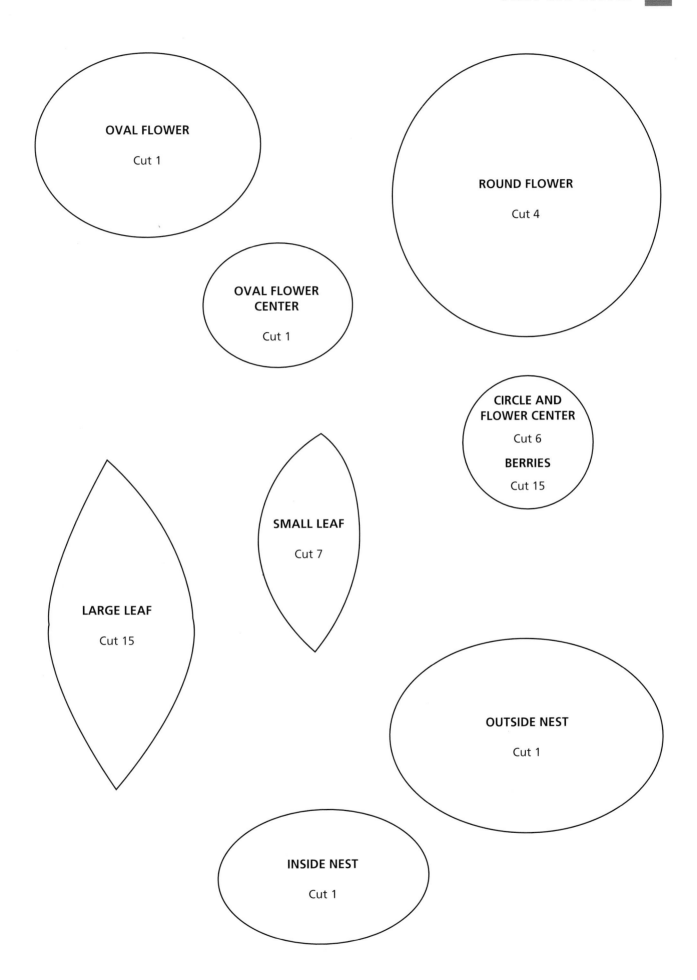

OVAL FLOWER

Cut 1

ROUND FLOWER

Cut 4

OVAL FLOWER
CENTER

Cut 1

CIRCLE AND
FLOWER CENTER

Cut 6

BERRIES

Cut 15

SMALL LEAF

Cut 7

LARGE LEAF

Cut 15

OUTSIDE NEST

Cut 1

INSIDE NEST

Cut 1

Quilt Diagram

I have a childlike fascination with sunflowers.
I remember spending summer days with my father out on country roads. We would stop to pick bunches of wild sunflowers growing alongside the road to take home to my mother. To this day, she remarks how the sunflower is still her favorite wildflower. I think of her every time I see them along the roadside. They are big, bold, strong, full of texture—and what great color! This small quilt is a perfect fall accessory, full of the rich colors of Indian summer. Sometimes I use it as a table topper with a huge black spatterware pail full of sunflowers, which I buy from a young woman at our local farmer's market.

SIZE

Wall quilt: 28 inches square (unquilted)

Finished block: 6 inches square.

FABRICS AND SUPPLIES

Yardage based on 44-inch-wide fabric.

$\frac{1}{2}$ yard of beige print background fabric

$\frac{7}{8}$ yard of green fabric for leaves and pieced outer border

$\frac{1}{2}$ yard of gold print fabric for flower petals, corner blocks, and pieced border

$\frac{1}{8}$ yard of black print fabric for flower center

$\frac{1}{2}$ yard of small black plaid fabric for lattice and inner border

$\frac{1}{2}$ yard of large black plaid fabric for binding

1 yard of fabric for quilt backing

1 yard of 16-inch-wide paper-backed fusible webbing (sewable)

Quilt batting, at least 32 inches square

Rotary cutter, mat, and see-through ruler

Template plastic

Black and gold embroidery floss

FABRIC KEY

 BEIGE PRINT

 GREEN PRINT

 GOLD PRINT

 BLACK PRINT

 SMALL BLACK PLAID

HINTS & HELPS

You may want to cut out the strips for the pieced border and outer border before cutting the sunflower appliqué pieces so you have the lengths needed for the borders.

GETTING READY

- Read instructions thoroughly before you begin.
- Prewash and press fabric.
- Use ¼-inch seam allowances throughout unless directions specify otherwise.
- Seam allowances are included in the cutting sizes given.
- Press seam allowance in the direction that will create the least bulk and, whenever possible, toward the darker fabric.
- Trace **Templates A, B,** and **C** (page 56) for sunflower appliqués onto template plastic and cut out.
- Cutting directions for each section of the quilt are given in the areas following the row of scissors. If you like to cut as you go, simply follow the directions as you get to them. If you'd rather cut all your pieces at once, skip ahead and look for the scissors to do all the cutting before you begin to sew.

SUNFLOWER BLOCKS
(Make 9)

Cutting for Sunflower Blocks

Trace **Templates A, B,** and **C** onto the paper side of the fusible webbing. Cut the shapes out loosely and fuse to the wrong side of the green, gold, and black print fabrics, following the manufacturer's directions.

From the beige fabric:
- Cut two 6½ × 44-inch strips. From these strips, cut nine 6½-inch squares.

From the green fabric with fusible webbing:
- Cut 36 of **Template A** for leaves

From the gold fabric with fusible webbing:
- Cut 72 of **Template B** for flower petals

From the black print fabric with fusible webbing:
- Cut 9 of **Template C** for flower centers

Appliquéing the Sunflower Blocks

Step 1. Peel off the paper backing from the appliqué shapes.

Step 2. Lay the background square on top of the **Block Diagram** on page 56 and trace the circles onto the fabric. Your traced lines will be covered by appliqué pieces, so you don't have to worry about erasing them.

Step 3. Position the leaves so the bottom edge is aligned with the Leaf Edge Placement circle. Press in place.

Step 4. Place four gold flower petals on top of the leaves with

Diagram 1

their bottom edges aligned with the Petal Edge Placement circle. See **Diagram 1.** Press petals in place.

Step 5. Place four more flower petals on the square, with the points between those of the first petals and the bottom edges aligned with the Petal Edge Placement circle. See **Diagram 2.** Press in place.

Step 6. Center the black print flower center over the petals, making sure the bottom raw edges of the petals are covered. Press in place. Your block should look like the one in **Diagram 3.**

Step 7. The appliqué shapes may be left as is, machine appliquéd with a satin or buttonhole stitch, or hand embellished with a small primitive stitch using two strands of embroidery floss. See "Machine Appliqué" on page 239 and "Primitive Appliqué" on page 239 for details on these techniques. If you choose to hand appliqué, use black embroidery floss for the leaf and petal pieces, and gold for the flower centers.

QUILT CENTER

Cutting for Lattice Pieces

From the small black plaid fabric:
• Cut two $1\frac{1}{2} \times 44$-inch strips. From these strips, cut twelve $1\frac{1}{2} \times 6\frac{1}{2}$-inch pieces.

From the gold print fabric:
• Cut four $1\frac{1}{2}$-inch squares

Quilt Center Assembly

Step 1. Arrange the Sunflower blocks, $6\frac{1}{2}$-inch lattice strips, and corner posts in rows, as shown in **Diagram 4.**

Step 2. Stitch three Sunflower blocks and two lattice strips together in a horizontal row. Make three of these rows.

Step 3. Stitch three lattice strips and two corner posts together to make a lattice row. Make two lattice rows.

Step 4. Stitch the rows together, as shown in **Diagram 5** on page 54, to make the quilt center.

Diagram 2

Make 9
Diagram 3

Diagram 4

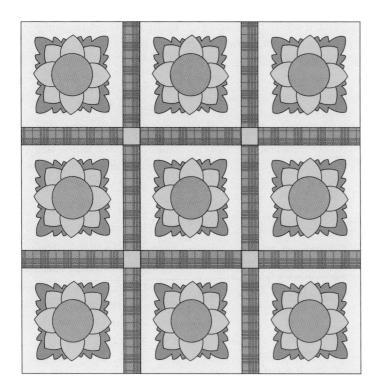

Diagram 5

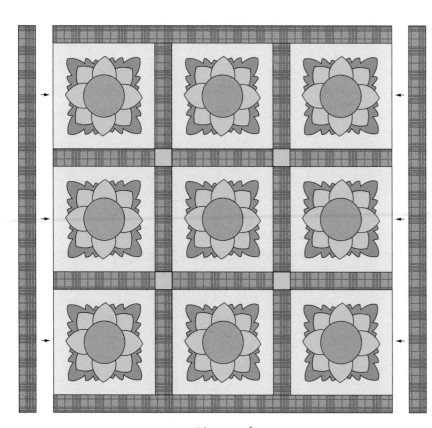

Diagram 6

BORDERS

Cutting for Borders

From the green print fabric:
• Cut two $1\frac{7}{8} \times 44$-inch strips for the pieced border
• Cut two $2\frac{1}{2} \times 24\frac{1}{2}$-inch strips for the outer border
• Cut two $2\frac{1}{2} \times 28\frac{1}{2}$-inch strips for the outer border

From the gold print fabric:
• Cut two $1\frac{7}{8} \times 44$-inch strips for the pieced border

From the small black plaid fabric:
• Cut two $1\frac{1}{2} \times 20\frac{1}{2}$-inch strips for the inner border
• Cut two $1\frac{1}{2} \times 22\frac{1}{2}$-inch strips for the inner border
• Cut four $1\frac{1}{2}$-inch squares

Attaching the Inner Border

Step 1. Sew the $1\frac{1}{2} \times 20\frac{1}{2}$-inch small black plaid strips to the top and bottom of the quilt, as shown in **Diagram 6.**

Step 2. Sew the $1\frac{1}{2} \times 22\frac{1}{2}$-inch small black plaid strips to the sides of the quilt. The quilt center should measure $22\frac{1}{2}$ inches square at this time.

Assembling the Pieced Border

Step 1. With right sides together, layer a $1\frac{7}{8}$-inch gold strip with a $1\frac{7}{8}$-inch green strip. Press strips together, but do not stitch. Layer the remaining gold and green strips into pairs in this fashion.

Step 2. Cut the layered strips into forty-four $1\frac{7}{8}$-inch squares. Cut the squares in half diagonally and stitch $\frac{1}{4}$ inch along the diagonal edge. Press seam allowances toward the green fabric to make $1\frac{1}{2}$-inch triangle-pieced squares.

Step 3. Sew two triangle-pieced squares together, positioning green fabric together, as shown in **Diagram 7.** Repeat to make 44 double triangle-pieced-square units. Sew 11 double triangle-pieced-square units together to make a pieced border for each side of the quilt. Refer to **Diagram 8.**

Step 4. Sew a pieced border to the top and bottom of the quilt. Make adjustments to the seams of triangle-pieced-square units as needed to make the border fit the quilt. Attach a 1½-inch small black plaid square to each end of the remaining pieced borders, as shown in **Diagram 9.** Adjust seam allowances if necessary to make the pieced borders fit, then sew them to the sides of the quilt.

HINTS & HELPS

Make small adjustments in many seams, rather than taking in or letting out a lot in just a few.

Outer Border

Attach the 2½ × 24½-inch green strips to the top and bottom of the quilt. Then sew the 28½-inch green strips to the sides of the quilt, referring to the **Quilt Diagram** on page 51.

QUILTING

Step 1. Cut the backing and batting so they are 4 inches larger than the quilt top.

Step 2. Mark the quilt top.

Step 3. Layer the backing, batting, and quilt top. Baste these layers together and quilt by hand or machine.

BINDING

The 3-inch binding strips will make a ½- to ⅝-inch-wide bias binding. If you want a wider or narrower binding, adjust the width of the strips you cut. (See page 247 for pointers on how to experiment with the binding width.) Refer to "Making and Attaching the Binding" on page 245 to complete your quilt.

Cutting for Bias Binding

From the large black plaid fabric:
• Cut enough 3-inch-wide bias strips to make a 135-inch strip

QUILTING IDEAS

◢ Hand quilt the sunflowers in the ditch to make them puff out a little.

◢ Add in-the-ditch quilting next to the lattice strips and in the pieced border.

◢ Quilt a simple chain in the outer border.

Diagram 7

Diagram 8

Diagram 9

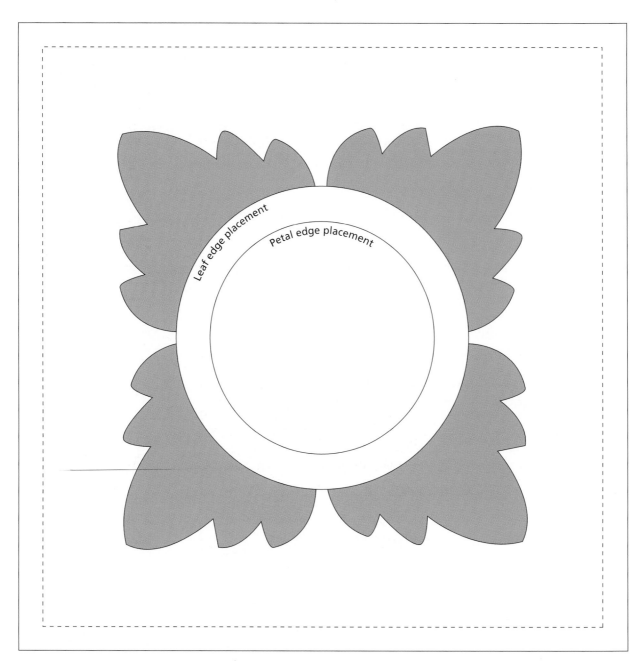

Block Diagram

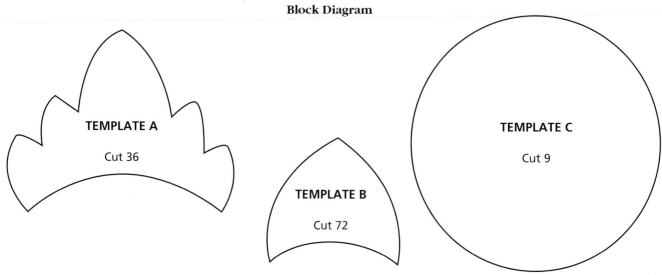

TEMPLATE A

Cut 36

TEMPLATE B

Cut 72

TEMPLATE C

Cut 9

PATCHWORK REMEMBERED

So many of us have childhood memories stitched together with needle and thread, a patchwork of hours spent watching a mother, grandmother, or favorite aunt work on blocks that grew to be quilts. Revisit the gentle spirit of those quilts and the people who made them by stitching one of these timeless and traditional designs.

DRESDEN SQUARE

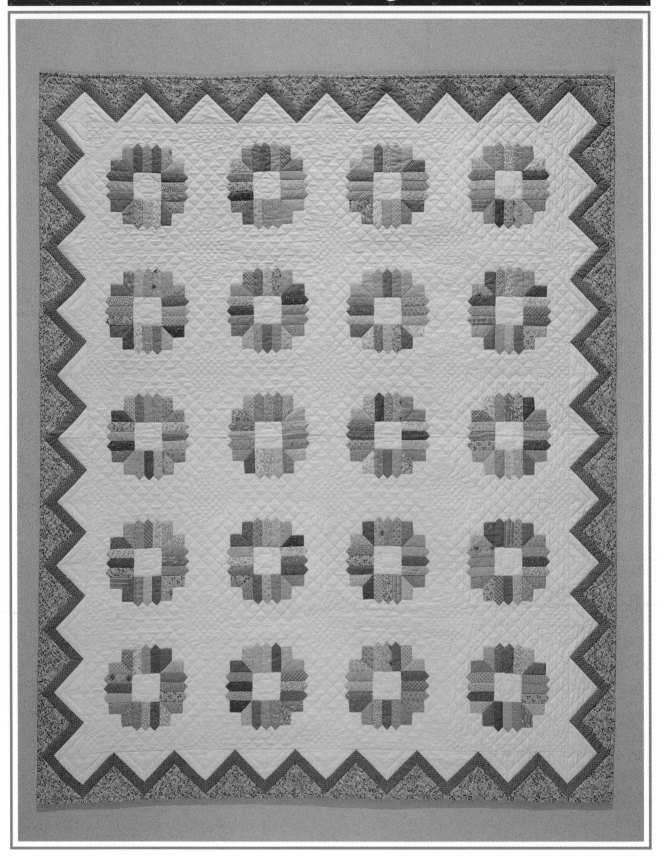

Quilt Diagram

SIZE

Bed quilt: 75 × 92 inches (unquilted)

Finished block: 16 inches square

FABRICS AND SUPPLIES

Yardage is based on 44-inch-wide fabric.

5¾ yards of beige fabric for background

2½ yards *total* of a variety of fabrics for Dresden Square pieces

1 yard of purple fabric for inner border

2 yards of green fabric for outer border and binding

5½ yards of fabric for quilt backing

Quilt batting, at least 79 × 96 inches

Template plastic

Rotary cutter, mat, and see-through ruler

Since so many of my quilts have a darker country look, when I wanted something softer for my daughter Kerry's room, I turned to my friend Marilyn Ginsburg. Her Dresden Square design was the perfect answer. She has made one for her daughter, too. I think this design is reminiscent of bygone days and lends itself nicely to sweet, old-fashioned prints. It is bound to become a family heirloom!

FABRIC KEY

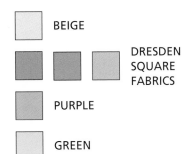

BEIGE

DRESDEN SQUARE FABRICS

PURPLE

GREEN

- Read instructions thoroughly before you begin.
- Prewash and press fabric.
- Use ¼-inch seam allowances throughout unless directions specify otherwise.
- Seam allowances are included in the cutting sizes given.
- Press seam allowance in the direction that will create the least bulk and, whenever possible, toward the darker fabric.
- Trace **Templates A, B,** and **C** (pages 62–63) onto template plastic and cut out.
- Cutting directions for each section of the quilt are given in the areas following the row of scissors. If you like to cut as you go, simply follow the directions as you get to them. If you'd rather cut all your pieces at once, skip ahead and look for the scissors to do all the cutting before you begin to sew.

DRESDEN SQUARE BLOCKS
(Make 20)

Cutting for Blocks

From the Dresden Square fabrics:
- Cut twenty-seven 1¾ × 44-inch strips. From these strips, cut two hundred forty 1¾ × 4¼-inch pieces (see **Diagram 1**). (These strips will be used for the pointed side pieces of the Dresden Square, shown in **Diagram 2**.)
- Cut sixteen 2 × 44-inch strips. Place **Template A** on the strips and cut off along the ends of the template (see **Diagram 3**). Cut 80 of **Template A** and 80 of **Template A Reverse.** On each piece, mark the two dots along the center line; these will become sewing guides.

From the beige fabric:
- Cut ten 17 × 44-inch strips. From these strips, cut twenty 17-inch squares for the background.

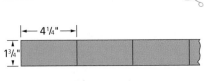

|← 4¼" →|

1¾"

Diagram 1

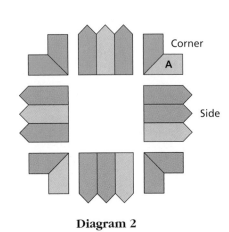

Corner

A

Side

Diagram 2

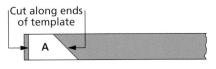

Cut along ends of template

A

Diagram 3

Piecing the Blocks

Step 1. Fold the 1¾ × 4¼-inch side pieces in half lengthwise, right sides together. Sew ¼ inch across one end. See **Diagram 4.** Trim seam allowance to ⅛ inch. Turn right side out, flatten, and press. This makes the end point.

Step 2. Sew these strips together in units of 3. Press seams toward the darker fabric. Make 4 of these units for each block. You will need a total of 80 units. See **Diagram 5.**

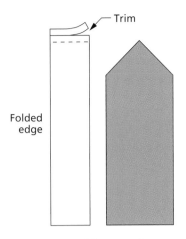

Diagram 4

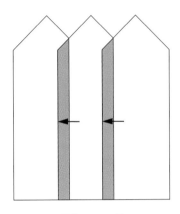

Diagram 5

Step 3. Sew the **Template A** and **Template A Reverse** pieces together along center line between the dots, having right sides together. It is important to sew only between the dots. Press seam toward the darker fabric. See **Diagram 6.** Make 4 of these corner units for each block. You will need a total of 80 corner units. Press under ¼ inch on the edges, as shown in the diagram. Baste.

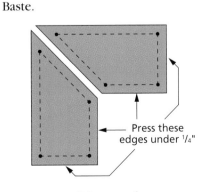

Diagram 6

Step 4. Sew four corner units to four side units. Sew from the top edge to the dots. See **Diagram 7.** Make 20 Dresden Square blocks in this manner.

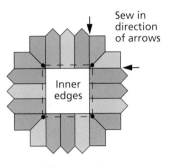

Diagram 7

Step 5. Turn under the four inner edges of the Dresden Square ¼ inch and baste, as shown in **Diagram 7.**

Step 6. Center a Dresden Square block on a 17-inch beige background square. To aid in the centering, lightly crease diagonal lines on the background square. Align the center lines of the corner units with these creases. See **Diagram 8.**

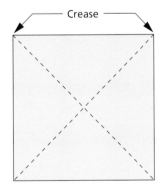

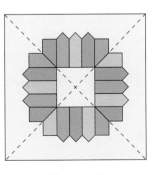

Diagram 8

Step 7. Baste in place and hand appliqué. Make 20 blocks. For instructions, see "Hand Appliqué" on page 238.

Step 8. Trim the blocks to measure 16½ inches square.

QUILT CENTER

Refer to the **Quilt Diagram** on page 59. Sew the quilt together in five horizontal rows of four Dresden Square blocks each.

BORDER

Cutting for Border

From the purple fabric:
• Cut sixteen 1¾ × 44-inch strips. Lay **Templates B** and **C** on these strips and cut off along the ends of the templates (see **Diagram 9**). Cut 36 of **Template B** and 36 of **Template B Reverse.** Cut 4 of **Template C.**

From the beige fabric:
• Cut five 4⅞ × 44-inch strips. From these strips, cut thirty-eight 4⅞-inch squares. Cut these squares in half diagonally to make 76 triangle pieces.

From the green fabric:
• Cut five 4⅞ × 44-inch strips. From these strips, cut thirty-six 4⅞-inch squares. Cut these squares in half diagonally to make 76 triangle pieces.
• Cut two 6⅝-inch squares. Cut these squares in half diagonally to make the corner blocks.

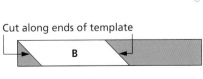

Diagram 9

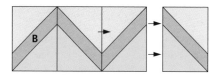

QUILTING IDEAS

☑ Quilt a simple box design in the center of the Dresden Square block as I did.

☑ Quilt in the ditch around the pieces of the Dresden Square block to make them puff out a little.

☑ Use a larger cross-hatching grid to fill in the background. See "Cross-Hatching Tips" on page 243.

☑ A lovely feathered wreath with cross-hatching was quilted at the block intersections.

☑ You can do echo quilting around the border strips.

Step 1. Refer to the **Quilt Diagram** on page 59 to see how the border looks. Sew a beige triangle to a purple strip cut from **Template B/B Reverse.** Then sew a green triangle to this unit, as shown in **Diagram 10.**

Diagram 10

Step 2. Sew the triangles and strips together to form the top, bottom, and side borders. Sew 16 units together for the top and bottom borders, and 20 units together for the side borders.

Step 3. To make the border corners, sew a beige triangle to a purple strip cut from **Template C.** Add a green triangle cut for the corners. Make four corners. See **Diagram 11.**

Diagram 11

Step 4. Sew the top and bottom borders to the quilt.

Step 5. Sew the border corners to the side borders. Sew these units to the sides of the quilt.

QUILTING

Step 1. Prepare the backing for the quilt. Cut the 5½ yards of backing material into two 2¾-yard lengths.

Step 2. Remove the selvages and sew the pieces together along the long edge. Press seam allowances open. Trim backing and batting so they are about 4 inches larger than the quilt top dimensions.

Step 3. Mark the quilt top for quilting.

Step 4. Layer the backing, batting, and quilt top. Baste together and quilt.

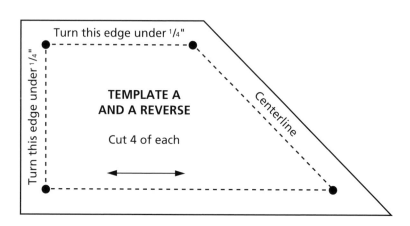

Turn this edge under ¼"

Turn this edge under ¼"

Centerline

TEMPLATE A AND A REVERSE

Cut 4 of each

BINDING

The 2¾-inch binding strips will produce a ⅜- to ½-inch-wide binding. If you want a wider or narrower binding, adjust the width of the strip you cut. (See page 247 for pointers on how to experiment with binding width.) Refer to "Making and Attaching the Binding" on page 245 to complete your quilt.

Cutting for Cross-Grain Binding

From the green fabric:
• Cut nine 2¾ × 44-inch strips

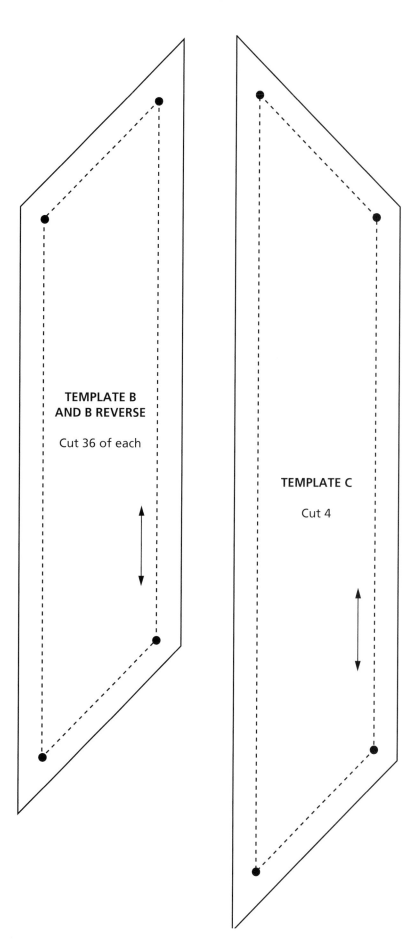

TEMPLATE B AND B REVERSE

Cut 36 of each

TEMPLATE C

Cut 4

Quilt Diagram

SIZE

Bed quilt: 78 × 102 inches (unquilted)

Finished block: 12 inches square

FABRICS AND SUPPLIES

Yardage is based on 44-inch-wide fabric.

3³/₈ yards of beige fabric for background

1²/₃ yards of medium brown fabric for Shadow blocks

2 yards *total* of a variety of colored fabrics for Windblown blocks

1 yard of dark brown print fabric for inner border

1³/₄ yards of red fabric for outer border

¹/₃ yard of dark blue fabric for corner squares

6 yards of fabric for quilt backing

1 yard of black-and-cream plaid fabric for bias binding

Quilt batting, at least 82 × 106 inches

Rotary cutter, mat, and see-through ruler

This is one of my favorite patchwork pieces! The brown alternate Shadow blocks echo each of the colorful Windblown blocks to create a soft feeling of movement. Keeping the same color in the Shadow blocks throughout the quilt gently accentuates the varied colors of the neighboring Windblown blocks. The plaid binding that I used offers a bold contrast against the red outer border and dark blue corner squares. Depending on your choice of fabrics, this quilt could look very contemporary or very traditional.

FABRIC KEY

BEIGE

MEDIUM BROWN

WINDBLOWN BLOCK FABRICS

DARK BROWN PRINT

RED

DARK BLUE

• Read instructions thoroughly before you begin.
• Prewash and press fabric.
• Use ¼-inch seam allowances throughout unless directions specify otherwise.
• Seam allowances are included in the cutting sizes given.
• Press seam allowance in the direction that will create the least bulk and, whenever possible, toward the darker fabric.
• Cutting directions for each section of the quilt are given in the areas following the row of scissors. If you like to cut as you go, simply follow the directions as you get to them. If you'd rather cut all your pieces at once, skip ahead and look for the scissors to do all the cutting before you begin to sew.

WINDBLOWN AND SHADOW BLOCKS
(Make 35)

Each block requires 16 triangle-pieced squares. The Shadow block and the Windblown block are organized exactly the same.

Cutting for Blocks

From the beige fabric:
• Cut twenty-nine 3⅞ × 44-inch strips

From the medium brown fabric:
• Cut fourteen 3⅞ × 44-inch strips

From the colored fabrics:
• Cut fifteen 3⅞ × 44-inch strips

Piecing the Shadow Blocks

Step 1. Layer the beige and medium brown 3⅞ × 44-inch strips with right sides together and press. Layer a total of 14 pairs of strips in this manner.

Step 2. Cut the layered strips into one hundred thirty-six 3⅞-inch squares. Cut these layered squares in half diagonally and stitch ¼ inch from the diagonal edges. Press seam allowances toward the darker fabric to make 272 triangle-pieced squares. See **Diagram 1.**

Diagram 1

Step 3. Assemble the blocks in four horizontal rows of four triangle-pieced squares each, as shown in **Diagram 2.** Press seam allowances in the direction of the arrows.

Press seams in direction of arrows

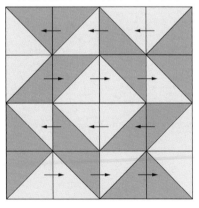

Diagram 2

Piecing the Windblown Blocks

Step 1. Layer the beige and colored 3⅞ × 44-inch strips with right sides together and press. Layer a total of 15 pairs of strips in this manner.

Step 2. Cut the layered strips into one hundred forty-four 3⅞-inch squares. Cut these layered squares in half diagonally and stitch ¼ inch from the diagonal edges. Press seam allowances toward the darker fabric to make 288 triangle-pieced squares.

Step 3. Assemble the blocks in four horizontal rows of four triangle-pieced squares each, as shown in **Diagram 2.** Press seam allowances in the direction of the arrows.

QUILT CENTER

Step 1. Sew the blocks together in seven horizontal rows of five blocks each. Odd-numbered rows have two Shadow blocks alternating with three Windblown blocks, starting and ending with the Windblown blocks. Even-numbered rows have two Windblown blocks alternating with three Shadow blocks, starting

and ending with the Shadow blocks. See **Diagram 3.**

Step 2. Press seams in alternating directions by rows so seams will fit snugly together with less bulk.

Step 3. Pin the blocks at the intersections and sew the rows together.

BORDERS

The yardage given allows for border pieces to be cut cross-grain. The inner and outer borders will be sewn together and attached to the quilt as one unit.

Cutting for Borders

From the dark brown fabric:
• Cut eight 3½ × 44-inch strips for the inner border

From the red fabric:
• Cut eight 6½ × 44-inch strips for the outer border

From the blue fabric:
• Cut one 9½ × 44-inch strip. From this strip, cut four 9½-inch squares.

Top and Bottom Borders

Step 1. Measure the quilt from left to right through the middle to determine the length of the top and bottom borders.

Step 2. Piece three 3½ × 44-inch dark brown strips diagonally and trim to the necessary length.

Step 3. Piece three 6½ × 44-inch red strips diagonally and trim to the necessary length.

Step 4. Sew the inner and outer borders for the top and bottom together.

Step 5. Attach the top and bottom border units to the quilt.

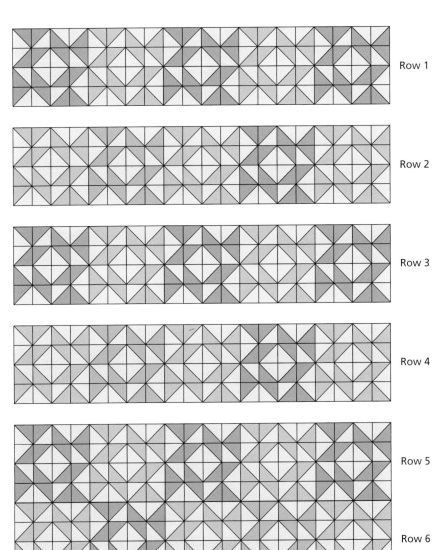

Row 1
Row 2
Row 3
Row 4
Row 5
Row 6
Row 7

Diagram 3

Side Borders

Step 1. Measure the quilt from top to bottom through the middle to determine the length of the side borders. Do *not* include the top and bottom borders.

Step 2. Piece five $3\frac{1}{2} \times 44$-inch dark brown strips diagonally and cut two strips to the necessary length.

Step 3. Piece five $6\frac{1}{2} \times 44$-inch red strips diagonally and cut two strips to the necessary length.

Step 4. Sew the red and brown side border strips together into two units.

Step 5. Sew two $9\frac{1}{2}$-inch dark blue corner squares to the ends of each of the side border units. See **Diagram 4.**

Diagram 4

Step 6. Attach the side border units to the quilt.

QUILTING

Step 1. Prepare the backing for the quilt by cutting the 6-yard length of backing fabric in half crosswise to make two 3-yard lengths. Remove the selvages.

Step 2. Sew the two lengths together with one center seam. Press seam allowance open. Trim backing and batting so they are about 4 inches larger than the quilt top.

Step 3. Mark the quilt top for quilting.

Step 4. Layer the backing, batting, and quilt top. Baste these layers together and quilt.

BINDING

The $2\frac{3}{4}$-inch plaid bias strip will produce a $\frac{3}{8}$-inch-wide binding. If you want a wider or narrower binding, adjust the width of the strip you cut. (See page 247 for pointers on how to experiment with binding width.) Refer to "Making and Attaching the Binding" on page 245 to complete your quilt.

Cutting for Bias Binding

From the plaid fabric:
• Cut enough $2\frac{3}{4}$-inch-wide bias strips to make a 380-inch strip

QUILTING IDEAS

☑ The background pieces are outline quilted $\frac{1}{4}$ inch away from the seam.

☑ Diagonal channel quilting was stitched in the border units and corner squares as shown.

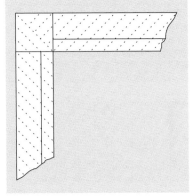

PINE GROVE BED QUILT

SIZE

Bed quilt: 88 × 106 inches (unquilted)

Finished block: 12 inches square

FABRICS AND SUPPLIES

Yardage is based on 44-inch-wide fabric.

1½ yards *total* of a variety of green, blue, and red fabrics for trees

½ yard of brown fabric for trunks

2 yards of beige fabric for background

1 yard of gold fabric for stars

2¾ yards of dark print fabric for lattice and inner border

2 yards of red fabric for side and corner triangles

3 yards of red check fabric for outer border and bias binding

7⅞ yards of fabric for quilt backing

Quilt batting, at least 92 × 110 inches

Rotary cutter, mat, and see-through ruler

Quilt Diagram

Evergreens remind me of the woods and lakes of northern Minnesota. They were my inspiration for this quilt. I've found that Pine Grove looks perfectly at home covering a bed at our lake cabin. The dark reds, greens, and blues I used for the pines create a strong, almost masculine feel. I chose gold for the stars to make them seem to sparkle throughout the thick grove of trees. The design of the Tree block is not as seasonal as a Christmas tree, which gives this quilt year-round appeal. I've included directions for pillows so you can create a coordinated set for your bed.

- Read instructions thoroughly before you begin.
- Prewash and press fabric.
- Use ¼-inch seam allowances throughout unless directions specify otherwise.
- Seam allowances are included in the cutting sizes given.
- Press seam allowance in the direction that will create the least bulk and, whenever possible, toward the darker fabric.
- Cutting directions for each section of the quilt are given in the areas following the row of scissors. If you like to cut as you go, simply follow the directions as you get to them. If you'd rather cut all your pieces at once, skip ahead and look for the scissors to do all the cutting before you begin to sew.

FABRIC KEY

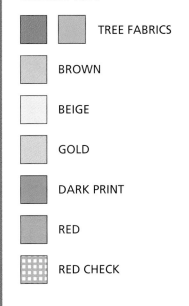

TREE FABRICS

BROWN

BEIGE

GOLD

DARK PRINT

RED

RED CHECK

TREE BLOCKS
(Make 18)

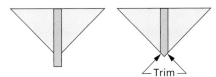

Cutting for Tree Blocks

From the tree fabrics:
- Cut six 5⅞ × 44-inch strips. From these strips, cut thirty-six 5⅞-inch squares. Cut these squares in half diagonally to make 72 triangles.

From the beige fabric:
- Cut five 5½ × 44-inch strips. From these strips, cut thirty-six 5½-inch squares. Cut these squares into quarters diagonally to make 144 triangles.
- Cut twenty-four 1½ × 44-inch strips

From the brown fabric:
- Cut eight 1½ × 44-inch strips. From these strips, cut seventy-two 1½ × 4½-inch pieces.

Piecing the Blocks

Step 1. Sew two beige background triangles to the 1½ × 4½-inch brown trunk pieces, as shown in **Diagram 1.** Trim the bottom edge of the trunk.

Step 2. Sew a green tree fabric triangle onto the trunk unit. See **Diagram 2.** The individual tree square should measure 5½ inches square. If it doesn't, double-check that the

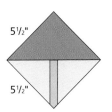

—Trim—

Diagram 1

5½"

5½"

Diagram 2

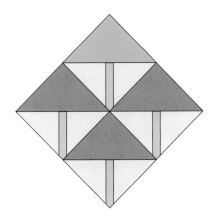

Diagram 3

pieces were cut correctly and that you used an accurate ¼-inch seam allowance. If any parts of the Tree block are off, the whole block can end up being uneven and distorted.

Step 3. Repeat Steps 1 and 2 to make four trees. Sew them together, as shown in **Diagram 3.**

HINTS & HELPS

You may want to wait to cut the dark print lattice pieces until after you have constructed the blocks. This will give you the opportunity to adjust the lattice length according to your block measurement.

Step 4. Stitch the beige 1½ × 44-inch background strips to the pieced Tree blocks in a Log Cabin piecing fashion. One 44-inch strip will complete the four borders for one block. Do *not* cut the strip into sections before sewing to the block. Stitch the borders clockwise onto the Tree block in the order shown by the numbers in **Diagram 4.** For the first border, with right sides together, stitch the 1½ × 44-inch beige strip to the block. Press seam allowance toward the block and trim the excess fabric. Using the excess strip, stitch the next border in the number 2 position on the block. Trim the excess, then continue to add the third and fourth borders onto the block in the same fashion. The Tree blocks should now measure 12½ inches square.

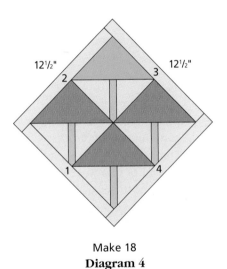

Make 18
Diagram 4

LATTICE

Before you cut the lattice pieces, measure the finished blocks. They should measure 12½ inches square. If not, adjust the length of the 3½-inch-wide dark print lattice pieces. Make sure *all* blocks measure the same and cut the lattice pieces to that measurement.

Cutting for Lattice

From the gold fabric:
• Cut three 3½ × 44-inch strips. From these strips, cut thirty-one 3½-inch squares.
• Cut ten 2 × 44-inch strips. From these strips, cut one hundred ninety-two 2-inch squares.

From the dark print fabric:
• Cut sixteen 3½ × 44-inch strips. From these strips, cut forty-eight 3½ × 12½-inch strips.

Piecing the Lattice

Step 1. With right sides together, place two 2-inch gold squares on opposite ends of each lattice piece. Draw a diagonal line from corner to corner on each square, referring to **Diagram 5.**

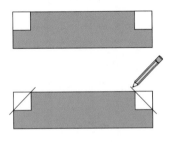

Diagram 5

Step 2. Do not stitch on top of the drawn line. Stitch just a hair to the outside edge of the line. Trim away corners leaving a ¼-inch seam allowance. See **Diagram 6.** Press the gold corners back onto the seam allowance.

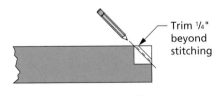

Trim ¼" beyond stitching

Diagram 6

Step 3. Repeat this process for the other two corners of the lattice piece with two more gold squares. The

lattice pieces will have star points on both ends. See **Diagram 7.**

Diagram 7

QUILT CENTER

Cutting Side and Corner Triangles

From the red fabric:
• Cut three 23-inch squares. Cut these squares into quarters diagonally to make 10 side triangles. (You will have two extra side triangles.)
• Cut two 15½-inch squares. Cut these squares in half diagonally to make 4 corner triangles.

Note: The side triangles and corner triangles will be larger than necessary and will be trimmed after they have been added to the pieced blocks.

Assembling the Quilt Center

You should have 18 Tree blocks and 48 lattice pieces with gold star points attached.

Step 1. Add the lattice pieces to the sides of the Tree blocks. See **Diagram 8.**

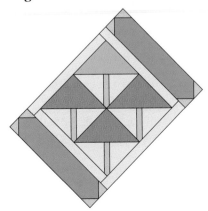

Diagram 8

Diagram 9

Cutting for Borders

From the dark print fabric:
• Cut nine $3\frac{1}{2} \times 44$-inch strips for the inner border

From the red check fabric:
• Cut ten $6\frac{1}{2} \times 44$-inch strips for the outer border

Inner Border

Step 1. Measure the quilt from left to right through the middle to determine the length of the top and bottom borders. Piece the dark print inner border strips with diagonal seams and cut to the necessary lengths.

Step 2. Sew the top and bottom dark print inner borders to the quilt.

Step 3. Measure the quilt from top to bottom through the middle, including the borders you just added, to determine the length of the inner side borders. Cut the remaining pieced inner border strip to the necessary lengths, and sew the dark print inner side borders to the quilt.

Outer Border

Step 1. Measure the quilt as you did in Step 1 under "Inner Border." Piece the red check outer border strips with diagonal seams and cut to the necessary lengths.

Step 2. Sew the top and bottom red check outer borders to the quilt.

Step 3. Measure the quilt as you did in Step 3 under "Inner Border." Cut the pieced outer border strip to the necessary lengths and sew the red check outer side borders to the quilt.

QUILTING

Step 1. Prepare the backing for the quilt by cutting the $7\frac{7}{8}$-yard length of backing fabric in thirds crosswise

Step 2. Sew the Tree blocks together in diagonal rows. Sew two rows of three blocks each and two rows of five blocks each, referring to **Diagram 9.**

Step 3. Sew the remaining lattice pieces and $3\frac{1}{2}$-inch gold squares together as needed for the lattice strips, as shown in **Diagram 10.** You will need two rows of three lattice pieces, two rows of five lattice pieces, and one row of six lattice pieces.

Diagram 10

Step 4. Assemble the Tree block strips and lattice strips in diagonal rows, as shown in **Diagrams 9** and

10. Sew the lattice strips to the Tree block strips. Add the red side triangles to each of the diagonal block rows as shown.

Step 5. Stitch the diagonal rows together. Add the red corner triangles last.

Step 6. Trim off excess fabric from the side and corner triangles, allowing $\frac{1}{4}$-inch seam allowances beyond block corners. Before you trim, be sure to see "Trimming Side and Corner Triangles" on page 236 to be certain you make these cuts accurately. Make sure the corners are accurate 90 degree angles.

BORDERS

The yardage given allows for border pieces to be cut cross-grain.

to make three 2⅝-yard lengths. Remove the selvages and sew the three lengths together so that the seams run horizontally. Press seams open.

Step 2. Trim the backing and batting so they are approximately 4 inches larger than the quilt top.

Step 3. Mark the quilt top for quilting.

Step 4. Layer the backing, batting, and quilt top. Baste these layers together and quilt.

BINDING

The 2¾-inch-wide red check bias strips will produce a ⅜- to ½-inch-wide binding. If you want a wider or narrower binding, adjust the width of the strip you cut. (See page 247 for pointers on how to experiment with binding width.) Refer to "Making and Attaching the Binding" on page 245 to complete your quilt.

Cutting for Bias Binding

From the plaid fabric:
• Cut enough 2¾-inch bias strips to make a 418-inch strip

QUILTING IDEAS

☑ The trees are quilted inside with an inverted V-shape, following the shape of the trees as shown.

☑ The outside edges of the trees are quilted in the ditch to make them puff out a bit.

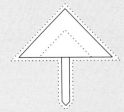

☑ Two rows of quilting spaced 1 inch apart are stitched in the dark lattice and inner border strips. The lattice and inner borders are also quilted in the ditch.

☑ Quilt from point to point through the star center. The outside edges of the stars were also quilted in the ditch.

☑ The side and corner triangles are crosshatched at 1-inch intervals.

☑ The outer border is crosshatched with a wider 2-inch grid. See "Cross-Hatching Tips" on page 243.

PINE GROVE PILLOW
Finished pillow: 17 inches square

FABRICS AND SUPPLIES FOR ONE PILLOW

Yardage is based on 44-inch-wide fabric.

¼ yard of green fabric or 6 × 6-inch scraps of four different fabrics for trees

2 × 20-inch piece of brown fabric for trunks

¼ yard of beige fabric for background

½ yard of red fabric for corner triangles

½ yard of fabric for pillow backing

½ yard of plaid fabric for bias binding

16 × 16-inch pillow form

Rotary cutter, mat, and see-through ruler

MAKING THE PILLOW

Before making the pillow, be sure to read "Getting Ready" for the Bed Quilt on page 71.

Cutting for Pillow Top

From the green fabric:
• Cut two 5⅞-inch squares. Cut these squares in half diagonally to make four triangles.

From the beige fabric:
• Cut two 5½-inch squares. Cut these squares into quarters diagonally to make eight triangles.
• Cut one 1½ × 44-inch strip for the block border

From the brown fabric:
• Cut one 1½ × 20-inch strip. From this strip, cut four 1½ × 4½-inch pieces.

From the red fabric:
• Cut two 13½-inch squares. Cut these squares in half diagonally to make four corner triangles.

Piecing the Pillow Top

Step 1. Follow Steps 1 through 4 under "Piecing the Blocks" on page 71 to make one Tree block.

Step 2. Stitch the four red corner triangles to the sides of the Tree block. See **Diagram 11**.

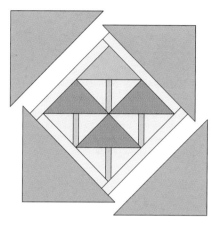

Diagram 11

Step 3. Trim the pillow block to 17 inches square

Step 4. Refer to "Quilting" for the Bed Quilt on page 73 if you wish to quilt the pillow top.

Pillow Back

Step 1. Cut two 17 × 19-inch pieces of pillow backing fabric. Fold the two pieces in half wrong sides together, forming two 9½ × 17-inch double-thickness pieces. Overlap

---

the two folded edges by 2 inches. See **Diagram 12**. Stitch across the edges where the folds overlap, ¼ inch from the edge, to secure.

Step 2. Layer the backing with the pieced pillow top facing up. Trim the backing if needed. Pin and stitch all thicknesses together ⅜ inch from all four edges.

BINDING

The raw edges of the pillow are bound with a contrasting binding.

Cutting for Bias Binding

From the plaid fabric:
• Cut enough 4½-inch bias strips to make an 83-inch strip

Step 1. Piece the 4¼-inch wide plaid bias strips with diagonal seams to get the length needed. Fold in half lengthwise, wrong sides together, and press.

Step 2. Having raw edges of the binding and pillow edges even, stitch a ½-inch seam. Fold binding to the back of the pillow and hand stitch the folded edge in place. This will give a nice heavy binding, much like a thick cording. Insert a high-quality 16-inch pillow form through the opening in the back.

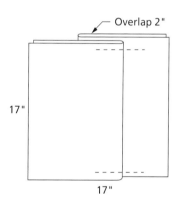

Diagram 12

Quilt Diagram

I love pine trees, so it's natural that the trees at our home should inspire a quilt design. Small Pines is a great little weekend project, and it's a perfect opportunity to experiment with color, texture, and design without a big investment of time. You can incorporate your favorite scraps to make each tree different, or use a planned color scheme. Either way, Small Pines will showcase your skills in a wall quilt that fits in many little spaces. It's a wonderful holiday accessory and belongs in every home all year long!

SIZE

Wall quilt: 18½ inches square (unquilted)

Finished block: 4½ inches square

FABRICS AND SUPPLIES

Yardage is based on 44-inch-wide fabric.

Scraps to total ¼ yard of assorted beige fabrics for Tree block background

⅓ yard of tan fabric for quilt background

⅓ yard *total* of a variety of green fabrics for trees

2 × 10-inch piece of brown fabric for tree trunks

⅓ yard of red fabric for inner border and binding

¼ yard of large check fabric for outer border

⅛ yard or 3 × 15-inch piece of small check fabric for corner squares

⅔ yard of fabric for quilt backing

Quilt batting, at least 22 × 22 inches

Rotary cutter, mat, and see-through ruler

Template plastic

FABRIC KEY

 BEIGE

 TAN

 TREE FABRICS

 BROWN

 RED

 LARGE CHECK

SMALL CHECK

HINTS & HELPS

Half of the Tree block must be cut with the templates reversed so that a right and left side is produced. To make sure you cut both left and right pieces, cut patches from a folded double thickness of fabric.

GETTING READY

• Read instructions thoroughly before you begin.
• Prewash and press fabric.
• Use ¼-inch seam allowances throughout unless directions specify otherwise.
• Seam allowances are included in the cutting sizes given.
• Press seam allowance in the direction that will create the least bulk and, whenever possible, toward the darker fabric
• Trace **Templates A** through **H** (page 81) onto template plastic and cut out.
• Cutting directions for each section of the quilt are given in the areas following the row of scissors. If you like to cut as you go, simply follow the directions as you get to them. If you'd rather cut all your pieces at once, skip ahead and look for the scissors to do all the cutting before you begin to sew.

TREE BLOCKS
(Make 5)

Piecing angle for quilt pieces:
A+H, A+G, B+G, C+G

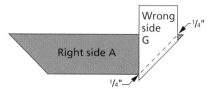

Cutting for Blocks

From the beige fabric:
• Cut ten of **Template E**
• Cut five of **Template F**
• Cut fifteen of **Template G**
• Cut fifteen of **Template G Reverse**
• Cut five of **Template H**
• Cut five of **Template H Reverse**

From the green fabric:
• Cut ten of **Template A**
• Cut ten of **Template A Reverse**
• Cut five of **Template B**
• Cut five of **Template B Reverse**
• Cut five of **Template C**
• Cut five of **Template C Reverse**

From the brown fabric:
• Cut five of **Template D**

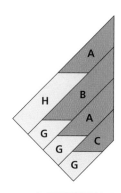

Diagram 1

Diagram 2

Piecing the Tree Blocks

Step 1. Sew A to H, B to G, A to G, and C to G, referring to **Diagram 1** for stitching angled seams. Then sew these four units together, referring to **Diagram 2** for placement. Press seams toward the top of the tree.

Step 2. Using the reverse pieces, assemble the pieces as you did in Step 1. Sew these four units together. Press seams toward the bottom of the tree.

Step 3. Sew the two tree halves together, stopping the stitching ¼-inch from the end of the seam near the base of the tree. See **Diagram 3.** Back stitch or tie off threads. Press center seam allowance open.

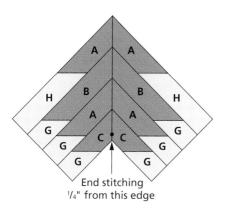

End stitching
¼" from this edge

Diagram 3

Step 4. Sew a piece E to each long side of piece D to make a triangle. Press seam allowances toward the trunk. Sew to triangle F; press seam toward F. See **Diagram 4.**

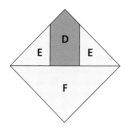

Diagram 4

Step 5. Set the trunk unit into the base of the tree. Referring to **Diagram 5,** match the edge of the trunk unit with the C/G edge of the tree. Starting with the needle ¼ inch in from the center top point of the trunk, stitch to the outer edge. Swing the other edge of the trunk to match the C Reverse/G Reverse edge of the tree. Stitch ¼ inch from the inner corner to the outer edge.

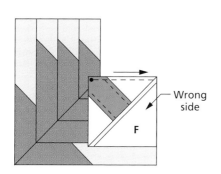

Wrong side

F

Diagram 5

QUILT CENTER

This quilt is assembled in diagonal rows. The rows will include the side triangles, which are slightly larger than necessary and will be trimmed after the quilt top has been assembled.

Cutting the Side and Corner Triangles

From the tan fabric:
• Cut one 9-inch square. Cut this square into quarters diagonally to make four side triangles.
• Cut two 6-inch squares. Cut these squares in half diagonally to make four corner triangles.

Step 1. Sew the blocks and side triangles together in rows 1, 2, and 3, as shown in **Diagram 6.** Do not attach the corner triangles yet. Press the seam allowances in rows 1 and 3 toward the side triangles. Press the seams in row 2 toward the center block.

Step 2. Join the rows, pinning at the seam intersections for accuracy.

Step 3. Sew on the four corner triangles, as shown in **Diagram 6,** to complete the quilt center.

Step 4. Trim off excess fabric from the side and corner triangles, allowing ¼-inch seam allowances beyond block corners. Before you trim, be sure to see "Trimming Side and Corner Triangles" on page 236 to be certain you make these cuts accurately. See **Diagram 7.** Make sure the corners are accurate 90 degree angles.

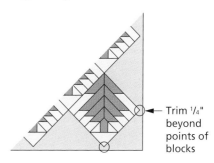

Trim ¼" beyond points of blocks

Diagram 7

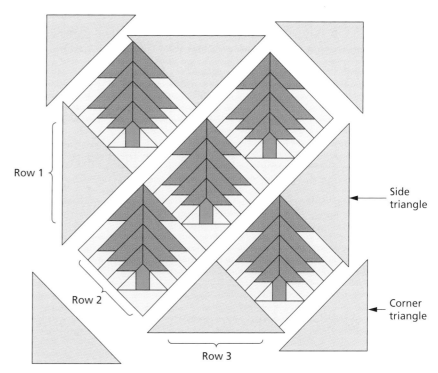

Row 1

Row 2

Row 3

Side triangle

Corner triangle

Diagram 6

BORDERS

Cutting for Borders

From the red fabric:
• Cut two $1\frac{1}{2} \times 44$-inch strips for inner border

From the large check fabric:
• Cut two $2\frac{1}{2} \times 44$-inch strips for outer border

From the small check fabric:
• Cut four $2\frac{1}{2}$-inch squares for corner blocks

Inner Border

Step 1. Measure the quilt from top to bottom through the middle to determine the length of the side borders. Cut two strips to the necessary measurement from the $1\frac{1}{2} \times 44$-inch strips of red fabric and sew the inner border strips to the sides of the quilt.

Step 2. Measure the quilt from left to right through the middle, including the borders you just added to determine the length of the top and bottom borders. Cut two strips from the red fabric to the necessary length and sew the red inner border to the top and bottom of the quilt.

Outer Border

Step 1. Measure the quilt from top to bottom, including the borders you just added. From the $2\frac{1}{2} \times 44$-inch large check fabric, cut two borders to the length needed and sew to the sides of the quilt.

Step 2. From the large check fabric, cut two border strips to the measurement taken in Step 1.

Step 3. Sew the corner blocks to each end of the large check top and bottom border strips. Sew the outer border units to the top and bottom of the quilt.

QUILTING

Step 1. Prepare the backing for the quilt. Trim the backing and batting so they are about 4 inches larger than the quilt top dimensions.

Step 2. Mark the quilt top for quilting.

Step 3. Layer the backing, batting, and quilt top. Baste these layers together and quilt.

BINDING

The red $2\frac{1}{2}$-inch binding strips will produce a $\frac{1}{4}$-inch-wide binding. If you want a wider binding, adjust the width of the strips you cut. (See page 247 for pointers on how to experiment with binding width.) Refer to "Making and Attaching the Binding" on page 245 to complete your quilt.

Cutting for Cross-Grain Binding

From the red fabric:
• Cut three $2\frac{1}{2} \times 44$-inch strips

QUILTING IDEAS

◢ The trees are quilted down the center of each tree piece with an inverted V-shape, following the shape of the trees as shown.

◢ The tree trunks and inner borders are quilted in the ditch.

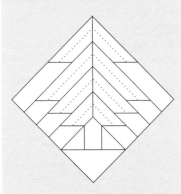

◢ Cross-hatching is done in the side and corner blocks at $\frac{1}{2}$-inch intervals. See "Cross-Hatching Tips" on page 243.

◢ A simple chain is quilted in the outer border.

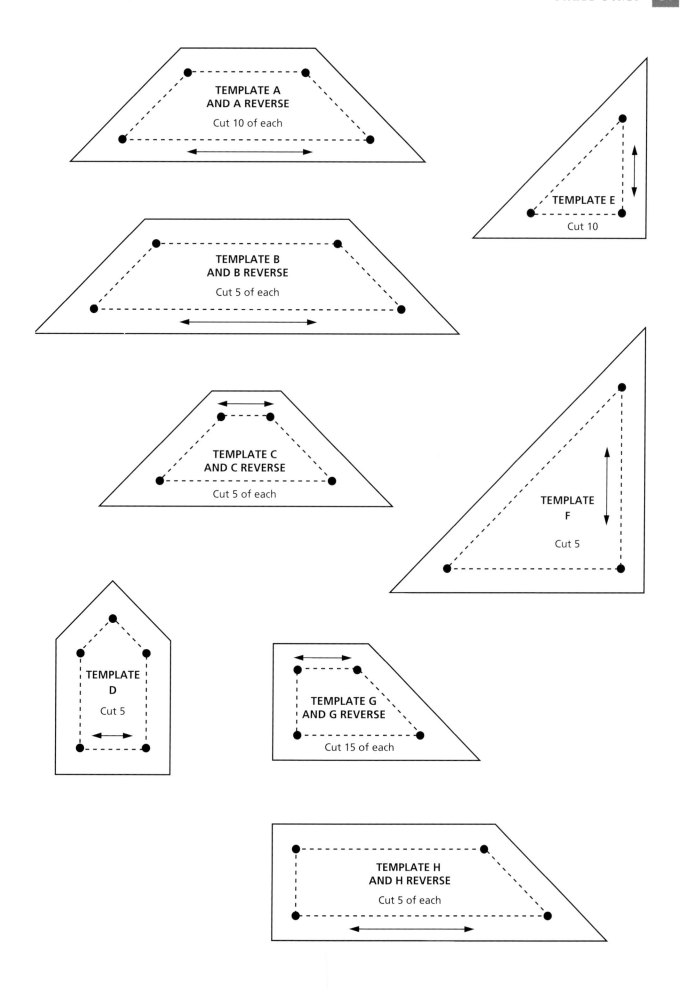

Quilt Diagram

SIZE

Twin-size quilt: 71 × 93 inches (unquilted)

Finished block: 8 inches square

FABRICS AND SUPPLIES

Yardage is based on 44-inch-wide fabric.

1½ yards *total* of a variety of dark fabrics for pieced blocks

2½ yards *total* of a variety of medium fabrics for pieced blocks

1½ yards *total* of a variety of light fabrics for pieced blocks

⅛ yard of medium brown fabric for stems

¼ yard of red fabric for apples

¼ yard of green fabric for leaves

1¼ yards of beige fabric for side triangles

¾ yard of dark brown fabric for inner border

2 yards of floral fabric for outer border

5½ yards of fabric for quilt backing

1 yard of red fabric for binding

Quilt batting, at least 75 × 97 inches

Freezer paper

Template plastic

Rotary cutter, mat, and see-through ruler

This is one of the first quilts I pull out in September to keep me cozy in the winter months to come. I especially love the warm, rich colors. This quilt gives the illusion of being difficult to make, with many tiny pieces, but the units are super easy to strip piece. Use as many fabrics as you can in different combinations to achieve the scrap look of antique quilts. And remember to use some "unlikely" fabrics now and then. Use more medium colors than darks or lights. If you prefer, you can eliminate the simple apple appliqué or you could use the apple shape for a quilting design in the triangles.

FABRIC KEY

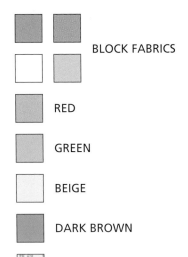

BLOCK FABRICS

RED

GREEN

BEIGE

DARK BROWN

FLORAL

GETTING READY

- Read instructions thoroughly from start to finish before you begin.
- Prewash and press fabric.
- Use ¼-inch seam allowances throughout unless directions specify otherwise.
- Seam allowances are included in the cutting sizes given.
- Press seam allowance in the direction that will create the least bulk and, whenever possible, toward the darker fabric.
- Trace the **Apple** and **Leaf Templates** (page 87) onto template plastic and cut out.
- Cutting directions for each section of the quilt are given in the areas following the row of scissors. If you like to cut as you go, simply follow the directions as you get to them. If you'd rather cut all your pieces at once, skip ahead and look for the scissors to do all the cutting before you begin to sew.
- Instructions are given for quick cutting and piecing the blocks. Note that for some of the pieces, the quick-cutting method will result in leftover fabric.

PIECED BLOCKS
(Make 59)

Cutting for Blocks

From the dark fabrics:
- Cut twenty-seven 1½ × 44-inch strips

From the medium fabrics:
- Cut fifty-four 1½ × 44-inch strips

From the light fabrics:
- Cut twenty-seven 1½ × 44-inch strips

Piecing the Blocks

Step 1. Sew a variety of different combinations of four strips to make strip sets. Each strip set will have one dark, one light, and two medium fabrics. Vary the combinations so darks, mediums, and lights appear in different orders. See **Diagram 1.** Make twenty-seven of these strip sets.

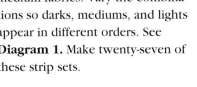

Diagram 1

Step 2. Cut each strip set into 4½-inch segments, referring to **Diagram 2.**

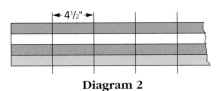

←4½"→

Diagram 2

HINTS & HELPS

The pieced blocks must have horizontal strips in the upper left hand corner and vertical strips in the upper right hand corner. Check each block to make certain the strips are in the correct position.

Step 3. Sew four segments together to make a pieced block. See **Diagram 3.**

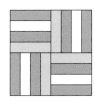

Make 59
Diagram 3

QUILT CENTER

Cutting for Triangles

From the beige fabric:
• Cut two 14 × 44-inch strips. From these strips, cut five 14-inch squares. Cut these squares into quarters diagonally to make 20 side triangles.
• Cut two 10-inch squares. Cut these squares in half diagonally to make 4 corner triangles.

Note: The side triangles and corner triangles will be larger than necessary and will be trimmed after they have been added to the pieced blocks.

Assembling the Quilt Center

Step 1. Referring to **Diagram 4,** arrange the pieced blocks in 11 diagonal rows. Add side triangles to the ends of the diagonal rows as needed. Stitch the blocks and side triangles together in diagonal rows.

Do not attach the corner triangles at this time.

Step 2. Press the new seam allowances in Row 1 in one direction. Press the new seam allowances in Row 2 in the opposite direction. Repeat alternating directions for the rest of the rows.

Step 3. Stitch the diagonal rows together to form the quilt center.

Step 4. Add the four corner triangles to the corners.

Step 5. Trim off excess fabric from the side and corner triangles, allowing ¼-inch seam allowances beyond block corners. Before you trim, be sure to see "Trimming Side and Corner Triangles" on page 236 to be certain you make these cuts accurately. Make sure the corners are accurate 90 degree angles.

INNER BORDER

The yardage given allows for border pieces to be cut cross-grain.

Cutting for Inner Border

From the dark brown fabric:
• Cut seven 2½ × 44-inch strips

Attaching the Inner Border

Step 1. Measure the quilt from left to right through the middle, to determine the length of the top and bottom borders.

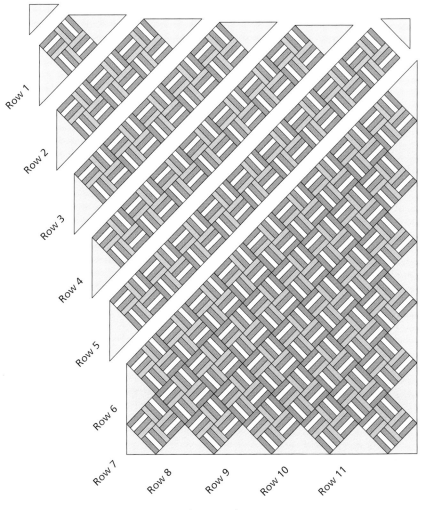

Row 1
Row 2
Row 3
Row 4
Row 5
Row 6
Row 7   Row 8   Row 9   Row 10   Row 11

Diagram 4

Step 2. Piece three of the $2\frac{1}{2} \times 44$-inch strips of brown fabric with diagonal seams and trim the ends to the necessary length for the quilt top and bottom.

Step 3. Sew the dark brown inner border strips to the top and bottom of the quilt.

Step 4. Measure the quilt from top to bottom through the middle, including the top and bottom borders you just added, to determine the length of the side borders. Piece four $2\frac{1}{2} \times 44$-inch strips of brown fabric with diagonal seams and trim the ends to the necessary length for the quilt sides.

Step 5. Sew the dark brown inner border strips to the sides of the quilt. The outer border is added after the apples have been appliquéd in place on the quilt top.

APPLIQUÉ

The apples, leaves, and stems can be hand appliquéd or machine appliquéd with a satin stitch. For hand appliqué, add $\frac{1}{8}$- to $\frac{1}{4}$-inch seam allowances to each appliqué piece, and read "Hand Appliqué," on the right, *before* you cut. For machine appliqué, the appliqué pieces should be cut with no seam allowances added.

Cutting for Appliqué Pieces

From the medium brown fabric:
• Cut one $1\frac{1}{4} \times 44$-inch strip

From the red fabric:
• Cut two 4×44-inch strips. From this strip, cut 20 pieces using the **Apple Template.**

From the green fabric:
• Cut two $3\frac{1}{2} \times 44$-inch strips. From this strip, cut 40 pieces using the **Leaf Template.**

Hand Appliqué

Refer to "Hand Appliqué" on page 238 if you need additional instructions.

Step 1. Stay stitch $\frac{1}{8}$ inch from the edges of the dark brown inner border to stabilize them for the appliqué process.

Step 2. Fold and press a brown stem strip in thirds lengthwise. Cut the stem strip into twenty 2-inch pieces. Fold the top edge under $\frac{1}{4}$ inch and press. The bottom raw edge will be covered by the apple.

Step 3. Cut 20 apple and 40 leaf appliqué shapes from freezer paper.

Step 4. Press the shiny side of freezer paper to the wrong side of the fabrics chosen for appliqué. Make sure to space the shapes $\frac{1}{2}$ inch apart so you will have enough fabric for seam allowances.

Step 5. Cut around the freezer paper shapes allowing $\frac{1}{8}$ to $\frac{1}{4}$ inch of fabric for seam allowances. Finger press seam allowances over the paper edge.

Step 6. Using the placement guide in **Diagram 5,** trace the appliqué shapes lightly onto the side triangles with a marking pencil that will come out.

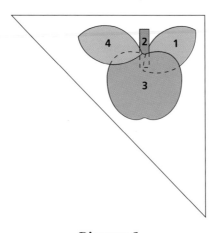

Diagram 5

Step 7. Secure the appliqué shapes to the beige triangles with pins. Hand appliqué the shapes in place, layering in order, following the numbers in **Diagram 5.** When there is about $\frac{1}{2}$ inch left to appliqué on each piece, remove the freezer paper and continue stitching.

Machine Appliqué

From the medium brown fabric, cut twenty $\frac{1}{2} \times 1\frac{1}{2}$-inch stems. Use the placement guide in **Diagram 5** as a reference and trace the appliqué shapes lightly onto the side triangles with a marking pencil that will come out. Refer to "Machine Appliqué" on page 239 to appliqué your apple, leaf, and stem pieces. Layer the appliqué shapes in order, following the numbers in the diagram.

OUTER BORDER

Cutting for Outer Border

From the floral fabric:
• Cut eight 8×44-inch strips

Attaching the Outer Border

Step 1. Measure the quilt from left to right through the middle, to determine the length of the top and bottom borders.

Step 2. Piece three 8×44-inch strips of the floral fabric with diagonal seams and trim to the necessary length for the top and bottom of the quilt.

Step 3. Sew the floral outer border strips to the top and bottom of the quilt.

Step 4. Measure the quilt from top to bottom through the middle, including the top and bottom borders you just added, to determine the length of the side borders.

Step 5. Piece five 8 × 44-inch strips of the floral fabric with diagonal seams and trim to the necessary length.

Step 6. Sew the floral outer border strips to the sides of the quilt.

QUILTING

Step 1. Prepare the backing for the quilt by cutting the 5½-yard length of backing fabric in half crosswise to make two 2¾-yard lengths. Remove the selvages.

Step 2. Sew the two lengths together with one center seam. Press seam allowances open. Trim backing and batting so they are about 4 inches larger than the quilt top dimensions.

Step 3. Mark the quilt top for quilting.

Step 4. Layer the backing, batting, and quilt top. Baste these layers together and quilt.

BINDING

The 3-inch binding strip will produce a ½-inch-wide binding. If you want a wider or narrower binding, adjust the width of the strip you cut. (See page 247 for pointers on how to experiment with the binding width.) Refer to "Making and Attaching the Binding" on page 245 to complete your quilt.

Cutting for Cross-Grain Binding

From the red fabric:
• Cut nine 3 × 44-inch strips

QUILTING IDEAS

◪ Quilt the appliqué pieces in the ditch to make them puff out a little.

◪ Quilt the pieced blocks in the ditch.

◪ Use a simple chain design for the inner border.

◪ Quilt the outer border with 1½-inch cross-hatching. See "Cross-Hatching Tips" on page 243.

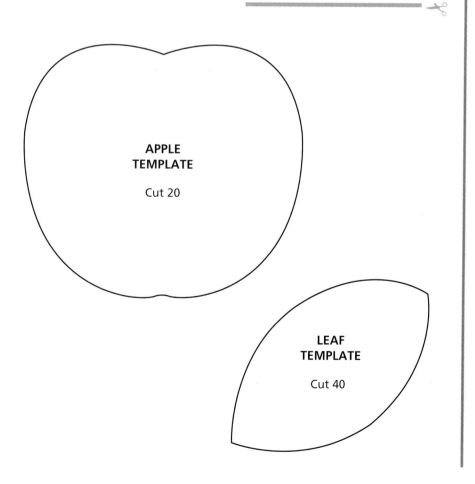

APPLE TEMPLATE

Cut 20

LEAF TEMPLATE

Cut 40

Quilt Diagram

SIZE

Lap quilt: 58 × 67 inches
(unquilted)

Finished block: 9 inches square

FABRICS AND SUPPLIES

Yardage is based on 44-inch-wide fabric.

1¼ yards of beige fabric for background and corner blocks

2 yards of fabric for paddle-wheels (**Note:** If you want a variety of fabrics, buy at least ⅛ yard of each to total 2¼ yards.)

1¼ yards of blue plaid fabric for inner and outer borders

1¼ yards of red fabric for middle border and binding

4 yards of fabric for quilt backing

Quilt batting, at least 62 × 71 inches

Rotary cutter, mat, and see-through ruler

Template plastic

Years ago, when I designed and made this quilt, I had to search high and low to find plaids and fabrics with a vintage look to give this the feel of an antique quilt. Now, thanks to all of the reproduction fabrics and plaids we can find in our fabric stores and quilt shops, it's easy to duplicate the old-fashioned look. This traditional Paddlewheel block is easy to sew, making the quilt a great project for beginners.

Have fun mixing prints and colors to create some scrappy Paddlewheel blocks. Be sure to notice the small pinwheels that appear wherever the background fabrics of the blocks intersect . . . that's why I named it Paddlewheels *and* Pinwheels.

FABRIC KEY

BEIGE

PADDLEWHEEL FABRICS

BLUE PLAID

RED

BROWN

GETTING READY

- Read directions thoroughly before you begin.
- Prewash and press fabric.
- Use ¼-inch seam allowances throughout unless directions specify otherwise.
- Seam allowances are included in the cutting sizes given.
- Press seam allowance in the direction that will create the least bulk and, whenever possible, toward the darker fabric.
- Trace **Templates A** and **B** (page 92) onto template plastic and cut out. Note that Template A is 3⅝ inches. Cutting strips to this width eliminates extra trimming.
- Cutting directions for each quilt section are given in the areas following the row of scissors. If you like to cut as you go, simply follow the directions as you get to them. If you'd rather cut all pieces at once, skip ahead and look for the scissors to do all the cutting before you begin to sew.

PADDLEWHEEL BLOCKS
(Make 30)

Cutting for Blocks

To cut pieces A and B for the Paddlewheel blocks, it is easiest first to cut fabric strips the width of the pieces. Then lay the templates on the strip and trim fabric along both ends of the template. For the most efficient use of your fabric, see the cutting layouts in **Diagram 1.** Cut pieces A and B out of a single thickness of fabric so all the "paddles" in the blocks are going in the same direction.

From the beige fabric:
- Cut ten 3 × 44-inch strips. From these strips, cut 120 of **Template B.**

From the paddlewheel fabric(s):
- Cut eighteen 3⅝ × 44-inch strips. From these strips, cut 120 of **Template A.**

Piecing the Blocks

Step 1. Construct the blocks in quarters; sew one piece A to one piece B, as shown in **Diagram 2,** for each quarter-square triangle.

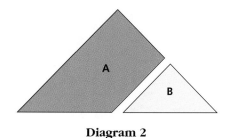

Diagram 2

Step 2. Sew two quarters together, as shown in **Diagram 3,** to make a half-square triangle.

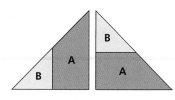

Diagram 3

Cut 120

Cut 120

Diagram 1

Step 3. Sew two halves together, as shown in **Diagram 4,** to make a Paddlewheel block.

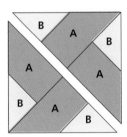

Make 30
Diagram 4

Step 4. Measure all the blocks to make sure they are the same dimensions. They should measure 9½ inches square. If any blocks deviate a by more than ⅛ inch, correct your seam allowances before sewing the blocks together.

QUILT CENTER

Step 1. Sew Paddlewheel blocks together in rows. Make six horizontal rows with five blocks in each row.

Step 2. Join rows, pinning at block intersections. It is important that your block intersections are exact for the small beige pinwheel design to be effective.

Step 3. Press all the horizontal seam allowances in one direction.

BORDERS

The yardage given allows for border pieces to be cut cross-grain. The inner, middle, and outer borders will be sewn together as one border unit. This unit will then be attached to the quilt.

Cutting for Borders

From the beige fabric:
• Cut one 7 × 44-inch strip. From this strip, cut four 7-inch squares.

From the blue fabric:
• Cut twelve 3 × 44-inch strips for the inner and outer borders

From the red fabric:
• Cut six 2 × 44-inch strips for the middle border

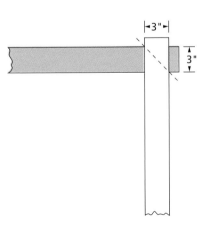

Diagram 5

Inner Border

Step 1. Measure the quilt from left to right through the middle to determine the length of the top and bottom borders. Piece three of the 3 × 44-inch strips of blue fabric together with diagonal seams, as shown in **Diagram 5.** From this strip, cut two strips to the length of the quilt top and bottom.

Step 2. Measure the quilt from top to bottom through the middle to determine the length of the side borders. Piece three blue fabric strips together with diagonal seams. From this strip, cut two strips to the length of the quilt sides.

Middle Border

Piece the strips of red fabric together as for the inner border. Cut the strips to the same lengths as the blue fabric for the top and bottom and the side borders.

Outer Border

Piece the remaining blue plaid strips together as for the inner border. Cut the strips to the same lengths as the top and bottom and the side borders.

Attaching the Borders

Step 1. Arrange the inner, middle, and outer borders in the correct order and lengths, as shown in **Diagram 6.** Sew the border strips together. Press seam allowances toward the blue fabric.

Step 2. Attach the top and bottom border units to the quilt. Press seam allowances toward the inner borders.

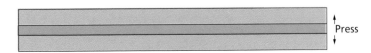

Press

Diagram 6

Diagram 7

QUILTING IDEAS

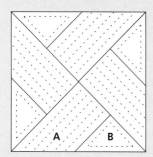

■ For a traditional look, the blocks were quilted with the design shown.

■ The inner and outer borders were quilted with three lengthwise rows of quilting spaced ½ inch apart.

■ The middle border has two lengthwise rows of quilting spaced ½ inch apart.

■ Quilt a crosshatched grid of ½-inch intervals in the corner blocks. See "Cross-Hatching Tips" on page 243.

Step 3. Sew the four 7-inch beige squares to the ends of the two side border units, referring to **Diagram 7**. Press seam allowances toward the border unit.

Step 4. Attach the side border units to the quilt. Press seam allowances toward the inner borders.

QUILTING

Step 1. Prepare the backing for the quilt by cutting the 4-yard length of backing fabric in half crosswise to make two 2-yard lengths. Remove the selvages.

Step 2. Sew the two lengths together with one center seam. Press seam allowances open. Trim the backing and batting so they are 4 inches larger than the quilt top.

Step 3. Mark the quilt top for quilting.

Step 4. Layer the backing, batting, and quilt top. Baste these layers together and quilt.

BINDING

The 2¾-inch binding strips will produce a ⅜- to ½-inch-wide binding. If you want a wider or narrower binding, adjust the width of the strips you cut. (See page 247 for pointers on how to experiment with binding width.) See "Making and Attaching the Binding" on page 245 to complete your quilt.

Cutting for Cross-Grain Binding

From the red fabric:
• Cut seven 2¾ × 44-inch strips

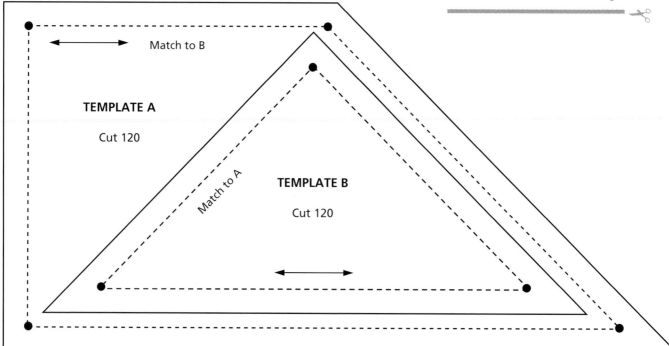

Match to B

TEMPLATE A

Cut 120

Match to A

TEMPLATE B

Cut 120

TWINKLING STARS

Star light, star bright, let the quilts your loved ones sleep under tonight be ones you've made. After all, what could bring more comfort and warmth in the dark of night than one of these simply heavenly star quilts, stitched with care by you?

Wall Quilt Diagram

STAR PATCH WALL QUILT

SIZE

Wall quilt: 60 inches square (unquilted)

Finished block: 16 inches square

FABRICS AND SUPPLIES

Yardage is based on 44-inch-wide fabric.

$2\frac{1}{4}$ yards of red check fabric for inner star, outer border, and binding

$1\frac{3}{8}$ yards of red fabric for outer star and inner border

$1\frac{1}{4}$ yards of beige fabric for Nine Patch blocks and star triangles

$1\frac{1}{4}$ yards *total* of a variety of green fabrics for the Nine Patch blocks

$3\frac{3}{4}$ yards of fabric for quilt backing

Quilt batting, at least 64 × 64 inches

Rotary cutter, mat, and see-through ruler

I use the Star Patch table runner year-round. It complements every table I use, from my primitive pine work table to this more refined cherry table. I think it adds such warmth to a room setting. I also use it draped over the back of an easy chair to change the look of a room. The star motif my friend and fellow quilt designer Marilyn Ginsburg used in these projects is one of my favorites. By changing the color scheme and omitting the lattice strips as I did in the wall quilt, the original stars blend with the background while a secondary design emerges.

FABRIC KEY

 RED CHECK

 RED

BEIGE

 GREENS

- Read instructions thoroughly before you begin.
- Prewash and press fabric.
- Use ¼-inch seam allowances throughout unless directions specify otherwise.
- Seam allowances are included in the cutting sizes given.
- Press seam allowance in the direction that will create the least bulk and, whenever possible, toward the darker fabric.
- Cutting directions for each section of the quilt are given in the areas following the row of scissors. If you like to cut as you go, simply follow the directions as you get to them. If you'd rather cut all your pieces at once, skip ahead and look for the scissors to do all the cutting before you begin to sew.
- Instructions are given for quick cutting and piecing the blocks. Note that for some of the pieces, the quick-cutting method will result in leftover fabric.

STAR/NINE PATCH BLOCKS
(Make 9)

Cutting for Star/Nine Patch Blocks

From the red check fabric:
- Cut one $4\frac{1}{2} \times 44$-inch strip. From this strip, cut nine $4\frac{1}{2}$-inch squares.
- Cut three $2\frac{7}{8} \times 44$-inch strips

From the red fabric:
- Cut five $2\frac{1}{2} \times 44$-inch strips. From these strips cut thirty-six $2\frac{1}{2} \times 4\frac{1}{2}$-inch pieces.
- Cut six $2\frac{7}{8} \times 44$-inch strips

From the beige fabric:
- Cut eleven $2\frac{1}{2} \times 44$-inch strips
- Cut three $2\frac{7}{8} \times 44$-inch strips

From the green fabrics:
- Cut thirteen $2\frac{1}{2} \times 44$-inch strips

Piecing the Nine Patch Blocks

Step 1. Make Strip Set 1. With right sides together, sew a green $2\frac{1}{2} \times 44$-inch strip to each side of a $2\frac{1}{2} \times 44$-inch beige strip. See **Diagram 1.** Press seams toward the green fabric. Make five of these strip sets. Crosscut the strip sets into 72 segments $2\frac{1}{2}$ inches wide.

Step 2. Make Strip Set 2. With right sides together, sew a $2\frac{1}{2} \times 44$-inch beige strip to each side of a $2\frac{1}{2}$-inch green strip, as shown in **Diagram 2.**

Press seam allowances toward the green fabric. Make three of these strip sets. Crosscut the strip sets into 36 segments $2\frac{1}{2}$ inches wide.

Step 3. Sew a Strip Set 1 segment to the top and bottom of a Strip Set 2 segment to make 36 Nine Patch blocks, as shown in **Diagram 3.**

Strip Set 1

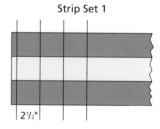

$2\frac{1}{2}$"

Diagram 1

Strip Set 2

$2\frac{1}{2}$"

Diagram 2

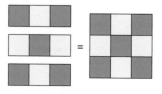

Make 36
Diagram 3

Piecing the Star Sections

Step 1. Layer the $2^7/8 \times 44$-inch strips of red check and red fabric with right sides together. You will have three pairs. Press; cut into 36 pairs of $2^7/8$-inch squares.

Step 2. Cut the layered squares in half diagonally. Stitch the red check and red triangles together $1/4$ inch from the diagonal edge to make 72 triangle-pieced squares, as shown in **Diagram 4.**

Diagram 4

Step 3. Sew the triangle-pieced squares together in pairs, as shown in **Diagram 5** to make 36 units.

Diagram 5

Step 4. Layer the $2^7/8 \times 44$-inch strips of red and beige fabric with right sides together. You will have three pairs. Press together and cut the layered strips into 36 pairs of $2^7/8$-inch squares.

Step 5. Cut the layered squares in half diagonally. Stitch the triangles together $1/4$ inch from the diagonal edge to make 72 triangle-pieced squares.

Step 6. Sew the triangle-pieced squares together in pairs, as shown in **Diagram 6** to make 36 units.

Diagram 6

Step 7. Sew the units made in Step 3 to the bottom of the $2^1/2 \times 4^1/2$-inch red rectangles. See **Diagram 7.** Sew

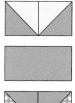

Diagram 7

the units made in Step 6 to the top of the rectangles, as shown.

Assembling the Star/Nine Patch Blocks

Step 1. Assemble the Star/Nine Patch block, as shown in **Diagram 8.** For rows 1 and 3, sew a star section between two Nine Patch blocks.

Step 2. Sew a $4^1/2$-inch red square between two star sections for row 2. Sew the three rows together to make the Star/Nine Patch block. Repeat to make nine Star/Nine Patch blocks.

QUILT CENTER

Assemble the quilt center in three vertical rows of three blocks each, as shown in **Diagram 9.** Sew the three vertical rows together.

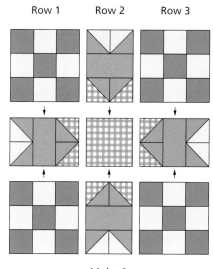

Make 9
Diagram 8

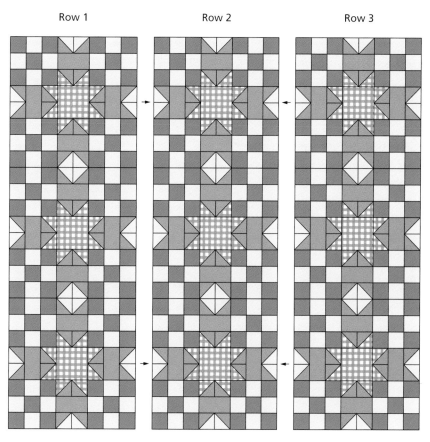

Diagram 9

BORDERS

Cutting for Borders

From the red fabric:
• Cut six $1\frac{1}{2} \times 44$-inch strips for the inner border

From the red check fabric:
• Cut six $5\frac{1}{2} \times 44$-inch strips for the outer border

Attaching the Borders

Step 1. Piece the red inner border strips together with diagonal seams. Measure the quilt from left to right through the middle to determine the length of the top and bottom borders. Cut the long red inner border strip to the length needed for the top and bottom borders and sew them to the quilt.

Step 2. Measure the quilt from top to the bottom through the middle, including the borders you just added, to determine the length of the side borders. Cut the remaining red inner border strip to the lengths needed and sew the strips to the sides of the quilt.

Step 3. Piece the red check outer border strips together with diagonal seams. Measure as you did for the inner border; cut to the lengths needed. Sew top and bottom red check outer border strips to the quilt first, followed by the side borders.

QUILTING

Step 1. Prepare the backing for the wall quilt by cutting the $3\frac{3}{4}$-yard length of backing fabric in half crosswise to make two $1\frac{7}{8}$-yard lengths. Remove the selvages. Sew the two lengths together with one center seam. Press seam allowances open.

Step 2. Trim the backing and batting so they are 4 inches larger than the quilt top dimensions.

Step 3. Mark the quilt top.

Step 4. Layer the backing, batting, and quilt top. Baste the layers together and quilt by hand or machine.

BINDING

The $2\frac{3}{4}$-inch strips will make a $\frac{3}{8}$- to $\frac{1}{2}$-inch-wide binding. If you want a wider or narrower binding, adjust the width of the strips you cut. (See page 247 for pointers on how to experiment with binding width.) See "Making and Attaching the Binding" on page 245 to complete your quilt.

Cutting for Cross-Grain Binding

From the red check fabric:
• Cut seven $2\frac{3}{4} \times 44$-inch strips

QUILTING IDEAS

☑ You may choose to hand quilt the wall quilt.

☑ Quilt the 4-inch center square of the star diagonally from corner to corner.

☑ Quilt a large V in the outer star to give it definition.

☑ Quilt the outside edges of the entire star in the ditch to make the star puff out a little.

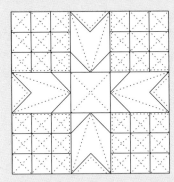

☑ Stitch all of the Nine Patch blocks diagonally, so the stitching extends into the lattice and border strips.

☑ The quilt in the photo was quilted by machine in an allover meandering design for a contemporary look. See "Meander and Stipple Quilting" on page 246 for tips.

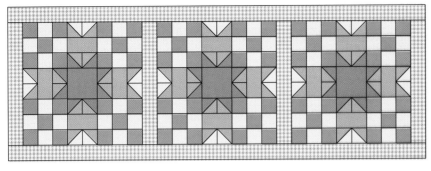

Table Runner Diagram

FABRIC KEY

DARK RED

RED

BEIGE

BLUES

BLUE CHECK

STAR PATCH TABLE RUNNER

SIZE

Table runner: 20 × 56 inches (unquilted)

Finished block: 16 inches square

FABRICS AND SUPPLIES

Yardage is based on 44-inch-wide fabric.

⅓ yard of dark red fabric for inner star

½ yard of medium red fabric for outer star

½ yard of beige fabric for Nine Patch blocks

½ yard *total* of a variety of medium blue fabrics for Nine Patch squares

½ yard of blue check fabric for lattice and border

¼ yard of dark blue fabric for accent binding

½ yard of plaid fabric for bias binding

1½ yards of fabric for table runner backing

Quilt batting, at least 24 × 60 inches

Rotary cutter, mat, and see-through ruler

Before making the table runner, be sure to read "Getting Ready" for the Wall Quilt on page 96.

STAR/NINE PATCH BLOCKS
(Make 3)

Cutting for Star/Nine Patch Blocks

From the dark red fabric:
• Cut one 4½ × 16-inch strip. From this strip, cut three 4½-inch squares.
• Cut one 2⅞ × 44-inch strip

From the medium red fabric:
• Cut two 2½ × 44-inch strips. From these strips, cut twelve 2½ × 4½-inch pieces.
• Cut two 2⅞ × 44-inch strips

From the beige fabric:
• Cut four 2½ × 44-inch strips
• Cut one 2⅞ × 44-inch strip

From the medium blue fabrics:
• Cut five 2½ × 44-inch strips

Piecing the Nine Patch Blocks

Step 1. Make Strip Set 1. With right sides together, sew a 2½ × 44-inch medium blue strip to each side of a 2½ × 44-inch beige strip. Press seam allowances toward the blue fabric. Make two of these strip sets. Crosscut the strip sets into 24 segments 2½ inches wide, as shown in **Diagram 10.**

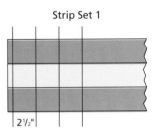

Strip Set 1

2½"

Diagram 10

Step 2. Make Strip Set 2. With right sides together, sew a 2½ × 44-inch beige strip to each side of a 2½ × 44-inch medium blue strip. Press seam allowances toward the blue strip. Cut the strip set into twelve 2½-inch-wide segments, as shown in **Diagram 11.**

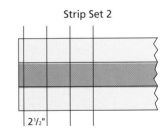

Strip Set 2

2½"

Diagram 11

Step 3. Sew a Strip Set 1 segment to the top and bottom of a Strip Set 2 segment to make 12 Nine Patch blocks, as shown in **Diagram 12** on page 100.

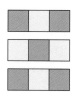

Diagram 12

Piecing the Star Sections

Step 1. Layer the $2\frac{7}{8} \times 44$-inch strips of dark red and red fabric with right sides together. Press the layers together and cut into 12 pairs of $2\frac{7}{8}$-inch squares.

Step 2. Cut the layered squares in half diagonally. Stitch the dark red and medium red triangles together $\frac{1}{4}$ inch from the diagonal edge to make 24 triangle-pieced squares, as shown in **Diagram 13.**

Diagram 13

Step 3. Sew the triangle-pieced squares together in pairs, as shown in **Diagram 14** to make 12 units.

Diagram 14

Step 4. Layer the $2\frac{7}{8} \times 44$-inch strips of red and beige fabric with right sides together. Press together and cut the layered strips into 12 pairs of $2\frac{7}{8}$-inch squares.

Step 5. Cut the layered squares in half diagonally. Stitch the triangles together $\frac{1}{4}$ inch from the diagonal edge to make 24 triangle-pieced squares.

Step 6. Sew the triangle-pieced squares together in pairs, as shown in **Diagram 15** to make 12 units.

Diagram 15

Step 7. Sew the units made in Step 3 to the bottom of the $2\frac{1}{2} \times 4\frac{1}{2}$-inch medium red rectangles, referring to **Diagram 16.** Sew the units made in Step 6 to the top of the rectangles, as shown.

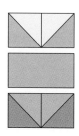

Diagram 16

Assembling the Star/Nine Patch Blocks

Step 1. Assemble the Star/Nine Patch block in rows, as shown in **Diagram 17.** For rows 1 and 3 of the block, sew a star section between two Nine Patch blocks.

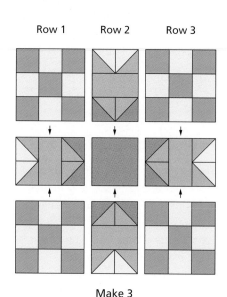

Row 1   Row 2   Row 3

Make 3
Diagram 17

Step 2. Sew a $4\frac{1}{2}$-inch dark red square between two star sections for row 2. Sew these three rows together to make the Star/Nine Patch block. Repeat to make three Star/Nine Patch blocks.

TABLE RUNNER TOP

Cutting for Lattice Strips and Borders

From the blue check fabric:
• Cut five $2\frac{1}{2} \times 44$-inch strips

Step 1. Measure your blocks. They should be $16\frac{1}{2}$ inches square. Cut four strips of this measurement from the $2\frac{1}{2}$-inch blue check lattice strips. Sew a lattice strip to two opposite sides of a Star/Nine Patch block. Sew a Star/Nine Patch block to either side of the lattice strips to make a row, as shown in **Diagram 18.**

Step 2. Add the lattice strips to the ends of the runner to make a border.

Step 3. Measure the length of the runner through the center, including the borders you just added, to determine the measurement for the top and bottom borders. Piece three 44-inch blue check border strips together with diagonal seams and cut two pieces to the length of the runner. Add these border strips to the runner.

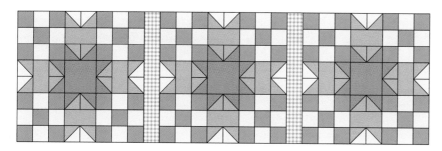

Diagram 18

QUILTING

Step 1. Prepare the backing for the table runner by cutting the 1½-yard piece of backing fabric in half to make two 27 × 44-inch pieces. Remove the selvages and sew the two pieces together along the 27-inch edge. Press the seam allowances open.

Step 2. Trim the backing fabric and batting so they are 4 inches larger than the runner dimensions.

Step 3. Mark the table runner.

Step 4. Layer the backing, batting, and pieced top. Baste the layers together and quilt by hand or machine.

BINDING

The table runner pictured has a binding accent trim that is added before the final binding is applied.

Cutting for Binding

From the plaid fabric:
• Cut enough 2¾-inch-wide bias strips to make a 167-inch strip

From the dark blue fabric:
• Cut four 1 × 44-inch strips for the accent trim

Attaching the Binding

Step 1. To add the accent trim, piece the trim strips with diagonal seams as necessary to obtain the lengths needed for the edges of your runner. Fold the trim in half lengthwise, *wrong* sides together. With raw edges even, machine baste an accent strip to each end of the runner using a ¼-inch seam. Next machine baste a similar strip to each side of the runner. The ends of the accent strips will overlap at the corners, as shown in **Diagram 19.**

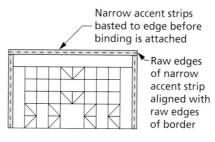

Narrow accent strips basted to edge before binding is attached

Raw edges of narrow accent strip aligned with raw edges of border

Diagram 19

Step 2. To add the 2¾-inch-wide plaid bias binding, see "Making and Attaching the Binding" on page 245. Approximately ¼ inch of the accent trim will be exposed once the final bias binding is applied. You do not need to tack down this trim. It is so narrow that it will lay flat, similar to a piping.

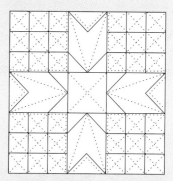

QUILTING IDEAS

☑ You may choose to hand quilt the table runner.

☑ Quilt the 4-inch center square of the star diagonally from corner to corner.

☑ Quilt a large V in the outer star to give it definition.

☑ Quilt the outside edges of the entire star in the ditch to make the star puff out a little.

☑ Quilt by machine in an allover meandering design for a contemporary look. See "Meander and Stipple Quilting" on page 246 for details on this technique.

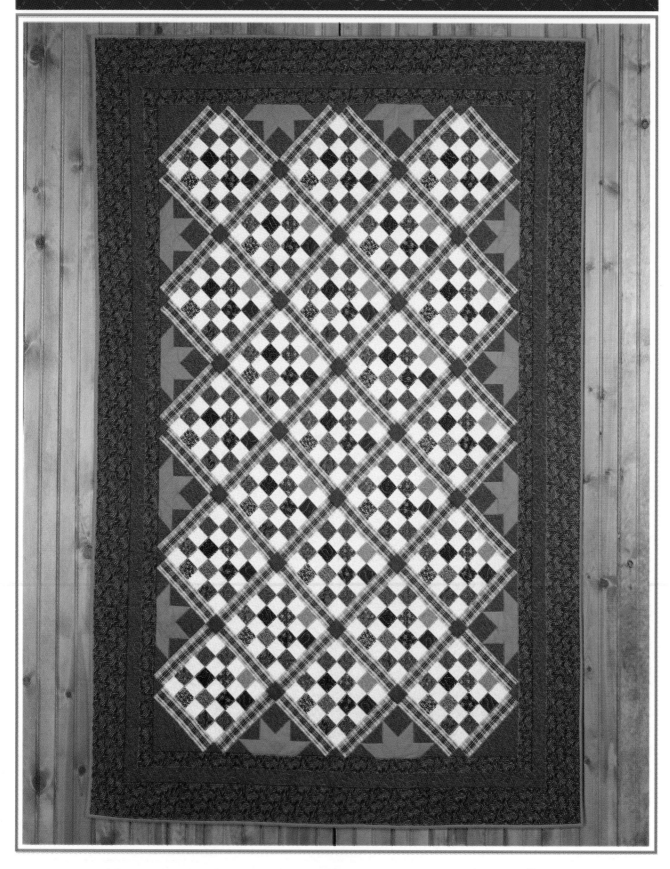

Quilt Diagram

Bed quilt: 68 × 103 inches unquilted

Finished block: 10 inches square

FABRICS AND SUPPLIES

Yardage is based on 44-inch-wide fabric.

2 yards of cream print fabric for pieced blocks

¼ yard *each* of 12 blue print fabrics for pieced blocks

1⅛ yards of gold fabric for Half-Star blocks and binding

1¾ yards of dark red print fabric for lattice posts, Half-Star blocks, side triangles, and middle border

1⅝ yards of blue plaid fabric for lattice strips

2 yards of dark blue print fabric for inner and outer borders

6 yards of fabric for quilt backing

Quilt batting, at least 72 × 107 inches

Rotary cutter, mat, and see-through ruler

Template plastic

Scrappy Five Patch blocks in a wonderful array of homespun plaids and indigo blues make this quilt a perfect complement for the antiques in my home. I included a warm touch of country red and gold in the Half-Star blocks that frame the patchwork. I'm most attracted to the understated nature of this quilt. It fits in so comfortably with my home that it's almost as if it came with the house!

FABRIC KEY

 CREAM

 BLUE FABRICS

 GOLD

 DARK RED PRINT

 BLUE PLAID

DARK BLUE PRINT

GETTING READY

- Read instructions thoroughly before you begin.
- Prewash and press fabric.
- Use ¼-inch seam allowances throughout unless directions specify otherwise.
- Seam allowances are included in cutting sizes.
- Press seam allowance in the direction that will create the least bulk and, whenever possible, toward the darker fabric.
- Trace **Templates A, B,** and **C** (page 109) onto template plastic and cut out. When cutting your fabric, you may want to skip ahead and cut the strips you need before you cut using the templates.
- Cutting directions for each section of the quilt are given in the areas following the row of scissors. If you like to cut as you go, simply follow the directions as you get to them. If you'd rather cut all your pieces at once, skip ahead and look for the scissors to do all the cutting before you begin to sew.
- Instructions are given for quick cutting and piecing the blocks and borders. Note that for some of the pieces, the quick-cutting method will result in leftover fabric.

FIVE PATCH BLOCKS
(Make 23)

Cutting for Five Patch Blocks

From the cream fabric:
- Cut twenty-six 2½ × 44-inch strips

From *each* of the 12 blue print fabrics:
- Cut two 2½ × 44-inch strips. Number each of these fabrics, 1 through 12.

Making the Strip Sets

The blocks are made up of a combination of five strip sets, as shown in **Diagram 1.** The strip sets are identified by the letters A, B, C, D, and E. Once you have arranged the strips by color combinations, sew the five-piece strip sets together. Place strips right sides together and stitch along

the 44-inch sides. After stitching, these strip sets must measure 10½ inches wide. Check and adjust seam allowances as needed. Accuracy is a must, or the outside Half-Star blocks will not fit the quilt center. Press all seams toward the blue fabric. Make two of each strip set.

HINTS & HELPS

When you are stitching long strips together, be careful not to pull or stretch them while you're sewing. This may cause them to become wavy, which can distort your final strip set. Also, press the strip sets perpendicular to your ironing board to help prevent the rainbow effect.

Strip Set A: Use one strip each of blue print fabrics 1 and 2 and three cream strips, as shown in **Diagram 2.** Make two Strip Set As.

Strip Set B: Use one strip each of blue print fabrics 3, 4, and 5 and two cream strips, as shown in **Diagram 3.** Make two Strip Set Bs.

Strip Set A		1	2	
Strip Set B	3	4		5
Strip Set C		6	7	
Strip Set D	8	9		10
Strip Set E		11	12	

Diagram 1

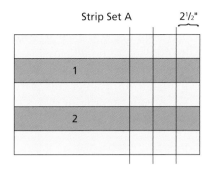

Diagram 2

Diagram 3

Strip Set C: Use one strip each of blue print fabrics 6 and 7 and three cream strips, as shown in **Diagram 4.** Make two Strip Set Cs.

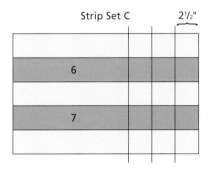

Diagram 4

Strip Set D: Use one strip each of blue print fabrics 8, 9, and 10 and two cream strips, as shown in **Diagram 5.** Make two Strip Set Ds.

Strip Set E: Use one strip each of blue print fabrics 11 and 12 and three cream strips, as shown in **Diagram 6.** Make two Strip Set Es.

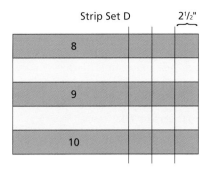

Diagram 5

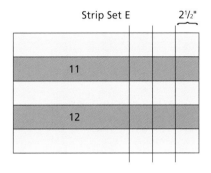

Diagram 6

Quick-Cutting the Pieced Strip Sets

Step 1. With the right side of the fabric facing up, lay Strip Set A on your cutting mat. Using a see-through ruler and rotary cutter, cut the strip set into $2\frac{1}{2} \times 10\frac{1}{2}$-inch segments. Refer to the cutting lines in **Diagrams 2** through **6.**

Step 2. After a few cuts, you may need to straighten the cut edge of the strip set again with the ruler and mat. Cut each of the strip sets in this manner, cutting twenty-three $2\frac{1}{2}$-inch segments of each combination.

Assembling the Blocks

Step 1. Lay out the Strip Set A, B, C, D, and E segments, as shown in **Diagram 1.**

Step 2. With right sides together, stitch a Strip Set A and a Strip Set B segment together. Sew strip set segments C, D, and E to the block in this same manner, following the order shown in **Diagram 1.** The

completed block should measure $10\frac{1}{2}$ inches square. Adjust seam allowances if needed. Press.

Step 3. Sew the rest of the strip set segments together in this manner to make 23 pieced blocks. Press.

HALF-STAR BLOCKS
(Make 12)

HINTS & HELPS

If you use plastic or cardboard templates, make a hole at each of the corner dots where the sewing lines intersect. Use a sturdy darning needle or $\frac{1}{8}$-inch paper punch. With the tip of a pencil, mark the exact corner points on the fabric pieces as you cut them out.

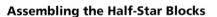

Cutting for Half-Star Blocks

As you cut out each piece, mark the corner points by making a dot on the sewing line to help you with assembly.

From the gold fabric:
• Cut 48 of **Template A**

From the dark red print fabric cut:
• Cut 12 of **Template B**
• Cut 48 of **Template C**

Assembling the Half-Star Blocks

The red squares and triangles that frame the star must be set into the angles created by the star, as shown in **Diagram 7.**

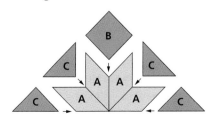

Diagram 7

Step 1. Join two piece As together, stitching from the edge of the pieces on one end and ending at the dot on the other, as shown in **Diagram 8.** Repeat for a second pair of star points.

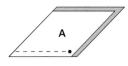

Diagram 8

Step 2. Join the two pairs of star points together, stitching from the center to the dot at the other end of the A piece, referring to **Diagram 9.**

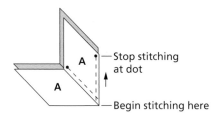

Diagram 9

Step 3. Square B is set between the two center star points. Pin one edge of square B to piece A, right sides together, matching the dots. Begin stitching from the dot at the inner corner to the outer edge, as shown in **Diagram 10.**

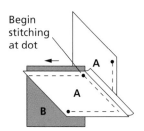

Diagram 10

Step 4. Position the adjacent edge of square B on top of the adjacent edge of the A piece with right sides together and raw edges even. Stitch from the dot at the inner corner to the outer edge, as shown in **Diagram 11.**

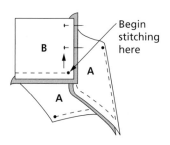

Diagram 11

Step 5. Set in two C triangles next to the center star points. Pin one edge of the C triangle to the A piece, right sides together, matching the dots, as shown in **Diagram 12.** Stitch from the dot at the inner corner to the outer edge.

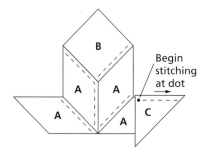

Diagram 12

Position the adjacent edge of the C triangle on top of the adjacent edge of the A piece, with right sides together and raw edges even. Stitch from the dot at the inner corner to the outer edge. Repeat for the second C triangle.

Step 6. Sew a C triangle to each of the remaining two corners of the Half-Star block, as shown in **Diagram 13.**

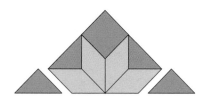

Diagram 13

Step 7. Repeat Steps 1 through 6 to make a total of 12 Half-Star blocks.

QUILT CENTER

Cutting for Lattice and Corner Triangles

From the blue plaid fabric:
• Cut sixteen $2\frac{1}{2} \times 44$-inch strips. From these strips, cut sixty $2\frac{1}{2} \times 10\frac{1}{2}$-inch pieces.

From the dark red print fabric:
• Cut two $2\frac{1}{2} \times 44$-inch strips. From these strips, cut twenty-two $2\frac{1}{2}$-inch squares for lattice posts.
• Cut one 5×44-inch strip. From this strip, cut four 5-inch squares. Cut these squares into quarters diagonally to make 16 half-posts for the lattice.
• Cut two $11\frac{1}{2}$-inch squares. Cut these squares in half diagonally to make four corner triangles.

Assembling the Quilt Center

Step 1. Referring to **Diagram 14,** prepare eight lattice rows, adding lattice posts and half-posts to the lattice pieces as necessary to complete the strips. Note that two of these lattice rows will not have any lattice posts, only half-posts on each end.

Step 2. Lay out the quilt blocks and lattice strips in diagonal rows, as shown in **Diagram 14.** Sew the 10½-inch lattice pieces and blocks together to make the rows.

Step 3. Referring to **Diagram 14,** add Half-Star blocks to each end of the diagonal block rows as required.

Step 4. Stitch the rows of blocks and lattice strips together to make the quilt top.

Step 5. Add the corner triangles.

Step 6. You will need to trim the excess fabric from the corner triangles and the half-post triangles on the ends of the lattice strips. Before you trim, be sure to read "Trimming Side and Corner Triangles" on page 236 to be certain you make these cuts accurately.

Using a see-through ruler, cutting mat, and rotary cutter, leave ¼-inch seam allowances beyond the block corners. Be careful to keep your corners accurate 90 degree angles as you cut. Press all seams.

BORDERS

Cutting for Borders

From the dark blue print fabric:
• Cut eight 2½ × 44-inch strips for the inner border
• Cut nine 5½ × 44-inch strips for the outer border

From the dark red print fabric:
• Cut eight 2½ × 44-inch strips for the middle border

Inner Border

Step 1. Piece three 2½-inch dark blue print inner border strips together with diagonal seams for the top and bottom borders, and piece five strips together with diagonal seams for the side borders.

Step 2. Measure the quilt from left to right through the middle to determine the length of the top and bottom borders. Cut the top and bottom inner border strip to the necessary lengths and sew the dark blue print inner border to the top and bottom of the quilt.

Step 3. Measure the quilt from top to bottom through the middle, including the borders you just added, to determine the length of the side borders. Cut the side inner border strip to the necessary lengths and sew the dark blue print inner border to the sides of the quilt.

Middle Border

Step 1. Piece the 2½-inch red middle border strips with diagonal seams.

Diagram 14

Step 2. Measure your quilt as you did for the inner border to determine the length needed for the middle border strips. Sew the top and bottom dark red print middle border strips to the quilt first, followed by the side borders.

Outer Border

Step 1. Piece the 5½-inch blue outer border strips with diagonal seams.

Step 2. Measure your quilt as you did for the inner border to determine the length needed for the outer border strips. Sew the top and bottom dark blue print outer border strips to the quilt first, followed by the side borders.

QUILTING

Step 1. Prepare the backing for the quilt by cutting the 6-yard length of backing fabric in half crosswise to make two 3-yard lengths. Remove the selvages and sew the two lengths together with one center seam. Press the seam open.

Step 2. Trim the backing and batting to measure 4 inches larger than the quilt top dimensions.

Step 3. Mark the quilt top.

Step 4. Layer the backing, batting, and quilt top. Baste the layers together and quilt by hand or machine.

BINDING

The 2¾-inch strips will produce a ⅜- to ½-inch-wide binding. If you want a wider or narrower binding, adjust the width of the strips you cut. (See page 247 for pointers on how to experiment with binding width.) See "Making and Attaching Binding" on page 245 to complete your quilt.

Cutting for Cross-Grain Binding

From the gold fabric:
• Cut eight 2¾ × 44-inch strips

QUILTING IDEAS

◿ The quilt in the photograph was machine quilted in an overall meandering pattern, but the stars were left unquilted to make them stand out. The borders have a feather quilting design surrounded by meander quilting.

◿ You could quilt in the ditch around the blue and cream squares in the Five Patch blocks. Stitch on the side of the seam line that does not have the seam allowance.

◿ Quilt in the ditch around the Half-Star blocks along all the seam lines.

◿ The star points could also be outline quilted ¼ inch in from the seam lines.

◿ The lattice pieces could have two rows of stitching about ⅝ inch apart, dividing the lattice strips lengthwise into thirds. When these stitching lines intersect in the lattice posts you'll form an interesting stitched Nine Patch effect.

◿ Try vertical channel quilting in the border.

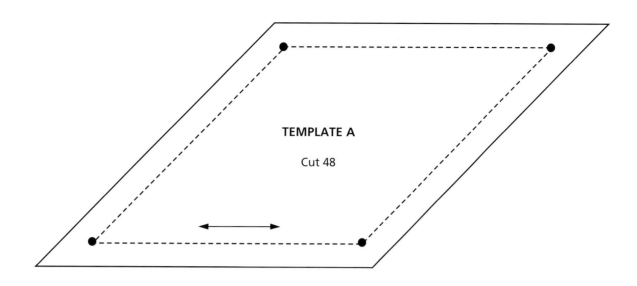

TEMPLATE A

Cut 48

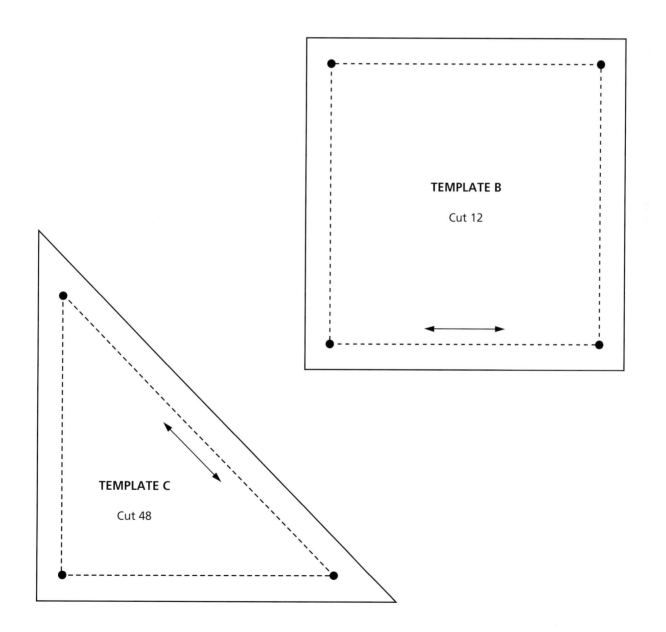

TEMPLATE B

Cut 12

TEMPLATE C

Cut 48

MIDNIGHT SKY

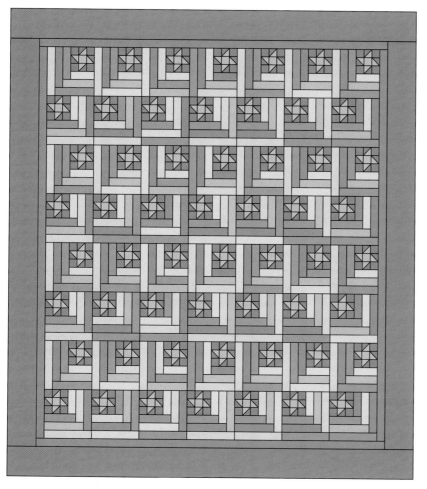

Quilt Diagram

SIZE

Bed quilt: 77 × 86 inches (unquilted)

Finished block: 9 inches square

FABRICS AND SUPPLIES

Yardage is based on 44-inch-wide fabric.

3⅓ yards *total* of variety of red and blue fabrics for Log Cabin strips

¾ yard of gold fabric for stars

½ yard of red print fabric for inner border

1⅓ yards of blue check fabric for star background

2½ yards of blue homespun plaid for outer border

⅞ yard blue star fabric for binding

5¼ yards of fabric for quilt backing

Quilt batting, at least 81 × 90 inches

Rotary cutter, mat, and see-through ruler

My original design of Midnight Sky used all blue prints around the gold stars. In the quilt shown here, shades of red have been added to give the quilt an Americana feel. Follow this example and change colors and fabrics to adapt this design to any theme or holiday. Piece this quilt in reproduction vintage fabrics for a wonderful antique feel. Use pastels for baby; bright primary colors for kids; holiday red and green for Christmastime; or rich earth colors such as deep golds, fiery reds, and mossy greens to celebrate the brief but vibrant colors of fall. The simple star and Log Cabin piecing make this quilt very easy to put together.

FABRIC KEY

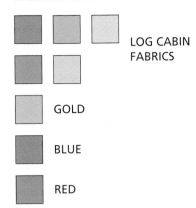

LOG CABIN
FABRICS

GOLD

BLUE

RED

- Read instructions thoroughly before you begin.
- Prewash and press fabric.
- Use ¼-inch seam allowances throughout unless directions specify otherwise.
- Seam allowances are included in the cutting sizes given.
- Press seam allowance in the direction that will create the least bulk and, whenever possible, toward the darker fabric.
- Cutting directions for each section of the quilt are given in the areas following the row of scissors. If you like to cut as you go, simply follow the directions as you get to them. If you'd rather cut all your pieces at once, skip ahead and look for the scissors to do all the cutting before you begin to sew.
- Instructions are given for quick cutting and piecing the blocks and borders. Note that for some of the pieces, the quick-cutting method will result in leftover fabric.

STAR BLOCKS AND LOG CABIN STRIPS
(Make 56)

Each block is made from a pieced star surrounded on two sides by strips of fabric.

Cutting for Stars and Log Cabin Strips

From the gold fabric:
- Cut three 2 × 44-inch strips. From these strips, cut fifty-six 2-inch squares.
- Cut seven 2⅜ × 44-inch strips

From the blue check fabric:
- Cut eleven 2 × 44-inch strips. From these strips, cut two hundred twenty-four 2-inch squares.
- Cut seven 2⅜ × 44-inch strips

From a variety of red and blue fabrics:
- Cut fifty-six 2 × 44-inch Log Cabin strips

Piecing the Star Blocks

Step 1. With right sides together, layer a gold 2⅜ × 44-inch strip and a blue check 2⅜ × 44-inch strip. Press together. Layer the remaining gold and blue check strips into pairs but do not stitch. Cut the layered strips into 112 squares, each 2⅜ inches.

Step 2. Cut the layered squares in half diagonally, as shown in **Diagram 1.** Stitch ¼-inch from the diagonal edge. Press seam allowances toward the blue fabric to make a 2-inch triangle-pieced square. Repeat to make 224 triangle-pieced squares.

Diagram 1

Step 3. Sew a 2-inch blue check square to either side of a 2-inch triangle-pieced square, as shown in **Diagram 2.** Repeat to make 112 of these units.

Diagram 2

Step 4. Sew a 2-inch triangle-pieced square to either side of a 2-inch gold square, referring to **Diagram 3.** Repeat to make 56 of these units.

Diagram 3

Step 5. Sew a unit made in Step 3 to either side of a unit made in Step 4. Refer to **Diagram 4.** Press. Repeat to make 56 stars.

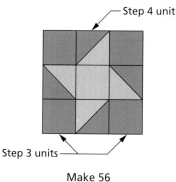

Step 4 unit

Step 3 units

Make 56
Diagram 4

Adding the Log Cabin Strips

Add a variety of strips to the Star blocks in a random fashion so the fabrics appear in different positions in each block.

Step 1. Sew a 44-inch strip onto a Star block, as shown in **Diagram 5.** Press the seam allowance toward the strip just added and then trim the strip even with the edge of the Star block.

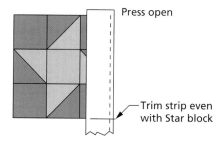

Press open

Trim strip even with Star block

Diagram 5

Step 2. Turn the Star block a quarter turn to the left. Sew the next strip to the block. Press and trim the strip even with the edge of the block, as shown in **Diagram 6.**

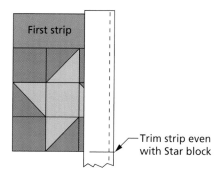

First strip

Trim strip even with Star block

Diagram 6

Step 3. Add the third strip to the same side of the block as the first strip. Continue to add strips to the Star block in the same fashion, making sure your strips are added to only two sides of each block. Trim the excess from each consecutive strip, as shown in **Diagram 7.** When six strips have been added, your block should measure 9½-inches square. Make sure you press and square up your blocks as you go. Make seam allowance adjustments if necessary.

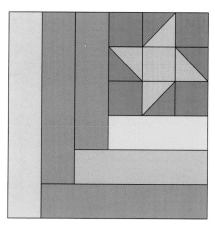

Make 56
Diagram 7

QUILT TOP

Sew the blocks together in rows. Make eight horizontal rows of seven blocks each. Rotate the blocks a quarter turn in every other row so that the star alternates positions. See **Diagram 8.** Sew the rows together.

BORDERS

The yardage given allows for the inner border pieces to be cut cross-grain and the outer borders to be cut lengthwise.

Cutting for Borders

From the red print fabric:
• Cut seven 2 × 44-inch strips for the inner border

From the blue plaid fabric:
• Cut two 6 × 81-inch strips for the outer border
• Cut two 6 × 90-inch strips for the outer border

Diagram 8

Attaching the Borders

Step 1. Piece three red print inner border strips with diagonal seams.

Step 2. Measure the quilt from top to bottom through the middle to determine the length of the side borders. Cut the pieced border strip into two strips of the necessary length. Sew the red print inner border strips to the sides of your quilt.

Step 3. Piece together four red print inner border strips with diagonal seams.

Step 4. Measure the quilt from side to side through the middle, including the borders you just added, to determine the length of the top and bottom borders. Cut the pieced red print inner border strip into two strips of the necessary length and sew the strips to the top and bottom of the quilt.

Step 5. Measure the quilt as you did in Step 2. Cut the 81-inch blue plaid outer border strips to the necessary length and sew them to the sides of the quilt.

Step 6. Measure the quilt as you did in Step 4. Cut the 90-inch blue plaid outer border strips to the necessary length and sew them to the top and bottom of the quilt.

Note: Outside borders may vary in size to accommodate a particular bed. In the quilt shown on page 110, the top and bottom borders are a bit wider than the side borders.

QUILTING

Step 1. Prepare the backing for the quilt by cutting the 5¼-yard length of backing fabric in half crosswise to make two 2⅝-yard lengths. Remove the selvages. Sew the two lengths together with one center seam. Press seam allowance open.

Step 2. Trim backing and batting so they are 4 inches larger than the quilt top.

Step 3. Mark the quilt top.

Step 4. Layer the backing, batting, and quilt top. Baste these layers together and quilt by hand or machine.

BINDING

The 2¾-inch strips will make a ⅜- to ½-inch-wide binding. If you want a wider or narrower binding, adjust the width of the strips you cut. (See page 247 for pointers on how to experiment with binding width.) See "Making and Attaching the Binding" on page 245 to complete your quilt.

Cutting for Cross-Grain Binding

From the blue star fabric:
• Cut nine 2¾ × 44-inch strips

QUILTING IDEAS

▨ The quilt in the photograph was machine quilted in an overall meandering pattern. See "Meander and Stipple Quilting" on page 246.

▨ Instead of covering the quilt with meander stitching, another option would be to quilt in the ditch around the stars and Log Cabin strips to make them puff out a little.

▨ You could also quilt in the ditch along the inner border to define it.

▨ Vertical channel quilting would be very effective in the outer border.

HOMEWARD BOUND

These quilts beckon you to sit down and take a few minutes to enjoy the soothing comfort of the place you call home. Chat with your family and friends and make time just to relax. For a quilter, this also means making time to retreat to the sewing room to enjoy the pleasures of piecing together color and cloth.

Wall Quilt Diagram

MY FRIEND'S HOUSE WALL QUILT

SIZE

Wall quilt: 38 × 48 inches (unquilted)

Finished House block: 6 × 7 inches

Finished Star block: 4 inches square

FABRICS AND SUPPLIES

Yardage is based on 44-inch-wide fabric.

¾ yard *total* of a variety of fabrics for houses and roofs

⅛ yard of gold solid fabric for windows

⅔ yard of beige solid fabric for background

⅓ yard of gold print fabric for stars

½ yard of black print fabric for lattice center strip and inner border

¾ yard of dark print fabric for outer border (or ¼ yard *each* of four fabrics)

⅝ yard of plaid fabric for bias binding

1½ yards of fabric for quilt backing

Quilt batting, at least 42 × 52 inches

Rotary cutter, mat, and see-through ruler

This rustic charmer is a perfect friendship quilt project because the block design is simple enough for anyone to have fun with. I designed this as a group project when I was the outgoing president of Quilters Along the Yellowstone Trail. It is the custom for members to sew blocks for the outgoing president as a remembrance of her year in office. I have a huge quilt full of signature blocks from the members. It's always fun to take time out to read over the names. I'm so pleased to have a memory stitched by each person. My Friend's House is just as delightful to make by yourself, using lots of colors and prints from your scrap bag.

FABRIC KEY

HOUSE FABRICS

ROOF FABRICS

GOLD SOLID

BEIGE

GOLD PRINT

BLACK PRINT

DARK PRINTS

- Read instructions thoroughly before you begin.
- Prewash and press fabric.
- Use ¼-inch seam allowances throughout unless directions specify otherwise.
- Seam allowances are included in the cutting sizes given.
- Press seam allowance in the direction that will create the least bulk and, whenever possible, toward the darker fabric.
- Cutting directions for each section of the quilt are given in the areas following the row of scissors. If you like to cut as you go, simply follow the directions as you get to them. If you'd rather cut all your pieces at once, skip ahead and look for the scissors to do all the cutting before you begin to sew.

HOUSE BLOCKS
(Make 16)

Cutting for House Blocks

From the house fabrics:
- Cut two 1½ × 44-inch strips. From these strips (or from scraps), cut thirty-two 1½ × 2½-inch pieces.
- Cut two 4½ × 44-inch strips. From these strips (or from scraps), cut thirty-two 2½ × 4½-inch pieces.

From the roof fabrics:
- Cut two 3⅞ × 44-inch strips. From these strips (or from scraps), cut sixteen 3⅞-inch squares.

From the beige fabrics:
- Cut two 3⅞ × 44-inch strips. From these strips, cut sixteen 3⅞-inch squares.

From the gold solid fabric:
- Cut one 2½ × 44-inch strip. From this strip, cut sixteen 2½-inch squares.

Piecing the House Blocks

Step 1. With right sides together, layer a 3⅞-inch beige square and a 3⅞-inch roof fabric square. Press together. Cut this layered square in half diagonally. See **Diagram 1**. Stitch ¼-inch from the diagonal edge. Press seam allowances toward the roof fabric to make a 3½-inch triangle-pieced square. Repeat to make 32 triangle-pieced squares.

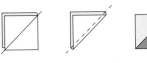

Diagram 1

Step 2. Sew two triangle-pieced squares together to form a roof section, as shown in **Diagram 2**. Repeat to make 16 roof sections.

Diagram 2

Step 3. Sew a 1½ × 2½-inch house fabric piece to the top and bottom of a 2½-inch gold solid square to make a window unit. Add a 2½ × 4½-inch house fabric piece to the left and right sides of the window unit to make a house base. See **Diagram 3**. Repeat to make 16 house bases.

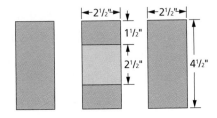

Diagram 3

Step 4. Sew the roof sections to the top of the house bases, as shown in **Diagram 4.**

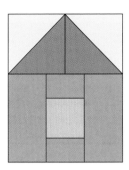

Make 16
Diagram 4

STAR BLOCKS
(Make 16)

Cutting for Star Blocks

From the gold print fabric:
- Cut three $1\frac{7}{8} \times 44$-inch strips.
- Cut one $2\frac{1}{2} \times 44$-inch strip. From this strip, cut sixteen $2\frac{1}{2}$-inch squares.

From the beige fabric:
- Cut three $1\frac{7}{8} \times 44$-inch strips.
- Cut three $1\frac{1}{2} \times 44$-inch strips. From these strips, cut sixty-four $1\frac{1}{2}$-inch squares.

Piecing the Star Blocks

Step 1. With right sides together, layer the $1\frac{7}{8} \times 44$-inch gold print strips and the $1\frac{7}{8} \times 44$-inch beige strips in pairs. Press together. Cut the layered strips into 64 pairs of $1\frac{7}{8}$-inch squares. Cut the layered squares in half diagonally. Stitch $\frac{1}{4}$ inch from the diagonal edge. Press seam allowances toward the gold fabric. Repeat to make 128 triangle-pieced squares.

HINTS & HELPS

If you are making My Friend's House as a friendship quilt and the number of house blocks does not work out evenly for your group, simply piece extra house blocks to make a larger quilt. Identify each block with the group name, hometown, or other special notation. Add extra yardage for borders and backing fabric if you are making a larger quilt.

Step 2. Sew two of the triangle-pieced squares together, as shown in **Diagram 5.** Repeat with the remaining triangle-pieced squares to make 64 star point units.

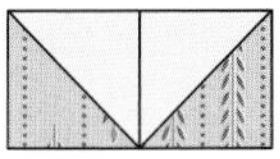

Diagram 5

Step 3. Sew a star point unit to the top and bottom of a $2\frac{1}{2}$-inch gold print square, referring to **Diagram 6.** Repeat to make 16 units.

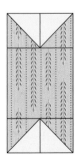

Diagram 6

Step 4. Sew a $1\frac{1}{2}$-inch beige square to the left and right of each of the remaining star point units. See **Diagram 7.** Sew these units to the left and right sides of the units created in Step 3 to make 16 stars, as shown in **Diagram 8.**

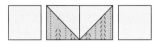

Diagram 7

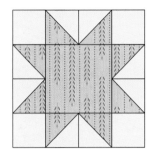

Make 16
Diagram 8

JOINING THE BLOCKS

Step 1. Sew three Star blocks together, side by side. Make four of these units. The four "extra" Star blocks will be used in the quilt corners.

Step 2. Sew four House blocks together, two on top of two, matching the seam intersections. Make four of these units.

Step 3. Sew the House and Star block units in two vertical rows, as shown in **Diagram 9** on page 120. To make Row 1, sew a Star block unit to the bottom of a House block unit. Repeat to make one more unit like this, and then join the two units together vertically.

Step 4. To make Row 2, sew a House block unit to the bottom of a Star block unit. Repeat for one more unit, and then join the two units together vertically, as shown in **Diagram 9** on page 120.

Row 1   Row 2

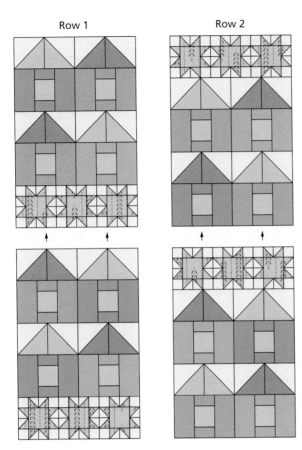

Diagram 9

LATTICE AND BORDERS

The yardage given allows for the border pieces to be cut cross-grain.

Cutting for Lattice and Borders

From the black print fabric:
• Cut five 2½ × 44-inch strips for the lattice and inner border

From the dark print fabric:
• Cut four 4½ × 44-inch strips for the outer border

Attaching the Lattice and Borders

Step 1. Measure the two house/star rows. They must be the same length. Adjust seam allowances if needed. Cut a 2½-inch-wide black print lattice strip to this measurement. Sew the lattice center strip vertically between the two rows of houses and stars.

Step 2. For the side inner borders, use the measurement taken in Step 1. Cut the black print inner border strips to the necessary lengths and sew to the sides of the quilt.

Step 3. For the top and bottom inner borders, measure the quilt from side to side through the middle, including the borders just added. Cut the black print border strips to the necessary lengths, and sew them to the top and bottom of the quilt.

Step 4. For the top and bottom outer border, measure as you did for the inner border in Step 3. Trim the dark print outer border strips to the necessary lengths and sew to the top and bottom of the quilt.

Step 5. For the side outer borders, measure the quilt from top to bottom. *Do not* include the top and bottom dark print outer borders in your measurement. Add ¼ inch on each end for seam allowances. Sew one of the four remaining star blocks to each end of the dark print side outer border strips. Add the side outer border units to the quilt.

QUILTING

Step 1. Trim the backing and batting so they are about 4 inches larger than the quilt top.

Step 2. Mark the quilt top.

Step 3. Layer the backing, batting, and quilt top. Baste these layers together and quilt by hand or machine.

BINDING

The 2¾-inch bias strips will produce a ⅜-inch-wide binding. If you want a wider or narrower binding, adjust the width of the strips you cut. (See page 247 for pointers on how to experiment with binding width.) See "Making and Attaching the Binding" on page 245 to complete your quilt.

Cutting for Bias Binding

From the plaid fabric:
• Cut enough 2¾-inch-wide bias strips to make a 200-inch strip

QUILTING IDEAS

▨ I used overall meander quilting on the quilt in the photograph. The beige background areas were stipple quilted. See "Meander and Stipple Quilting" on page 246 for tips.

▨ Quilt the House and Star blocks in the ditch to define these elements.

▨ Quilt a simple chain in the vertical lattice and inner borders.

▨ Quilt the outer border of the quilt with a larger chain design to complement the inner border design.

Miniature Quilt Diagram

FABRIC KEY

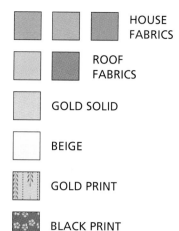

HOUSE FABRICS

ROOF FABRICS

GOLD SOLID

BEIGE

GOLD PRINT

BLACK PRINT

MY FRIEND'S HOUSE MINIATURE QUILT

SIZE

Miniature quilt: 19 × 25 inches (unquilted)

Finished House block: 6 × 7 inches

Finished Star block: 4 inches square

FABRICS AND SUPPLIES

⅓ yard *total* of a variety of fabrics for houses and roofs

⅛ yard of gold solid fabric for windows

¼ yard of beige solid fabric for background

⅛ yard *each* of three gold print fabrics or scraps for stars

½ yard of black print fabric for border

⅜ yard of red fabric for binding

¾ yard of fabric for quilt backing

Quilt batting, at least 23 × 29 inches

Rotary cutter, mat, and see-through ruler

HOUSE BLOCKS

(Make 4)

Be sure to read "Getting Ready" for the Wall Quilt on page 118 before you begin.

Cutting for House Blocks

From the house fabrics:
• Cut one 1½ × 21-inch strip. From this strip (or from scraps), cut eight 1½ × 2½-inch pieces.
• Cut one 2½ × 44-inch strip. From this strip (or from scraps), cut eight 2½ × 4½-inch pieces.

From the roof fabrics:
• Cut one 3⅞ × 17-inch strip. From this strip (or from scraps), cut four 3⅞-inch squares.

From the gold solid fabric:
• Cut one 2½ × 12-inch strip. From this strip, cut four 2½-inch squares.

From the beige fabric:
• Cut one 3⅞ × 17-inch strip. From this strip, cut four 3⅞-inch squares.

Piecing the House Blocks

Follow Steps 1 through 4 under "Piecing the House Blocks" for the Wall Quilt on page 118. You will make eight triangle-pieced squares, four roof sections, and four house bases to make four House blocks.

STAR BLOCKS
(Make 3)

Cutting for Star Blocks

From the gold print fabric:
• Cut one $2\frac{1}{2} \times 12$-inch strip. From this strip (or from scraps), cut three $2\frac{1}{2}$-inch squares.
• Cut one $1\frac{7}{8} \times 26$-inch strip. From this strip, cut twelve $1\frac{7}{8}$-inch squares.

From the beige fabric:
• Cut one $1\frac{7}{8} \times 26$-inch strip. From this strip, cut twelve $1\frac{7}{8}$-inch squares.
• Cut one $1\frac{1}{2} \times 20$-inch strip. From this strip, cut twelve $1\frac{1}{2}$-inch squares.

Piecing the Star Blocks

Step 1. With right sides together, layer the twelve $1\frac{7}{8}$-inch gold squares and the twelve $1\frac{7}{8}$-inch beige squares in pairs. Press

together. Cut the layered squares in half diagonally. Stitch $\frac{1}{4}$ inch from the diagonal edge. Press seams toward the gold fabric to make 24 triangle-pieced squares.

Step 2. Follow Steps 2 through 4 under "Piecing the Star Blocks" on page 119 for the wall quilt. You will make 12 star point units for three Star blocks.

QUILT CENTER

Step 1. Sew the three Star blocks together, side by side. Sew the four House blocks together, two on top of two, matching seam intersections.

Step 2. Sew the Star block unit to the top of the House block unit, as shown in the **Miniature Quilt Diagram** on page 121.

BORDERS

Cutting for Borders

From the black print fabric:
• Cut three 4×44-inch strips

Attaching the Borders

Step 1. Measure the quilt from left to right through the middle to determine the length of the top and

bottom borders. Cut a black print border strip to the necessary lengths and sew to the top and bottom of the quilt.

Step 2. Measure the quilt from top to bottom through the middle, including the borders you just added, to determine the length of the side borders. Trim the border strips to the necessary length and sew to the sides of the quilt.

QUILTING

See "Quilting" and "Quilting Ideas" for the Wall Quilt on page 120.

BINDING

The $2\frac{3}{4}$-inch binding strips will make a $\frac{3}{8}$-inch-wide binding. If you want a wider or narrower binding, adjust the width of the strips you cut. (See page 247 for pointers on how to experiment with binding width.) See "Making and Attaching Binding" on page 245 to complete your quilt.

Cutting for Cross-Grain Binding

From the red fabric:
• Cut three $2\frac{3}{4} \times 44$-inch strips

THERE'S
no place like
HOME

*T*he red patches in these
Log Cabin quilt blocks
symbolize warmth and
hospitality, two qualities
that are at the heart of
any quiltmaker's home.
I bought this little wooden
dollhouse, with its chimney
and shuttered windows,
because it reminds me
of the home we now live
in. It also makes me think
of a little girl stitching
quilts for a family of dolls
with all the same love and
care we put into our
quilts today.

PINE VIEW

Pine View is a strong, masculine design with an understated country flavor. I selected small- to medium-scale prints in similar color values (the same degree of lightness and darkness) and a lot of tone-on-tone prints. All of the tree trunks are the same fabric, which guides your eyes over the entire surface. Long, narrow, dark brown print strips beside the Tree blocks set off the lighter background fabrics. The fabric in the vertical stripes between the rows of trees is a larger print that does not distract from the trees. The pieced stars at the top and the bottom bring the center colors out into the dark borders.

Size

Bed Quilt: 92 × 104 inches (unquilted)

Finished Block: 5 inches square

Fabrics and Supplies

Yardage is based on 44-inch-wide fabric.

1½ yards *total* of a variety of green, red, blue, and brown fabrics for trees

1 yard beige fabric for tree background

1⅞ yards dark brown fabric for trunks and narrow border

2½ yards beige/black print fabric for side and corner triangles

1¾ yards of chestnut print fabric for lattice strips

4 yards red print fabric for border

¼ yard *each* of three gold print fabrics for stars

1 yard red print fabric for binding

8¼ yards fabric for quilt backing

Quilt batting, at least 96 × 108 inches

Rotary cutter, mat, and see-through ruler with ⅛-inch markings

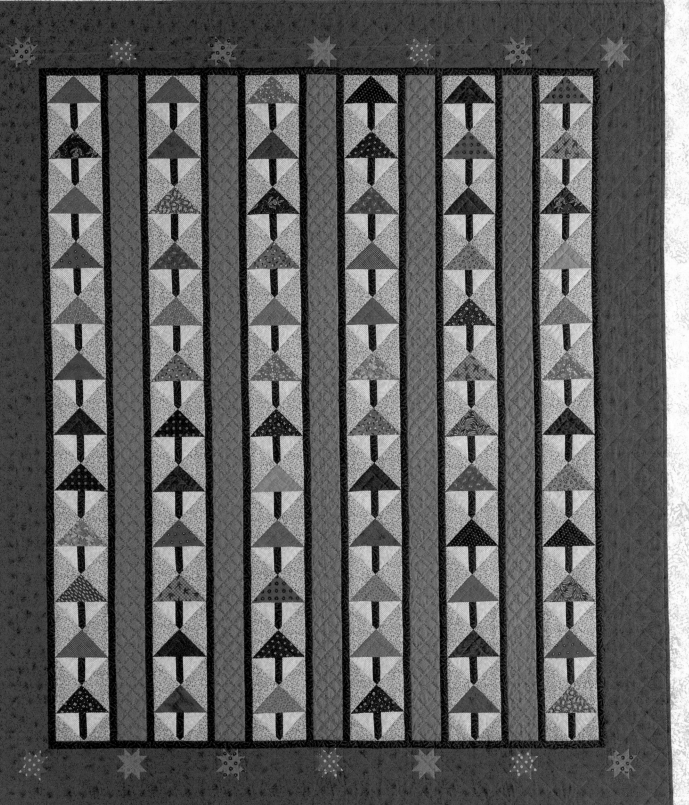

G e t t i n g   R e a d y

- READ instructions thoroughly before you begin.
- PREWASH and press fabric.
- USE ¼-inch seam allowances throughout unless directions specify otherwise.
- SEAM ALLOWANCES are included in the cutting sizes given.
- PRESS seam allowances in the direction that will create the least bulk, and whenever possible, press toward the darker fabric.
- CUTTING DIRECTIONS for each section of the quilt are given individually. If you like to cut as you go, simply follow the directions as you get to them. If you'd rather cut all your pieces at the same time, skip ahead to find each of the cutting sections and do all the cutting before you begin to sew. ✎

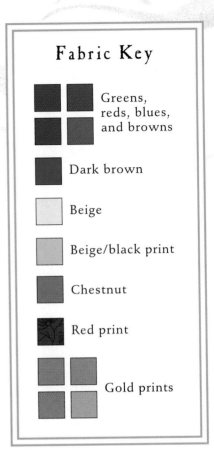

Fabric Key

Greens, reds, blues, and browns

Dark brown

Beige

Beige/black print

Chestnut

Red print

Gold prints

WHEN ORGANIZING a large group of fabrics for a scrap quilt, gather more than you'll actually need. Spread out your background fabric and start laying on top of it fabrics you know you want to use. Step back and view them from a distance to see how they look together. Then continue adding fabrics until you have found just the right mix for the look you want to achieve.

TIPS AND TRICKS

Tree Blocks
(MAKE 72)

C U T T I N G

From the green, red, blue, and brown tree fabrics:
- Cut six 5⅞ × 44-inch strips; from these strips, cut thirty-six 5⅞-inch squares. Cut these squares in half diagonally to make 72 triangles.

From the dark brown fabric:
- Cut eight 1½ × 44-inch strips; from these strips, cut seventy-two 1½ × 4½-inch pieces.

From the beige fabric:
- Cut five 5½ × 44-inch strips; from these strips, cut thirty-six 5½-inch squares. Cut these squares into quarters diagonally to make 144 triangles.

Piecing the Tree Blocks

1 Sew two beige background triangles to a 1½ × 4½-inch brown trunk piece, as shown in DIAGRAM 1. Trim the bottom edge of the trunk, as shown. Repeat for each trunk unit.

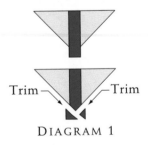

Trim — ——— Trim

DIAGRAM 1

2 Sew a tree fabric triangle onto each trunk unit, as shown in DIAGRAM 2. The individual tree square should measure 5½ inches square. If it

doesn't, check to make sure that the pieces were cut correctly and that you used accurate ¼-inch seam allowances.

DIAGRAM 2

Quilt Center

CUTTING

From the beige/black print fabric:
• Cut eight 9 × 44-inch strips; from these strips, cut thirty-three 9-inch squares. Cut these squares diagonally into quarters to form 132 side triangles.
• Cut two 5½ × 44-inch strips; from these strips, cut twelve 5½-inch squares. Cut these squares in half to form 24 corner triangles.

From the dark brown fabric:
• Cut thirty-one 1½ × 44-inch strips for narrow borders.

From the chestnut fabric:
• Cut eleven 4½ × 44-inch strips for lattice strips.

NOTE: The side triangles and corner triangles will be larger than necessary and will be trimmed before the narrow borders are added.

Piecing the Quilt Center

1 Referring to DIAGRAM 3, sew the side triangles to the Tree blocks. Make six vertical rows of 12 Tree blocks each. Be sure to match the seams of the Tree blocks. Add the corner triangles to the top and bottom of each row, as shown.

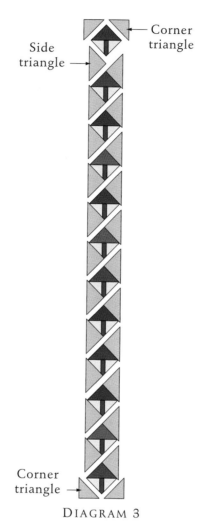

Side triangle

Corner triangle

Corner triangle

DIAGRAM 3

2 Trim off excess fabric from the side and corner triangles, taking care to allow for the ¼-inch seam allowances beyond the block corners. Before you trim, be sure to read through "Trimming Side and Corner Triangles" on page 211 to be certain you make these cuts accurately. Make sure that the corners measure accurate 90 degree angles and that all six rows measure the same.

3 Piece the short ends of the 1½ × 44-inch dark brown strips together diagonally, as shown in DIAGRAM 4. Trim the seam allowances to ¼ inch and press them open.

Trim to ¼"

DIAGRAM 4

4 Measure the length of your tree block rows, and trim 12 dark brown border strips to that length. Sew a border strip to each side of the tree rows, as shown in DIAGRAM 5.

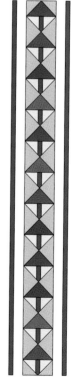

DIAGRAM 5

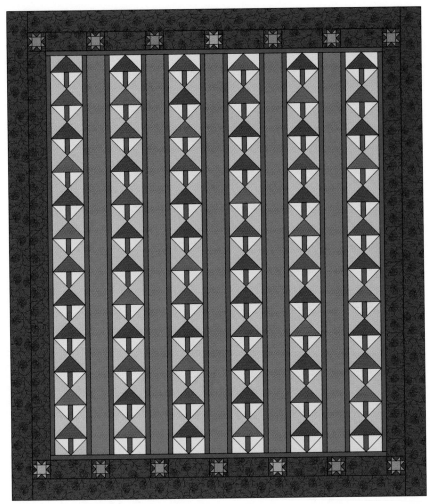

QUILT ASSEMBLY DIAGRAM

Star Blocks
(MAKE 14)

for each Star Block

From one of the gold print fabrics:
• Cut one 2½-inch square
• Cut one 1⅞ × 9-inch strip

From the red print border fabric:
• Cut four 1½-inch squares
• Cut one 1⅞ × 9-inch strip

Piecing
the Star Blocks

5 Piece the short ends of the 4½ × 44-inch chestnut strips together diagonally. Trim seam allowances to ¼ inch and press them open. Trim five chestnut lattice strips to the same length as your bordered tree rows. Sew a bordered tree row to each side of the lattice strips, as shown in the QUILT ASSEMBLY DIAGRAM. Press seam allowances toward the dark brown narrow borders.

6 Measure the quilt from left to right, through the center, to determine the length of the top and bottom dark brown borders. Trim two dark brown borders to the necessary length and sew them to the top and bottom of the quilt, as shown in the QUILT ASSEMBLY DIAGRAM.

7 Measure the quilt from top to bottom through the center to determine the length of the dark brown side borders. Trim two dark brown borders to the necessary length, and sew them to the sides of the quilt, as shown in the QUILT ASSEMBLY DIAGRAM.

1 With right sides together, layer the 1⅞ × 9-inch gold print strips and the 1⅞ × 9-inch red print strips in pairs. Press each pair of strips together. Cut each of the layered strips into four 1⅞-inch squares, as shown in DIAGRAM 6. Cut the layered squares in half diagonally, and stitch a seam ¼ inch in from the diagonal edges, as shown. Press seam allowances toward the gold print fabric. Make a total of eight triangle-pieced squares for each Star block.

DIAGRAM 6

2 Sew two triangle-pieced squares together, as shown in DIAGRAM 7. Repeat to make a total of four star-point units for each Star block.

DIAGRAM 7

3 Sew a star-point unit to the top and bottom of each 2½-inch gold print square, as shown in DIAGRAM 8.

DIAGRAM 8

4 Sew a 1½-inch red print square to the sides of the remaining star-point units, as shown in DIAGRAM 9, and sew these units to the sides of the Star blocks. The Star blocks should now measure 4½ inches square.

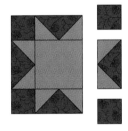

DIAGRAM 9

Borders

The yardage given allows for borders to be cut cross-grain.

From the red print border fabric:
• Cut eight 4½ × 44-inch strips for inner border
• Cut eleven 5 × 44-inch strips for outer border

Assembling the Inner Border

1 Measure the quilt from top to bottom through the center to determine the length of the side borders. Piece the short ends of five 4½-inch-wide red print strips together diagonally. Trim seam allowances and press them open. Trim two 4½-inch-wide red print borders to the necessary length, and sew them to the sides of the quilt. Press seam allowances toward the borders.

2 Measure the width of a Tree block row with two dark brown border strips attached. Cut twelve 4½-inch-wide red print rectangles to this measurement.

3 Referring to the QUILT ASSEMBLY DIAGRAM on the opposite page, sew seven stars and six 4½-inch-wide rectangles together. Press seam allowances toward the red print rectangles. Make one of these pieced border units for the top and one for the bottom inner border.

4 Sew the pieced border units to the top and bottom of the quilt. Press seam allowances toward the borders.

5 Measure the quilt from left to right through the middle to determine the length of the top and bottom outer borders. Piece together the short ends of the 5-inch-wide red print strips together with diagonal seams. Trim seam allowances to ¼ inch and press them open. Cut a top and bottom border to the length needed. Sew the borders to the top and bottom of the quilt.

Press seam allowances toward the borders.

6 Measure the quilt from top to bottom through the middle, including the borders you just added, to determine the length of the side borders. Cut the red print outer border strips to the necessary length and sew them to the quilt sides in the same manner as for the top and botttom borders. Press seam allowances toward the borders.

Putting It All Together

1 Prepare the backing by cutting the 8¼-yard length of backing fabric into thirds crosswise to make three 2¾-yard lengths. Remove the selvage edges. Sew the long edges of the three lengths together and press seam allowances open.

2 Trim the backing and batting so they are 4 inches larger than the quilt top dimensions.

3 Mark quilting designs on the quilt top.

4 Layer the backing, batting, and quilt top. Baste these layers together and quilt.

5 When quilting is complete, remove the basting stitches, and trim the excess backing and batting even with the quilt top.

Binding

NOTE: The 2¾-inch-wide binding strip will produce a ⅜-inch-wide finished binding. If you want a wider or narrower binding, adjust the width of the strips you cut. (See page 216 for pointers on how to experiment with binding width.) Refer to "Making and Attaching the Binding" on page 215 to complete your quilt.

CUTTING

From the red print binding fabric:
• Cut eleven 2¾ × 44-inch strips for cross-grain binding

WHEN APPLYING double-fold binding to a quilt, slip stitch the binding to the back side of the quilt by hand. To do this, slip your needle into the quilt back, sliding the needle approximately ¼ inch. Bring it out of the fabric again and catch a few threads in the fold of the binding. At exactly the same point from which the needle emerged, insert it into the quilt back again, and take the next stitch. It's a good idea to take a double stitch approximately every 6 to 8 inches to anchor the binding.

Quilting DESIGNS

FOR HAND QUILTING:

🌀 Quilting in the ditch of each seam always helps to emphasize patchwork shapes in any quilt. Stitching in the ditch around the Tree blocks is a good choice for this quilt.

🌀 You may find a purchased quilting stencil with a simple chain design will be effective in the narrow vertical strips of fabric in Pine View.

🌀 Quilting in the ditch on each side of the narrow brown border strips will make them visually more prominent.

🌀 Cross-hatching always produces a nice quilted texture. It is a good choice for large borders or for prints in areas where you want to camouflage your quilting stitches. In the large unpieced borders of this quilt, quilt diagonal cross-hatching lines spaced at 3-inch intervals for an easy, allover pattern that is simple to quilt.

FOR MACHINE QUILTING:

🌀 Follow the same quilting suggestions as for hand quilting, replacing the chain design in the long, narrow vertical strips and the cross-hatching in the large unpieced borders with gentle meander quilting. Meander quilting is a continuous, free-motion type of stitching that requires no marking beforehand.

TEA TIME

This whimsical design brightens my dining room, accompanying an antique doll cupboard filled with a blue and white toy tea set I've had since I was five years old. I chose fabrics in colors and prints that remind me of the floral prints depicted in some of the teapots in my own collection. The appliqué designs on the teapots spill into the outer borders, almost as if the flowers were floating on the edge of the quilt. This creates the effect of a large printed fabric in the border areas. Black buttonhole stitching adds a strong edge to the appliqués and a three-dimensional feel to each of the shapes.

Size

Wall Quilt: 34 inches square (unquilted)

Finished Block: 8 inches square

Fabrics and Supplies

Yardage is based on 44-inch-wide fabric.

¾ yard beige print fabric for background

⅜ yard multicolor floral fabric for corner squares

⅜ yard deep rose print fabric for flower petal appliqués and inner border

1⅓ yards blue print fabric for teapot appliqué and outer border

¼ yard medium rose print fabric for flower petal appliqués

⅛ yard gold print for flower center appliqués

¼ yard green print fabric for leaf and stem appliqués

1 yard fusible web

2 skeins black embroidery floss

½ yard blue print fabric for binding

1⅛ yards backing fabric

Quilt batting, at least 38 inches square

Rotary cutter, mat, and see-through ruler with ⅛-inch markings

SIZE

Wall quilt: 66 inches square (unquilted)

Finished pieced block: 6 inches square

Finished alternate block: 12 inches square

FABRICS AND SUPPLIES

Yardage is based on 44-inch-wide fabric.

$\frac{1}{3}$ yard of fabric for House 1

$\frac{1}{4}$ yard of fabric for House 2

$\frac{1}{4}$ yard of fabric for House 3

$\frac{1}{8}$ yard of white fabric for church

Scraps of black print fabrics to total $\frac{1}{4}$ yard for windows, doors, and chimneys

Scraps of gray and brown fabrics to total $\frac{1}{4}$ yard for roofs

$\frac{3}{4}$ yard of beige fabric for House and Church block backgrounds and Nine Patch, or scraps of different light colored fabrics to total $\frac{3}{4}$ yard

$\frac{1}{4}$ yard of dark green fabric for trees

$\frac{1}{4}$ yard of light green fabric for tree background

$\frac{1}{8}$ yard of dark brown for tree trunks

$\frac{1}{4}$ yard of dark blue fabric for Nine Patch

$1\frac{1}{2}$ yards of beige print fabric for alternate blocks

2 yards *total* of a variety of browns, rusts, golds, and blacks for bricks

4 yards of fabric for quilt back

$\frac{3}{4}$ yard of black print fabric for binding

Quilt batting, at least 70 × 70 inches

Rotary cutter, mat, and see-through ruler

Template plastic

Quilt Diagram

Thinking back to my childhood spent growing up in a small town, I was inspired to design Around Town with its unusual pieced lattice. From picturesque houses to the church steeple rising above the wide open spaces, this quilt reminds me of all of the relaxed comforts of life in a small town. To make the neighborhood in this wall quilt truly your own, why not add a few of your favorite scraps, or choose fabrics that capture the look of your hometown? As a finishing touch, stitch your name and date in a brick "cornerstone" in the border!

GETTING READY

- Read instructions thoroughly before you begin.
- Prewash and press fabric.
- Use ¼-inch seam allowances throughout unless directions specify otherwise.
- Seam allowances are included in the cutting sizes given.
- Press seam allowance in the direction that will create the least bulk and, whenever possible, toward the darker fabric.
- Trace **Templates A** through **Q** (pages 132–135) onto template plastic and cut out.
- Cutting directions for each section of the quilt are given in the areas following the row of scissors. If you like to cut as you go, simply follow the directions as you get to them. If you'd rather cut all your pieces at once, skip ahead and look for the scissors to do all the cutting before you begin to sew.
- Instructions are given for quick cutting and piecing the windows, chimneys, doors, and tree trunks. Note that for some of the pieces, the quick-cutting method will result in leftover fabric.

HOUSE 1 BLOCKS
(Make 7)

Cutting for House 1 Blocks

Use **Templates H, I, J,** and **K** and refer to **Diagram 1** on page 126 as you work for easier cutting.

From the beige block background fabric:
- Cut seven *each* of **Templates I** and **J**

From the gray and brown roof fabrics:
- Cut seven of **Template H**

From the black chimney fabrics:
- Cut seven of **Template K**
- Cut one 1½ × 24-inch strip

From House 1 fabric:
- Cut one 3½ × 44-inch strip. From this strip, cut fourteen 1½ × 3½-inch pieces and seven 2½ × 3½-inch pieces.
- Cut two 1½ × 24-inch strips

Piecing the House 1 Blocks

Step 1. To make the roof unit, refer to **Diagram 1** on page 126 and join piece J to piece K. Stitch this unit to piece H. Press seam toward H. Stitch piece I to H. Press. Repeat to make seven roof units.

Step 2. To make the window units, sew the 1½ × 24-inch black strip lengthwise between two 1½ × 24-inch strips of House 1 fabric.

Step 3. With the joined strip set face up on your cutting mat, crosscut fourteen 1½-inch-wide segments, referring to **Diagram 2** on page 126.

Step 4. To make the house base, sew a 2½ × 3½-inch rectangle of House 1 fabric between two window units, referring to **Diagram 1** on page 126. Add a 1½ × 3½-inch piece of the same house fabric to the outside of each window unit. Repeat to make seven house bases.

Step 5. Sew the roof units to the house bases to complete the blocks. Press.

FABRIC KEY

- HOUSE 1
- HOUSE 2
- HOUSE 3
- CHURCH
- BLACK
- ROOF FABRICS
- BEIGE
- DARK GREEN
- LIGHT GREEN
- DARK BROWN
- DARK BLUE
- BEIGE PRINT
- BRICK FABRICS (BORDERS)

HINTS & HELPS

Accuracy is a must for this pattern. Measure seam allowances every now and then to make sure they are accurate and consistent. Make adjustments as necessary to save time—and headaches—when it comes time to fit your lattice strips to your blocks.

House 1

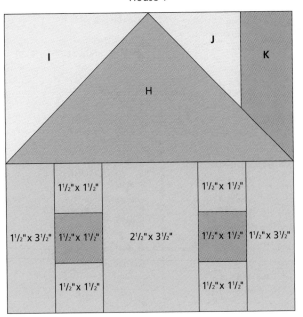

1½"x 1½"

1½"x 3½" 1½"x 1½" 2½"x 3½" 1½"x 1½" 1½"x 3½"

1½"x 1½"

Dimensions are cut sizes, not finished sizes

Make 7
Diagram 1

Cutting lines

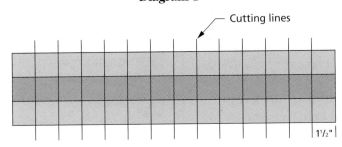

1½"

Window Units
Diagram 2

House 2

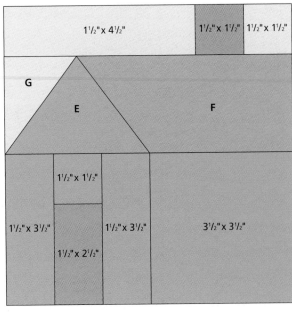

1½"x 4½" 1½"x 1½" 1½"x 1½"

G

E F

1½"x 1½"

1½"x 3½" 1½"x 3½" 3½"x 3½"

1½"x 2½"

Dimensions are cut sizes, not finished sizes

Make 5
Diagram 3

HOUSE 2 BLOCKS
(Make 5)

Cutting for House 2 Blocks

Use **Templates E, F,** and **G** and refer to **Diagram 3** for easier cutting.

From the beige block background fabric:
• Cut five of **Template G**
• Cut one 1½ × 8-inch strip
• Cut one 4½ × 8-inch strip

From the gray and brown roof fabrics:
• Cut five of **Template F**

From the black chimney fabric:
• Cut one 1½ × 8-inch strip
• Cut one 2½ × 8-inch strip

From the House 2 fabric:
• Cut one 3½ × 44-inch strip. From this strip, cut ten 1½ × 3½-inch pieces and five 3½-inch squares
• Cut one 1½ × 8-inch strip
• Cut five of **Template E**

Piecing the House 2 Blocks

Step 1. To make the roof unit, join pieces G and F to piece E, as shown in **Diagram 3.** Set this aside until the entire block is ready to be pieced.

Step 2. To make the chimney units, sew a 1½ × 8-inch black strip between a 1½ × 8-inch beige strip and a 4½ × 8-inch beige strip. With the strip set face up on your cutting mat, crosscut five 1½-inch-wide sections from this strip set, as shown in **Diagram 4.**

Step 3. For the door units, sew a 1½ × 8-inch strip of House 2 fabric to a 2½ × 8-inch black strip, as shown in **Diagram 5.** Crosscut five 1½-inch wide segments from this strip set.

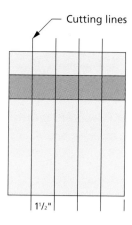

Chimney Units
Diagram 4

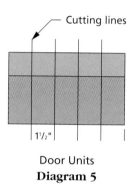

Door Units
Diagram 5

Step 4. Referring to **Diagram 3**, sew a door unit between two 1½ × 3½-inch House 2 fabric pieces for the house base. Add a 3½-inch square of house fabric to the right side of this unit. Make five House 2 base units.

Step 5. Stitch the roof sections to the tops of the house base units. Then sew the chimney units to the tops of the roof units to complete the blocks. Press.

HOUSE 3 BLOCKS
(Make 4)

Cutting for House 3 Blocks

Use **Templates L, M, N,** and **N Reverse** and refer to **Diagram 6** for easier cutting.

From the beige block background fabric:
• Cut four *each* of **Templates N** and **N Reverse**

From the gray and brown roof fabrics:
• Cut four of **Template M**

From the House 3 fabric:
• Cut one 3½ × 24-inch strip. From this strip, cut eight 1½ × 3½-inch pieces and four 2½ × 3½-inch pieces.
• Cut four of **Template L**
• Cut one 1½ × 24-inch strip. From this strip, cut three 8 × 1½-inch pieces.

From a black chimney fabrics:
• Cut one 1½ × 8-inch strip
• Cut one 2½ × 8-inch strip

Piecing the House 3 Blocks

Step 1. To make the roof units, refer to **Diagram 6** and join piece N to L and piece N Reverse to M. Then join piece L to M. Repeat to make four roof units.

Step 2. To make the door units, refer to Step 3 under "House 2 Blocks." You will need to crosscut only four of these units, however. See **Diagram 5**.

Step 3. For the window units, sew a 1½ × 8-inch black strip between two 1½ × 8-inch House 3 fabric strips. Crosscut four 1½-inch-wide segments from this strip set.

Step 4. To make the house base, sew a 1½ × 3½-inch House 3 fabric piece to the left side of the door unit. Sew a 2½ × 3½-inch house fabric piece to the left side of the window unit. Add a 1½ × 3½-inch house unit to the right side of the window unit. Join the two sections together, with the door section on the left and the window section on the right, as shown in **Diagram 6**. Repeat to make four House 3 bases.

Step 5. Sew the roof units to the house bases to complete the blocks. Press.

House 3

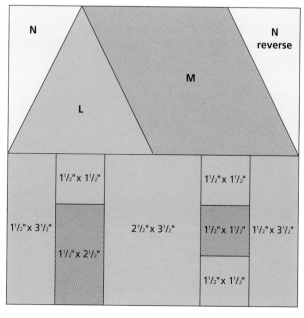

Dimensions are cut sizes, not finished sizes

Make 4
Diagram 6

CHURCH BLOCK
(Make 1)

The church is basically the same as House 3 (**Diagram 6**) with the steeple added to the top. Use **Templates L, M, N, N Reverse, O, P,** and **Q.** Refer to **Diagram 7** as you work for easier cutting.

Cutting for Church Block

From the beige block background fabric:
• Cut one *each* of **Template N, N Reverse, P,** and **Q**
• Cut one $1\frac{1}{2} \times 6\frac{1}{2}$-inch strip
• Cut one 2-inch square
• Cut one $2 \times 3\frac{1}{2}$-inch rectangle

From the white fabric:
• Cut one $1\frac{1}{2} \times 13$-inch strip. From this strip, cut two $1\frac{1}{2} \times 3\frac{1}{2}$-inch pieces and three $1\frac{1}{2}$-inch squares.
• Cut one $2\frac{1}{2} \times 3\frac{1}{2}$-inch rectangle
• Cut one *each* of **Templates L** and **O**

From the gray and brown roof fabrics:
• Cut one of **Template M**
• Cut one 2-inch square

From the black chimney fabrics:
• Cut one $1\frac{1}{2} \times 2\frac{1}{2}$-inch rectangle
• Cut one $1\frac{1}{2}$-inch square

Piecing the Church Block

Step 1. To make the roof unit, refer to **Diagram 6** on page 127 and join piece N to L, and piece N Reverse to M. Then attach piece L to piece M.

Step 2. To make the church door unit, sew a $1\frac{1}{2}$-inch white square to the top of a $1\frac{1}{2} \times 2\frac{1}{2}$-inch black rectangle. See **Diagram 6** on page 127.

Step 3. For the window unit, sew a $1\frac{1}{2}$-inch black square between two $1\frac{1}{2}$-inch white squares.

Step 4. To make the church base, refer to **Diagram 6.** Sew a $1\frac{1}{2} \times 3\frac{1}{2}$-inch white piece to the left side of the door unit. Sew a $2\frac{1}{2} \times 3\frac{1}{2}$-inch white rectangle to the left side of the window unit. Add a $1\frac{1}{2} \times 3\frac{1}{2}$-inch white rectangle to the right side of the window. Join the two sections together with the door unit on the left and the window unit on the right. Sew the church base to the bottom of the roof unit.

Step 5. To make the steeple unit, refer to **Diagram 7** and join piece P to the left side of piece O, then add piece Q to the right side of piece O.

Step 6. Add a $1\frac{1}{2} \times 6\frac{1}{2}$-inch beige strip to the top of the steeple unit. Sew a 2-inch beige square to the left of a 2-inch roof square. Add a $2 \times 3\frac{1}{2}$-inch background piece to the right of the roof square. Sew this strip to the bottom of the steeple unit. Join the steeple unit to the top of the church roof. Press.

TREE BLOCKS
(Make 6)

Cutting for Tree Blocks

Use **Templates A, B, B Reverse, C, D,** and **D Reverse** and refer to **Diagram 8** for easier cutting.

From the dark green tree fabric:
• Cut six *each* of **Templates A** and **C**

From the light green background fabric:
• Cut six *each* of **Templates B, B Reverse, D,** and **D Reverse**
• Cut two 3×15-inch strips

From the dark brown trunk fabric:
• Cut one $1\frac{1}{2} \times 15$-inch strip

Piecing the Tree Blocks

Step 1. Sew pieces B and B Reverse to piece A. Stitch pieces D and D Reverse to piece C. Repeat to make six of each unit. Press seams toward the tree fabric. Sew the A/B units to the tops of the C/D units.

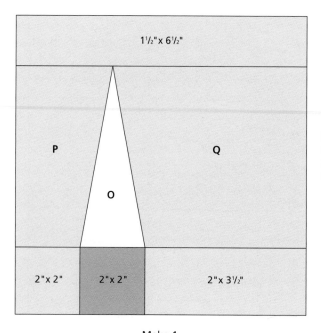

Dimensions are cut sizes, not finished sizes

Make 1
Diagram 7

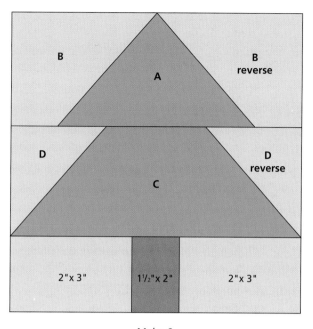

Dimensions are cut sizes, not finished sizes

Make 6
Diagram 8

Step 2. To make the trunk unit, sew the 1½ × 15-inch dark brown trunk strip lengthwise between two 3 × 15-inch background strips. Crosscut six 2-inch-wide sections from this strip set, as shown in **Diagram 9.**

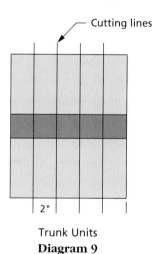

Cutting lines

Trunk Units
Diagram 9

Step 3. Sew a trunk unit to the bottom of each tree to complete the blocks. Press.

NINE PATCH BLOCKS
(Make 4)

The Nine Patch block is made from two different strip sets. The fabrics are first cut into strips. These strips are then sewn together and cut into segments for the block.

Cutting for Nine Patch Blocks

From the dark blue fabric:
• Cut two 2½ × 24-inch strips
• Cut one 2½ × 13-inch strip

From the beige background fabric:
• Cut one 2½ × 24-inch strip
• Cut two 2½ × 13-inch strips

Piecing the Nine Patch Blocks

Step 1. Make Strip Set 1. Sew a 2½ × 24-inch dark blue strip to the top and bottom of a 2½ × 24-inch beige strip. Crosscut this strip set into eight 2½-inch segments. See **Diagram 10.**

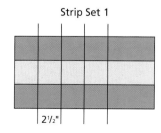

Strip Set 1

Diagram 10

Step 2. Make Strip Set 2. Sew a 2½ × 13-inch beige strip to the top and bottom of a 2½ × 13-inch dark blue strip. Crosscut this strip set into four 2½-inch segments, as shown in **Diagram 11.**

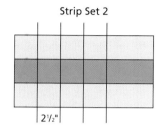

Strip Set 2

Diagram 11

Step 3. Sew the units together matching block intersections, as shown in **Diagram 12** to make four Nine Patch blocks.

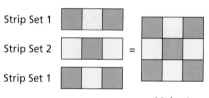

Strip Set 1
Strip Set 2
Strip Set 1

Make 4
Diagram 12

QUILT CENTER

Use **Diagram 13** on page 130 as a reference to construct the quilt center. You will be sewing the blocks together into sections to make three vertical rows.

Cutting for Alternate Blocks

From the beige print fabric:
• Cut three 12½ × 44-inch strips. From these strips, cut nine 12½-inch squares.

Row 1

Step 1. Sew a House 1 block to the right side of a Tree block. Sew this unit to the bottom of a 12½-inch alternate block.

The directions here tell you how to assemble the quilt shown in the photo on page 123. But don't be afraid to experiment. Depending on your fabrics, you may want to change some of the locations of your houses and trees. (It's more fun to move a pine tree here than it is in your yard!) Before you stitch your blocks together, lay them out and play with their locations. Stand back and check for good color placement and overall eye appeal. Keep track of your layout as you sew blocks together.

Step 2. Sew a House 1 block to the top of a House 2 block. Sew a Nine Patch block to the bottom of this unit. Sew this three-block unit to the right side of the alternate block unit made in Step 1.

Step 3. Sew a Tree block to the right side of a House 1 block. Sew this unit to the bottom of a 12½-inch alternate block.

Step 4. Sew a House 2 block to the top of a House 3 block. Sew a Nine Patch block to the bottom of this unit. Sew this three-block unit to the right side of the alternate block unit made in Step 3.

Step 5. Sew a House 3 block to the top of a Tree block. Sew this unit to the right side of an alternate block.

Step 6. Sew the three sections together, as shown in **Diagram 13,** to complete Row 1.

Row 2

Step 1. Sew a House 1 block to the right side of a Tree block. Sew this unit to the bottom of a 12½-inch alternate block.

Step 2. Sew a House 3 block to the right side of a House 2 block. Sew this unit to the bottom of a 12½-inch alternate block.

Step 3. Sew the two sections together with a 12½-inch alternate block, as shown in **Diagram 13,** to complete Row 2.

Row 3

Step 1. Sew a House 2 block to the right side of a House 3 block. Sew this unit to the bottom of a 12½-inch alternate block.

Step 2. Sew a House 1 block to the top of a House 2 block. Sew a Nine Patch block to the bottom of this unit. Sew this three-block unit to the left side of the alternate block unit made in Step 1.

Step 3. Sew a Tree block to the right side of a House 1 block. Sew this unit to the bottom of a 12½-inch alternate block.

Step 4. Sew the Church block to the top of a Nine Patch block. Sew this unit to the left side of the alternate block unit made in Step 3.

Step 5. Sew a Tree block to the top of a House 1 block. Sew this unit to the left side of a 12½-inch alternate block.

Step 6. Sew the three sections together, as shown in **Diagram 13,** to complete Row 3.

Sewing the Rows Together

Sew the three rows together, as shown in **Diagram 13,** to complete the quilt center.

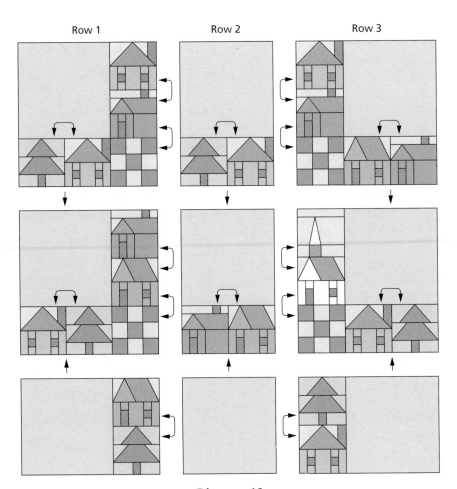

Diagram 13

BRICK BORDERS

Cutting for Bricks

From the brick fabrics:
• Cut nineteen $3\frac{1}{2} \times 44$-inch strips. From these strips, cut one hundred fourteen $3\frac{1}{2} \times 6\frac{1}{2}$-inch pieces.

Assembling the Brick Borders

Step 1. Stitch eight $3\frac{1}{2} \times 6\frac{1}{2}$-inch bricks together along the short ends. Make two of these brick strips. Sew one strip to the top of the quilt and one to the bottom. See **Diagram 14.**

Step 2. Sew nine bricks together end to end. Make two of these units. Sew one brick strip to each side of the quilt, as shown in **Diagram 14.**

Step 3. For the middle brick border, make two brick strip sets with 9 bricks and two sets with 10 bricks.

Sew the 9-brick strips to the top and bottom of the quilt. Sew the 10-brick strips to the sides of the quilt.

Step 4. To make the outer brick border, repeat Step 3, adding one extra brick to each strip, so top and bottom borders have 10 bricks and side borders have 11 bricks.

QUILTING

Step 1. Prepare the backing for the quilt by cutting the 4-yard length of backing fabric in half to make two 2-yard lengths. Remove the selvages.

Step 2. Sew the two lengths together with one center seam. Press seam open. Trim the backing and batting so they are 4 inches larger than the quilt top dimensions.

Step 3. Mark the quilt top for quilting.

Step 4. Layer the backing, batting, and quilt top, baste, and quilt.

BINDING

The 3-inch strips will produce a $\frac{1}{2}$-inch-wide binding. If you want a wider or narrower binding, adjust the width of the strips you cut. (See page 247 for pointers on how to experiment with binding width.) See "Making and Attaching the Binding" on page 245 to complete your quilt.

Cutting for Cross-Grain Binding

From the black print fabric:
• Cut seven 3×44-inch strips

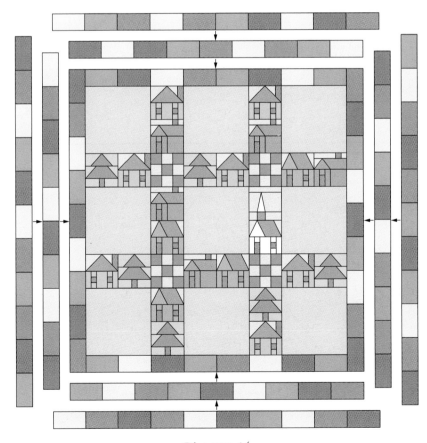

Diagram 14

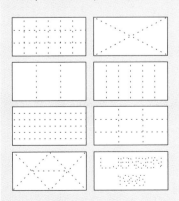

QUILTING IDEAS

☑ Use cross-hatching or a large floral design in the large alternate blocks.

☑ Quilt the smaller pieced blocks in the ditch so the houses and tree shapes puff out a bit.

☑ Use a variety of different designs to add interest to the bricks. I used vertical lines, horizontal lines, Xs, stars, and more, as shown.

☑ Quilt your name and the date into one of the bricks.

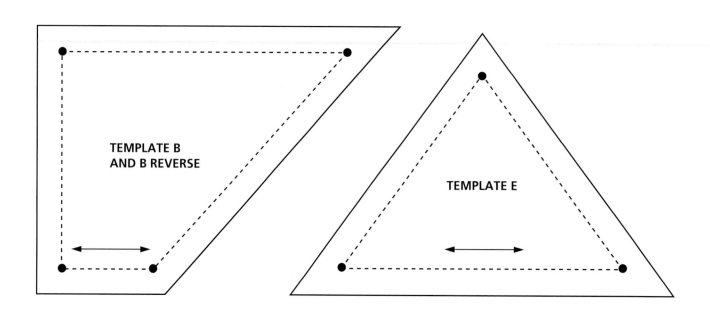

**TEMPLATE D
AND
D REVERSE**

Cut 6 of each

**TEMPLATE
A**

TEMPLATE C

**TEMPLATE B
AND B REVERSE**

TEMPLATE E

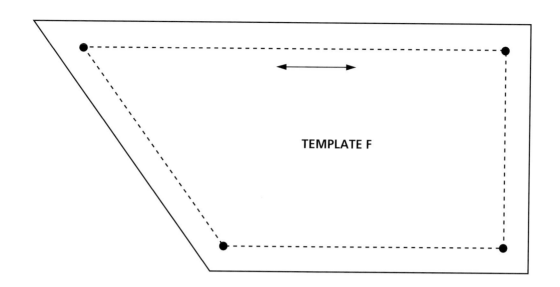

TEMPLATE F

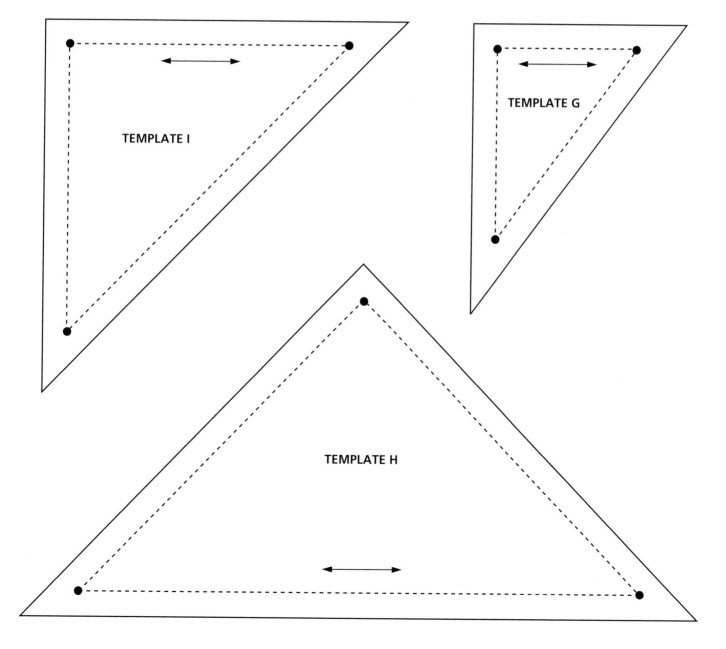

TEMPLATE I

TEMPLATE G

TEMPLATE H

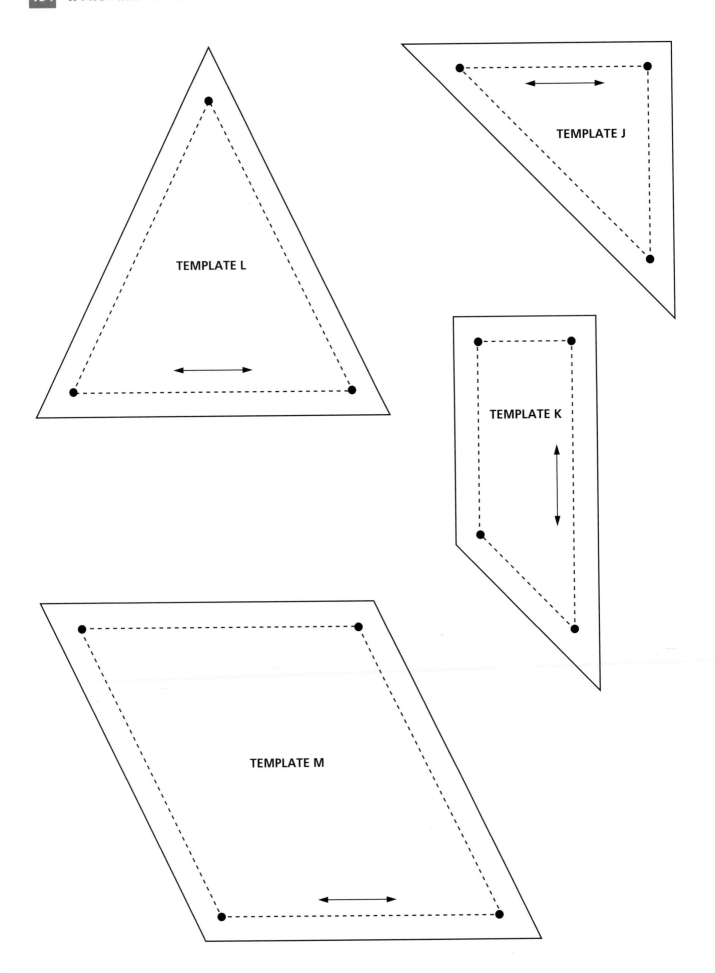

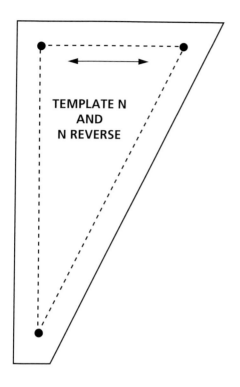

TEMPLATE N
AND
N REVERSE

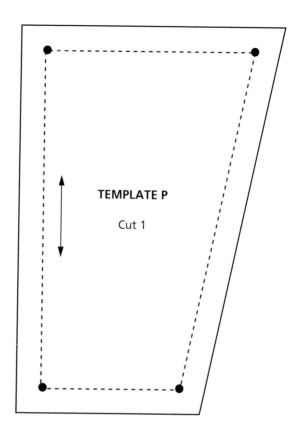

TEMPLATE P

Cut 1

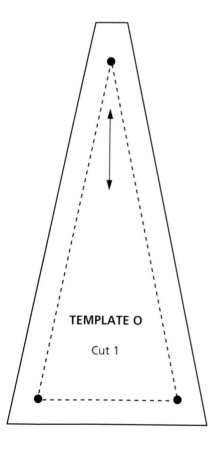

TEMPLATE O

Cut 1

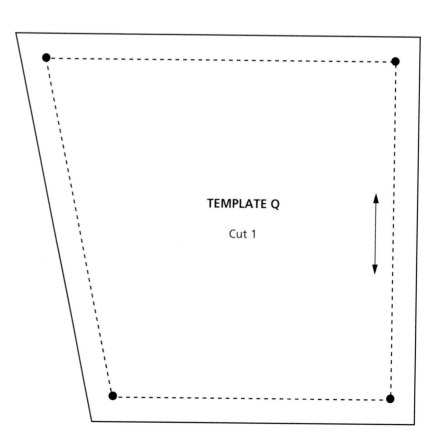

TEMPLATE Q

Cut 1

TWILIGHT VILLAGE

Tree, House, and Star Table Runner Diagram

Iuse these table accessories in fun combinations with my dishes and linens. Sometimes I use them on their own on my antique pine farm table, but often I place them on top of a plaid or country check tablecloth. I use plain creamy beige plates and an assortment of blue, antique, salt-glazed pottery for serving pieces. The easy-to-piece Milky Way Star block twinkles in the center of the runners and place mats. For a coordinated look, put the large runner in the center of your table surrounded by a set of place mats and arrange the tree and star runner on a sideboard.

TWILIGHT VILLAGE TREE, HOUSE, AND STAR TABLE RUNNER

SIZE

Finished table runner: 26 × 38 inches (unquilted)

Finished Tree and House block: 6 inches square

Finished Star block: 3 inches square

FABRICS AND SUPPLIES

Yardage is based on 44-inch-wide fabric.

¼ yard *each* of six coordinating colors, in prints and plaids, for houses and roofs

⅛ yard of gold solid fabric for house windows

⅛ yard of black print fabric for chimneys and doors

¼ yard of gold print fabric for stars

⅓ yard of green fabric for trees (or a variety of green fabrics)

⅛ yard of brown fabric for trunks (or a variety of brown fabrics)

¾ yard of beige print fabric for background

½ yard of dark print fabric for border

⅓ yard of contrasting fabric for binding

1 yard of fabric for the runner backing

Quilt batting, at least 30 × 42 inches

Rotary cutter, mat, and see-through ruler

Template plastic

FABRIC KEY

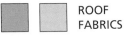

HOUSE FABRICS

ROOF FABRICS

GOLD SOLID

GOLD PRINT

BLACK PRINT

GREEN PRINT

BROWN PRINT

BEIGE PRINT

DARK PRINT

- Read instructions thoroughly before you begin.
- Prewash and press fabrics.
- Use ¼-inch seam allowances throughout unless directions specify otherwise.
- Seam allowances are included in the cutting sizes given.
- Press seam allowance in the direction that will create the least bulk and, whenever possible, toward the darker fabric.
- Trace **Templates A** through **N** (pages 132–135 in "Around Town") onto template plastic and cut out.
- Cutting directions for each section of the quilt are given in the areas following the line of scissors. If you like to cut as you go, simply follow the directions as you get to them. If you'd rather cut all your pieces at once, skip ahead and look for the scissors to do all the cutting before you begin to sew.
- Instructions are given for quick cutting and piecing the windows, chimneys, doors, and tree trunks. Note that for some of the pieces, the quick-cutting method will result in leftover fabric.

TREE BLOCKS
(Make 6)

Cutting for Tree Blocks

Use **Templates A, B, B Reverse, C, D,** and **D Reverse** and refer to **Diagram 1** for easier cutting.

From the green fabric(s):
- Cut six *each* of **Templates A** and **C**

From the beige print fabric:
- Cut six *each* of **Templates B, B Reverse, D,** and **D Reverse**
- Cut two 3 × 15-inch strips

From the brown fabric(s):
- Cut one 1½ × 15-inch strip

Tree Block

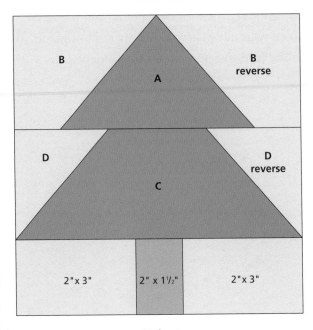

Dimensions are cut sizes, not finished sizes

Make 6
Diagram 1

Piecing the Tree Blocks

Step 1. Referring to **Diagram 1**, sew pieces B and B Reverse to an A piece and pieces D and D Reverse to a C piece. Press seams toward the tree fabric. Sew the A/B units to the top of the C/D units. Repeat to make six tree units.

Step 2. To make the trunk unit, sew a beige strip lengthwise to each side of the brown trunk strip. Press. With the fabric strip set right side up on your cutting mat, crosscut six 2-inch-wide segments, as shown in **Diagram 2**.

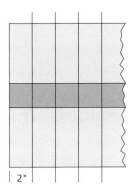

| 2" |

Diagram 2

Step 3. Sew a trunk unit to the bottom of a tree unit. Repeat to make six Tree blocks.

HINTS & HELPS

Accuracy is a must for this pattern. Be careful not to stretch fabrics when sewing bias seams for trees and rooftops. Measure seam allowances often to make sure they are accurate and consistent.

HOUSE 1 BLOCKS
(Make 2)

Cutting for House 1 Blocks

Use **Templates H, I, J,** and **K** and refer **Diagram 3** as you work for easier cutting.

From the roof fabrics:
• Cut two of **Template H**

From the black print fabric:
• Cut two of **Template K**

From the beige print fabric:
• Cut two *each* of **Templates I** and **J**

From the gold solid fabric:
• Cut one $1\frac{1}{2} \times 7$-inch strip

From the house fabric:
• Cut one $1\frac{1}{2} \times 30$-inch strip. From this strip, cut two $1\frac{1}{2} \times 7$-inch pieces and four $1\frac{1}{2} \times 3\frac{1}{2}$-inch pieces.
• Cut two $2\frac{1}{2} \times 3\frac{1}{2}$-inch rectangles

Piecing the House 1 Blocks

Step 1. Referring to **Diagram 3**, join piece J to piece K. Sew this unit to piece H. Join piece I to piece H. Repeat to make two roof units.

Step 2. To make the window unit, sew the 7-inch gold solid strip lengthwise between the 7-inch house fabric strips. Press. Crosscut four $1\frac{1}{2}$-inch-wide segments from this strip set to make the window units, as shown in **Diagram 4**.

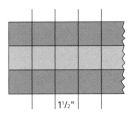

| $1\frac{1}{2}$" |

Diagram 4

Step 3. To make the house base, refer to **Diagram 3** and sew a window unit to either side of a $2\frac{1}{2} \times 3\frac{1}{2}$-inch rectangle of house fabric.

House 1

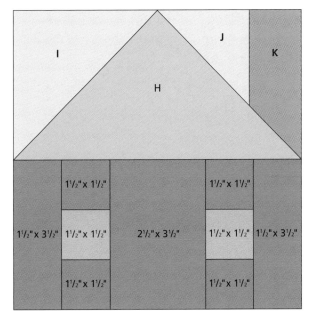

Dimensions are cut sizes, not finished sizes

Make 2
Diagram 3

Add a $1\frac{1}{2} \times 3\frac{1}{2}$-inch piece of house fabric to the outside of each window unit.

Step 4. Sew a roof unit to the top of a house base. Repeat to make two House 1 blocks.

HOUSE 2 BLOCKS
(Make 2)

Cutting for House 2 Blocks

Use **Templates E, F,** and **G** and refer to **Diagram 5** as you work for easier cutting.

From the house fabrics:
• Cut two of **Template E**
• Cut one $1\frac{1}{2} \times 20$-inch strip. From this strip cut one $1\frac{1}{2} \times 4$-inch piece and four $1\frac{1}{2} \times 3\frac{1}{2}$-inch pieces.
• Cut two $3\frac{1}{2}$-inch squares

From the black print fabric:
• Cut one $1\frac{1}{2} \times 4$-inch piece
• Cut one $2\frac{1}{2} \times 4$-inch piece

From the beige print fabric:
• Cut two of **Template G**
• Cut one $1\frac{1}{2} \times 4$-inch piece
• Cut one $4 \times 4\frac{1}{2}$-inch piece

From the roof fabrics:
• Cut two of **Template F**

Piecing the House 2 Blocks

Step 1. To make the roof unit, refer to **Diagram 5** and stitch piece G to the left of piece E. Join piece F to the right of piece E. Repeat to make two roof units.

Step 2. To make the chimney unit, sew the $4 \times 4\frac{1}{2}$-inch beige piece to one side of the $1\frac{1}{2} \times 4$-inch black piece. Sew the $1\frac{1}{2} \times 4$-inch beige strip on the other side, as shown in **Diagram 6.** Crosscut two $1\frac{1}{2}$-inch-wide segments from this strip set. Sew these units to the roof units, with the chimney toward the right side.

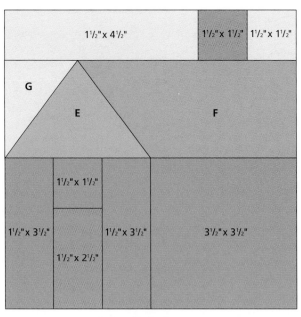

House 2

$1\frac{1}{2}" \times 4\frac{1}{2}"$ $1\frac{1}{2}" \times 1\frac{1}{2}"$ $1\frac{1}{2}" \times 1\frac{1}{2}"$

G

E

F

$1\frac{1}{2}" \times 1\frac{1}{2}"$

$1\frac{1}{2}" \times 3\frac{1}{2}"$ $1\frac{1}{2}" \times 3\frac{1}{2}"$ $3\frac{1}{2}" \times 3\frac{1}{2}"$

$1\frac{1}{2}" \times 2\frac{1}{2}"$

Dimensions are cut sizes, not finished sizes

Make 2
Diagram 5

Step 3. To make the door unit, sew the $1\frac{1}{2} \times 4$-inch strip of house fabric to the $2\frac{1}{2} \times 4$-inch black strip. Crosscut two $1\frac{1}{2}$-inch-wide segments from this strip set, as shown in **Diagram 7.**

Step 4. To make the house base, sew a door unit between two $1\frac{1}{2} \times 3\frac{1}{2}$-inch house fabric pieces. Add a $3\frac{1}{2}$-inch square of house fabric to the right side of this unit.

Step 5. Sew a roof unit to the top of this house base. Repeat to make two House 2 blocks.

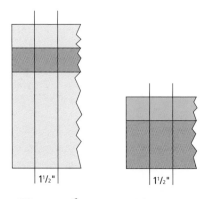

$1\frac{1}{2}"$ $1\frac{1}{2}"$

Diagram 6   **Diagram 7**

HOUSE 3 BLOCKS
(Make 2)

Cutting for House 3 Block

Use **Templates L, M,** and **N** and refer to **Diagram 8** as you work for easier cutting.

From the beige print fabric:
• Cut two *each* of **Templates N** and **N Reverse**

From the roof fabrics:
• Cut two of **Template M**

From the house fabrics:
• Cut two of **Template L**
• Cut one $1\frac{1}{2} \times 44$-inch strip. From this strip cut eight $1\frac{1}{2} \times 3\frac{1}{2}$-inch pieces and three $1\frac{1}{2} \times 4$-inch pieces.

From the gold solid fabric:
• Cut one $1\frac{1}{2} \times 4$-inch piece

From the black print fabric:
• Cut one $2\frac{1}{2} \times 4$-inch piece

House 3

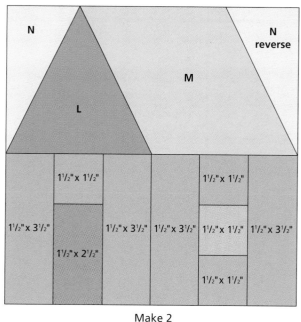

Dimensions are cut sizes, not finished sizes

Make 2
Diagram 8

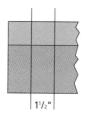

Diagram 9   **Diagram 10**

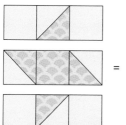

Make 6
Diagram 11

Piecing the House 3 Blocks

Step 1. To make the roof unit, join piece N to piece L, and piece N Reverse to piece M. Then join piece L to piece M, referring to **Diagram 8.** Repeat to make two roof units.

Step 2. To make the window unit, sew the $1\frac{1}{2} \times 4$-inch gold solid piece between two $1\frac{1}{2} \times 4$-inch house fabric pieces along the 4-inch sides. Crosscut two $1\frac{1}{2}$-inch-wide segments from this strip set, as shown in **Diagram 9.**

Step 3. To make the door unit, sew a $1\frac{1}{2} \times 4$-inch house fabric strip to a $2\frac{1}{2} \times 4$-inch black strip. Crosscut two $1\frac{1}{2}$-inch-wide segments from this strip set, as shown in **Diagram 10.**

Step 4. To make the house base, sew a door unit between two $1\frac{1}{2} \times 3\frac{1}{2}$-inch house fabric pieces. Sew a window unit between two $1\frac{1}{2} \times 3\frac{1}{2}$-inch house fabric pieces. Join these sections together with the door on the left and the window on the right.

Step 5. Sew a roof unit to the top of a house base. Repeat to make two House 3 blocks.

STAR BLOCKS
(Make 6)

Cutting for Star Blocks and Alternate Blocks

From the gold print fabric:
• Cut one $1\frac{1}{2} \times 10$-inch strip. From this strip cut six $1\frac{1}{2}$-inch squares.
• Cut one $1\frac{7}{8} \times 24$-inch strip

From the beige print fabric:
• Cut one $1\frac{1}{2} \times 38$-inch strip. From this strip cut twenty-four $1\frac{1}{2}$-inch squares.
• Cut one $1\frac{7}{8} \times 24$-inch strip
• Cut six $3\frac{1}{2}$-inch squares for alternate blocks

Piecing the Star Blocks

Step 1. With right sides together, layer the $1\frac{7}{8} \times 24$-inch gold print and beige strips. Press together. Cut into twelve $1\frac{7}{8}$-inch squares. Cut the squares in half diagonally and stitch $\frac{1}{4}$ inch from the diagonal edge. Press seam allowances toward the gold print fabric. Make twenty-four $1\frac{1}{2}$-inch triangle-pieced squares.

Step 2. Sew a beige square to either side of a triangle-pieced square, as shown in **Diagram 11.** Sew a triangle-pieced square to either side of a gold print square, as shown. Sew a beige square to either side of a triangle-pieced square. Sew the rows together to make a Star block. Repeat to make six Star blocks.

TABLE RUNNER CENTER

Step 1. Sew the Star blocks and $3\frac{1}{2}$-inch beige squares together to form two rows for the center of the table runner. Each row is made of six blocks. The first row starts with an alternate block and ends with a Star block. The second row starts with a Star block and ends with an alternate block. See **Diagram 12** on page 142. Sew the two rows together.

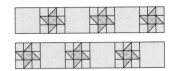

Diagram 12

Step 2. Make two rows of houses by sewing a House 1, House 2, and House 3 side to side, following the **Tree, House, and Star Table Runner Diagram** on page 137 for placement. Attach these rows to the runner's star center, making sure the rooftops point toward the stars.

Step 3. Make two rows of Tree blocks, sewing three trees together to make a row. Attach the tree rows to the ends of the star/house center, with the treetops pointing toward the stars.

BORDER

Cutting for Border

From the dark print fabric:
• Cut three 4½ × 44-inch strips

Attaching the Border

Step 1. Measure the width of the runner (the narrower way) through the middle from side to side to determine the length of the end borders. Cut two strips to the necessary length. Sew the strips to the ends of the runner.

Step 2. Measure the runner from left to right through the middle, including the borders you just added, to determine the length of the side borders. Cut two strips to the necessary length. Sew the strips to the sides of the runner.

QUILTING IDEAS

■ The projects in the photograph were machine quilted with an allover meandering design. See "Meander and Stipple Quilting" on page 246 for tips on how to do this.

■ Quilting in the ditch around the stars, houses, and trees will make them puff out a little.

■ A simple chain could be hand quilted in the borders of any of these projects.

QUILTING

Step 1. Cut the backing and batting so they are about 4 inches larger than the pieced top dimensions.

Step 2. Mark the pieced top for quilting.

Step 3. Layer the backing, batting, and pieced top. Baste the layers together and quilt by hand or machine.

BINDING

The 2½-inch binding strip will produce a ⅜-inch-wide binding. If you want a wider or narrower binding, adjust the width of the strips you cut. (See page 247 for pointers on how to experiment with binding width.) Refer to "Making and Attaching Binding" on page 245 to complete the table runner.

Cutting for Cross-Grain Binding

From the binding fabric:
• Cut four 2½ × 44-inch strips

TWILIGHT VILLAGE TREE AND STAR TABLE RUNNER

SIZE

Table runner: 24 × 33½ inches (unquilted)

Finished Tree block: 6 inches square

Finished Star block: 3 inches square

FABRICS AND SUPPLIES

Yardage is based on 44-inch-wide fabric.

⅓ yard of green print fabric for trees (or a variety of greens)

⅛ yard of brown fabric for trunks (or a variety of browns)

⅓ yard of gold print fabric for stars

½ yard of beige print fabric for background

½ yard of dark print fabric for border

⅓ yard of contrasting fabric for binding

¾ yard of fabric for runner back

Quilt batting, at least 30 × 37 inches

Rotary cutter, mat, and see-through ruler

Template plastic

TREE BLOCKS
(Make 6)

Be sure to read "Getting Ready" for the Tree, House, and Star Table Runner on page 138 before you begin. For this table runner, you will need to use **Templates A, B, C,** and **D** on page 132 in "Around Town." Follow the cutting and piecing instructions under "Tree Blocks" for the Tree, House, and Star Table Runner. Make six Tree blocks.

Tree and Star Table Runner Diagram

FABRIC KEY

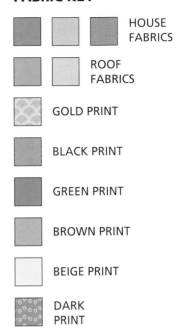

HOUSE FABRICS

ROOF FABRICS

GOLD PRINT

BLACK PRINT

GREEN PRINT

BROWN PRINT

BEIGE PRINT

DARK PRINT

STAR BLOCKS
(Make 15)

Cutting for Star Blocks

From the gold print fabric:
• Cut one $1\frac{1}{2} \times 24$-inch strip. From this strip cut fifteen $1\frac{1}{2}$-inch squares.
• Cut two $1\frac{7}{8} \times 44$-inch strips

From the beige print fabric:
• Cut three $1\frac{1}{2} \times 44$-inch strips. From these strips, cut sixty $1\frac{1}{2}$-inch squares.
• Cut two $1\frac{7}{8} \times 44$-inch strips
• Cut fifteen $3\frac{1}{2}$-inch squares for alternate blocks

Piecing the Star Blocks

Step 1. With right sides together, layer the $1\frac{7}{8} \times 44$-inch gold and beige strips. Press together. Cut the strips into thirty $1\frac{7}{8}$-inch squares. Cut the squares in half diagonally and stitch $\frac{1}{4}$ inch from the diagonal edge. Press seams toward the gold to make 60 triangle-pieced squares.

Step 2. Following **Diagram 11** on page 141, sew a beige square to either side of a triangle-pieced square, as shown. Sew a triangle-

pieced square to either side of a gold square. Sew a beige square to either side of a triangle-pieced square. Sew the rows together to make a Star block. Repeat to make 15 Star blocks.

TABLE RUNNER CENTER

Step 1. Sew the Star blocks and $3\frac{1}{2}$-inch beige alternate blocks together to form six rows for the center of the table runner. Each row is made of five blocks. Refer to the **Tree and Star Table Runner Diagram** and **Diagram 13.**

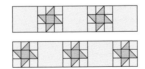

Diagram 13

Step 2. Referring to the **Tree and Star Table Runner Diagram,** sew the six rows together, alternating the rows so the stars are staggered.

Step 3. Make two rows of Tree blocks, with three trees per row. Attach these rows to the ends of the star center, making sure the treetops point toward the stars.

BORDER

Cutting for Border

From the dark print fabric:
• Cut three $3\frac{1}{2} \times 44$-inch strips

Attaching the Border

Step 1. Measure the runner from left to right (the narrower way) through the middle to determine the length of the end borders. Cut two strips to the necessary length and sew them to the ends of the runner.

Step 2. Measure the runner from left to right through the middle, including the borders you just added, to determine the length of the side borders. Cut two strips to the necessary length and sew them to the sides of the runner.

QUILTING

See "Quilting" for the Tree, House, and Star Table Runner on the opposite page.

BINDING

The 2½-inch strips will produce a ⅜-inch-wide binding. If you want a wider or narrower binding, adjust the width of the strips you cut. (See page 247 for pointers on how to experiment with binding width.) Refer to "Making and Attaching Binding" on page 245 to complete the table runner.

Cutting for Cross-Grain Binding

From the binding fabric:
• Cut four 2½ × 44-inch strips

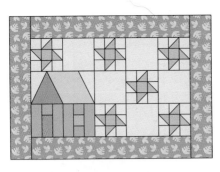

House Place Mat Diagram

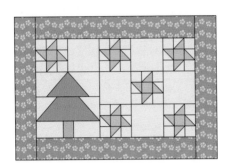

Tree Place Mat Diagram

FABRIC KEY

HOUSE FABRICS

ROOF FABRICS

GOLD PRINT

BLACK PRINT

GREEN PRINT

BROWN PRINT

BEIGE PRINT

DARK PRINTS

TWILIGHT VILLAGE HOUSE AND TREE PLACE MATS

SIZE

Place mat: 13 × 19 inches (unquilted)

Finished House and Tree blocks: 6 inches square

Finished Star block: 3 inches square

FABRICS AND SUPPLIES

(for two house place mats)

Yardage is based on 44-inch-wide fabric.

4 fat quarters (18 × 22-inch pieces) of coordinating prints, plaids, or solids for houses

Scraps of contrasting fabric for doors and windows (either very dark or much lighter than houses)

¼ yard of gold print fabric for stars

½ yard of beige print fabric for background

½ yard of dark print fabric for border

¼ yard of contrasting fabric for binding

½ yard of fabric for place mat backing

Quilt batting, at least 23 × 34 inches

Rotary cutter, mat, and see-through ruler

Template plastic

FABRICS AND SUPPLIES

(for two tree place mats)

Yardage is based on 44-inch-wide fabric.

⅛ yard of green print fabric for trees (or a variety of greens)

Scraps of brown fabric for trunks

¼ yard of gold print fabric for stars

½ yard of beige print fabric for background

½ yard of dark print fabric for border

⅓ yard of contrasting fabric for binding

½ yard of fabric for place mat backing

Quilt batting, at least 23 × 34 inches

Rotary cutter, mat, and see-through ruler

Template plastic

MAKING THE PLACE MATS

The directions that follow are for making four place mats, two each of a tree and house place mat. If you plan to set your whole table with place mats, using a mixture of all the house designs will add interest. Be sure to read "Getting Ready" for the Tree, House, and Star Table Runner on page 138 before you begin.

TREE BLOCKS

(Make 2)

Cutting for Tree Blocks

From the green fabric(s):
• Cut two *each* of **Templates A** and **C**

From the beige print fabric:
• Cut two *each* of **Templates B, B Reverse, D,** and **D Reverse**
• Cut two 3 × 5-inch strips

From the brown fabric:
• Cut one 1½ × 5-inch strip

Piecing the Tree Blocks

Follow Steps 1 through 3 under "Piecing the Tree Blocks" for the Tree, House, and Star Table Runner on page 139. Make two blocks and cross-cut the trunk strip set into two 2-inch pieces.

HOUSE BLOCKS

(Make 2)

Follow the cutting and piecing instructions under "House 1 Blocks," "House 2 Blocks," *or* "House 3 Blocks" for the Tree, House, and Star Table Runner, beginning on page 139.

STAR BLOCKS

(Make 6)

Follow the cutting and piecing instructions under "Star Blocks" for the Tree, House, and Star Table Runner on page 141. You will need only five alternate blocks.

PLACE MAT CENTERS

Step 1. Make three rows of Star blocks and alternate blocks, as shown in **Diagram 14.**

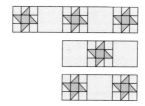

Diagram 14

Step 2. Referring to the **Tree Place Mat Diagram** and the **House Place Mat Diagram,** assemble the place mats. Sew the two shorter star rows together and attach either a House or Tree block to the left of this two-row unit.

Step 3. Sew the long row of Star and alternate blocks to the top of the unit from Step 2. Repeat to make all four place mats.

BORDERS

Cutting Borders for Two Place Mats

From the dark print fabric:
• Cut four 2½ × 44-inch strips

Attaching the Borders

Step 1. Measure the place mat from left to right through the middle to determine the length of the top and bottom borders. Cut two strips to the necessary length and sew to the top and bottom of the place mat.

Step 2. Measure the place mat from top to bottom through the middle, including the borders just added, to determine the length of the side borders. Cut two strips to the necessary length and sew to the sides of the place mat. Repeat Steps 1 and 2 for each place mat.

QUILTING

See for "Quilting" for the Tree, House, and Star Table Runner on page 142.

BINDING

The 2½-inch strips will produce a ⅜-inch-wide binding. If you want a wider or narrower binding, adjust the width of the strips you cut. (See page 247 for pointers on how to experiment with binding width.) Refer to "Making and Attaching the Binding" on page 245 to complete the place mats.

Cutting for Cross-Grain Binding

From the binding fabric:
• Cut four 2½ × 44-inch strips

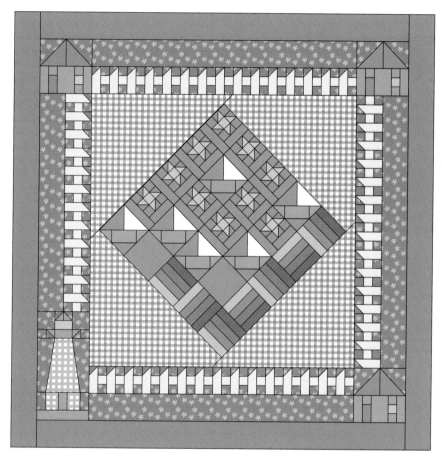

Quilt Diagram

Seashore bungalows, small bayside villages, salty mist in the air, sailboats drifting by . . . all of these things inspired me to design Harbor Town while on vacation. The striking contrast of the white picket fence against the background frames the center nicely, and the corner houses and lighthouse just hint that a village is near. If you enjoy the seashore as much as I do, this is a wonderful way to capture your vacation memories!

SIZE

Wall quilt: 48 inches square (unquilted)

Finished block size: 4 inches square

FABRICS AND SUPPLIES

Yardage is based on 44-inch-wide fabric.

¼ yard of white fabric for sails

¼ yard of gold print fabric for stars, lighthouse light, and windows

⅓ yard of red print fabric for boats and houses

¼ yard of red check fabric for lighthouse

¼ yard of brown #1 fabric for wharf and house roofs

¼ yard of brown #2 fabric for wharf, doors, and lighthouse details

⅛ yard of brown #3 fabric for wharf

⅛ yard of brown #4 fabric for wharf

½ yard of blue-green print fabric for water

⅝ yard of red plaid fabric for large corner triangles

⅝ yard of cream fabric for fence

1¼ yards of blue print fabric for border with fence

⅝ yard of green print fabric for outside border

1 yard of red/brown plaid fabric for binding

3 yards of fabric for quilt backing

Quilt batting, at least 52 inches square

Rotary cutter, mat, and see-through ruler

Template plastic

FABRIC KEY

WHITE

GOLD

RED PRINT

RED CHECK

BROWN #1

BROWN #2

BROWN #3

BROWN #4

BLUE-GREEN

RED PLAID

CREAM

BLUE PRINT

GREEN PRINT

GETTING READY

- Read instructions thoroughly before you begin.
- Prewash and press fabric.
- Use ¼-inch seam allowances throughout unless directions specify otherwise.
- Seam allowances are included in the cutting sizes given.
- Press seam allowance in the direction that will create the least bulk and, whenever possible, toward the darker fabric.
- Trace **Templates A** and **B** (page 153) onto template plastic and cut out.
- Cutting directions are given for each section of the quilt in the areas following the row of scissors. If you like to cut as you go, simply follow the directions as you get to them. If you'd rather cut all your pieces at once, skip ahead and look for the scissors to do all the cutting before you begin to sew.
- Instructions are given for quick cutting and piecing the blocks and borders. Note that for some of the pieces, the quick-cutting method will result in leftover fabric.

STAR BLOCKS
(Make 10)

Cutting for Star Blocks

From the gold fabric:
- Cut one 1⅞ × 44-inch strip
- Cut one 1½ × 44-inch strip. From this strip, cut thirteen 1½-inch squares. Ten of these squares will be used for the Star blocks; the other three will be used in the House blocks.

From the blue-green fabric:
- Cut one 1⅞ × 44-inch strip
- Cut four 1½ × 44-inch strips. From these strips, cut forty 1½-inch squares, ten 1½ × 3⅓-inch pieces, and ten 1½ × 4½-inch pieces.

Piecing the Star Blocks

Step 1. With right sides together, layer the gold and the blue-green 1⅞ × 44-inch strips. Press strips together, but do not stitch.

Step 2. Cut the layered strips into twenty 1⅞-inch squares. Cut the layered squares in half diagonally, being careful not to move your fabric layers while cutting. Stitch ¼ inch from the diagonal edges of the

triangles. Press the seam allowances toward the blue-green fabric. Make forty 1½-inch triangle-pieced squares, as shown in **Diagram 1.**

Diagram 1

Step 3. Sew a 1½-inch blue-green square to either side of a 1½-inch triangle-pieced square. See **Diagram 2.** Repeat to make 20 of these units.

Diagram 2

Step 4. Sew a 1½-inch triangle-pieced square to either side of a 1½-inch gold square. See **Diagram 3.** Repeat to make 10 of these units.

Diagram 3

Step 5. Sew a unit from Step 3 to the top and bottom of a unit from Step 4, as shown in **Diagram 4.** Press. Repeat to make 10 stars.

Diagram 4

Step 6. Sew a $1\frac{1}{2} \times 3\frac{1}{2}$-inch blue-green piece to the right side of each star. Then stitch a $1\frac{1}{2} \times 4\frac{1}{2}$-inch blue-green strip to the bottom of each star to complete the Star blocks. See **Diagram 5.**

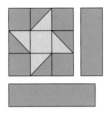

Make 10
Diagram 5

SAILBOAT BLOCKS
(Make 6)

Cutting for Sailboat Blocks

From the blue-green fabric:
• Cut two $5\frac{1}{4}$-inch squares. Cut these squares into quarters diagonally to make eight triangles. You will have two extra triangles.
• Cut three $2\frac{7}{8}$-inch squares. Cut these squares in half diagonally to make six triangles.

From the white fabric:
• Cut two $5\frac{1}{4}$-inch squares. Cut these squares into quarters diagonally to make eight triangles. You will have two extra triangles.

From the red print fabric:
• Cut one 2×44-inch strip. From this strip, cut six $2 \times 3\frac{3}{8}$-inch pieces.
• Cut three $3\frac{1}{4}$-inch squares. Cut these squares into quarters diagonally to form 12 triangles.

Piecing the Sailboat Blocks

Step 1. With right sides together, layer a white triangle and a blue-green triangle cut from the $5\frac{1}{4}$-inch squares, as shown in **Diagram 6.** Stitch as shown to make a sail unit that has the white sail on the right.

Diagram 6

Step 2. Sew a red print triangle to either side of a $2 \times 3\frac{3}{8}$-inch red print rectangle to make a boat unit. See **Diagram 7.**

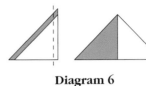

Diagram 7

Step 3. Stitch a sail unit to the top of a boat unit. Add a smaller blue-green triangle to the bottom of the boat. See **Diagram 8.**

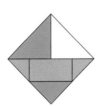

Make 6
Diagram 8

WHARF BLOCKS
(Make 7)

Cutting for Wharf Blocks

From *each* of the four brown fabrics:
• Cut one $1\frac{1}{2} \times 44$-inch strip. From *each* strip, cut seven $1\frac{1}{2} \times 4\frac{1}{2}$-inch pieces.

Piecing the Wharf Blocks

Each block consists of four strips, one from each of the brown fabrics. Sew the four strips together along the long edges in random order. You will create more interest if all your Wharf blocks are not the same. See **Diagram 9.**

Make 7
Diagram 9

QUILT CENTER

Cutting for Water and Corner Blocks

From the blue-green fabric:
• Cut two $4\frac{1}{2}$-inch squares

From the red plaid fabric:
• Cut two $16\frac{3}{4}$-inch squares. Cut these squares in half diagonally to form four triangles.

Assembling the Quilt Center

Step 1. Arrange the Star, Boat, Wharf, and Water blocks, as shown in **Diagram 10** on page 150.

Step 2. Sew the blocks together in rows, pressing the seam allowances of adjacent rows in opposite directions. Join the five rows together and press. The quilt center should measure $20\frac{1}{2}$ inches square.

Step 3. Mark the center point of the long edge on each of the four red plaid triangles. Also mark the center point on each side of the quilt center.

Step 4. Referring to **Diagram 11** on page 150, stitch the side triangles to the sides of the quilt,

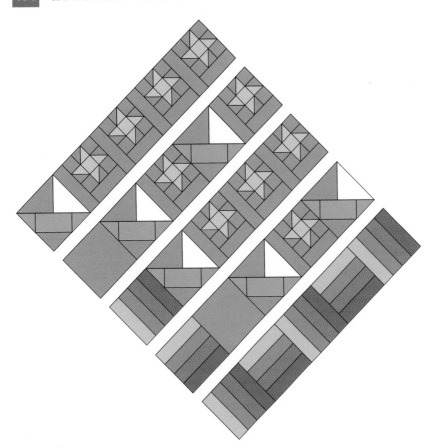

Diagram 10

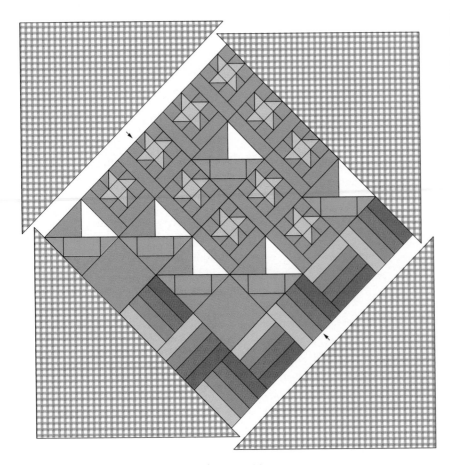

Diagram 11

matching center points and being careful not to stretch the bias edge of the triangles. Press seams toward the red plaid. The quilt center should now measure 30½ inches square.

FENCE BORDER

Cutting for Fence Border

From the cream fabric:
• Cut three 1½ × 44-inch strips
• Cut three 2½ × 44-inch strips. From these strips, cut fifty-seven 1½ × 2½-inch pieces.
• Cut two 1⅞ × 44-inch strips

From the blue fabric:
• Cut six 1½ × 44-inch strips
• Cut two 1⅞ × 44-inch strips
• Cut four 3½ × 44-inch strips. Cut three of these strips to 30½ inches and cut one strip to 24½ inches.

Piecing the Fence Border

Step 1. Sew a 1½ × 44-inch inch blue strip to each side of a 1½ × 44-inch cream strip, as shown in **Diagram 12.** Press the seam allowances toward the blue fabric. Repeat to make three of these strip sets. Cut these strip sets into 57 units, each 1½ inches wide, to make fence spacing units.

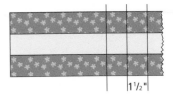

Diagram 12

Step 2. With right sides together, layer a 1⅞ × 44-inch cream strip with a 1⅞ × 44-inch blue strip. Press together, but do not stitch. Make another set of layered cream and blue print strips in the same manner. Cut the layered strips into 29 squares, each 1⅞ inches. Cut the layered squares in half diagonally. Stitch ¼ inch from the diagonal edge. Press the seam allowances toward the blue fabric. Make 58 triangle-pieced squares. (You will only need 57 of these squares.)

Step 3. Sew a triangle-pieced square to the top of a 1½ × 2½-inch cream piece, as shown in **Diagram 13**. Repeat for all 57 fence posts, making sure all points are going in the same direction.

Diagram 13

Step 4. Sew the fence units together, starting with a pointed fence post and alternating with the fence spacing units. See **Diagram 14**. Construct three fence sections with 15 fence posts and 15 fence spacing units. Make one fence section with 12 of each unit. The three long fence sections should measure 30½ inches and the shorter section should measure 24½ inches. Adjust seam allowances if necessary to achieve these measurements.

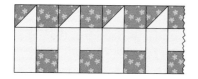

Diagram 14

Step 5. Sew the 3½-inch-wide blue strips to the fence sections, matching lengths. The blue strips will be sewn to the bottom of three fence rows and to the top of one fence row. Refer to the **Quilt Diagram** on page 147. Press seam allowances toward the blue fabric.

Step 6. Referring to the **Quilt Diagram** for correct positioning of

pointed fence posts, sew the top and bottom fence borders to the quilt. Press seams toward the red plaid triangles. The side fence sections will be added later.

HOUSE AND LIGHTHOUSE BLOCKS

Cutting for House and Lighthouse Blocks

You will now need the three gold 1½-inch squares left over from cutting for the Star blocks.

From the gold fabric:
• Cut one 1½ × 2½-inch rectangle

From the red print fabric:
• Cut one 3½ × 20-inch strip. From this strip, cut three 2½ × 3½-inch pieces and six 1½ × 3½-inch pieces.
• Cut one 1½ × 20-inch strip. From this strip, cut nine 1½-inch squares.

From the brown #1 fabric:
• Cut three 3⅞-inch squares. Cut these squares in half diagonally to make six triangles.

From the brown #2 fabric:
• Cut one 1⅞ × 44-inch strip. From this strip, cut two 1⅞-inch squares. Trim the remainder of the 1⅞-inch strip to 1½ inches wide. From this strip, cut three 1½ × 2½-inch pieces and one 1½ × 6½-inch piece.

From the blue fabric:
• Cut three 3⅞-inch squares. Cut these squares in half diagonally to form six triangles.
• Cut one 3 × 44-inch strip. From this strip, cut one of **Template B,** one of **Template B Reverse,** two 2½-inch squares, two 1½-inch squares, two 1⅞-inch squares, and two 1½ × 2½-inch pieces.

From the red check fabric:
• Cut one of **Template A**
• Cut two 2 × 2½-inch rectangles

Piecing the House Blocks
(Make 3)

Step 1. Sew a 1½-inch red print square to the top of each brown #2 piece to make the door units.

Step 2. Sew a 1½-inch red print square to the top and bottom of each 1½-inch gold square to make the window units.

Step 3. Using two 1½ × 3½-inch red print pieces and one 2½-inch red print piece, assemble the house base, as shown in **Diagram 15**. Stitch together and press. Repeat to make the other two house bases.

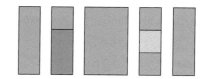

Diagram 15

Step 4. Sew the brown #1 triangles to the blue triangles along their long edges. Press seam allowances toward the roof fabric. Stitch two of these triangle-pieced squares together to make a roof. See **Diagram 16.** Sew the roof units to the house bases to complete the houses. (Refer to the

Diagram 16

Quilt Diagram on page 147 to see the completed houses.)

Piecing the Lighthouse Block
(Make 1)

Step 1. With right sides together, layer a 1⅞-inch brown #2 square with a 1⅞-inch blue square. Press together and cut in half diagonally to form two sets of layered triangles. Stitch the triangles together, sewing ¼ inch from the diagonal edge. Press seam allowances toward the brown fabric. Repeat with the other blue and brown #2 squares.

Step 2. Sew two of the triangle-pieced squares together to form the lighthouse roof. See **Diagram 17.**

Diagram 17

Step 3. Referring to **Diagram 18,** make row 1 of the block by attaching the lighthouse roof to the long side of the 1½ × 2½-inch gold rectangle. Press the seam allowance toward the gold fabric. Sew a 2½-inch blue square to the left and right sides of the roof and light unit you just made.

Step 4. For row 2, attach the two remaining blue and brown #2 triangle-pieced squares to the sides of the 1½ × 2½-inch brown #2 piece. See **Diagram 18.** Sew a 1½-inch blue print square to each end of this section.

Step 5. Sew the blue B and B Reverse pieces to either side of the red check A piece to make row 3, as shown in **Diagram 18.** Press seams toward the red check fabric.

Step 6. To make row 4, sew the 1½ × 2½-inch brown #2 piece between two 2 × 2½-inch red check pieces. Next sew a 1½ × 2½-inch blue piece to each side of this unit.

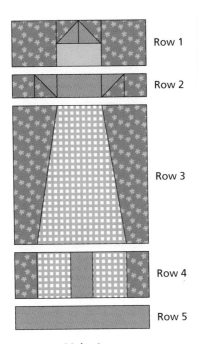

Row 1

Row 2

Row 3

Row 4

Row 5

Make 1
Diagram 18

Step 7. Assemble the Lighthouse block in rows, referring to **Diagram 18.** Sew the rows together, pressing seams as you go. Add the 1½ × 6½-inch brown #2 piece (row 5) to the bottom of the lighthouse, pressing the seam allowance toward the brown fabric.

BORDERS

Cutting for Outer Border

From the green fabric:
• Cut five 3½ × 44-inch strips

Assembling the Pieced Border

Step 1. Referring to the **Quilt Diagram** on page 147, sew a House block to each end of the right side fence border.

Step 2. Sew a House block to the top of the left side fence border. Sew the Lighthouse block to the bottom of this border. Attach the left and right borders to the quilt sides. Press seams toward the red plaid triangles.

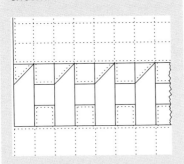

QUILTING IDEAS

☑ Quilt in the ditch around the stars, sailboats, wharf, fence, houses, and lighthouse. The borders have 1-inch channel quilting, as shown.

☑ In the large open area of the plaid triangles, you could crosshatch a 1-inch grid as I did, or use a large quilt stencil design. For more information, refer to "Cross-Hatching Tips" on page 243.

☑ A simple chain design could be quilted in both the blue and the green borders.

Attaching the Outer Border

Step 1. Measure the quilt from left to right through the middle to determine the length of the top and bottom borders. Cut two 3½ × 44-inch green outer border strips to the necessary length and sew to the top and bottom of the quilt.

Step 2. Piece the remaining three green border strips together with diagonal seams. Cut this long strip in half crosswise.

Step 3. Measure the quilt from top to bottom, including the borders you just added, to determine the length of the side borders. Trim the two strips to the necessary length and sew to the sides of the quilt.

QUILTING

Step 1. Prepare the backing for the quilt. Cut the 3-yard backing fabric crosswise into two $1\frac{1}{2}$-yard lengths. Remove the selvages and sew the two pieces together along the long edge. Press the seam open.

Step 2. Trim the backing and batting to measure 4 inches larger than the quilt top.

Step 3. Mark the quilt top.

Step 4. Layer the backing, batting, and quilt top. Baste the layers together and quilt by hand or machine.

BINDING

The 3-inch strips will produce a $\frac{1}{2}$-inch-wide bias binding. If you want a wider or narrower binding, adjust the width of the strips you cut. (See page 247 for pointers on how to experiment with binding width.)

See "Making and Attaching the Binding" on to page 245 to complete your quilt.

Cutting for Bias Binding

From the red/brown plaid fabric:
• Cut enough 3-inch-wide bias strips to make a 216-inch strip

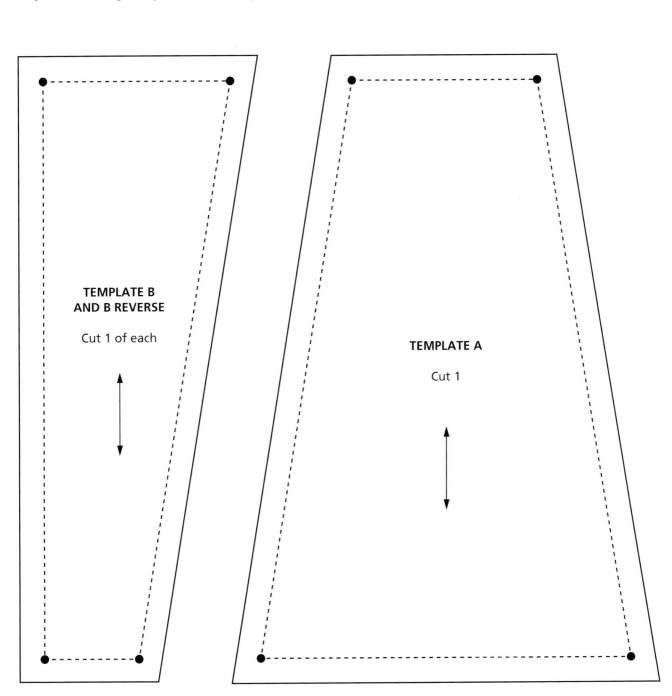

TEMPLATE B AND B REVERSE

Cut 1 of each

TEMPLATE A

Cut 1

Lap Quilt Diagram

BIRDHOUSE ROW LAP QUILT

SIZE

Lap quilt: 56 × 68 inches (unquilted)

Finished block: 7½ inches square

FABRICS AND SUPPLIES

Yardage is based on 44-inch-wide fabric.

1 yard of red print fabric for birdhouses

½ yard of brown print fabric for roofs

⅛ yard of black print fabric for holes

1⅔ yards of beige print fabric for side and corner triangles

2½ yards of brown floral print fabric for lattice, outer border, and binding

⅔ yard of blue print fabric for inner border

4 yards of fabric for quilt backing

Quilt batting, at least 60 × 72 inches

Rotary cutter, mat, and see-through ruler

Template plastic or cardboard

Fusible webbing (optional)

I love antique birdhouses. To me they are the best example of true folk art—meaning art of the common person. Whenever I see an antique birdhouse, I try to imagine the process the builder went through. I am always amazed at how such a very simple design can be so pleasing. It was the simplest of birdhouses from my collection that inspired this quilt. I organized the birdhouses in rows between the floral fabric strips as if the birdhouses were tucked in among the blossoms of trees and bushes.

FABRIC KEY

 RED PRINT

 BROWN PRINT

 BLACK PRINT

 BEIGE PRINT

 BROWN FLORAL PRINT

 BLUE PRINT

GETTING READY

- Read instructions thoroughly before you begin.
- Prewash and press fabric.
- Use ¼-inch seam allowances throughout unless directions specify otherwise.
- Seam allowances are included in the cutting sizes given.
- Press seam allowance in the direction that will create the least bulk and, whenever possible, toward the darker fabric.
- Trace **Template A** (page 161) onto template plastic and cut out.
- If you choose to use fusible webbing to attach the birdhouse holes, follow the manufacturer's directions.
- Cutting directions for each section of the quilt are given in the areas following the row of scissors. If you like to cut as you go, simply follow the directions as you get to them. If you'd rather cut all your pieces at once, skip ahead and look for the scissors to do all the cutting before you begin to sew.

BIRDHOUSE BLOCKS
(Make 15)

Cutting for Birdhouse Blocks

From the red fabric:
- Cut three 6½ × 44-inch strips. From these strips, cut fifteen 6½-inch squares.

From the beige fabric:
- Cut one 3 × 44-inch strip. From this strip, cut fourteen 3-inch squares.
- Cut 1 additional 3-inch square

From the brown print fabric:
- Cut six 2 × 44-inch strips

From the black fabric:
- Cut 15 of **Template A**

Piecing the Birdhouse Blocks

Step 1. With right sides together, place a 3-inch beige square on one corner of a 6½-inch red square, as shown in **Diagram 1.** Stitch diagonally from corner to corner. Trim seam allowance to ¼-inch. Repeat for all 15 birdhouses.

Step 2. With right sides together, stitch a 2 × 44-inch brown roof strip

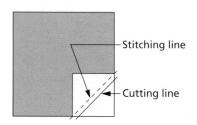

Stitching line

Cutting line

Diagram 1

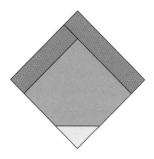

Diagram 2

Make 15
Diagram 3

to the top left side of a red bird-house square, as shown in **Diagram 2.** Trim the strip even with the house edge.

Step 3. Stitch the roof strip to the top right side to complete the birdhouse roof. Trim the strip even with the house and roof edge. See **Diagram 3.** Add roof strips in this manner to all 15 birdhouses.

Step 4. Hand appliqué the hole onto the birdhouse. To do this, run a small basting stitch a scant ¼ inch from the outside edge of the black print circle. Pull very slightly to encourage the edges to turn under. See the **Lap Quilt Placement Guide** on page 162 and use it to make sure you position the holes consistently. Place the black circle on the birdhouse and hand appliqué in place with matching thread. See "Hand Appliqué" on page 238 and "Appliqué Tips and Tricks" above. Repeat for all birdhouses.

HINTS & HELPS

To get a perfect circle for ap-pliqué, use a thin cardboard or plastic template. Trace around it on the fabric and cut out the shape, adding ¼ inch for seam allowance. Stitch around the circle a scant ¼ inch from the edge in a hand or machine gathering stitch. Place the template in the center of the circle and draw up the gather-ing stitches around the tem-plate. Fasten by tying the threads. Press lightly and care-fully slip the template out of the circle.

Appliqué Tips and Tricks

❖ Using the **Miniature Quilt Placement Guide** on page 161 and the **Lap Quilt Placement Guide** on page 162, trace the upper portion of the birdhouse onto paper and cut out the hole. Lay this pattern on your pieced birdhouses and mark where the hole belongs so that your blocks will be consistent.

❖ You can machine appliqué the hole with a satin stitch, using matching thread. When you cut out **Template A,** be sure to eliminate the seam allowance on the circle. See "Machine Appliqué" on page 239.

❖ Or you can use fusible webbing and an iron to attach the holes. For this, eliminate the seam allowance when you cut out **Template A.**

QUILT CENTER

Cutting for Background and Lattice

From the beige print fabric:
• Cut two 14 × 44-inch strips. From these strips, cut six 14-inch squares. Cut these squares diagonally into quarters to form 24 side triangles.
• Cut two 9 × 44-inch strips. From these strips, cut six 9-inch squares. Cut these squares in half to form 12 corner triangles.

From the brown floral fabric:
• Cut two 4½ × 44-inch strips

Note: The side triangles and corner triangles will be larger than neces-sary and will be trimmed after they have been added to the pieced blocks.

Piecing the Quilt Center

Step 1. Referring to **Diagram 4,** sew the side triangles to the bird-houses. Make three vertical rows of five birdhouses each. Be sure to match the seams of the birdhouses. Add the corner triangles to the top and bottom of each row.

Step 2. Trim off excess fabric from the side and corner triangles, allowing ¼-inch seam allowances beyond block corners. Before you trim, be sure to see "Trimming Side

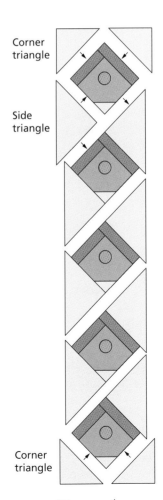

Corner triangle

Side triangle

Corner triangle

Diagram 4

and Corner Triangles" on page 236 to be certain you make these cuts accurately. Make sure the corners are accurate 90 degree angles and all three rows measure the same.

Step 3. Measure the length of the birdhouse rows. Trim the two $4\frac{1}{2} \times$ 44-inch brown floral lattice strips to that length. Sew a lattice strip lengthwise to each side of one birdhouse row, as shown in **Diagram 5.** Press all the seams toward the lattice strips. Sew the remaining two birdhouse rows to the other sides of the lattice strips to complete the center portion of the quilt top.

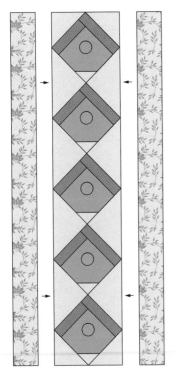

Diagram 5

BORDERS

Cutting for Borders

The yardage given allows for borders to be cut cross-grain.

From the blue fabric:
• Cut five $2\frac{1}{2} \times 44$-inch strips for the inner border

From the brown floral fabric:
• Cut six $6\frac{1}{2} \times 44$-inch strips for the outer border

Attaching the Borders

Step 1. Measure the quilt from left to right through the middle to determine the length of the top and bottom borders. Cut the blue inner border strips to the necessary length and sew to the top and bottom of the quilt.

Step 2. Measure the quilt from top to bottom through the middle, including the borders you just added, to determine the length of the side borders. Piece the remaining three blue strips together with diagonal seams and cut to the length needed. Attach the side inner borders.

Step 3. Measure the quilt from left to right as you did for the inner border. Cut two brown floral outer border strips to the necessary length and sew to the top and bottom of your quilt.

Step 4. Piece the remaining brown floral strips together with diagonal seams. Measure the quilt from top to bottom, as before, and cut the brown floral outer border strips to the necessary length and sew to the quilt sides.

QUILTING

Step 1. Prepare the backing by cutting the 4-yard length of backing fabric in half crosswise to make two 2-yard lengths. Remove the selvages. Sew the two lengths together with one center seam. Press seam allowances open.

Step 2. Trim the backing and batting so they are 4 inches larger than the quilt top dimensions.

Step 3. Mark the quilt top.

QUILTING IDEAS

☑ Quilt in the ditch around the holes, roofs, and birdhouses to define these features.

☑ The birdhouses are filled with vertical rows of quilting spaced $1\frac{3}{4}$ inches apart and the beige background has diagonal rows of quilting $1\frac{1}{2}$ inches apart.

☑ Add interest to the vertical lattice by quilting a large chain or feather design.

☑ The outer borders have parallel lines of quilting 2 inches apart.

Step 4. Layer the backing, batting, and quilt top. Baste these layers together and quilt.

BINDING

The $2\frac{3}{4}$-inch-wide strip will produce a $\frac{3}{8}$-inch-wide binding. If you want a wider or narrower binding, adjust the width of the strips you cut. (See page 247 for pointers on how to experiment with binding width.) Refer to the "Making and Attaching the Binding" on page 245 to complete your quilt.

Cutting for Cross-Grain Binding

From the brown floral fabric:
• Cut seven $2\frac{3}{4} \times 44$-inch strips

Miniature Quilt Diagram

FABRIC KEY

 RED CHECK

 BROWN PRINT

 BLACK PRINT

BEIGE PRINT

 BLUE FLORAL PRINT

BIRDHOUSE ROW MINIATURE QUILT

SIZE

Miniature quilt: 23 × 27 inches (unquilted)

Finished block: 4¼ inches square

FABRICS AND SUPPLIES

Yardage is based on 44-inch-wide fabric.

¼ yard of red small check fabric for birdhouses

¼ yard of brown print fabric for roofs and inner border

4 × 8-inch piece of black print fabric for holes

½ yard of beige print fabric for side and corner triangles

⅔ yard of blue floral print fabric for lattice and outer border

½ yard of plaid fabric for bias binding

¾ yard of fabric for quilt backing

Quilt batting, at least 27 × 31 inches

Rotary cutter, mat, and see-through ruler

Template plastic

Fusible webbing (optional)

BIRDHOUSE BLOCKS

(Make 6)

Before starting the miniature quilt, be sure to read "Getting Ready" for the Lap Quilt on page 156. Then trace **Template B** (page 161) onto template plastic and cut out.

Cutting for Birdhouse Blocks

From the red check fabric:
• Cut one 4 × 26-inch strip. From this strip, cut six 4-inch squares.

From the beige print fabric:
• Cut one 1½ × 15-inch strip. From this strip, cut six 1½-inch squares.

From the brown print fabric:
• Cut two 1½ × 44-inch strips

From the black fabric:
• Cut six of **Template B**

Piecing the Birdhouse Blocks

Step 1. With right sides together, place a 1½-inch beige square on one corner of a 4-inch red square, as shown in **Diagram 6**. Stitch from

corner to corner diagonally. Trim the seam allowance to ¼-inch. Repeat for all the birdhouses.

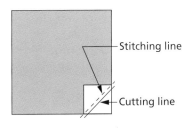

Stitching line

Cutting line

Diagram 6

Step 2. With right sides together, stitch a 1½ × 44-inch brown roof strip to the top left side of the red birdhouse square. See **Diagram 7**. Trim the strip even with the house edge.

Diagram 7

Step 3. Stitch the roof strip to the top right side to complete the birdhouse roof. Trim the strip even with the house and roof edge, as shown in **Diagram 8.** Add roof strips to all the birdhouses in the same manner.

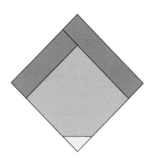

Make 6
Diagram 8

Step 4. To appliqué the birdhouse holes, follow Step 4 under "Piecing the Birdhouse Blocks" for the lap quilt, using the **Miniature Quilt Placement Guide.**

QUILT CENTER

Cutting for Background and Lattice

From the beige fabric:
• Cut two 8-inch squares. Cut these squares in quarters diagonally to form eight side triangles.
• Cut one 6 × 26-inch strip. From this strip, cut four 6-inch squares. Cut these squares in half diagonally to form eight corner triangles.

From the blue fabric:
• Cut one 3 × 20-inch strip

Note: The side triangles and corner triangles will be larger than necessary and will be trimmed after they have been added to the pieced blocks.

Piecing the Quilt Center

Step 1. Referring to **Diagram 9,** sew the side triangles to the birdhouses. Make two vertical rows of three birdhouses each. Add the corner triangles to the top and bottom of each row.

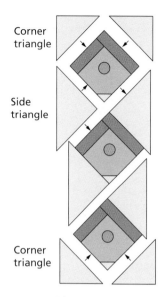

Corner triangle

Side triangle

Corner triangle

Diagram 9

Step 2. Trim off excess fabric from the side and corner triangles, allowing ¼-inch seam allowances beyond block corners. Before you trim, be sure to see "Trimming Side and Corner Triangles" on page 236 to be certain you make these cuts accurately. Make sure the corners are accurate 90 degree angles and both rows measure the same.

Step 3. Measure the length of your birdhouse rows. Trim the 3 × 20-inch floral lattice strip to that

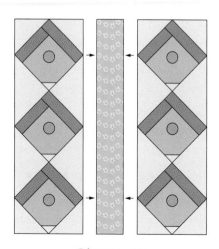

Diagram 10

length. Sew a birdhouse row lengthwise onto each side of the lattice strip to complete the center portion of the quilt top. See **Diagram 10.**

BORDERS

Cutting for Borders

The yardage given allows for borders to be cut cross-grain.

From the brown fabric:
• Cut two 1¼ × 44-inch strips for the inner borders

From the blue fabric:
• Cut three 4½ × 44-inch strips for the outer borders

Attaching the Borders

Step 1. Measure the quilt from left to right through the middle to determine the length of the top and bottom borders. One strip of the brown fabric will be enough to make both of these inner borders. Cut to the necessary length and sew the brown inner borders to the quilt.

Step 2. The side borders will also be cut from one strip of brown fabric. Measure the quilt from top to bottom through the middle, including the borders you just added, to determine the length of the side borders. Cut to the necessary length and sew the brown inner borders to the quilt.

Step 3. Measure the quilt from left to right, as before, and cut one of the blue strips to the necessary length for the top and bottom borders. Sew the blue outer border strips to the top and bottom of your quilt.

Step 4. Measure the quilt from top to bottom, as before, and cut the remaining two blue outer border strips to the length needed for the side outer borders. Sew the borders to the quilt sides.

QUILTING

Step 1. Prepare the backing by cutting a 28 × 32-inch piece from the backing fabric.

Step 2. Trim the backing and batting so they are 4 inches larger than the quilt top dimensions.

Step 3. Mark the quilt top.

Step 4. Layer the backing, batting, and quilt top. Baste these layers together and quilt.

BINDING

The 2¾-inch strips will produce ⅜-inch-wide binding. If you want a wider or narrower binding, adjust the width of the strips you cut. (See page 247 for pointers on how to experiment with binding width.) Refer to "Making and Attaching Binding" on page 245 to complete your quilt.

Cutting for Bias Binding

From the plaid fabric:
• Cut enough 2¾-inch-wide bias strips to make a 120-inch strip

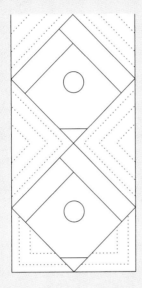
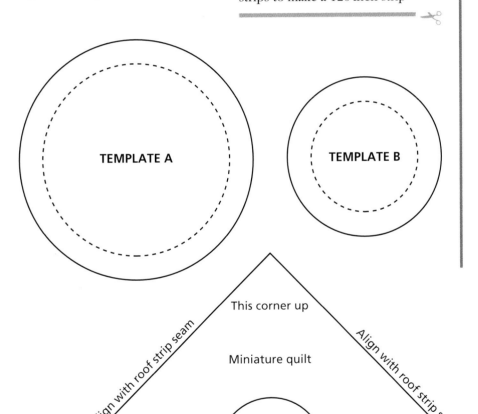

TEMPLATE A

TEMPLATE B

Align with roof strip seam

This corner up

Miniature quilt

Align with roof strip seam

Placement of finished hole

**MINIATURE QUILT
PLACEMENT GUIDE**

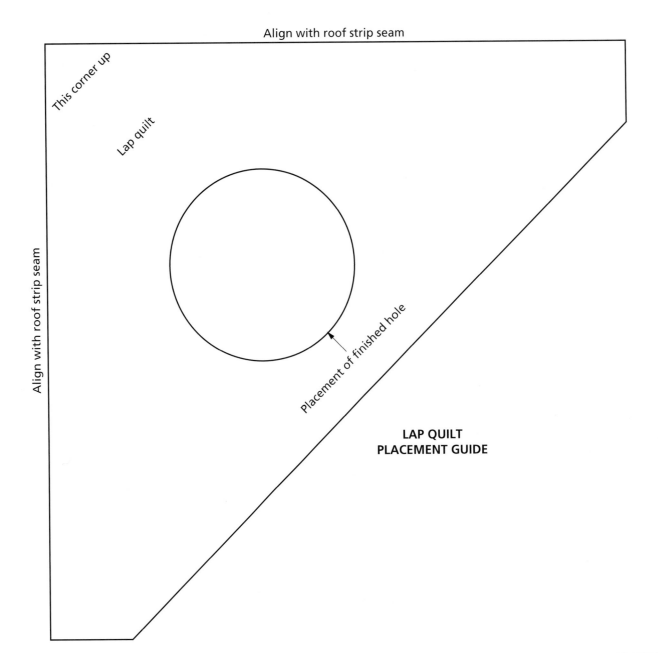

Align with roof strip seam

This corner up

Lap quilt

Align with roof strip seam

Placement of finished hole

**LAP QUILT
PLACEMENT GUIDE**

DECK THE HALLS

Add to the magic of the season with quilts and accessories you've created. As a gift to yourself and your holiday home, why not plan to make one new project from this section each year? Your collection of Christmas decorations will grow, and you'll get to enjoy the holidays surrounded by your own handiwork.

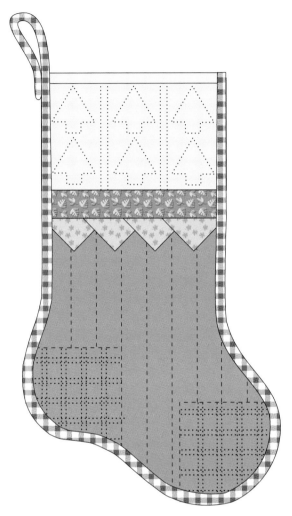

Stocking Diagram

FABRICS AND SUPPLIES
(for 1 stocking)

Some parts of the stocking require only small amounts of fabric. You may already have scraps of fabric on hand that will work well. If not, buy an interesting assortment of fat quarters.

Yardage is based on 44-inch-wide fabric.

- ³/₄ yard of dark red print fabric for stocking front and back
- ¹/₄ yard of cream fabric for cuff and top binding
- ¹/₈ yard of red print fabric for cuff band (or 2 × 8-inch strip)
- ¹/₈ yard of green print fabric for prairie points (or 4 × 10-inch strip)
- ¹/₂ yard of muslin for lining
- ¹/₂ yard of plaid fabric for bias binding
- 1 yard of quilt batting
- Five ¹/₂-inch jingle bells
- Two 1-inch jingle bells
- 1 yard of ¹/₄-inch-wide green satin ribbon
- 2 yards *each* of green, red, gold, and black embroidery floss
- Rotary cutter, mat, and see-through ruler
- Template plastic

$\mathbf{A}$s a child, I loved the sweet sound of jingle bells, and these stockings prove that I have never outgrown that love! The tradition of hanging Christmas stockings to be filled with treasures is a simple but sure-fire way to remind everyone that Christmas is almost here! My Jingle Socks feature hand quilting, a bold plaid binding, and heels and toes filled with "darning" stitches to add texture and design.

FABRIC KEY

 DARK RED PRINT

 CREAM

 RED PRINT

 GREEN PRINT

- Read instructions thoroughly before you begin.
- Prewash and press fabric.
- Use ¼-inch seam allowances throughout unless directions specify otherwise.
- Seam allowances are included in the cutting sizes given.
- Press seam allowance in the direction that will create the least bulk and, whenever possible, toward the darker fabric.
- Trace **Templates A, B,** and **C** (page 169–172) onto template plastic and cut out.
- Cutting directions for each section of the quilt are given in the areas following the row of scissors. If you like to cut as you go, simply follow the directions as you get to them. If you'd rather cut all your pieces at once, skip ahead and look for the scissors to do all the cutting before you begin to sew.

STOCKING FRONT

Cutting for Stocking Front

From the dark red fabric:
- Cut one 12-inch square. From this square, cut one of **Template C.**

From the green fabric:
- Cut four 3-inch squares

From the cream fabric:
- Cut one of **Template A**
- Cut one 3 × 9-inch piece for stocking front binding

From the red print fabric:
- Cut one of **Template B**

From *each* of the muslin and batting:
- Cut one 12 × 18-inch rectangle

Making the Prairie Points

Step 1. Fold a 3-inch green square in half diagonally, with *wrong* sides

together. Press. Fold in half diagonally again. Press, as shown in **Diagram 1.** Repeat with the remaining three squares.

Step 2. With the dark red stocking front (piece C) facing up, position the four folded prairie points along the top edge of the stocking. Overlap the ends of the prairie points, starting at the left side, as shown in **Diagram 2.** The corner tips of the end prairie points should be even with the side edges of the stocking, as shown in **Diagram 3.**

HINTS & HELPS

I like the nice strong diagonal lines of the overlapping prairie points, and it's much easier than trying to tuck one into the fold of the one next to it.

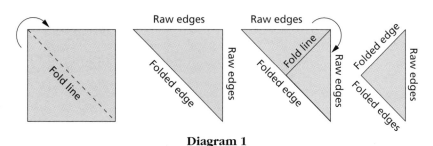

Diagram 1

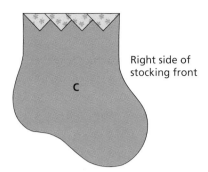

Right side of
stocking front

Diagram 2

Diagram 3

Step 3. Pin prairie points in place. Machine baste them to the stocking with a ¼-inch seam.

Attaching the Cuff to the Stocking

Step 1. With right sides together, stitch the red print rectangle (piece B) to the top edge of the stocking front, where the prairie points have been basted in place. See **Diagram 4.** Press seam allowance toward the cuff band.

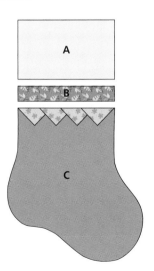

Diagram 4

Step 2. With right sides together, stitch the cream rectangle (piece A) to the top edge of the red print cuff

band. Press seam allowance toward the red print fabric.

Quilting the Stocking Front

Step 1. Layer the muslin, batting, and pieced stocking front. Pin or baste the three layers together, as shown in **Diagram 5.**

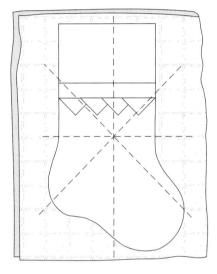

Diagram 5

Step 2. See suggested quilt designs in **Diagram 6.** Trace around the **Tree Quilting Design** on page 169 to mark the cuff, as shown. Between these rows of trees, draw pairs of vertical lines. Use two strands of embroidery floss for quilting. Use green floss for trees and red floss for

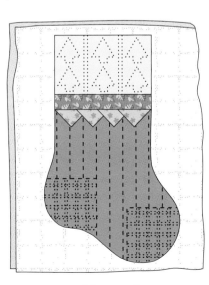

Diagram 6

vertical lines. Quilt the heel and toe with a ½-inch grid. Refer to **Template C** on pages 170–171 for placement lines. Use black floss to quilt the grid. Use gold floss to stitch another grid ¹⁄₁₆ inch away from the black floss grid. Channel quilt the remainder of the stocking with vertical quilting lines that are 1 inch apart.

Step 3. Machine baste around the stocking, ¼ inch from the edges.

Step 4. Trim the lining and batting even with the raw edge of the stocking front.

Binding for Stocking Top

Step 1. Fold the 3 × 9-inch cream piece in half lengthwise with wrong sides together. Press.

Step 2. With the raw edges of the binding and the stocking top even, stitch together using a ¼-inch seam, as shown in **Diagram 7.**

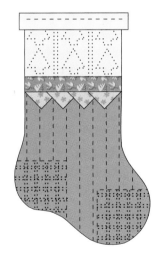

Diagram 7

Step 3. Fold the binding to the lining side of the stocking and hand stitch just to the edge of the stocking, as shown in **Diagram 8** on page 168.

Step 4. Trim the ends of the binding even with the sides of the stocking, being careful not to cut your hand stitches.

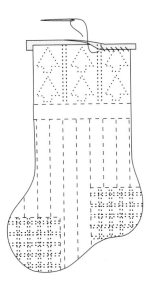

Diagram 8

STOCKING BACK

Do not cut the stocking shape from the fabrics designated for stocking back. The technique that follows treats the stocking back as a rectangular unit of layered fabric and batting. This technique is much easier and more accurate than trying to align so many layers and cut edges. Read through the directions carefully before proceeding.

Cutting for Stocking Back

From the dark red print fabric:
• Cut one 12 × 18-inch rectangle

From the muslin:
• Cut one 12 × 18-inch rectangle

From the batting:
• Cut one 12 × 18-inch rectangle

From the cream fabric:
• Cut one 3 × 12-inch rectangle

Assembling the Stocking Back

Step 1. Layer the dark red print backing, batting, and muslin lining together. Pin together along the top edge and machine baste, as shown in **Diagram 9.**

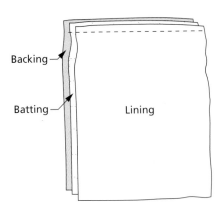

Diagram 9

Step 2. Fold the 3 × 12-inch cream binding strip in half lengthwise, wrong sides together as you did for the front binding.

Step 3. With right sides together, pin the binding along the top edge of the backing fabric with raw edges even. Stitch a ¼-inch seam.

Step 4. Fold the binding over to the lining side and hand stitch in place, as shown in **Diagram 10.**

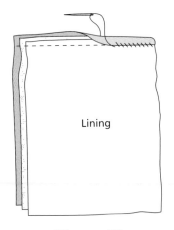

Diagram 10

STOCKING ASSEMBLY

Step 1. Lay the stocking back unit on the table with the lining facing up.

Step 2. Lay the stocking front unit on top of the stocking back unit, right side up. (Linings are facing each other; see **Diagram 11.**) Be sure the top bindings are even.

Step 3. Pin the stocking front to the back assembly.

Step 4. Hand baste the stocking front to the back assembly with a ¼-inch seam.

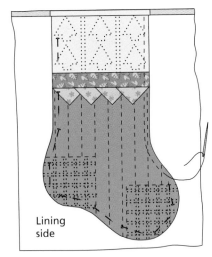

Diagram 11

Step 5. Trim the stocking back layers even with the stocking front.

BINDING

Cutting for Bias Binding

From the plaid fabric:
• Cut enough 3-inch-wide bias strips to make a 55-inch strip

Step 1. Piece the bias strips, using diagonal seams, to make one long 55-inch binding strip.

Step 2. Fold the plaid binding strip in half lengthwise, wrong sides together. Press.

HINTS & HELPS

You will be binding the stocking as you would a quilt. A plaid binding cut on the bias not only adds a charming country look to the stocking but also enables you to bind all of the curves of the stocking.

Step 3. Lay the binding on the upper right side of the stocking front, with raw edges even. Extend the binding ¹⁄₂-inch beyond the top of the stocking, as shown in **Diagram 12.**

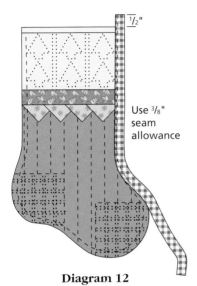

Diagram 12

Step 4. Stitch the binding to the stocking using a ³⁄₈-inch seam allowance, easing in extra binding fabric at the heel and toe.

Step 5. Continue sewing the binding around the stocking. *Do not cut off the excess binding on the left side.* The extra binding will become the stocking hanger.

Step 6. Turn the binding to the back side of the stocking and hand stitch in place. Continue stitching the folded edges of the extended binding for about 5 inches more.

Step 7. Trim the extended binding to 5¹⁄₂-inches beyond the stocking top, as shown in **Diagram 13.**

Step 8. Fold the extended binding to the back of the stocking to form a loop hanger about 2¹⁄₂-inches long. Fold the raw edge of the binding end under ¹⁄₂-inch and stitch in place, as shown in **Diagram 14.**

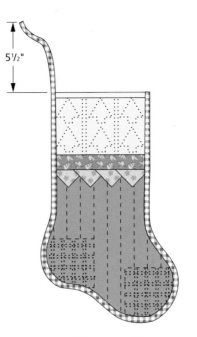

Diagram 13

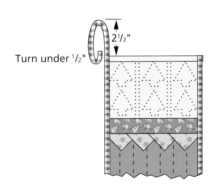

Diagram 14

ADDING THE FINISHING TOUCHES

Step 1. Sew five ¹⁄₂-inch jingle bells in place along the binding edge. See **Template C** on pages 170–171 for placement.

Step 2. Tie a 1-inch jingle bell on each end of the satin ribbon.

Step 3. Tie the ribbon into a bow around the base of the stocking hanger.

Step 4. Hang your stocking and you're ready for Santa!

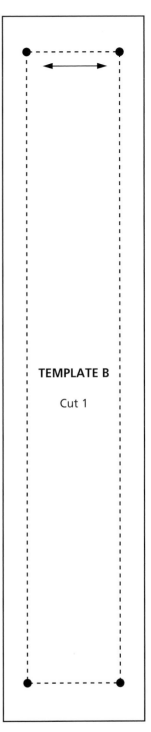

TEMPLATE B

Cut 1

TREE QUILTING DESIGN

Jingle bell
placement

TEMPLATE C
(SECTION 1 OF 2)

1" channel
quilting lines

Match with Section 2

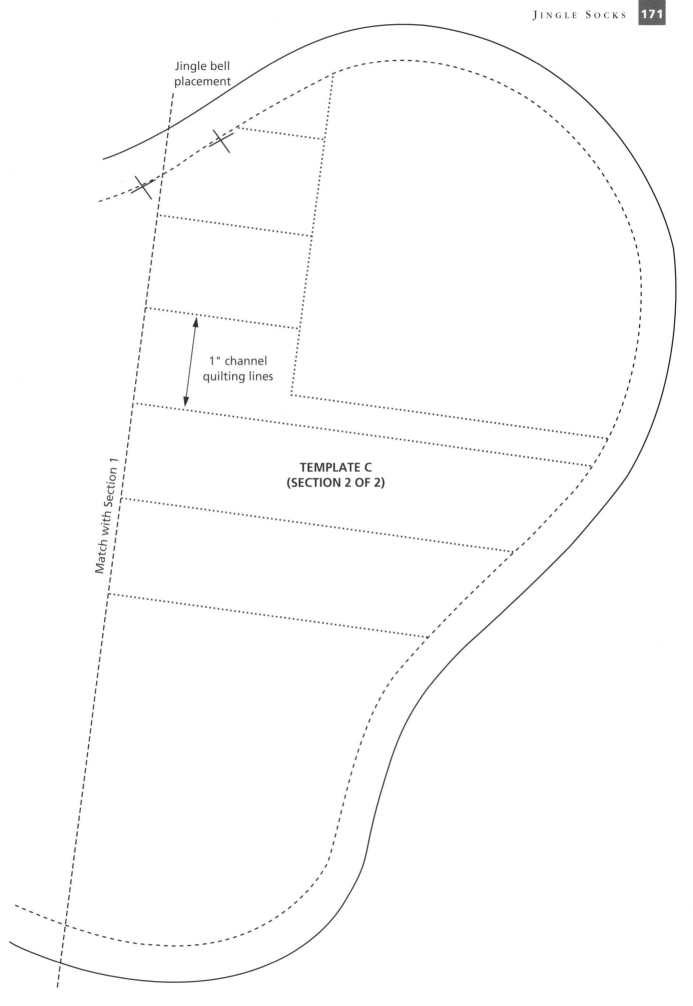

Jingle bell
placement

1" channel
quilting lines

Match with Section 1

**TEMPLATE C
(SECTION 2 OF 2)**

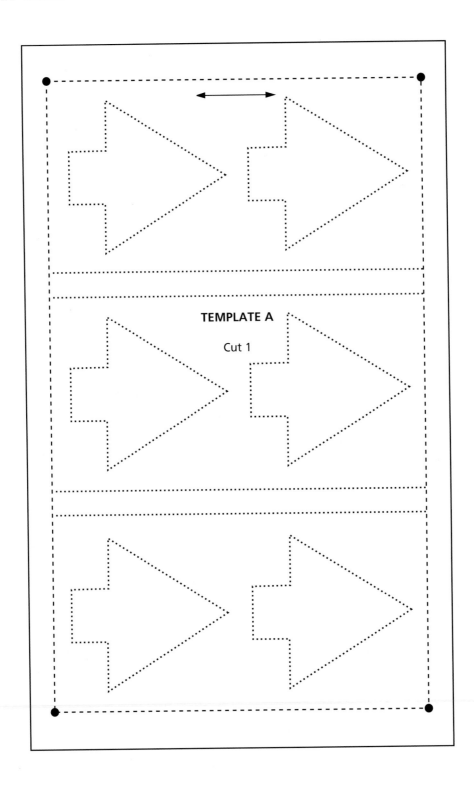

TEMPLATE A

Cut 1

SIZE

Tree skirt: 17 inches in diameter

FABRICS AND SUPPLIES

Yardage is based on 44-inch-wide fabric.

¾ yard of beige fabric for center, backing, and bias binding

⅓ yard *total* of assorted prints for wedges

½ yard of ¼- to ⅜-inch grosgrain ribbon

Quilt batting, at least 21 × 21 inches

Rotary cutter, mat, and see-through ruler

Template plastic

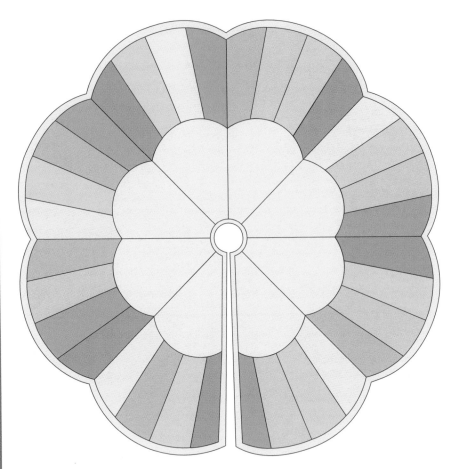

Tree Skirt Diagram

This tree skirt was designed to be used with my antique feather tree, which stands 30 inches tall. It is, however, the perfect accessory for any miniature tree trimmed with tiny holiday ornaments. I also like to use this little skirt under baskets or large crock bowls filled with apples. I place the bowl or basket just off center a bit to cover the back opening and ties and let the remainder fan out. This project gives you the chance to reach into your scrap bag for bits of your favorite fabrics. Because it goes together so quickly, it makes a perfect weekend project. You'll create a holiday heirloom without months of work!

GETTING READY

- Read instructions thoroughly before you begin.
- Prewash and press fabric.
- Use ¼-inch seam allowances throughout unless directions specify otherwise.
- Seam allowances are included in the cutting sizes given.
- Press seam allowance in the direction that will create the least bulk and, whenever possible, toward the darker fabric.
- Trace **Templates A, B,** and **C** (page 177) onto template plastic and cut out.
- Cutting directions for each section of the quilt are given in the areas following the row of scissors. If you like to cut as you go, simply follow the directions as you get to them. If you'd rather cut all your pieces at once, skip ahead and look for the scissors to do all the cutting before you begin to sew.

FABRIC KEY

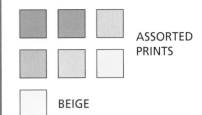

ASSORTED PRINTS

BEIGE

MAKING THE TREE SKIRT

Cutting for Tree Skirt

From the assorted print fabrics:
- Cut 8 of **Template A**
- Cut 8 of **Template A Reverse**
- Cut 8 of **Template B**
- Cut 8 of **Template B Reverse**

From the beige fabric:
- Cut 8 of **Template C**
- Cut one 20 × 20-inch piece for the backing

Piecing the Tree Skirt

Step 1. Sew two piece As and two piece Bs together, as shown in **Diagram 1.** Press seams in one direction. Make eight of these wedge units.

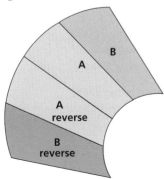

Diagram 1

Step 2. On the inside edge of the wedge units, turn under a ¼-inch

seam allowance and baste. Hand sew this unit to piece C with an invisible stitch along the placement line, referring to **Diagram 2.** Remove the basting stitches. Repeat for all eight wedge units.

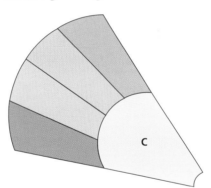

Diagram 2

Step 3. Sew the eight wedge units together leaving one seam open, as shown in **Diagram 3** on page 176. Cut off a ¼-inch seam allowance on the two wedge units next to the opening. You should have a scalloped circle that lies flat.

HINTS & HELPS

If your tree skirt does not lie flat, adjust the seam allowances so it does. You may need to take them in, let them out, or both, if an exact ¼-inch seam allowance wasn't used.

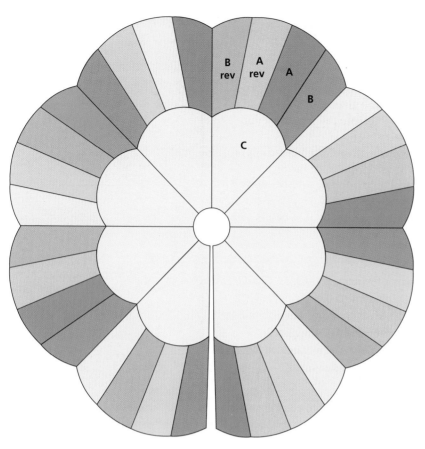

Leave open and trim
off ¼" on each side

Diagram 3

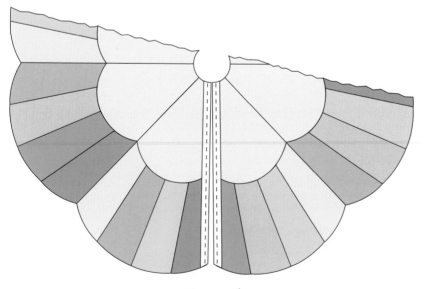

Diagram 4

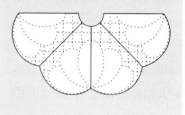

QUILTING IDEAS

◪ The tree skirt pictured
was hand quilted in the ditch
along the wedges. A small
feathered design with cross-
hatching was used in the
center section.

QUILTING

Step 1. Mark the tree skirt for
quilting. Layer the backing, batting,
and tree skirt together. Baste and
quilt up to the edge of the opening.

Step 2. Carefully cut the slit and
center circle through the backing
and batting using your pieced tree
skirt as a guide. The center circle
will be approximately ¾ inch in
diameter. The center circle can be
cut larger if necessary to fit around
your tree.

Step 3. Trim away extra batting and
backing, making them even with
the pieced tree skirt.

BINDING

Cutting for Bias Binding

From the beige fabric:
• Cut two 1 × 8½-inch strips for the
bias binding of the slit edges
• Cut enough 1-inch-wide bias strips
to make a 55-inch strip for the outer
edge
• Cut one ¾ × 4-inch bias strip for
the center circle edge

Step 1. Begin with the two slit edges. Bind these edges with the 1 × 8½-inch bias strips, as shown in **Diagram 4.** With right sides together and raw edges even, sew the binding to the tree skirt with a ¼-inch seam allowance. Turn under raw edge of binding ¼ inch and slip stitch this folded edge in place over the seam line on the back of the tree skirt. Trim the binding even with the upper and lower edges.

Step 2. Bind the outer edge of the tree skirt with the 1 × 55-inch bias strip using the same method as described in Step 1. Leave approximately ½ inch extra at the start and finish of the binding. Fold in the raw edges of these ends, then tuck them around to the back at the edges of the opening and stitch in place, as shown in **Diagram 5.** See "Attaching Binding to Scalloped Edges" on page 194 for hints on how to do this.

Step 3. Bind the center circle with the ¾ × 4-inch bias strip. This circle is so small you will need to fold in both long edges of the binding ⅛ inch and press in place; refer to **Diagram 6.** Then fold the binding in half lengthwise, wrong sides together. Press. Open the binding and hand sew it in place around the circle on the front, with right sides together. Bring the binding around to the back and hand stitch in place turning in the ends to finish off.

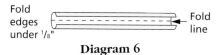

Fold edges under ⅛" • Fold line

Diagram 6

Step 4. Tack two 9-inch pieces of ribbon near the center opening of the tree skirt. Use this ribbon to tie the skirt around your tree.

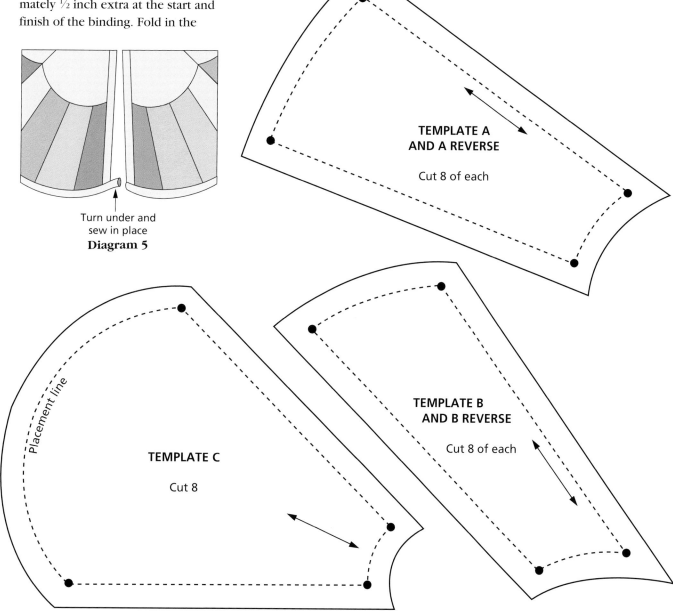

Turn under and sew in place
Diagram 5

TEMPLATE A
AND A REVERSE

Cut 8 of each

Placement line

TEMPLATE C

Cut 8

TEMPLATE B
AND B REVERSE

Cut 8 of each

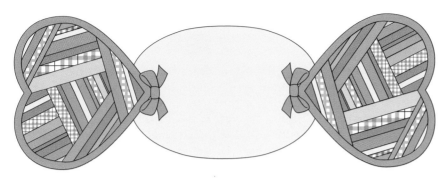

Table Runner Diagram

The idea for this project started years ago, when I designed a heart-shaped pillow top. Using the same piecing configuration, I made a 2½-inch miniature version of the pillow and turned it into a necklace for my daughter. My friend Marilyn Ginsburg always loved the necklace and decided to design a table accessory using the technique. Once the runner was designed, the chair pads seemed like a natural way to adapt the same design. The strip piecing is as simple as can be. I like this piecing technique because it is possible to combine so many fabrics, tucking in the smallest and most unusual scraps.

SIZE

Table runner: 16 × 46 inches (unquilted)

Chair pad: 16 inches square (unquilted)

FABRICS AND SUPPLIES

Yardage is based on 44-inch-wide fabric.

Table Runner

⅛ yard *each* of 10 coordinating fabrics for hearts (select dark-, medium-, and light-colored fabrics in a variety of prints)

⅛ yard of red fabric for bows

2 yards of beige fabric for center oval, table runner backing, and bias binding for center oval

½ yard of plaid fabric for heart bias binding

1 yard of needlepunch batting, at least 36 inches wide, for batting

Chair Pad

Yardage is based on 44-inch-wide fabric and is for one chair pad.

⅛ yard *each* of 10 coordinating fabrics for hearts (select dark-, medium-, and light-colored fabrics in a variety of prints)

⅜ yard of red fabric for ties

½ yard of fabric for backing

½ yard of plaid fabric for bias binding

½ yard of needlepunch batting

Rotary cutter, mat, and see-through ruler

Template plastic

GETTING READY

- Read instructions thoroughly before you begin.
- Prewash and press fabric.
- Use ¼-inch seam allowances throughout unless directions specify otherwise.
- Press seam allowances in the direction that will create the least bulk and, whenever possible, toward the darker fabric
- Trace **Heart Templates 1** through **6** (pages 183–186) onto paper and fit together to create the heart pattern. See **Guide for Completed Heart Pattern** on page 183 to help you put all the pieces together.
- For the table runner, enlarge the **Oval Pattern** (page 187) to make the oval pattern. Use the **Guide for Completed Oval Pattern** on page 187 to help you put the pieces together.

HEART
(Directions for making 1)

In this project, strip piecing is used to stitch many fabric strips of varying widths together, directly onto the batting. This time-saving method lets you simultaneously create a design and quilt as you go.

Use at least 10 different fabrics of dark, medium, and light prints. The more fabrics you use, the more interesting your finished project will be. Needlepunch is recommended for the foundation of your strip piecing because it is a dense batting with low loft that offers much more stability than regular batting.

Strip Piecing the Heart

Step 1. Trace the completed heart pattern onto an 18-inch square of needlepunch batting. A felt-tipped pen will work well. Do not cut out the heart shape yet.

Step 2. Mark the dividing lines on the heart using the pattern as a guide. These lines divide the heart into sections that are numbered in the order in which the sections should be constructed.

Step 3. Cut strips of fabric from the dark, medium, and light fabrics ranging in width from ¾ to 1½ inches. Begin sewing with the full length of the strips and trim as you go. You can

cut the strips to around 20 inches long if you find that more manageable or are working with scraps.

Step 4. Begin the strip piecing by constructing section 1 and referring to **Diagram 1.** The arrows on the diagram indicate in which direction the strips should be placed. Place the first fabric strip right side up at the edge of section 1, but do not stitch.

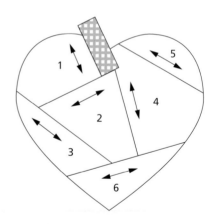

Diagram 1

Step 5. Place a second strip on the first strip, with right sides facing each other, referring to **Diagram 2.** Machine stitch through all thicknesses, ¼ inch from the raw edges of your strips. **Note:** Do not stitch beyond the lines marking the sections. Also, make sure the fabric strips extend beyond the outer edge of the heart shape a bit.

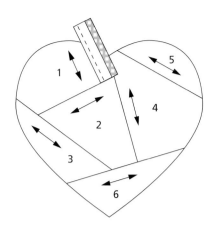

Diagram 2

Step 6. Turn the second strip right side up, finger press or press lightly with an iron. Continue adding strips in this manner, making sure you vary the widths and prints. Continue until section 1 is completely covered.

Step 7. Continue to add strips in the other sections. Use the arrows to determine the direction for placing the strips. With right sides together, line up the raw edge of the first strip in each new section with the raw edges of the stitched strips in the previous section, as shown in **Diagram 3**. It is important always to start each new section in this way; the first strip you add in the new section should cover the raw edges of a previously pieced section. Do not stitch beyond the lines marking the

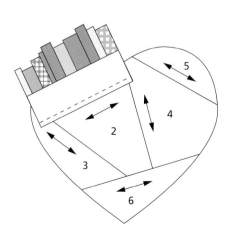

Diagram 3

sections. Trim the strips even with these lines as you add each new strip. Continue to let the fabric strips extend a little beyond the heart outline. It's always good to have extra to trim. It makes a nice even edge.

Step 8. When all the sections are covered, trim excess needlepunch and fabric strips along the outline of the heart shape.

Step 9. With wrong sides together, baste the pieced heart to a square of backing fabric along the outer edge. Trim the backing even with the pieced heart, as shown in **Diagram 4.**

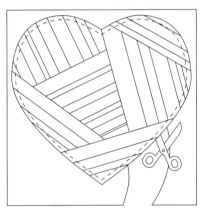

Trim backing even with
edge of heart
Diagram 4

BINDING THE HEART

Cutting for Binding

From the plaid fabric:
• Cut enough 2½-inch-wide bias strips to make a 52-inch strip

Step 1. Piece the 2½-inch-wide plaid bias binding strips with diagonal seams to obtain the length needed (approximately 52 inches). Press seams open. Fold the strip in half lengthwise, wrong sides together, and press.

Step 2. Stitch the raw edges of the binding to the raw edges of the heart with a ¼-inch seam. Bring the folded edge of the binding to the back of the heart and slip stitch in place.

TABLE RUNNER

Step 1. Make two strip-pieced hearts as described above.

Step 2. Trace the completed oval pattern onto the beige fabric, allowing a few extra inches on all sides.

Step 3. Mark the center of the oval for quilting.

Step 4. Cut the backing and needlepunch batting so they are about 4 inches larger than the oval shape. Layer the backing, needlepunch batting, and beige oval. Baste these layers together and quilt. Trim the oval shape.

BINDING THE OVAL

Cutting for Bias Binding

From the beige fabric:
• Cut enough 2½-inch-wide bias strips to make a 63-inch strip

Step 1. Cut and piece the 2½-inch-wide bias binding strips as instructed in Step 1 under "Binding the Heart."

Step 2. Stitch the raw edges of the binding to the raw edges of the oval with a ¼-inch seam. Bring the folded edge of the binding to the back of the oval and slip stitch in place.

MAKING THE BOWS

Cutting for Bows

From the red fabric:
• Cut two 2½ × 19-inch strips

Step 1. Fold one strip in half lengthwise, right sides together. Stitch a ¼-inch seam along the long raw edge, leaving an opening for turning. Taper the stitching at an angle at each end, as shown in **Diagram 5.**

Leave open

Trim seam allowance
Diagram 5

Step 2. Trim the seam allowance and turn the strip right side out. Press and slip stitch the opening closed. Tie into a bow. Tack the bow by hand through the point of the heart where it will be attached to the oval, as shown in **Diagram 6.** Repeat to make another bow for the other heart. Tack the hearts in place by hand at the ends of the oval.

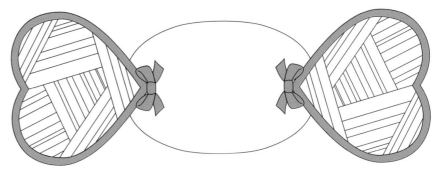

Diagram 6

HINTS & HELPS

It's easy to adjust the length of the runner to fit your table. To lengthen, place the hearts closer to the edge of the center oval. To shorten, move the hearts in toward the center of the oval.

CHAIR PAD
(Directions for making 1)

Cutting for Ties

From the red fabric:
• Cut four 3 × 28-inch red strips

Step 1. Follow the directions under "Strip Piecing the Heart" on page 180. Make one heart for each chair pad, but don't attach the binding yet.

Step 2. To make the ties, fold each 3-inch strip in half lengthwise, right

---

HINTS & HELPS

For a firmer chair pad, stitch the strips to two thickness of needlepunch batting. To stitch through the two layers, pin closely and stitch slowly so that you can control the pieces . . . don't let them push you around!

---

sides together, as shown in **Diagram 7.** Stitch a ¼-inch seam along the raw edges of each tie, leaving one end open for turning. Taper the stitching at an angle on the other end.

Trim seam allowance
Diagram 7

Step 3. Trim seam allowances, turn ties right side out, and press.

Step 4. Position ties on the back of the heart before stitching the binding. Place a pair of ties on either side of the curve of the heart, as shown in **Diagram 8.** To determine the exact location of the ties, pin them in place first, then tie the pad to your chair. Make any necessary adjustments.

Diagram 8

Step 5. Attach the binding as described in "Binding the Heart" on page 181. Be sure to catch the raw edges of each tie in the seam when stitching the binding to the hearts.

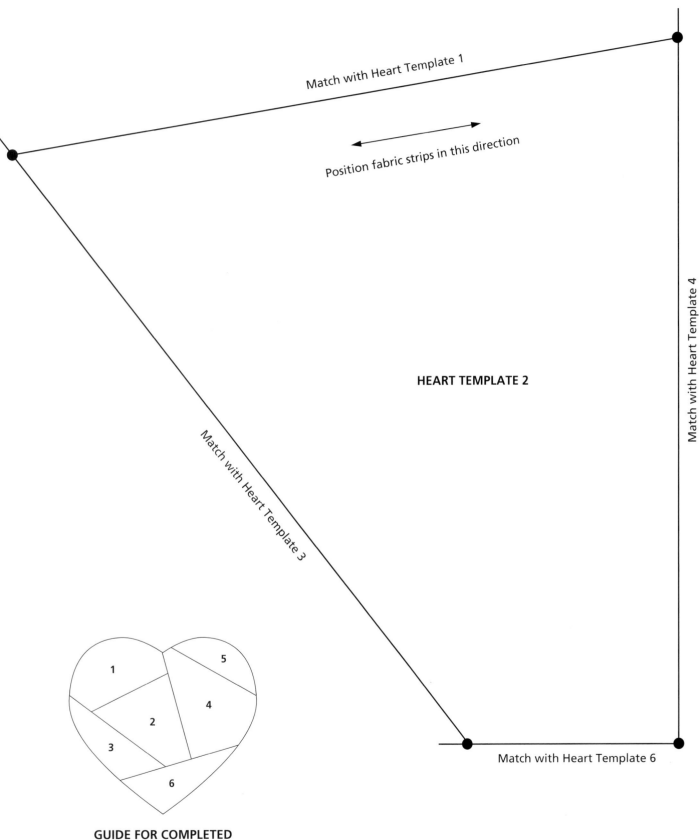

Match with Heart Template 1

Position fabric strips in this direction

Match with Heart Template 4

HEART TEMPLATE 2

Match with Heart Template 3

Match with Heart Template 6

1

5

4

2

3

6

**GUIDE FOR COMPLETED
HEART PATTERN**

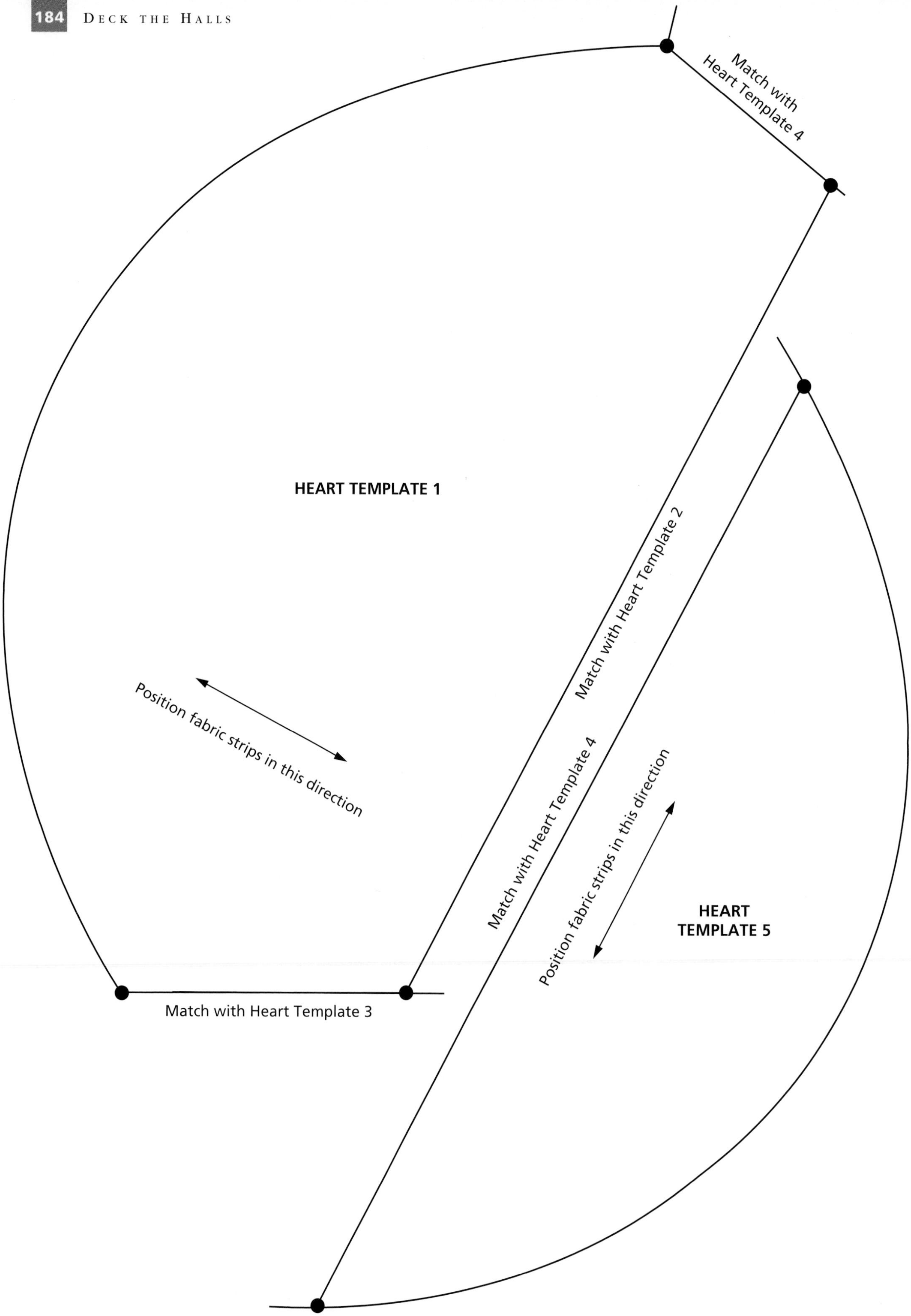

Match with Heart Template 4

HEART TEMPLATE 1

Match with Heart Template 2

Position fabric strips in this direction

Match with Heart Template 4

Position fabric strips in this direction

HEART TEMPLATE 5

Match with Heart Template 3

Match with Heart Template 1

Match with Heart Template 2

Position fabric strips in this direction

Match with Heart Template 5

HEART TEMPLATE 4

Match with Heart Template 6

**GUIDE FOR COMPLETED
HEART PATTERN**

1

2

3

4

5

6

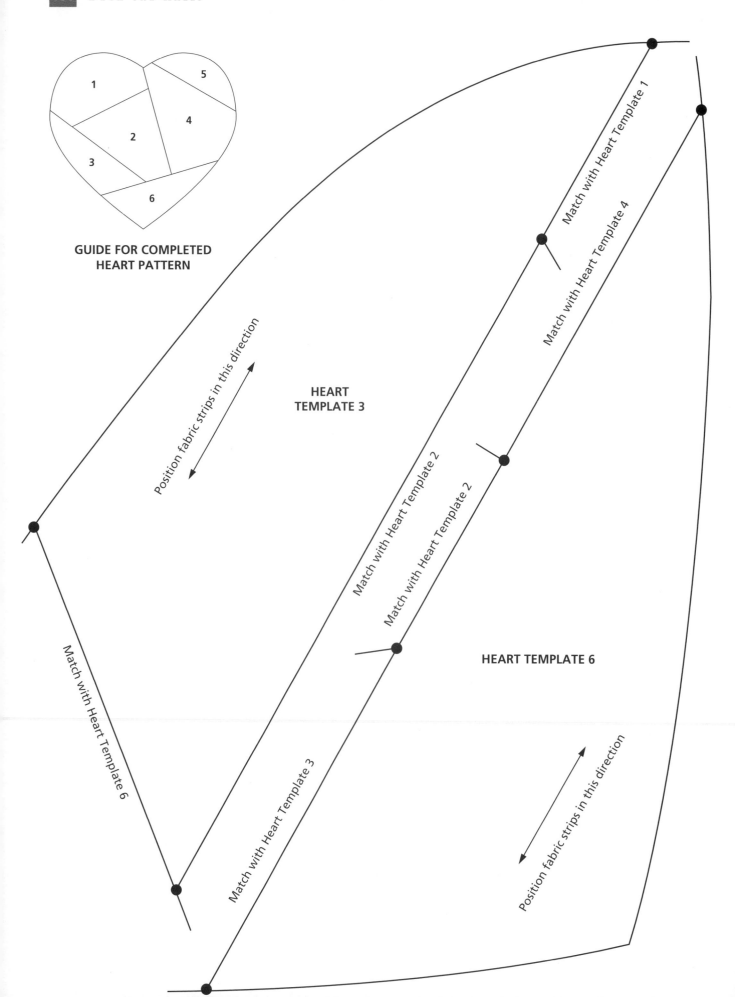

**GUIDE FOR COMPLETED
HEART PATTERN**

1

5

4

2

3

6

Position fabric strips in this direction

**HEART
TEMPLATE 3**

Match with Heart Template 1

Match with Heart Template 4

Match with Heart Template 2

Match with Heart Template 2

Match with Heart Template 6

Match with Heart Template 3

HEART TEMPLATE 6

Position fabric strips in this direction

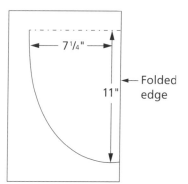

1. Place template on fold of paper and trace

7 1/4"

11"

Folded edge

OVAL PATTERN

Enlarge this pattern 150% on a photocopier to obtain the dimensions shown in the Guide for Completed Oval Pattern. This is one-quarter of the oval pattern.

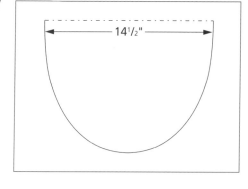

2. Trace the half-oval to duplicate

14 1/2"

3. Tape pieces together to complete

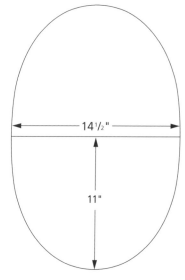

14 1/2"

11"

GUIDE FOR COMPLETED OVAL PATTERN

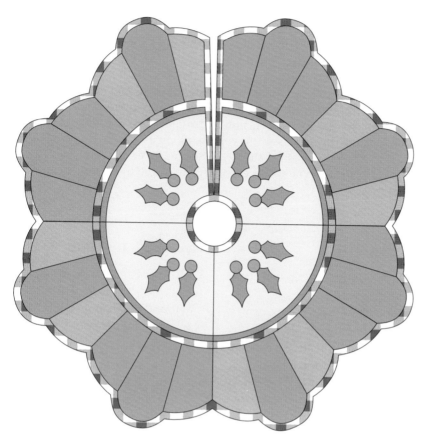

Tree Skirt Diagram

SIZE

Tree skirt: 42 inches in diameter

FABRICS AND SUPPLIES

Yardage is based on 44-inch-wide fabric.

½ yard of nondirectional light print fabric for the center of the tree skirt

⅓ yard *each* of three red print fabrics (two medium and one dark)

1 yard of plaid fabric for bias trim and binding

½ yard of green print fabric for bias trim and holly appliqué

1⅓ yards of fabric for backing

Quilt batting, at least 46 × 46 inches

½ yard of 16-inch-wide sewable, fusible webbing

Black embroidery floss

Rotary cutter, mat, and see-through ruler

Template plastic

Holly Tree Skirt is just the right size for the Christmas trees I put up each year. I love the way the red scallop frames the base of the tree. I used three very similar red prints to create a subtly shaded effect. For more of a scrap look, choose red fabrics that have greater contrast. My friend Marilyn Ginsburg and I put our heads together on this project and felt the holly appliqué with an old-fashioned buttonhole stitch and black embroidery floss was just the right amount of detail to make it special. I added the plaid binding because I like the way it "dances" around the tree, showing off the gentle scalloped edge.

FABRIC KEY

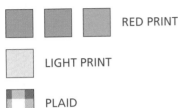

RED PRINT

LIGHT PRINT

PLAID

GREEN PRINT

GETTING READY

- Read instructions thoroughly before you begin.
- Prewash and press fabric.
- Use ¼-inch seam allowances throughout unless directions specify otherwise.
- Seam allowance are included in the cutting sizes given.
- Press seam allowances in the direction that will create the least bulk and, whenever possible, toward the darker fabric.
- Enlarge **Template A** and trace **Templates B** and **C** and the **Berry** and **Holly Templates** (pages 194–196) onto template plastic and cut out.
- Cutting directions for each section of the quilt are given in the areas following the row of scissors. If you like to cut as you go, simply follow the directions as you get to them. If you'd rather cut all your pieces at once, skip ahead and look for the scissors to do all the cutting before you begin to sew.

TREE SKIRT TOP

The tree skirt is made up of a center section and a pieced border. The border units are made up of two different combinations of red fabrics using **Templates B** and **C.** Both border units consist of a piece B in the center with a piece C on the left and a piece C Reverse on the right. All piece Bs will be cut from your darkest red fabric. Pieces C and C Reverse will be cut from both of the other two red fabrics. Combination 1 will use pieces C and C reverse cut from one of the lighter red fabrics. Combination 2 will use these pieces cut from the other red fabric.

Cutting for Tree Skirt

From the light print fabric:
- Cut four of **Template A**

From the darkest red fabric:
- Cut eight of **Template B**

From red print fabric #1:
- Cut four of **Template C**
- Cut four of **Template C Reverse**

From red print fabric #2:
- Cut four of **Template C**
- Cut four of **Template C Reverse**

Piecing the Tree Skirt

Step 1. Sew the red prints together to make four Combination 1 units and four Combination 2 units, as shown in **Diagram 1.**

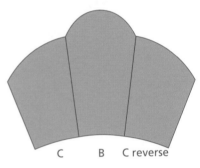

C B C reverse

Combination 1
Make 4

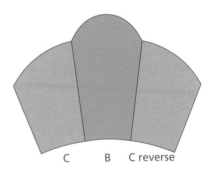

C B C reverse

Combination 2
Make 4
Diagram 1

Step 2. Sew a Combination 1 unit to the left side of a Combination 2 unit, as shown in **Diagram 2.** Make four of these units.

Diagram 2

Step 3. Sew a light print piece A to each of the four units from Step 2, as shown in **Diagram 3.**

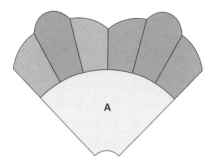

A

Diagram 3

Step 4. Join the four units into a circle, leaving one seam open, as shown in **Diagram 4.**

ADDING THE HOLLY TRIM

Step 1. Cut a $4\frac{1}{2} \times 24$-inch strip of green print fabric.

Step 2. Following the manufacturer's instructions, adhere fusible webbing to the strip of green fabric and to scraps of each of the red fabrics. See "Primitive Appliqué" on page 239 for directions on how to use fusible appliqué.

Step 3. Using the **Holly Template,** cut out 12 holly leaves; using the **Berry Template,** cut out 12 berries (four from each of the three red fabrics). Fuse the holly leaves and berries to the tree skirt using the **Tree Skirt Diagram** on page 189 as a placement guide.

Step 4. Using three strands of black embroidery floss, appliqué the holly leaves and berries to the tree skirt using the buttonhole stitch, as shown in **Diagram 5.**

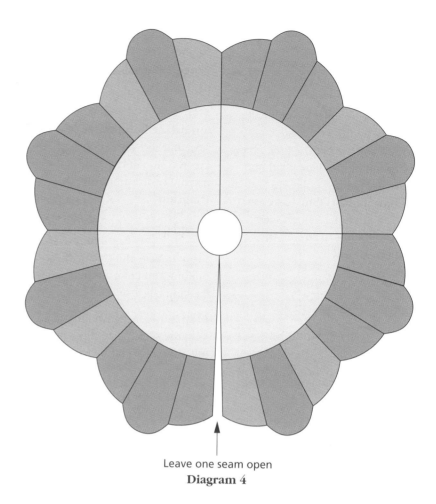

Leave one seam open
Diagram 4

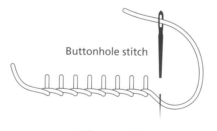

Buttonhole stitch

Diagram 5

HINTS & HELPS

It is best to work with 18-inch lengths of embroidery floss. Longer pieces tangle too easily. After cutting your floss into 18-inch lengths, separate it into two sections of three strands each by separating the strands in the center and pulling apart gently toward both ends.

THE BIAS STRIPS

You will need to piece together bias strips to get the length needed for your tree skirt. Refer to "Making and Attaching Binding" on page 245 for directions on cutting and piecing bias strips.

Cutting for Bias Strips

From the plaid fabric:
• Cut enough 2-inch-wide bias strips to make an 80-inch strip
• Cut two $2\frac{1}{4} \times 18$-inch bias strips
• Cut enough $2\frac{1}{4}$-inch-wide bias strips to make a 135-inch strip
• Cut enough 3-inch-wide bias strips to make a 56-inch strip

From the green print fabric:
• Cut enough $1\frac{1}{4}$-inch-wide strips to make an 80-inch strip

BIAS TRIM

Step 1. Press the green print 1¼ × 80-inch bias strip in half lengthwise, with wrong sides together. Press the plaid 2 × 80-inch bias strip in half lengthwise, with wrong sides together. Lay the narrow green bias strip on top of the wide plaid bias strip, matching raw edges, as shown in **Diagram 6**. Machine baste raw edges together in a ¼-inch seam, being careful not to stretch the fabric as you sew.

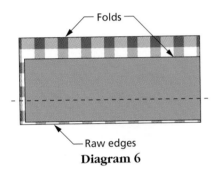

Folds

Raw edges

Diagram 6

Step 2. Beginning at the opening in the tree skirt, lay the bias trim on the tree skirt, matching the raw edges of the trim to the seam line of the background and border section. The plaid fabric should be on top, and the green trim should be facing the tree skirt, as shown in **Diagram 7**. Machine stitch the bias trim to

the tree skirt on top of the basting stitches. Trim the bias strips even with the raw edge at the opening of the tree skirt.

Step 3. Press only the plaid trim toward the border edge of the tree skirt and slip stitch in place. The green trim will lay flat and provide a narrow contrasting trim. See **Diagram 7.**

QUILTING

Step 1. Mark the tree skirt for quilting and cut a 44-inch square of backing fabric and batting.

Step 2. Layer the backing, batting, and tree skirt. Baste these layers together and quilt by hand or machine.

Step 3. After quilting, machine or hand baste a scant ¼ inch in from the edge of the tree skirt. This will ensure that all the layers remain securely aligned while sewing on the binding.

Step 4. Trim away the excess backing and batting. Cut the backing and batting along the open edge of the tree skirt and trim them away around the center.

BINDING

Step 1. For the side edges, fold the two 2¼ × 18-inch plaid bias binding strips in half lengthwise, with wrong sides together. Press. Then, with raw edges even, stitch one length of binding to the top side of each edge of the tree skirt using a ¼-inch seam. Fold the binding to the back and slip stitch the folded edge in place.

Step 2. For the lower edge, fold the 2¼ × 135-inch plaid bias strip in half lengthwise, with wrong sides together and press. With raw edges even, stitch the binding to the lower edge of the tree skirt with a ¼-inch seam, pivoting at the scallops. Fold the binding to the back and slip stitch the folded edge in place. See "Attaching Binding to Scalloped Edges" on page 194.

Step 3. For the center binding, fold the 3 × 56-inch plaid bias strip in half lengthwise, with wrong sides together and press. Mark the

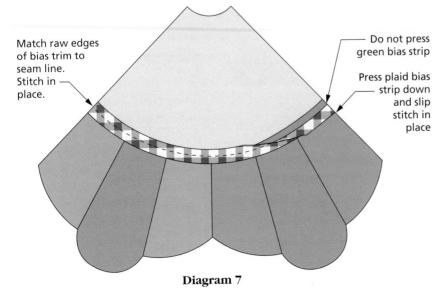

Match raw edges of bias trim to seam line. Stitch in place.

Do not press green bias strip

Press plaid bias strip down and slip stitch in place

Diagram 7

midpoint of the binding and the tree skirt center. Pin the binding to the tree skirt center, with raw edges even and midpoints matching, as shown in **Diagram 8.**

Step 4. Using a ⅜-inch seam allowance, stitch the binding to the skirt center leaving the excess binding free for ties. Bring the folded edge of the binding to the back of the tree skirt and slip stitch to the backing. Fold the raw ends of the ties under ½-inch and slip stitch the folded edges together along the length of the ties.

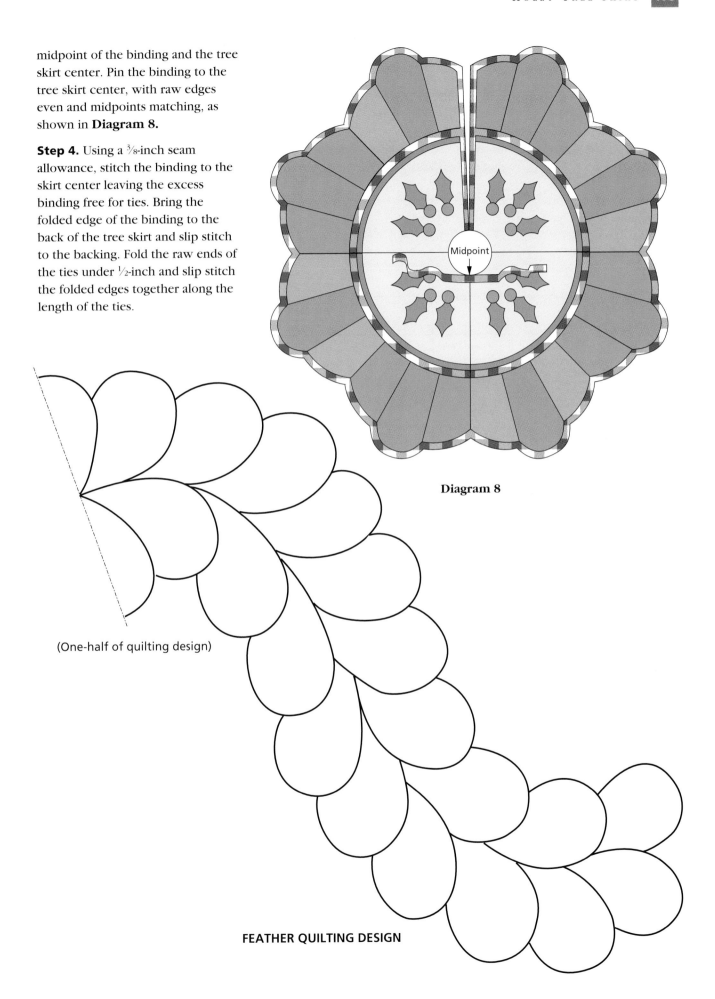

Diagram 8

(One-half of quilting design)

FEATHER QUILTING DESIGN

Attaching Binding to Scalloped Edges

Always use bias binding for a nice, smooth binding around curves. Pin the raw edge of the bias binding to the edge of the tree skirt. Do not pin the entire binding on, but just a few inches ahead as you stitch the binding on. As you stitch, gently ease a little extra binding onto the outer curved edge. This will prevent the scalloped edges from "cupping" when finished. This happens when you stretch the binding when you are first stitching it on.

At the inside point of the scallops, raise your presser foot and pivot, changing direction of the presser foot slightly. Lower the presser foot and continue stitching. With the tip of a pin or needle, push the edge of the binding strip, making sure it continues to meet the edge of the tree skirt. When you are finished stitching, turn the binding to the back and hand stitch the folded edge in place. This is a gentle scallop and should be fairly easy to bind if you follow these suggestions.

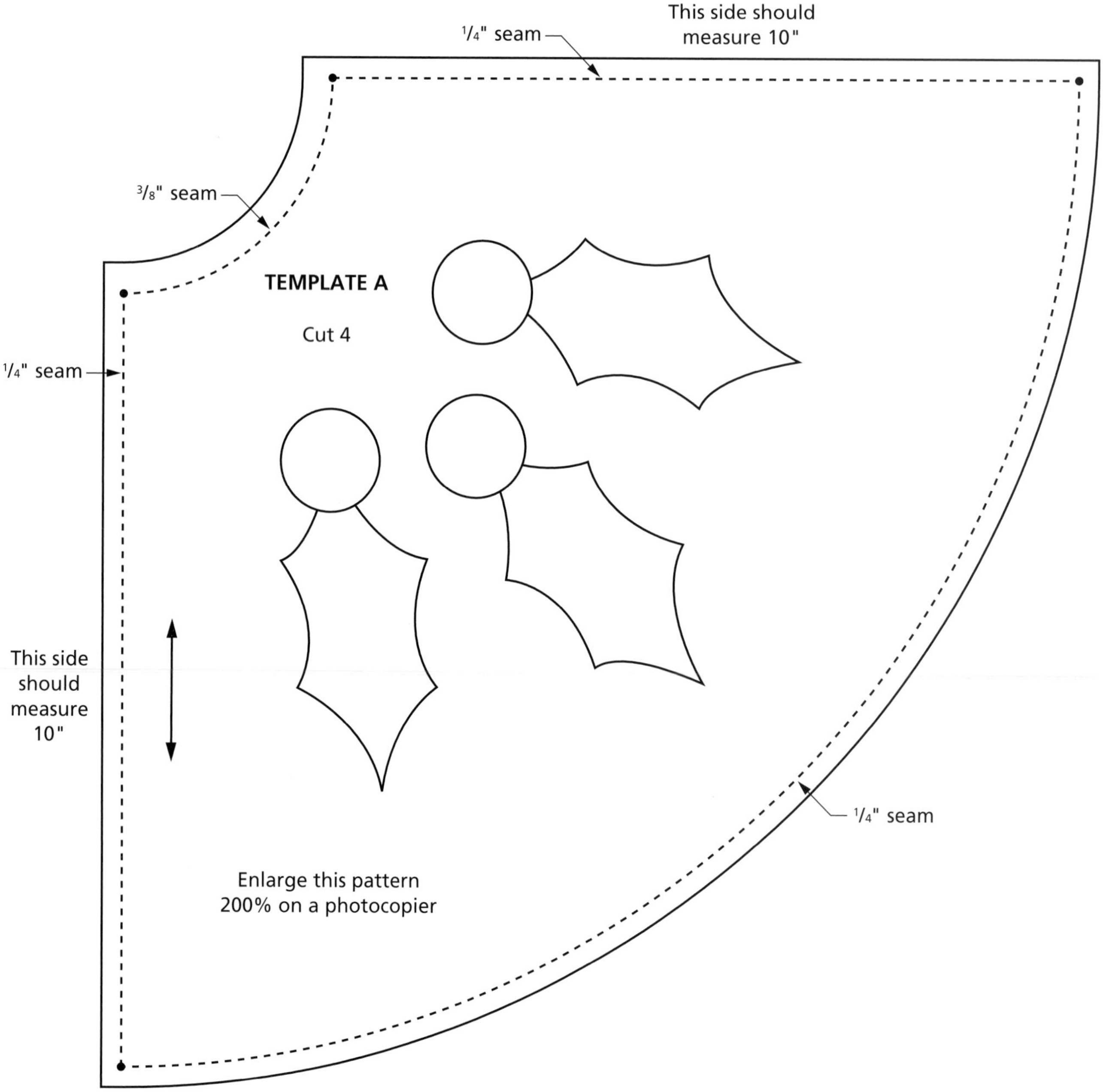

This side should measure 10"
1/4" seam
3/8" seam
TEMPLATE A
Cut 4
1/4" seam
This side should measure 10"
1/4" seam
Enlarge this pattern 200% on a photocopier

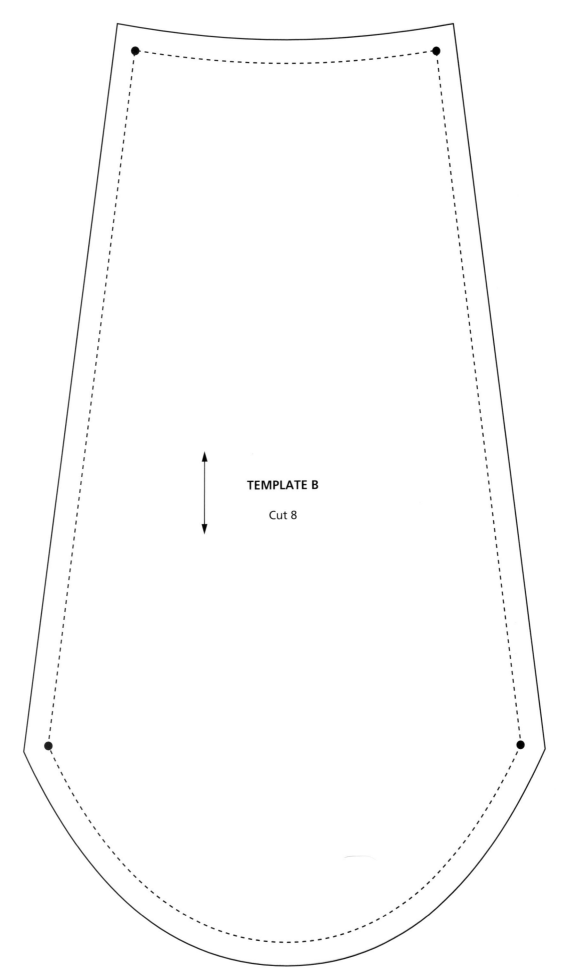

TEMPLATE B

Cut 8

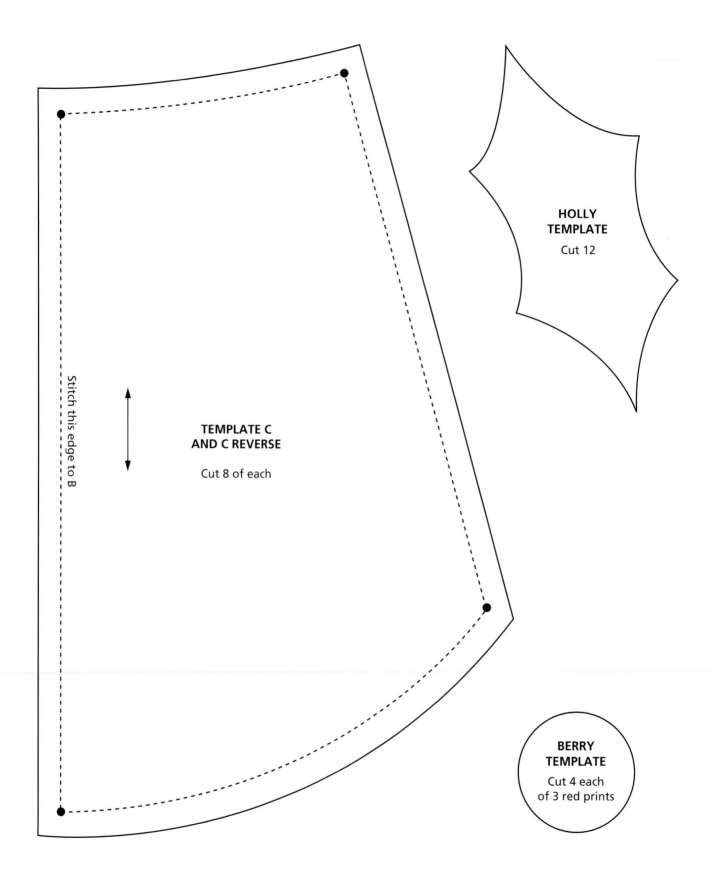

HOLLY
TEMPLATE
Cut 12

Stitch this edge to B

TEMPLATE C
AND C REVERSE

Cut 8 of each

BERRY
TEMPLATE
Cut 4 each
of 3 red prints

WELCOME CHRISTMAS!

When friends and family walk through your front door at Christmastime, welcome them with a warm fire, a cup of hot chocolate, and a soft and cozy quilt to curl up in. Although the quilts in this section have a touch of Christmas in their colors or design, they could be made for year-round enjoyment as well.

HOLLY RIBBONS

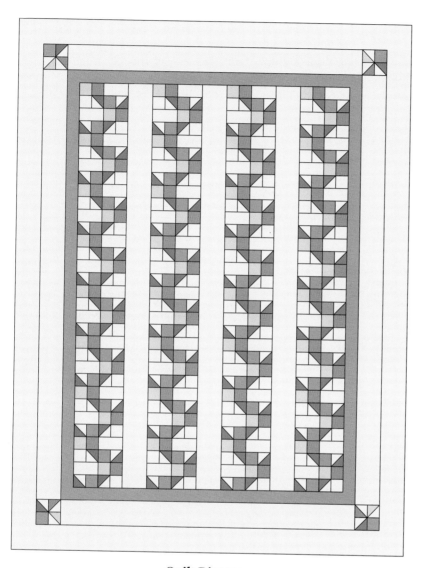

Quilt Diagram

SIZE

Lap quilt: 64 × 84 inches
(unquilted)

Finished block: 8 inches square

FABRICS AND SUPPLIES

Yardage is based on 44-inch-wide fabric.

1¼ yards *total* of a variety of green fabrics for leaves

1⅔ yards of red fabric for berries, inner border, and binding

3¾ yards of cream fabric for background, lattice strips, and outer borders

5 yards of fabric for quilt backing

Quilt batting, at least 68 × 88 inches

Rotary cutter, mat, and see-through ruler

This easy-to-make Christmas lap quilt is a wonderful addition to your holiday heirlooms. A variety of green prints gives the holly leaves depth and interest against the warm cream background. The holly design is created by combining blocks of simple squares and triangles. I think Holly Ribbons is a great companion quilt to display layered on a bed with other quilts or used on a table with your holiday linens. It goes well with other more complicated designs and looks right at home with plaid and print upholstery fabrics. I think it adds a classy, understated touch to holiday decorating.

FABRIC KEY

GREEN PRINT

RED

CREAM

- Read instructions thoroughly before you begin.
- Prewash and press fabric.
- Use ¼-inch seam allowances throughout unless directions specify otherwise.
- Seam allowances are included in the cutting sizes given.
- Press seam allowances in the direction that will create the least bulk and, whenever possible, toward the darker fabric.
- Cutting directions are given for each section of the quilt in the areas following the row of scissors. If you like to cut as you go, simply follow the directions as you get to them. If you'd rather cut all your pieces at once, skip ahead and look for the scissors to do all the cutting before you begin to sew.
- Instructions are given for quick cutting and piecing the blocks and borders. Note that for some of the pieces, the quick-cutting method will result in leftover fabric.

HOLLY BLOCKS AND CORNER BLOCKS

Cutting for Holly Blocks

From the green fabric:
- Cut five 2⅞ × 44-inch strips
- Cut eight 2½ × 44-inch strips. From these strips, cut one hundred twenty-eight 2½-inch squares.

From the red fabric:
- Cut four 2½ × 44-inch strips. From these strips, cut sixty-eight 2½-inch squares (four of these squares will be used for the corner blocks).

From the cream fabric:
- Cut five 2⅞ × 44-inch strips
- Cut eleven 2½ × 44-inch strips. From these strips, cut sixty-four 2½-inch squares and sixty-four 2½ × 4½-inch pieces.

Making the Triangle-Pieced Squares

Step 1. To make the triangle-pieced squares, layer the green and cream 2⅞ × 44-inch strips, with right sides together. Press together and cut these layered strips into 2⅞-inch squares. Repeat with remaining 2⅞-inch strips until you have cut 70 pairs of 2⅞-inch squares.

Step 2. Cut these layered squares in half diagonally, as shown in **Diagram 1.** Stitch the green and cream triangles together ¼ inch from the diagonal edge. Press seams toward the green fabric to make 140 triangle-pieced squares. Set aside 12 of these triangle-pieced squares for the corner blocks.

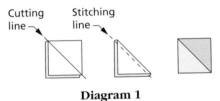

Diagram 1

Piecing the Holly Blocks
(Make 32)

Step 1. Refer to **Diagram 2** for piecing the blocks. All the blocks are pieced in this order.

Step 2. Sew the block pieces together in horizontal rows beginning with row 1. Press the seam allowances in the opposite direction from row to row. This allows the seams to nestle together and create less bulk when the rows are joined.

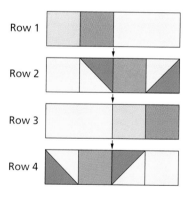

Diagram 2

Step 3. Join the horizontal rows, pinning at the seams, referring to **Diagram 3.** The blocks should measure 8½ inches square at this point. See **Diagram 4.**

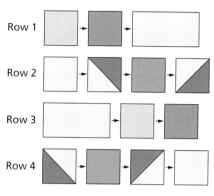

Diagram 3

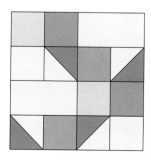

Make 32
Diagram 4

Piecing the Corner Blocks
(Make 4)

Step 1. Using the red squares and the twelve triangle-pieced squares made earlier, assemble the horizontal rows for the corner blocks, as shown in **Diagram 5.** Remember to press the seams for each row in the opposite direction of the other one.

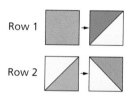

Diagram 5

Step 2. Join the horizontal rows, pinning at the seams, referring to **Diagram 6.** The corner blocks should measure 4½ inches square at this time. See **Diagram 7.**

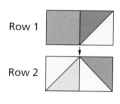

Diagram 6

Make 4
Diagram 7

QUILT CENTER

Cutting for Vertical Lattice

From the cream fabric:
• Cut five 4½ × 44-inch strips

Step 1. Sew four vertical rows of eight Holly blocks each, referring to **Diagram 8.**

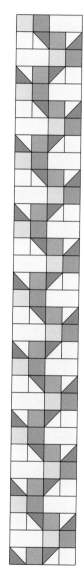

Diagram 8

Step 2. Make sure the four vertical holly rows are the same length. Adjust seam allowances if needed. Piece the 4½ × 44-inch cream lattice strips with diagonal seams. Cut to make three lattice strips that are the same length as the vertical holly rows.

Step 3. Sew the holly rows and the lattice strips together to make the quilt center, as shown in **Diagram 9.** Press seams toward the lattice strips.

BORDERS

Cutting for Borders

From the red fabric:
• Cut six to seven $2\frac{1}{2} \times 44$-inch strips for the inner border

From the cream fabric:
• Cut six to seven $4\frac{1}{2} \times 44$-inch strips for the middle border
• Cut seven $4\frac{1}{2} \times 44$-inch strips for the outer border

Inner Border

Step 1. Measure the quilt from left to right through the middle to determine the length of the top and bottom borders. Piece the red inner border strips with diagonal seams and cut to the necessary lengths.

Step 2. Sew the red inner border strips to the top and bottom of the quilt.

Step 3. Measure the quilt from top to bottom through the middle, including the borders you just added, to determine the length of the side borders. Piece the red inner border strips with diagonal seams and cut to the necessary lengths. This will also be the measurement for the side middle borders.

Step 4. Sew the red inner border strips to the sides of the quilt.

Middle Border

Step 1. Measure the quilt from left to right through the middle to determine the length of the top and bottom borders.

Step 2. Piece the $4\frac{1}{2} \times 44$-inch cream strips with diagonal seams and cut to the necessary length for the top and bottom of the quilt. Sew the border strips to the top and bottom of the quilt.

Step 3. Piece the $4\frac{1}{2} \times 44$-inch cream strips with diagonal seams and cut two border strips the length of the measurement taken in Step 3 under "Inner Border."

Step 4. Add the corner blocks to each end of the side middle border strips, as shown in **Diagram 10.** Make sure the holly berries are positioned correctly. Sew the

pieced middle border strips to the sides of the quilt.

Outer Border

Step 1. Measure the quilt from left to right as you did for the inner border. Piece the cream outer border strips diagonally and cut to the necessary length.

Step 2. Sew the cream outer border strips to the top and bottom of the quilt.

Step 3. Measure the quilt from top to bottom as before. Piece the cream outer border strips diagonally and cut to the necessary length. Sew

Diagram 9

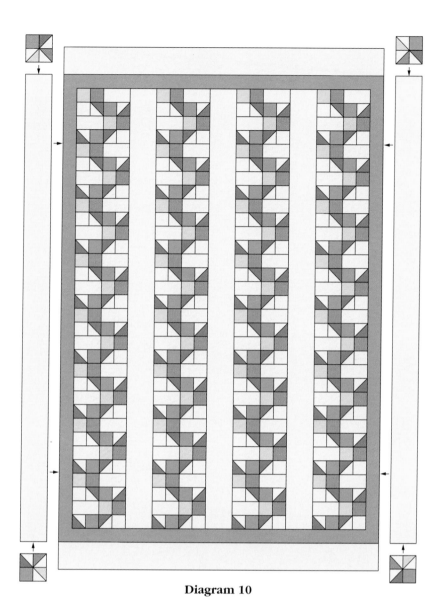

Diagram 10

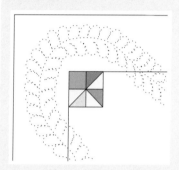

QUILTING IDEAS

◢ On my quilt, shown in the photograph, a feather design was machine quilted in the lattice strips and borders. Machine stippling was done in all of the background areas.

◢ To hand quilt, you could quilt in the ditch around the holly pieces to make them puff out a little. A feather or chain design could be quilted in the lattice strips and borders.

◢ Use cross-hatching at $1\frac{1}{4}$-inch intervals to fill in the background.

the outer border strips to the sides of the quilt.

QUILTING

Step 1. Prepare the backing for the quilt by cutting the 5-yard length of backing fabric in half crosswise to make two $2\frac{1}{2}$-yard lengths. Remove the selvages.

Step 2. Sew the two lengths together with one center seam. Press seam allowance open. Trim backing and batting so they are 4 inches larger than the quilt top.

Step 3. Mark the quilt top for quilting.

Step 4. Layer the backing, batting, and quilt top. Baste these layers together and quilt.

BINDING

The 3-inch binding strips will produce a $\frac{3}{8}$- to $\frac{1}{2}$-inch-wide binding. If you want a wider or narrower binding, adjust the width of the strips you cut. (See page 247 for pointers on how to experiment with binding width.) Refer to "Making and Attaching the Binding" on page 245 to complete your quilt.

Cutting for Cross-Grain Binding

From the red fabric:
• Cut eight 3 × 44-inch strips

Quilt Diagram

SIZE

Lap quilt: 66 × 80 inches (unquilted)

Finished Nine Patch block with border: 10 inches square

FABRICS AND SUPPLIES

Yardage is based on 44-inch-wide fabric.

4 yards of green plaid flannel for block borders, lattice posts, outer border, and bias binding

1¼ yards of black fine pinwale corduroy for blocks and narrow border

1¾ yards of red fabric for blocks, lattice pieces, and corner blocks

½ yard of tan fabric for blocks and lattice posts

4½ yards of flannel for quilt backing

Quilt batting, at least 70 × 84 inches

Rotary cutter, mat, and see-through ruler

Template plastic or manila folder

3 skeins of #5 gold pearl cotton for reindeer, stars, and outline quilting

3 skeins of #5 black pearl cotton for tying blocks and quilting

2 skeins of #5 green pearl cotton for pine sprigs

Note: You can substitute regular cotton fabrics for the flannel and corduroy if desired.

Each skein is approximately 27 yards long. Embroidery floss or other comparable thread could be used.

Τhis is my family's all-time favorite quilt. It just begs to be cuddled with its mix of flannel, fine pinwale corduroy, and soft cotton calicoes. You can just imagine reading Christmas stories under this quilt, snuggled up next to the fire in your favorite chair. Its rustic folk-art charm is played up by quilted reindeer prancing among stars around the borders and quilted pine sprigs decorating the lattices and corner squares. Besides being wonderfully inviting, this quilt is easy to piece and goes together quickly. For a fun project, get everyone in the family to put in a few of the chunky quilting stitches. What happy memories can be created in those stitches!

FABRIC KEY

 GREEN PLAID

 BLACK

 RED

 TAN

HINTS & HELPS

This quilt is casual and comfortable, so don't worry about nap on the corduroy when cutting and piecing. When buying the flannel, be generous in the yardage. It may shrink more when prewashed than regular cottons. Don't feel you must use these fabrics, however. I have seen many wonderful Fireside Cozy quilts made from homespun and other fabrics.

GETTING READY

- Read instructions thoroughly before you begin.
- Prewash and press fabric.
- Use ¼-inch seam allowances throughout unless directions specify otherwise.
- Seam allowances are included in the cutting sizes given.
- Press seam allowance in the direction that will create the least bulk and, whenever possible, toward the darker fabric.
- Trace the **Star, Pine Sprig,** and **Reindeer Quilting Designs** (pages 210–211) onto template plastic and cut out. Or use manila folders, like I did, to make the templates. The deer and star shapes were cut out and traced around. The pine sprigs were carefully cut out and a pencil line was drawn onto the fabric through the cutout slits.
- Cutting directions for each section of the quilt are given in the areas following the row of scissors. If you like to cut as you go, simply follow the directions as you get to them. If you'd rather cut all your pieces at once, skip ahead and look for the scissors to do all the cutting before you begin to sew.
- Instructions are given for quick cutting and piecing the blocks and borders. Note that for some of the pieces, the quick-cutting method will result in leftover fabric.

NINE PATCH BLOCKS
(Make 12)

Each block consists of a Nine Patch center with borders and corner posts. The Nine Patch square is made from two different strip sets. To minimize cutting and piecing, the fabrics are first cut into strips. These strips are then sewn together and cut into segments for the block assembly.

Cutting for Nine Patch Blocks

From the green fabric:
- Cut eight 2½ × 44-inch strips. From these strips, cut forty-eight 2½ × 6½-inch pieces.

From the black fabric:
- Cut seven 2½ × 44-inch strips. From three of these strips, cut forty-eight 2½-inch squares.

From the red fabric:
- Cut four 2½ × 44-inch strips

From the tan fabric:
- Cut one 2½ × 44-inch strip

Piecing the Nine Patch Blocks

Step 1. For Strip Set 1, sew a black strip to each side of a tan strip, as shown in **Diagram 1**. Press seam allowances toward the black fabric.

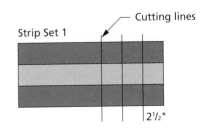

Diagram 1

Step 2. For Strip Set 2, sew a red strip to each side of a black strip, as shown in **Diagram 2**. Press seam allowances toward the black fabric. Make two of Strip Set 2.

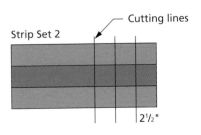

Diagram 2

Step 3. With the right side of the fabric facing up, lay Strip Set 1 on the cutting mat. Using your ruler and rotary cutter, cut the strip set into 2½-inch segments, as indicated by the cutting lines in **Diagram 1.**

Step 4. After a few cuts you may need to straighten the cut edge of the strip set again with the ruler and mat. Cut twelve 2½-inch segments from Strip Set 1.

Step 5. Cut twenty-four 2½-inch segments from Strip Set 2, as explained in Step 3, referring to the cutting lines in **Diagram 2.**

Step 6. Sew a Strip Set 2 segment to the top and bottom of a Strip Set 1 segment to make a Nine Patch square. See **Diagram 3.** Press seam allowance toward the center row. Repeat to make 12 Nine Patch squares.

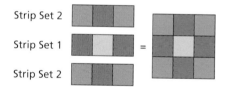

Strip Set 2

Strip Set 1

Strip Set 2

Diagram 3

Step 7. Sew a 2½ × 6½-inch green block border piece to the top and bottom of each Nine Patch square, as shown in **Diagram 4.** Press seams toward the borders.

Diagram 4

Step 8. Sew a 2½-inch black square to each end of a 2½ × 6½-inch green piece, as shown in **Diagram**

5, to make a block border unit. Make 24 of these block border units. Press seam allowances toward the green fabric.

Diagram 5

Step 9. Sew a block border unit to the left and right sides of each Nine Patch square. See **Diagram 6.** Press seam allowances toward the borders. Repeat to make 12 completed Nine Patch blocks.

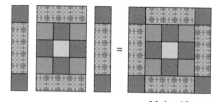

Make 12

Diagram 6

QUILT CENTER

Cutting for Lattice and Lattice Posts

From the green fabric:
• Cut two 3⅜ × 44-inch strips. From these strips, cut twenty 3⅜-inch squares.

From the red fabric:
• Cut eight 4½ × 44-inch strips. From these strips, cut thirty-one 4½ × 10½-inch pieces.

From the tan fabric:
• Cut three 2⅞ × 44-inch strips. From these strips, cut forty 2⅞-inch squares. Cut these squares in half diagonally to form 80 post triangles.

Constructing the Lattice Posts

Step 1. Sew a tan triangle to two opposite sides of a green square, as shown on the left in **Diagram 7.** Press seam allowances toward the triangles.

Diagram 7

Step 2. Sew tan triangles to the remaining two sides of the green square, as shown in the middle in **Diagram 7.** Press seam allowances toward the triangles.

Step 3. Repeat Steps 1 and 2 to make 20 lattice posts.

Attaching the Lattice

Step 1. Assemble the lattice strips. Each strip is made up of three lattice pieces and four lattice posts, as shown in **Diagram 8.**

Step 2. Assemble the rows of Nine Patch blocks. Each row has three Nine Patch blocks and four lattice pieces, as shown in **Diagram 9.**

Make 5

Diagram 8

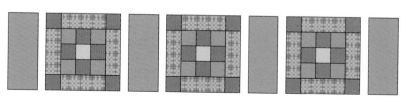

Diagram 9

Step 3. Referring to **Diagram 10**, lay out the lattice strips and rows of Nine Patch blocks, beginning and ending with a lattice strip. Pin at the block intersections so that the lattice strips and rows of Nine Patch blocks stay aligned. Stitch the lattice and block rows together to form the quilt center.

BORDERS

The yardage given allows for the border pieces to be cut cross-grain.

Cutting for Borders

From the green fabric:
• Cut seven $8\frac{1}{2} \times 44$-inch strips for the outer border

From the black fabric:
• Cut seven $2\frac{1}{2} \times 44$-inch strips for the inner border

From the red fabric:
• Cut one $8\frac{1}{2} \times 44$-inch strip. From this strip, cut four $8\frac{1}{2}$-inch squares for the corner blocks.

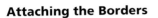

Attaching the Borders

Step 1. Measure the quilt from left to right through the middle to determine the length of the top and bottom borders. Piece three $2\frac{1}{2} \times 44$-inch strips of black fabric with diagonal seams and cut to the length needed for the quilt top and bottom.

Step 2. Sew the top and bottom black inner borders to the quilt.

Step 3. Measure the quilt from top to bottom through the middle, including borders you just added, to determine the length of the side borders. Piece four $2\frac{1}{2} \times 44$-inch strips of black fabric with diagonal seams and cut to the necessary lengths for the quilt sides.

Step 4. Sew the side black inner borders to the quilt.

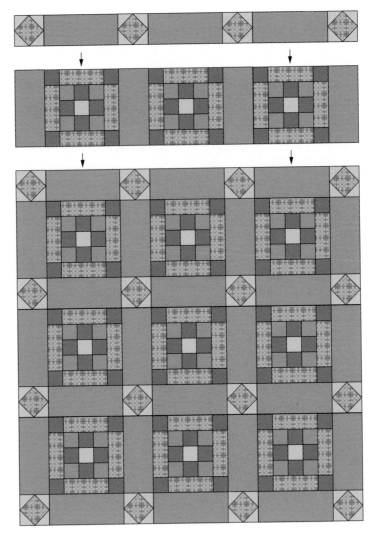

Diagram 10

Tying Your Quilt

❖ Use a crewel needle or a darning needle, which has a sharp point and a large eye for holding thicker threads.

❖ Thread your needle with a 30-inch strand of pearl cotton. You can experiment to see what length works best for you. Do not knot the end.

❖ Take a small stitch (about $\frac{1}{8}$ inch long) at the position where you want the tie. Be sure the stitch goes through all layers.

❖ Pull up the pearl cotton leaving a 3- to 4-inch tail. Leave the needle threaded and tie the ends securely in a square knot.

❖ Clip the thread ends to the length you desire.

Because pearl cotton has a sheen, sometimes the knots do not stay tied. I have found that a dab of Fray Check (made by Dritz) will secure the knot. It is a liquid that dries clear.

HINTS & HELPS

When quilting with pearl cotton, use a needle with a larger eye to accommodate the thicker thread. Knot the thread as you normally do and pull it through the top layer of fabric as you would with a knot made with regular quilting thread. You may need to separate the threads of the fabric a bit with the tip of your needle to allow the knot to pop through. Rock the needle up and down the same way you always do, but make large instead of small quilting stitches. Quilting with pearl cotton is fun and fast!

Step 5. Measure the quilt as you did in Step 1, including the borders you just added, to determine the length of the top and bottom outer borders. Piece the green outer border strips with diagonal seams and cut to the necessary length. Sew the green outer borders to the quilt top and bottom.

Step 6. Measure the quilt as you did in Step 3, not including the borders you just added. Add ½ inch to the measurement to include seam allowances for the corner blocks. Cut the pieced green outer border strips to the necessary length.

Step 7. Sew a large red corner block to the ends of each side outer border. Matching seam intersections, attach the side outer borders to the quilt.

QUILTING

Step 1. Prepare the backing for the quilt by cutting the 4½-yard length of backing fabric in half crosswise to make two 2¼-yard lengths. Remove the selvages.

Step 2. Sew the two lengths together with one center seam. Press seam allowance open.

Step 3. Trim the backing and batting so they are 4 inches larger than the quilt top.

Step 4. Mark your quilt top for quilting.

Step 5. Layer the backing, batting, and quilt top. Baste the layers together and quilt.

BINDING

The 2¾-inch bias binding strips will produce a ⅜-inch-wide binding. If you want a wider or narrower binding, adjust the width of the strips you cut. (See page 247 for pointers on how to experiment with the binding width.) See "Making and Attaching the Binding" on page 245 to complete your quilt.

Cutting for Bias Binding

From the green fabric:
• Cut enough 2¾-inch-wide bias strips to make a 350-inch strip

QUILTING IDEAS

▰ My Fireside Cozy features "chunky" quilting stitches that I made large on purpose to carry out the folk-art look of the quilt. I used pearl cotton instead of regular quilting thread to make the stitches more noticeable.

▰ The block intersections were tied with pearl cotton.

▰ Stitch an X in the Nine Patch blocks with black pearl cotton.

▰ Quilt a pine sprig with green pearl cotton in each lattice piece and in the four large corner blocks. Use the **Pine Sprig Quilting Design** template you cut out earlier.

▰ Gold pearl cotton was used to quilt the reindeer in the borders. Quilt three reindeer in the shorter borders and five in the longer borders, using your **Reindeer Quilting Design** template.

▰ Randomly quilt gold stars between the deer and in the center of each lattice post. Use your **Star Quilting Design** template.

▰ The borders and corner blocks were stitched in the ditch with gold pearl cotton.

STAR QUILTING DESIGN

PINE SPRIG QUILTING DESIGN

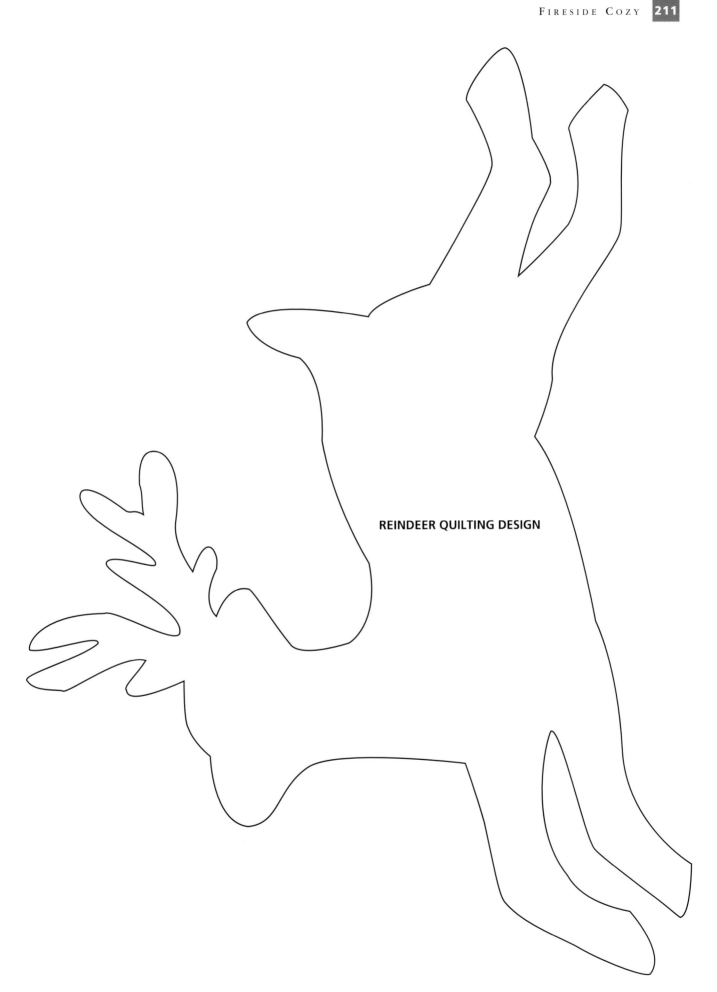

REINDEER QUILTING DESIGN

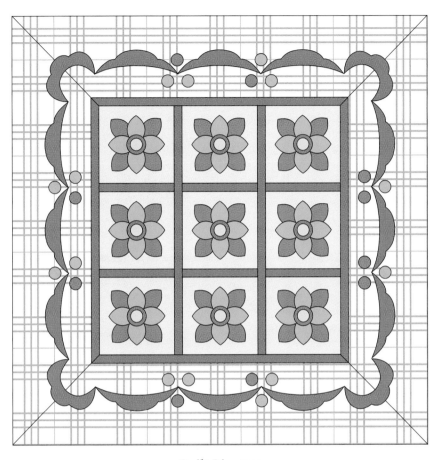

Quilt Diagram

WINTER POSIES WALL QUILT

SIZE

Wall quilt: 50 inches square (unquilted)

Finished block: 9½ inches square

FABRICS AND SUPPLIES

Yardage is based on 44-inch-wide fabric.

1 yard of beige fabric for background

1 yard of dark red fabric for flowers, berries, and binding

⅜ yard of medium red fabric for flowers and berries

⅛ yard of black fabric for flower centers

⅛ yard of gold fabric for small flower centers

1⅛ yards of green fabric for lattice, inner border, and swag

2¾ yards of plaid fabric for outer border and bias binding

3 yards of fabric for quilt backing

Quilt batting, at least 54 × 54 inches

Rotary cutter, mat, and see-through ruler

Template plastic

I love this design from my friend Marilyn Ginsburg. It has a strong graphic design that really shows off the fabrics. I just had to use one of my favorite red plaids for the border. I think it adds a warm, interesting background for the traditional holiday motifs of green swags with clusters of deep red berries.

The layered petals and flower centers add dimension and make the flowers look as if you could pick them right off the quilt. I use this as a holiday table covering but find that I display it throughout the year as well. Extra blocks make handsome coordinating pillows that are on my couch year-round.

FABRIC KEY

BEIGE

DARK RED

MEDIUM RED

GOLD

BLACK

PLAID

GREEN

- Read instructions thoroughly before you begin.
- Prewash and press fabric.
- Use ¼-inch seam allowances throughout unless directions specify otherwise.
- Seam allowances are included in the cutting sizes given.
- Press seam allowance in the direction that will create the least bulk and, whenever possible, toward the darker fabric.
- Trace **Templates A** through **F** (pages 218–219) onto template plastic and cut out.
- Cutting directions for each section of the quilt are given in the areas following the row of scissors. If you like to cut as you go, simply follow the direction as you get to them. If you'd rather cut all your pieces at once, skip ahead and look for the scissors to do all the cutting before you begin to sew.

FLOWER BLOCKS
(Make 9)

Cutting for Flower Blocks

From the beige fabric:
- Cut three 11 × 44-inch strips. From these strips cut nine 11-inch squares for the background. (These will be trimmed to 10 inches square after the appliqué is completed.)

From the dark red fabric:
- Cut 36 of **Template A**

From the medium red fabric:
- Cut 36 of **Template B**

From the black fabric:
- Cut nine of **Template C**

From the gold fabric:
- Cut nine of **Template D**

Step 1. Using one of the appliqué methods described on pages 238–240, prepare the appliqué pieces. The freezer paper appliqué method works well for these large, simple shapes, but you can use the method you prefer.

Step 2. Appliqué a small gold circle (piece D) to the center of each of the large black circles (piece C),

referring to **Diagram 1.** You will have completed nine flower centers. Set these aside.

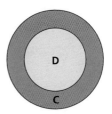

Diagram 1

Step 3. You are now ready to appliqué the flowers to the 11-inch beige squares. To aid in the centering of the design, finger crease the background block in half, in both directions and diagonally. The points of your flower petals should line up with these creased lines, as shown in **Diagram 2.**

Step 4. Refer to **Diagram 3** as a placement guide. Position and appliqué the A pieces first, then the B petals, and finally the flower centers. Check to be certain the black flower center covers the inner curved raw edges of the petals.

Step 5. Trim the blocks to 10 inches square.

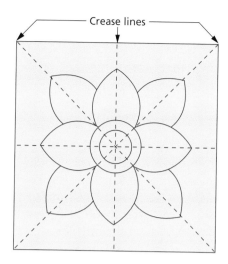

Diagram 2

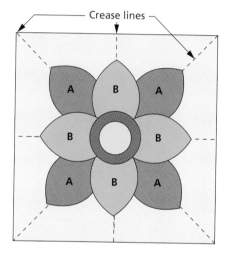

Diagram 3

QUILT TOP

Cutting for Lattice

From the green fabric:
• Cut four 1½ × 44-inch strips. From two of these strips, cut six 1½ × 10-inch strips.

Step 1. Lay out the Flower blocks in three vertical rows of three blocks each. Sew a 1½ × 10-inch lattice strip to the top and bottom of the middle block in each row. Sew the blocks together. See **Diagram 4.**

Step 2. Measure the lengths of these three rows; they must all be the same length. Adjust the seam

allowances if necessary. Sew the lattice strips to both sides of the middle row of blocks. Trim even with the blocks and press seams toward the lattice.

Step 3. Sew the three rows together, as shown in **Diagram 5.**

BORDERS

The quilt in the photo has mitered borders. The yardage given allows for these border pieces to be cut lengthwise. If you use a plaid fabric for borders, see "Matching Plaids in Mitered Borders" on page 216.

Cutting for Borders

From the green fabric:
• Cut four 1½ × 44-inch strips for the inner border

From the plaid fabric:
• Cut four 9½ × 58-inch strips for the outer border

Mitered Inner and Outer Borders

Step 1. Measure the quilt top through the middle. The quilt

should measure the same from side to side and top to bottom.

Step 2. Cut and piece the 1½-inch green inner border strips with diagonal seams to make four 58-inch strips.

Step 3. Find and mark the center of each inner and outer border strip. Fold the strip in half crosswise and press lightly to mark the halfway point. Match the centers of the green inner border strips with the plaid strips, and sew together in pairs. They will be treated as one unit.

Step 4. With a ruler and pencil, mark the ¼-inch sewing line along the edge of the green inner border strips.

Step 5. Starting at the halfway point, measure out in each direction to one-half of the desired finished border length and make a mark on the sewing line.

Step 6. Use a ruler with a 45 degree angle line to mark the miter sewing line. Draw a line from the end mark made in Step 4 to the outer edge of the border strip. Mark a cutting line ¼ inch to the outside of the sewing line, as shown in **Diagram 6.** Don't

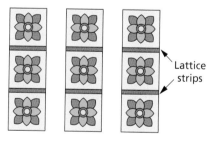

Diagram 4

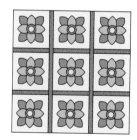

Diagram 5

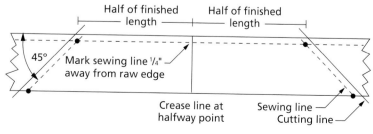

Diagram 6

Matching Plaids in Mitered Borders

This is always a bit tricky and works best if you use a woven plaid as opposed to a printed plaid fabric. A woven plaid is always on grain because the plaid design is actually formed by the horizontal and vertical threads. A printed plaid fabric may not be on grain and it is impossible to make it be so. You may be less successful in matching printed plaids. (It may be downright impossible!)

Cut *all* border strips so they have the same plaid pattern repeat. This usually means using scissors, not a rotary cutter, and actually following the plaid thread line. Depending on the plaid, you may have to waste a few inches between border strips to make sure they fall on the same pattern repeat.

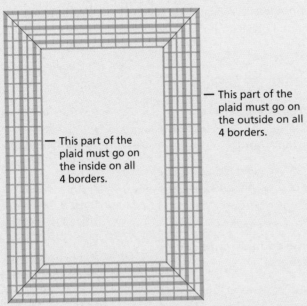

— This part of the plaid must go on the outside on all 4 borders.

— This part of the plaid must go on the inside on all 4 borders.

Next, you must remember to sew the border strips onto the quilt in the same fashion, paying attention to which part of the plaid should go next to the quilt and which should be on the outside edge. The more complicated the plaid, the more there is to watch.

If you follow these guidelines, the corners can't help but meet. See also "Tips for Plaid Borders" on page 241 for more information on plaid borders.

trim until after the border is sewn to the quilt top.

Step 7. Pin the marked border strip to the quilt top, matching the crease at the halfway point to the halfway point on the side of the quilt top. Position the end marks on the border strip ¼-inch in from the raw edges of the quilt top. Repeat for all remaining borders.

Step 8. Stitch the borders to the quilt top, starting and stopping exactly at the end marks ¼ inch from each end. Backstitch to secure the stitching. Press the seams away from the quilt top.

Step 9. To sew the miters, fold the quilt diagonally, right sides together, and align the marked miter lines on adjacent borders. Stitch from the

inner corner mark to the outer raw edge.

Step 10. Check the accuracy of your miter, then trim the seam.

BORDER APPLIQUÉS

Before you cut your fabric, use **Templates E** and **F** to check swag placement accuracy. The distance between the points of **Template E** should equal the distance between the centers of the lattice. See **Diagram 7.** The swag tips should be about 2¾ inches from the inner border.

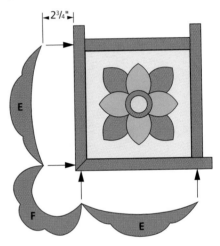

Diagram 7

Cutting for Appliqués

From the green fabric:
- Cut 12 of **Template E**
- Cut four of **Template F**

From the dark red fabric:
- Cut 12 of **Template D**

From the medium fabric:
- Cut 12 of **Template** D

Appliqué

Step 1. Using one of the appliqué methods described on pages 238–240, prepare the swag and berry appliqué pieces. The freezer paper appliqué method works well for these large, simple shapes.

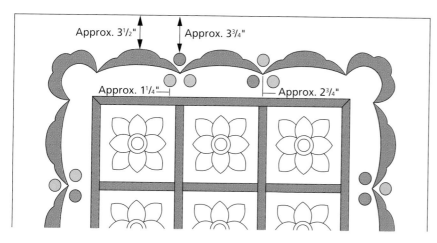

Approx. 3½"

Approx. 3¾"

Approx. 1¼"

Approx. 2¾"

Diagram 8

Step 2. Baste or pin the swag appliqué pieces in place on the border, following **Diagram 8** for placement. Appliqué the E and F pieces in place.

Step 3. Pin the berries in place on the border, referring to **Diagram 8** for placement. Appliqué in place.

QUILTING IDEAS

☑ In-the-ditch quilting was done around the flower petals, flower centers, lattice, swag, and berry appliqués.

☑ Detail quilting was done in the flower petals, as shown below.

☑ Cross-hatching fills in the outer border. Refer to "Cross-Hatching Tips" on page 243.

QUILTING

Step 1. Prepare the backing for the quilt by cutting the 3-yard length of backing fabric in half crosswise to make two 1½-yard lengths. Remove the selvages and sew the two lengths together with one center seam. Press seam allowance open.

Step 2. Trim backing and batting so they are about 4 inches larger than the quilt top.

Step 3. Mark the top for quilting.

Step 4. Layer the backing, batting, and quilt top. Baste these layers together and quilt.

BINDING

The 2¾-inch bias strips will produce a ⅜- to ½-inch-wide binding. If you want a wider or narrower binding adjust the width of the strips you cut. (See page 247 for pointers on how to experiment with binding width). Refer to "Making and Attaching the Binding" on page 245 to complete your quilt.

Cutting for Cross-Grain Binding

From the dark red fabric:
• Cut six 2¾ × 44-inch strips

WINTER POSIES PILLOW

SIZE

Pillow (without ruffle): 16 inches square (unquilted)

FABRICS AND SUPPLIES FOR ONE PILLOW

Yardage is based on 44-inch-wide fabric.

½ yard of beige fabric for background or one 12-inch square piece

⅛ yard of dark red fabric for flower

⅛ yard of medium red for flower

⅝ yard of black fabric for flower center and outer ruffle

2½-inch square of gold fabric for flower center

¼ yard of green fabric for border

⅞ yard of plaid fabric for inner ruffle and pillow back

16 × 16-inch pillow form (the 100 percent polyester Pop-in-Pillow by Fairfield Processing Corporation is my favorite)

Rotary cutter, mat, and see-through ruler

Template plastic

MAKING THE PILLOW

Before beginning the pillow, be sure to read "Getting Ready" for the Wall Quilt on page 214.

Cutting for the Pillow

From the beige fabric:
• Cut one 12-inch square for the background. (This block will be trimmed to 11 inches square after the appliqué is completed.)

From the dark red fabric:
• Cut four of **Template A**

From the medium red fabric:
• Cut four of **Template B**

From the black fabric:
• Cut one of **Template C**

• Cut four 3¾ × 44-inch strips for the outer ruffle

From the gold fabric:
• Cut one of **Template D**

From the green fabric:
• Cut two 3¼ × 44-inch strips. From these strips, cut two 3¼ × 11-inch strips and two 3¼ × 16½-inch strips.

From the plaid fabric:
• Cut four 2½ × 44-inch strips for inner ruffle
• Cut two 17 × 19-inch pieces for backing

PILLOW TOP

Step 1. Follow Steps 1 through 4 under "Flower Blocks" for the Wall Quilt on page 214. You will be working with a 12-inch background piece; make one block for each pillow. After the appliqué is completed, trim the block to 11 inches square.

Step 2. To add the borders, sew the 3¼ × 11-inch green strips to the top and bottom of the pillow square. Add the 3¼ × 16½-inch green strips to the sides of the pillow square.

PILLOW RUFFLE

Step 1. Piece the 2½ × 44-inch plaid strips together with diagonal seams. Piece the 3¾ × 44-inch black strips together with diagonal seams. Sew these strips together along the long edges, with right sides together, as shown in **Diagrams 9** and **10.**

Step 2. With right sides facing, sew the short raw edges together with diagonal seams to make a continuous ruffle strip. See **Diagram 10.** Trim the seam allowance to ¼ inch.

Step 3. Fold the strip in half lengthwise with wrong sides together. See **Diagram 11.** Run a gathering stitch ¼ inch from the raw edges.

Step 4. Pull up the gathering stitches so that the ruffle fits the

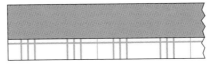

Diagram 9

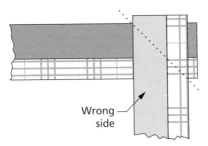

Wrong side

Diagram 10

Fold

Diagram 11

pillow square. Pin and sew a scant ¼ inch from the raw edges.

PILLOW BACK

Step 1. Fold the two plaid backing pieces in half with wrong sides together, to form two 9½ × 17-inch double-thickness back pieces. Overlap the two folded edges by 2 inches. See **Diagram 12.** Stitch across the folds, ¼ inch from the edge, to secure. The double-thickness pieces make the pillow back more stable and give it a nice finishing touch.

Step 2. Layer the back with the pillow top facing right side down. (The ruffle will be turned toward the center of the pillow at this time.) Pin the front to the back. Stitch together around all the outside edges using a ⅜-inch seam allowance.

Step 3. Trim the corner seam allowances if needed. Turn the pillow right side out and fluff up the ruffle. Insert the pillow form through the back opening.

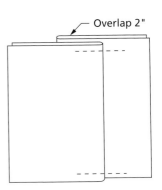

Overlap 2"

Diagram 12

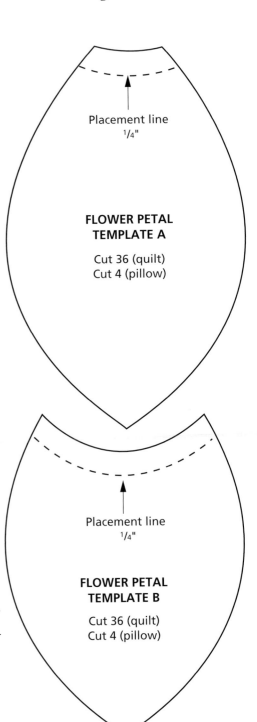

Placement line
¼"

**FLOWER PETAL
TEMPLATE A**

Cut 36 (quilt)
Cut 4 (pillow)

Placement line
¼"

**FLOWER PETAL
TEMPLATE B**

Cut 36 (quilt)
Cut 4 (pillow)

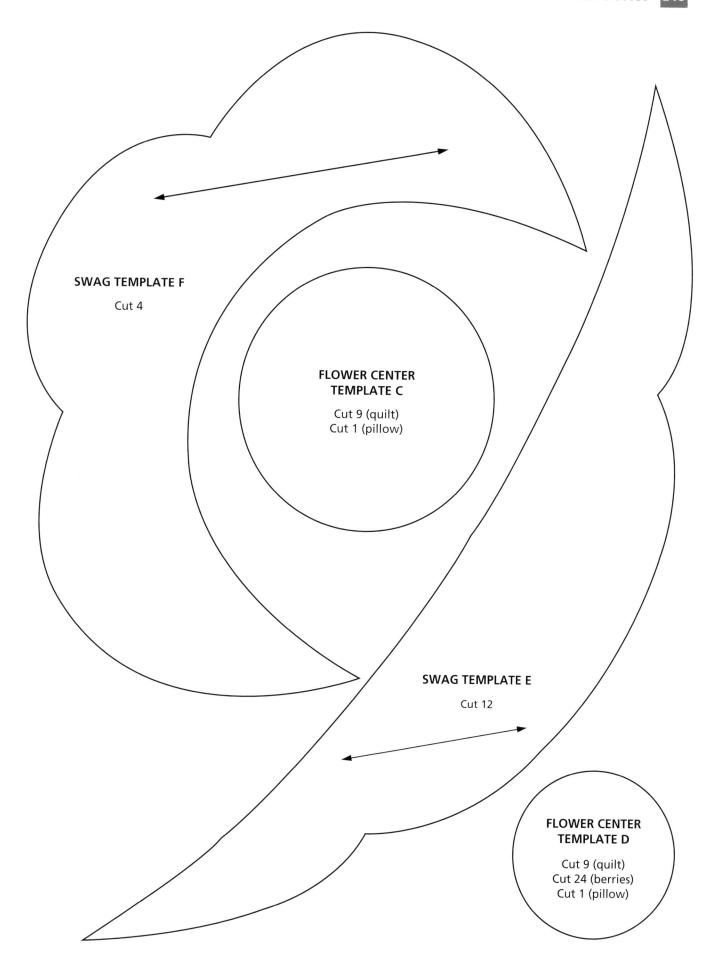

SWAG TEMPLATE F

Cut 4

**FLOWER CENTER
TEMPLATE C**

Cut 9 (quilt)
Cut 1 (pillow)

SWAG TEMPLATE E

Cut 12

**FLOWER CENTER
TEMPLATE D**

Cut 9 (quilt)
Cut 24 (berries)
Cut 1 (pillow)

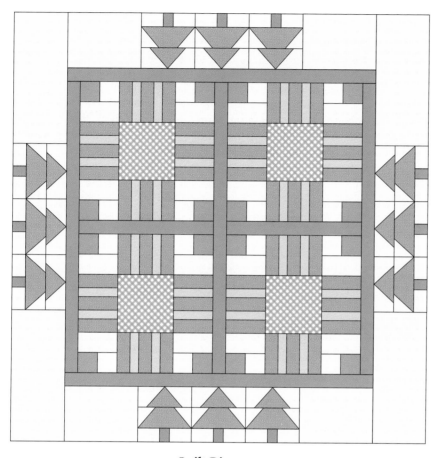

Quilt Diagram

SIZE

Wall quilt: 46½ inches square (unquilted)

Finished block: 14½ inches square

FABRICS AND SUPPLIES

Yardage is based on 44-inch-wide fabric.

1⅜ yards of cream fabric for blocks and outer border

⅛ yard of red solid fabric for small corner squares

1¼ yards of green fabric for blocks, trees, and binding

¼ yard of gold fabric for blocks

¼ yard of red print fabric for large center blocks

½ yard of brown fabric for lattice, trunks, and inner border

3 yards of fabric for quilt backing

Quilt batting, at least 51 × 51 inches

Rotary cutter, mat, and see-through ruler

Template plastic

I love the simple geometric design of antique game boards, and they were my inspiration for this wall quilt. A trio of trees in each border lends a holiday feel, but the use of rich colors contrasted with a creamy background print certainly encourages year-round display. For the Christmas season, use it as a table covering with an arrangement of pine boughs and pine cones in a wooden bowl for an easy holiday centerpiece. Set aside a weekend, and you'll be able to stitch up this simple yet appealing accessory for the holidays or anytime!

FABRIC KEY

CREAM

RED SOLID

GREEN

GOLD

RED PRINT

BROWN

- Read instructions thoroughly before you begin.
- Prewash and press fabric.
- Use ¼-inch seam allowances throughout unless directions specify otherwise.
- Seam allowances are included in the cutting sizes given.
- Press seam allowance in the direction that will create the least bulk and, whenever possible, toward the darker fabric.
- Trace **Templates A** through **D** (page 225) onto template plastic and cut out.
- Cutting directions for each section of the quilt are given in the areas following the row of scissors. If you like to cut as you go, simply follow the directions as you get to them. If you'd rather cut all your pieces at once, skip ahead and look for the scissors to do all the cutting before you begin to sew.
- Instructions are given for quick cutting and piecing the blocks and borders. Note that for some of the pieces, the quick-cutting method will result in leftover fabric.

SMALL CORNER BLOCKS
(Make 16)

Make 8   Make 8

Diagram 1

Cutting for Small Corner Blocks

From the cream fabric:
- Cut one 4½ × 44-inch strip. From this strip, cut sixteen 2½ × 4½-inch pieces.
- Cut one 2½ × 44-inch strip

From the red solid fabric:
- Cut one 2½ × 44-inch strip

Piecing the Small Corner Blocks

Step 1. Sew the 2½ × 44-inch cream strip and the 2½ × 44-inch red strip together along a long edge. Press seam allowance toward the red fabric. Cross-cut this strip into 2½-inch segments to make 16 units.

Step 2. With the red squares on top, sew a 2½ × 4½-inch cream rectangle to the side of each of these units. Notice the placement changes for the cream piece, as shown in **Diagram 1**: eight units have rectangles on the left and eight, on the right.

STRIP-PIECED BLOCKS
(Make 16)

Cutting for Strip-Pieced Blocks

From the green fabric:
- Cut six 2 × 44-inch strips

From the gold fabric:
- Cut four 1½ × 44-inch strips

Piecing the Strip Sets

Step 1. To construct the strip set, sew three green 2 × 44-inch strips and two gold 1½ × 44-inch strips together, alternating colors, as shown in **Diagram 2**. Sew remaining strip sets in this manner.

4½"

Diagram 2

Step 2. Press seam allowances toward the green strips.

Step 3. Cut the strip sets into sixteen 4½-inch units, as shown in **Diagram 2.**

ASSEMBLING THE GAME BOARD BLOCKS
(Make 4)

Cutting for Center Blocks

From the red print fabric:
• Cut one 7 × 44-inch strip. From this strip, cut four 7-inch squares.

Piecing the Blocks

Step 1. Sew a 4½-inch strip-pieced block to either side of a 7-inch red print center square, as shown in **Diagram 3.** Repeat to make four units.

Step 2. Sew a corner block to either side of a 4½-inch strip-pieced

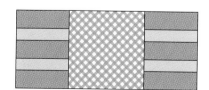

Diagram 3

Diagram 4

block, as shown in **Diagram 4.** Repeat to make eight units.

Step 3. Sew a unit from Step 2 to the top and bottom of each unit from Step 1, as shown in **Diagram 5.** Make sure the small red corner squares are positioned in the outside corners of your finished block. Repeat to make four blocks.

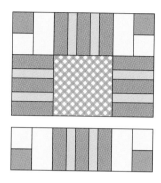

Make 4
Diagram 5

LATTICE AND INNER BORDER

Cutting for Lattice and Inner Border

From the brown fabric:
• Cut six 2 × 44-inch strips. From these strips, cut two 2 × 15-inch strips, three 2 × 31-inch strips, and two 2 × 34-inch strips.

Attaching the Strips

Step 1. Sew a 2 × 15-inch brown lattice strip between two Game Board blocks to make a row. Repeat for the remaining two blocks, as shown in **Diagram 6.** Press seam allowances toward the lattice.

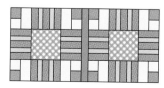

Diagram 6

Step 2. Sew one 2 × 31-inch brown lattice strip between the two rows of blocks.

Step 3. Sew two 2 × 31-inch brown inner border strips to the top and bottom of the quilt. Press seam allowances toward the borders. See **Diagram 7.**

Diagram 7

Step 4. Sew a 2 × 34-inch brown inner border strip to each side of the quilt. Press seam allowances toward the borders.

TREE BLOCKS AND OUTER BORDER

Cutting for Tree Blocks

From the cream fabric:
• Cut two 3 × 30-inch strips
• Cut two 3 × 44-inch strips. From these strips, cut 12 of **Template B** and 12 of **Template B Reverse**.
• Cut two 3½ × 44-inch strips. From these strips, cut 12 of **Template D** and 12 of **Template D Reverse**.

From the green fabric:
• Cut two 3 × 44-inch strips. From these strips, cut 12 of **Template A**.
• Cut two 3 × 44-inch strips. From these strips, cut 12 of **Template C**.

From the brown fabric:
• Cut one 1½ × 30-inch strip

Piecing the Tree Blocks

Step 1. Refer to **Diagram 8.** Sew a cream B and B Reverse piece to the two shorter sides of a green A triangle. In the same manner, sew a cream D and D Reverse piece to the sides of a green C piece. Press seams toward the green fabric. Next sew the A/B unit to the top of the C/D unit. Repeat to make 12 units.

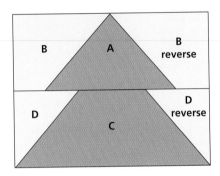

Diagram 8

Step 2. To make the tree trunk, sew a 3 × 30-inch cream strip to either side of a 1½ × 30-inch brown strip, as shown in **Diagram 9.** Press seam allowances toward the brown fabric.

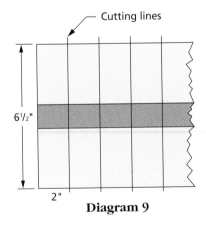

Diagram 9

Step 3. Cut the strip set into twelve 2-inch wide units, as shown in **Diagram 9,** and sew a tree trunk unit to the bottom of each tree unit.

Step 4. Sew three Tree blocks together for each outer border, as shown in **Diagram 10.**

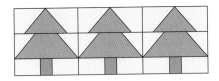

Diagram 10

Cutting for Outer Border

From the cream fabric:
• Cut three 6½ × 44-inch strips. From these strips, cut four 6½ × 8½-inch pieces and four 6½ × 14-inch pieces.

Piecing the Outer Border

Step 1. Sew a 6½ × 8½-inch cream piece to each end of a three-tree unit. Repeat for one more border.

Step 2. Sew these borders to the top and bottom of the quilt, with treetops pointing toward the center of the quilt. Press seam allowances toward the brown borders.

Step 3. Sew a 6½ × 14-inch cream piece to the ends of the two remaining three-tree units. Sew these borders to the sides of the quilt, with the treetops pointing toward the center of the quilt. Press seam allowances toward the brown borders.

QUILTING

Step 1. Prepare the backing for the quilt by cutting the 3-yard length of backing fabric in half crosswise to make two 1½-yard lengths. Remove selvages.

Step 2. Sew the two lengths together with one center seam. Press the seam allowance open. Trim backing and batting so they are 4 inches larger than the quilt top.

Step 3. Mark the quilt top for quilting.

Step 4. Layer the backing, batting, and quilt top. Baste these layers together, and quilt by hand or machine.

QUILTING IDEAS

☑ Quilt a floral design in the center of each large red print block.

☑ A feather design looks striking in the outer border. In my quilt, notice how the feather dips gracefully at the corners, as shown below.

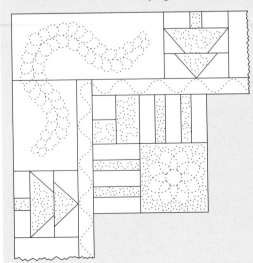

☑ Meander and stipple quilting were used to fill in the rest of the quilt.

☑ Outline quilting would be attractive in the strip sets, corner blocks, and Tree blocks.

☑ To define the lattice and narrow border, quilt in the ditch.

BINDING

The green 2¾-inch strips will produce a ⅜- to ½-inch-wide binding. If you want a wider or narrower binding, adjust the width of the strips you cut. (See page 247 for pointers on how to experiment with binding width.) See "Making and Attaching the Binding" on page 245 to complete your quilt.

Cutting for
Cross-Grain Binding

From the green fabric:
• Cut five 2¾ × 44-inch strips

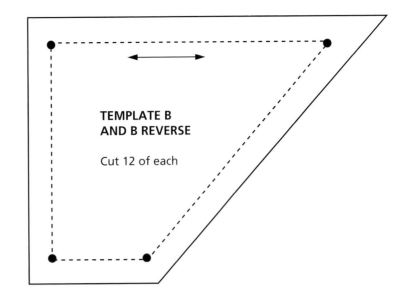

**TEMPLATE B
AND B REVERSE**

Cut 12 of each

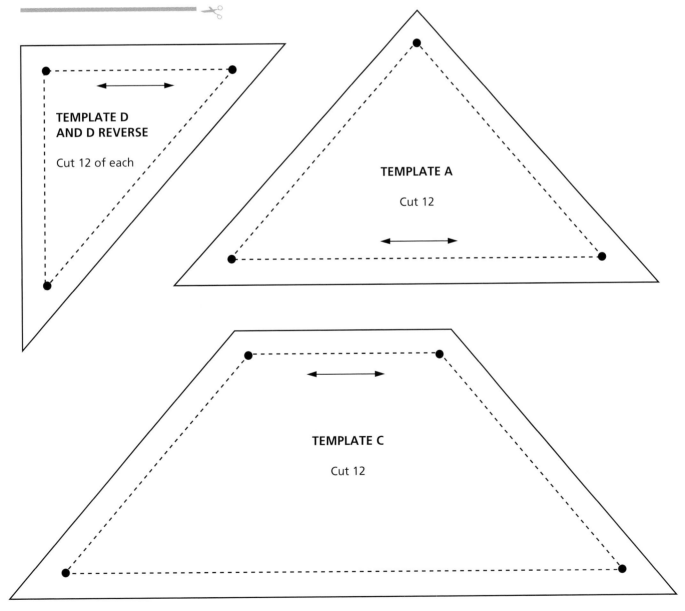

**TEMPLATE D
AND D REVERSE**

Cut 12 of each

TEMPLATE A

Cut 12

TEMPLATE C

Cut 12

Quilt Diagram

SIZE

Lap quilt: 46 × 54 inches (unquilted)

Finished block: 6 inches square

FABRICS AND SUPPLIES

Yardage is based on 44-inch-wide fabric.

1⅛ yards of red fabric for pinwheels and inner border

1¼ yards of cream fabric for background

2½ yards of red plaid fabric for alternate blocks, outer border, and bias binding

3¼ yards of fabric for quilt backing

Quilt batting, at least 50 × 58 inches

Rotary cutter, mat, and see-through ruler

Here's a perfect example of one of my basic approaches to quilt design—the most uncomplicated design is often the best. Sometimes I look at this quilt and think, this is what Christmas should be—simple and pure! The old-fashioned pinwheel design is perfectly suited to the use of just two colors, red and white. This quilt gives you a wonderful opportunity to enjoy the process of quiltmaking without worrying about fabric selection or tricky techniques. It makes a sweet baby quilt for all of the special little ones in your life. It would be especially nice for baby's first Christmas. (The size makes a perfect lap quilt for bigger people, too!)

FABRIC KEY

  RED

  CREAM

  RED PLAID

- Read instructions thoroughly before you begin.
- Prewash and press fabric.
- Use ¼-inch seam allowances throughout unless directions specify otherwise.
- Seam allowances are included in the cutting sizes given.
- Press seam allowance in the direction that will create the least bulk and, whenever possible, toward the darker fabric.
- Cutting directions for each section of the quilt are given in the areas following the row of scissors. If you like to cut as you go, simply follow the directions as you get to them. If you'd rather cut all your pieces at once, skip ahead and look for the scissors to do all the cutting before you begin to sew.

PINWHEEL BLOCKS
(Make 24)

Each Pinwheel block is made up of four triangle-pieced squares.

Cutting for Pinwheel Blocks

From the red fabric:
- Cut five 3⅞ × 44-inch strips

From the cream fabric:
- Cut five 3⅞ × 44-inch strips

Piecing the Pinwheel Blocks

Step 1. With right sides together, layer a 3⅞ × 44-inch red strip and a 3⅞ × 44-inch cream strip together. Layer the remaining 3⅞-inch strips into pairs of red and cream strips. Press together, but do not stitch.

Step 2. With your rotary cutter, cut the layered strips into 48 pairs of 3⅞-inch squares. (You will have a total of 96 squares, 48 each of red and cream fabrics.)

Step 3. Keeping edges even, cut the layered squares in half diagonally, as shown in **Diagram 1.** You will have 96 pairs of triangles. Stitch a ¼-inch seam along the diagonal edge of each pair to make a triangle-pieced square. Be careful not to stretch the fabric, since you will be sewing on the bias edge. Press seam allowance toward the red fabric. You will have 96 triangle-pieced squares.

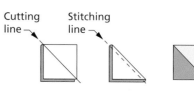

Cutting line ⟶   Stitching line ⟶

Diagram 1

Step 4. Join the triangle-pieced squares in pairs, positioning the red triangles, as shown in **Diagram 2.** Press the seam allowances toward the red fabric.

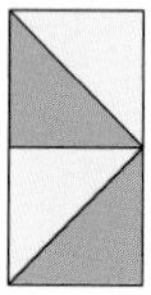

Diagram 2

Step 5. Sew two pairs of triangle-pieced squares together, turning one of the pairs upside down to position the fabrics, as shown in **Diagram 3.** This will create one Pinwheel block. Make 24 Pinwheel blocks; 20 for the quilt center and 4 for the corner blocks in the borders.

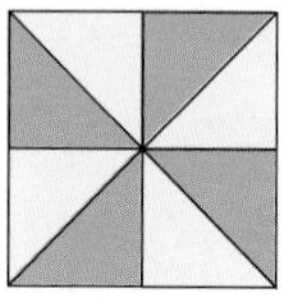

Make 24
Diagram 3

HINTS & HELPS

When joining the two pairs of triangle-pieced squares together, pin the center of these two sections to make all eight points meet. When you sew these two sections together, a fairly bulky seam is formed at the center. Instead of pressing seams to one direction, press them open to distribute the bulk evenly to both sides of the center.

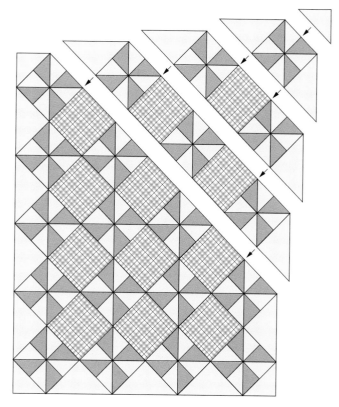

Diagram 4

ALTERNATE BLOCKS

Cutting for Alternate Blocks

From the red plaid fabric:
• Cut two 6½ × 44-inch strips. From these strips, cut twelve 6½-inch squares.

From the cream fabric:
• Cut one 10½ × 44-inch strip. From this strip, cut four 10½-inch squares. Cut these squares into quarters diagonally to form 16 side triangles. You will have two extra triangles.
• Cut one 7½ × 17-inch strip. From this strip cut two 7½-inch squares. Cut each square in half diagonally to form four corner triangles.

Note: The side triangles and corner triangles will be larger than necessary and will be trimmed after they have been added to the pieced blocks.

QUILT CENTER

Step 1. Referring to **Diagram 4**, arrange the Pinwheel blocks, alternate blocks, and side triangles in diagonal rows. The corner triangles will be added later in Step 4.

Step 2. Stitch the blocks together in diagonal rows, adding side triangles to the ends of diagonal block rows as needed.

Step 3. Stitch the rows of blocks and side triangles together to form the quilt center.

Step 4. Add the corner triangles to the four corners, as shown in **Diagram 4.**

Step 5. Trim off excess fabric from the side and corner triangles, allowing ¼-inch seam allowances beyond the block corners. Before you trim, be sure to see "Trimming Side and Corner Triangles" on page 236 to be certain you make these cuts correctly. Make sure the corners are accurate 90 degree angles.

BORDERS

The yardage given allows for the inner borders to be cut cross-grain and the outer borders to be cut lengthwise. The cutting directions give you the number of strips to cut for each border. See "Tips for Plaid Borders" on page 241.

Cutting for Borders

From the red fabric:
• Cut five 2½ × 44-inch strips for the inner border

From the red plaid fabric:
• Cut two 6½ × 40-inch strips *lengthwise* for top and bottom outer border
• Cut two 6½ × 48-inch strips *lengthwise* for side outer border

Inner Border

Step 1. Measure the quilt through the center from left to right to determine the length of the top and bottom borders. Trim two of the 2½ × 44-inch red strips to the length needed. Sew these red inner border strips to the top and bottom edges of the quilt.

Step 2. Measure the quilt through the center from top to bottom, including the border you just added. Piece the three remaining $2\frac{1}{2} \times 44$-inch red strips with diagonal seams. From this strip, cut two strips to the length needed. Sew the red inner border strips to the sides of the quilt.

Step 3. Measure the quilt from top to bottom at this point. You will use this measurement for cutting the plaid outer borders for the sides.

Outer Border

Step 1. Measure the quilt from right to left to determine the length needed for the top and bottom outer borders. Trim the two $6\frac{1}{2} \times 40$-inch plaid strips to the length needed and sew the plaid outer border to the top and bottom of your quilt.

Step 2. Using the measurement made in Step 3, trim the two $6\frac{1}{2} \times 48$-inch plaid strips to the length needed.

Step 3. Sew a Pinwheel block to each end of the side outer border strips. Sew the plaid outer borders to the sides of the quilt.

QUILTING

Step 1. Prepare the quilt backing by cutting the $3\frac{1}{4}$-yard length of backing fabric in half crosswise to make two $1\frac{5}{8}$-yard lengths.

Step 2. Remove the selvages and sew the two lengths together with one center seam. Press the seam open. Trim the backing and batting so they are 4 inches larger than the quilt top.

Step 3. Mark the quilt top for quilting.

Step 4. Layer the backing, batting, and quilt top. Baste these layers together and quilt.

BINDING

The $2\frac{3}{4}$-inch bias strips will produce a $\frac{3}{8}$- to $\frac{1}{2}$-inch-wide binding. If you want a wider or narrower binding, adjust the width of the strips you cut. (See page 247 for pointers on how to experiment with binding width.) See "Making and Attaching the Binding" on page 245 to complete your quilt.

Cutting for Bias Binding

From the red plaid fabric:
• Cut enough $2\frac{3}{4}$-inch-wide bias strips to make a 215-inch strip

QUILTING IDEAS

☑ Quilt in the ditch around the Pinwheel block triangles or outline quilt them ¼ inch from the seam line.

☑ Machine stipple quilting was added to the white parts of the Pinwheel blocks and to the white side and corner triangles.

☑ On my quilt, a simple floral design was used in the plaid alternate blocks. Half of the flower fits into the side triangles and one-quarter fits into the corner triangles. Cross-hatching in these areas could also be effective.

☑ Quilt a simple leaf chain design in the inner border.

☑ To add interest in the outer border, quilt a large chain or feathered vine.

QUILTMAKING BASICS

From selecting fabrics to the finishing stitches, here's everything you need to know to make a quilt you'll be proud of. Use this section to brush up on the basics and to make sure you have the tools you'll need. You'll find lots of helpful hints, tip, and techniques to use for any project in this book.

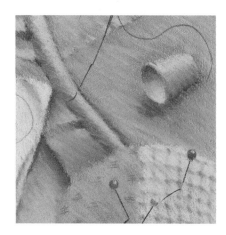

In "Thimbleberries Guide to Quilt-making" you'll find detailed instructions and information that you'll need to make the quilts in this book. You should read through this section and be familiar with the tools and techniques before beginning a project. It's a good opportunity to brush up on specifics, and you may discover some new hints that will be useful when you're in the middle of cutting, piecing, or quilting.

QUILTMAKING SUPPLIES

In each of the projects throughout the book, you'll find a list of specific materials and supplies needed for that particular quilt. Here is a list of basic items that you'll want to have on hand for making any quilt.

▨ **Straight Pins.** For piecing, you may want to use silk pins. These pins have a very fine shank that will slide easily into your fabric. When working with layers, the longer quilter's pins with colored plastic heads are helpful. At Thimbleberries, we like to use a magnetic pin holder, which only works with steel pins. This eliminates the problem of spilled pins, and it is always easy to

locate in a busy and sometimes cluttered sewing area. Make sure pins are not burred or rusted; they may leave marks in your fabric.

▨ **Needles.** For hand sewing and appliqué, use sharps in size 11 or 12. For hand quilting, use betweens. Start with a larger-size needle (#9) if you're just beginning, and move on to smaller ones as you gain experience. For both kinds of needles, the rule of thumb is the larger the number, the smaller the needle.

▨ **Scissors.** A good pair of sharp dressmaker's shears is essential for cutting fabrics. Use them *only* on fabric and have a pair of general scissors handy for cutting paper and template materials. Keep a pair of small, sharp embroidery scissors next to your sewing machine for trimming threads and clipping seam allowances.

▨ **Thread.** Use good quality thread for all your stitching. A 100 percent cotton or cotton-covered polyester thread is best for piecing. For quilting, use cotton or cotton-covered polyester quilting thread.

▨ **See-Through Ruler.** Heavy-duty plastic rulers come in many sizes and shapes. They are used in conjunction with rotary cutters and cutting mats. A 6 × 24-inch heavy-duty plastic ruler that is marked in inches, quarter inches, and eighth inches with 30, 45, and 60 degree angle lines is a good one to start out with. A square 12 × 12-inch ruler is handy to have on hand to help square up pieced blocks. We especially like the 6 × 12-inch ruler to cut smaller pieces and to cut strip sets into segments.

▨ **Rotary Cutter and Cutting Mat.** For quick and accurate cutting of strips and other pieces, you will need a rotary cutter and cutting mat. The larger rotary cutter is good for most cutting; the smaller one is nice to have for very small pieces and curves. Since you will be replacing the blades from time to time, you might want to keep old blades to cut paper, template plastic, and cardboard. Mark them with a permanent marker so you'll know which are the old ones. There are several brands of rotary cutting mats available in quilt and fabric shops. The mat will protect your work surface, and it is "self-healing," meaning that the cuts do not seem to be permanent. We prefer the 23 × 35-inch size, but an 18 × 24-inch size would be fine, too. With the larger mat, you don't have to handle and move the fabric as often, which increases accuracy. A mat with a grid is helpful, but don't use the lines for cutting guides. They are not accurate enough. I use the grid only to line up edges of fabric, folds, and selvages.

▨ **Sewing Machine.** Any sewing machine that does a reliable straight stitch is fine. Be sure that it is clean and in good working order.

▨ **Iron and Ironing Board.** Because pressing is so important for accurate piecing, you should keep your iron and ironing board as close to your sewing area as possible. This will save time and be more efficient.

▨ **Template Material.** You can use template plastic, cardboard, or manila folders to make your templates for patchwork, appliqué, and quilting. At Thimbleberries, straight-edge templates are cut with old rotary blades. Template plastic is nice because it is transparent and usually has a smooth side and a rough side. When you trace pattern pieces, mark on the smooth side of the plastic. When you place the template on the fabric, the rougher side lies next to the fabric. This helps keep the template from slipping. Template plastic is widely available in quilt shops and craft stores.

▨ Plastic-Coated Freezer Paper.

This ordinary grocery-store item has found its way into the homes of most quilters. The mention of "plastic" may sound alarming, but the shiny side is the side you adhere to fabric with an iron. It doesn't harm the fabric in any way or leave any residue. It can help stabilize fabrics, and we use freezer paper for hand appliqué.

▨ Thimble.

Find a thimble that fits you snugly on the finger that you will use to push the needle. There are many varieties on the market, from elegant gold and silver ones to soft leather versions. Try different ones until you settle on one that's right for you. The thimble should be snug enough that you can shake your hand and it will stay on your finger.

▨ Quilting Hoop or Frame.

For hand quilting you will need a hoop or floor frame to put tension on the quilt and keep the layers even. A standard 14-inch hoop is useful for most medium and large projects. There are also plastic Q-Snap frames that are portable and easy to assemble. Floor frames are a fairly big investment and require more space, so investigate them carefully before buying. The quilters who do our hand quilting prefer the traditional floor frame. It really keeps the borders nice and straight.

FABRIC FACTS

The quilts in this book are all made of 100 percent cotton fabrics.

Thimbleberries Rule of Fabric Buying

I buy fabric whenever I see something I like to add to my stash. It is from my collection that I like to create. I usually add something new, but I have the most fun combining fabrics from my cupboard.

I have a little rule that I have been following for years, and it has served me well. When I buy fabric, I never buy less than a yard. If I really, really like the piece, I buy 3 yards; this usually allows enough for piecing or for a background and maybe some lattice or border. If I think it is absolutely terrific, I will buy 6 yards. Friends who don't follow these guidelines end up in my fabric cupboard looking for more of their favorite fabrics!

Cotton is the preferred fabric for several reasons. It is easy to press because its "memory" allows it to retain a crease for some time. Cotton is also soft and lightweight, which makes it easier to quilt through three layers of a quilt sandwich. It can be manipulated to match tricky points, and it is flexible enough to ease around curves. For best results, stick with 100 percent cotton broadcloth or dress-weight fabrics.

Selecting Fabrics

Each of the quilt projects in the book includes complete lists for the fabrics and supplies you will need. If you need to purchase your fabric, visit a local quilt shop or fabric store. Take your book with you if you need assistance from the sales staff. If you will be using scraps you have on hand, be sure they are all cotton and of similar weight.

The yardages given for the quilts and projects in this book are based on 44-inch-wide fabric, but to allow for slight variations and possible shrinkage, we use 40 inches as the guideline for calculating required yardage. These yardages are adequate for the project, allowing up to $\frac{1}{4}$ yard extra. It's a measure of protection that you'll always have enough in case there's a cutting error or some other mishap. It's there if you need it, and if you don't, you can add it to your scrap

bag for future projects. The yardages have been double-checked for accuracy, but you may want to buy extra just to be safe. Even the most experienced quilters sometimes make mistakes. Check the fabric widths before you buy—the fabric may be narrower than 44 inches. You may also lose some yardage in the prewashing and preshrinking process.

COLOR COMFORT

I like strong colors that have some "age" to them, some depth, some character—colors that remind me of colors found in vintage items, whether antique quilts, pottery, toys, or books. They seem to be richer and maybe a little "muddy" or muted. I find that the deeper values

---

HINTS & HELPS

One of the most charming things I find in old quilts is the way the quiltmaker has "made do," a phrase that means doing the best you can with what you have available. To duplicate this look, make a block or two combining a mixture of colors—maybe using a scrap or two of fabrics that coordinate nicely but do not appear elsewhere in the quilt.

of a color make it easier to blend with other colors. If a pure shade of a certain color is not compatible with a group of other colors, try switching to a deeper value of the color that isn't working. Moving to a deeper value may be just the trick it takes to make it blend in. The colors I prefer also seem to be closer to nature than the vibrant, almost iridescent colors.

The colors I like are not trendy; they have a more timeless quality. I am pleased that my quilts look like family heirlooms rather than something quickly made or reflecting a fad. I like colors that quietly blend, complement, and are generally harmonious. It is always necessary to have some contrast between light and dark so that the shapes will stand out. But if you want something to be viewed as a unit, the colors should blend pleasantly and not distinguish themselves greatly.

I do encourage you to be creative. Thimbleberries' designs can be interpreted in any color combination. It is always so amazing to me to see the personality of a design change when someone else selects the fabric. I truly enjoy selecting and combining colors and prints. Over the years I have found that many quilters do not share this particular joy.

HINTS & HELPS

One of the strongest connections to the past is color. To achieve an antique country look for your quilt, select fabrics in "old colors"—deep values of blue, purple, green, red, brown, gold, and black. A touch of rich gold or brown always gives a quilt a warm, cozy appearance. Combine these colors with a medium neutral tone fabric for the background setting for true country style.

Color Reminders

❖ Pick colors that you enjoy being around—maybe favorite colors that you wear.

❖ Don't *always* be concerned about which bed a quilt will go on or the need to tie in with the color of the room. A quilt can be used in lots of places.

❖ Pick a print that has lots of colors in it and select colors from that print that you would like to emphasize—maybe even in about the same proportion as they appear in the print. Remember, the experts have already put these colors together for you.

❖ Don't worry so much. If it pleases you, maybe that should be enough!

❖ Observe lots of quilts and try to determine what it is that appeals to you. Soon you will see a pattern emerge of your personal color preferences.

There are some things you can do to give yourself more confidence in this area.

To help you make color selections, notice the colors you love to wear and decorate with. It is always more fun to work with colors that are pleasing to you. If you are using a large floral print, pick the colors from that print in about the same proportions. The experts have already done the work for you. They have chosen the correct value and scale.

To work with color, scale, and value for the quilts in this book, you can trace and enlarge the quilt diagram for the quilt you plan to make. Use colored pencils or markers to play around with the color scheme before buying fabrics. Or glue bits of fabrics down with a glue stick to make sure you like your color combinations before beginning.

You can also take classes on color at quilt shops. Consult books on color theory and learn how helpful a color wheel can be. Just keep learning and experimenting with different combinations. Sometimes if you're a little adventurous, you'll discover some new combinations you didn't expect to like. Remember, the print and color of a fabric is never as overpowering in a little patch as it may appear on the bolt.

Many of the old quilts that I love the most were not made for a particular room or with a planned color scheme. They were made for use from what was at hand, made to express an artistic urge, or were inspired by a piece of fabric or a life experience. I think people make quilts for hundreds of reasons, so just enjoy the process. I get as much pleasure out of the process of planning and making a quilt as I get from using it!

Scrap Quilts

I think an effective scrap quilt should have at least 30 different fabrics; 30 is the magic number at which your eye can no longer keep track of which print or color is where. I also think picking out or collecting that many fabrics forces you to select a wider variety of prints, not all the same scale or type—maybe novelty prints, diagonal plaids, or stripes. Usually not much of any one large print will show or be overwhelming.

I suggest selecting more medium-tone fabrics than very light or very dark. The medium ones coordinate darks and lights, and darks and lights demand more attention from your eye.

PRETREATING FABRICS

Always prewash, dry, and press your fabrics. Prewashing does a number of things. It shrinks your fabric slightly and removes any finishes and sizing, making the cloth softer and easier to handle. Washing will also let the fabric bleed, something you want to happen before you stitch the fabric into your quilt. To wash your fabric, use an automatic washer, warm water, and a mild detergent or a soap sold specifically for washing quilts. Dry fabrics on a medium setting in the dryer. I usually recommend that people treat the fabric they will be using in the quilt the same way they will treat the project when completed.

If you get in the habit of prewashing your fabric when you get home from the fabric store, you'll never have to wonder whether a fabric has been washed or not. Sometimes this is hard to do, so I always make a little clip at an angle in the selvage when a fabric has been prewashed. That way I don't have to rely on my memory.

Some quilters prefer the crisp feel of unwashed fabric, but they are taking a risk if the quilt will be washed after stitching. The colors may bleed.

MAKING THE CUT

The directions for most of the quilts in this book have been written for rotary cutting. Since this tool has become so popular, it is assumed that most quilters have one. A rotary cutter is faster and more accurate than the traditional method of making templates and using scissors to cut individual pieces. Some projects in the book that require templates combine them with rotary cutting. The rotary cutter is

To Use or Not to Use a Fabric

To test fabrics, especially deep reds, purples, blues, and greens for colorfastness, place the fabric in hot water for an hour. If color seeps into the water, you may want to try a commercial solution called Retayne that will set the dyes in fabric. Many quilt shops now carry this product. I wash all my fabrics with a soap sold specifically for washing quilts and rinse them until no dye comes out. If a fabric continues to bleed, I don't use it. I test the fabric by rubbing it against a wet tea towel or piece of muslin to see if any dye comes off.

used to cut strips of the correct width, and then a template is used on the strips.

Rotary Cutting Essentials

• Keep rotary cutters out of the reach of children. The blades are extremely sharp!

• Be sure to slide the blade guard into place as soon as you stop cutting.

• Always cut *away* from yourself.

• Square off the end of your fabric before measuring and cutting pieces, as shown in **Diagram 1.** Line up the selvages and place a ruled square on the fold. Place a 6 × 24-inch ruler against the side of the square to get a 90 degree angle. Hold the ruler in place, remove the square, and cut along the edge of the ruler. If you are left-handed, work from the other end of the fabric.

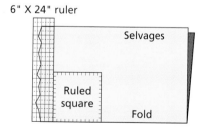

Diagram 1

• When cutting strips or rectangles, cut on the crosswise grain, as shown in **Diagram 2,** unless instructed otherwise. Strips can then be cut into squares as shown or smaller rectangles.

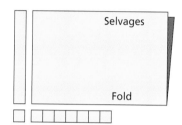

Diagram 2

• Check the strips often to make sure the fabric is square and the strips are straight. Your strips should be straight, not angled. If your strips are not straight, refold the fabric, square off the edge again, and begin cutting. See **Diagram 3.**

Diagram 3

Cutting Triangles from Squares

Cutting accurate triangles can be intimidating for beginners, but a see-through ruler, rotary cutter, and mat are all that are needed to make perfect triangles. The cutting instructions often direct you to cut strips, then squares, and then triangles, as in Cottage Flower, Mountain Flower, Star Patch, and many others. I like this method because it is very accurate and so simple. The size of the square (which is given in the project instructions) must be $7/8$ inch larger than the desired finished size of the triangle-pieced square.

For example, if you want a 2-inch finished triangle-pieced square, then each square should be $2\frac{7}{8} \times 2\frac{7}{8}$ inches. Cut a $2\frac{7}{8}$-inch-wide strip of each color in the triangle-pieced square. Layer the strips with right sides together and press. Cut the layered strips into $2\frac{7}{8}$-inch squares. You will get two triangle-pieced squares for each pair of squares you cut. Cut the layered squares in half diagonally to make perfect triangles. Sew together $\frac{1}{4}$ inch from the diagonal edge and press the seam allowances toward the darker fabric, as shown in **Diagram 4.**

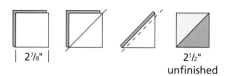

Diagram 4

Cutting Side and Corner Triangles

In projects with side and corner triangles, such as Baby Rosebud, Heart Blossom, Small Pines, Pine Grove, Apple Bars, and Peppermint Swirl, the instructions have you cut side and corner triangles larger than needed. This will allow you truly to square up the quilt and eliminates the frustration of ending up with precut side and corner triangles that don't match the size of your pieced blocks. I have found over the years of teaching that people like having this extra margin of error. Refer to "Trimming Side and Corner Triangles" on page 240.

To cut triangles, first cut squares. The project directions will tell you what size to make the squares and whether to cut them in half to make two triangles or to cut them in quarters to make four triangles, as shown in **Diagram 5.**

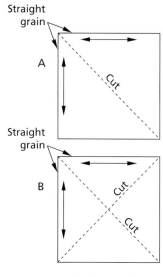

Diagram 5

This cutting method will give you side triangles that have the straight of grain on the outside edges of the quilt.

MAKING AND USING TEMPLATES

Most of the template patterns in this book are printed full size, so no enlarging or drafting is necessary. For the few that are too big to fit on a book page, we've given easy-to-follow directions for enlarging. At Thimbleberries, we use posterboard or manila folders for our templates, but of course plastic templates are very good.

Fine-point, permanent felt-tip pens are excellent for marking templates. The lines don't smear and the fine point helps ensure accuracy. Regular lead pencil also works well, but the lines may not be as easy to see.

To use cardboard or manila folders, place a sheet of tracing paper over the book page and trace the pattern. Glue the paper to the cardboard or manila folder and cut out the templates. Cut off the marking lines. If you cut beyond to the outside edge, you will be adding some size to the template when you trace onto fabric. Copy the identification

labels, grain lines, and any other information you need onto your templates. Check them against the printed pattern for accuracy. The thin, semitransparent template plastic makes excellent, durable templates. Another advantage is that you can lay the plastic directly over the book page and carefully trace the patterns onto the plastic. Then cut them out with scissors. Be as accurate as you can when tracing and cutting templates. It is critical to precise piecing.

HINTS & HELPS

We use a rotary cutter and our old blades to cut straightedge templates. Save blades that no longer cut fabric nicely to use on plastic and paper. The edges will be straight and accurate. Mark the blade with a permanent marker so you'll know right away that it is to be used only for this purpose.

The patchwork patterns in this book include seam allowances. They are printed with a solid outer line, which is the cutting line, and a dashed inner line, which is the sewing line. We've included dots at the seam intersections to help in matching up and pinning the pieces together for accurate placement. If you want to mark the seam intersections on your fabric, make holes in your templates at the dots with a heavy needle or $\frac{1}{8}$-inch paper punch. The holes need to be large enough for the point of a pencil or marker, as shown in **Diagram 6.** Draw around the templates on the

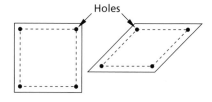

Diagram 6

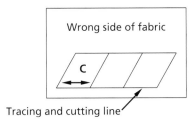

Wrong side of fabric

C

Tracing and cutting line

Diagram 7

wrong side of the fabric, as shown in **Diagram 7.** This line is the cutting line.

When we have labeled a template "Reverse," it is to give a left and right version of the same shape. For example, if you have a Template A and Template A Reverse with instructions to "cut 4 of each," you need to cut four shapes with the template right side up. Then turn the template over and cut four pieces for Template A Reverse. Parallelograms (used in Small Pines, Christmas Game Board, Around Town, and Twilight Village) and other asymmetrical shapes are often reversed. In the Tree block in Small Pines, four of the parallelograms that create the tree are reverse pieces. In Paddlewheels and Pinwheels, the shape repeats itself, so the template should not be flipped over.

HINTS & HELPS

If you cut your patches from a double thickness of fabric with right or wrong sides together, you automatically will get a left and a right version of the same shape.

PIECING PRECISELY

An exact ¼-inch seam allowance is extremely important in quiltmaking. A difference of as little as ¹⁄₁₆ inch on several pattern pieces can alter the dimensions of your quilt by as much as an inch or more.

Some sewing machines have a presser foot that measures exactly ¼ inch from the point where the needle goes into the fabric to the edge of the presser foot. Measure to determine whether this is true for your machine. If you cannot use your presser foot as a reliable seam guide, you may wish to mark an exact ¼-inch line on your machine. Lift the presser foot and measure over exactly ¼ inch from the needle. Lay a piece of ¼-inch masking tape at that point to help you guide your fabric.

The rule of thumb when assembling pieced blocks is to combine smaller pieces to make larger units. Join the larger units into rows or sections, and join sections to complete the blocks.

Before sewing a block, sew a test seam to make sure you are taking accurate ¼-inch seams. Adjust your machine to sew 10 to 12 stitches per inch. Select a neutral-color thread that blends well with the fabrics you are using. It is a good practice always to cut and piece a sample block before you cut all your fabrics. This will allow you to make certain your color choices work well together and that you are cutting the pieces accurately.

To join two pattern pieces, place them right sides together. Begin sewing the seam without backstitching and sew from edge to edge. It is not necessary to backstitch at the end of the seam if another seam will cross it at that point.

Press patchwork seams to one side toward the darker fabric, whenever possible, to prevent them from shadowing through lighter ones. Since seams will be stitched down when crossed with another seam, you will need to think about the direction in which you want them to lie. When you join blocks into rows, press the seam allowances in opposite directions from row to row. Then, when you join the rows, butt the pressed seam allowances together to produce precise intersections. For more information on pressing, see page 238.

Chain Piecing

In many quilts, you need to sew seemingly endless numbers of the same size or shape pieces together to create the blocks. Chain piecing or assembly-line piecing can help speed up this process. Run pairs of pieces or units through the sewing machine one after another without cutting the thread, as shown in **Diagram 8.** Once all the units you need have been sewn, snip them apart and press. You can continue to add on more pieces to these units in the same assembly-line fashion until the sections are complete.

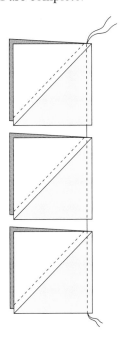

Diagram 8

Strip Piecing

When squares and rectangles are combined in a repeated pattern, you can simplify assembly by using strip piecing. This type of machine piecing eliminates monotonous cutting and significantly speeds up patchwork. In addition to saving time, strip piecing increases accuracy by eliminating the extra steps required by the traditional method of patchwork. Strip piecing is ideal for several quilts in this book, such as Apple Bars, Christmas Game Board,

Around Town, Harbor Town, Mountain Flower, Starbound, Fireside Cozy, and Twilight Village.

With strip piecing, you sew together a series of horizontal strips into a strip set. The strip set is then cut into segments. A rotary cutter, used with a see-through ruler with ⅛-inch markings, is ideal for this kind of straight-line cutting. Strips from the strip set are cut ½ inch wider than the finished size of the patch to allow for ¼-inch seam allowances.

When sewing strips of fabric together for strip sets, it is important to press the seam allowances nice and flat, usually to the darker fabric. Be very careful not to stretch as you press, causing a "rainbow effect." This will affect the accuracy and shape of the pieces cut from the strip set. I like to press on the wrong side first and with the strips perpendicular to the ironing board. Then I flip the piece over and press on the right side to prevent little pleats from forming at the seams. Laying the strip set lengthwise on the ironing board seems to encourage the rainbow effect, as shown in **Diagram 9.**

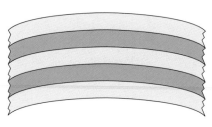

Diagram 9

PRESSING POINTERS

Pressing is an important step during piecing and assembling your quilt top. Some quilters prefer a dry iron, but I use a steam iron to press pieces. Experiment to see which works best for you. Be sure you press by bringing the iron down gently and firmly onto the fabric from above. Ironing your pieces by

sliding the iron back and forth across the fabric may stretch them out of shape.

Here are some other tips to help you press properly.

• Press a seam before crossing it with another seam.

• Press seam allowances to one side, not open.

• Whenever possible, press seams toward darker fabrics.

• Press seams of adjacent rows of blocks, or rows within blocks, in opposite directions so the pressed seams will abut as the rows are joined. See **Diagram 10.**

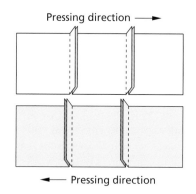

Diagram 10

• Press appliqués very gently from the back side of the background fabric. They are prettiest when slightly puffed, rather than flat.

HAND APPLIQUÉ

Several quilts in this book include appliqué, sometimes in combination with patchwork. There are three popular techniques for hand appliqué that you can choose from. I use the freezer paper method, which is especially effective for larger appliqué pieces.

Use a thread that matches the appliqué pieces and stitch the appliqué to the background fabric with a blind hem or appliqué stitch, as shown in **Diagram 11.** The stitches should be a snug ⅛ inch

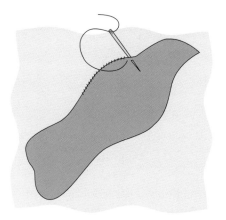

Diagram 11

apart, or closer. Use a long, thin needle—called a sharp—in size number 11 or 12.

When making appliqué blocks, always work from the background to the foreground. When one appliqué piece will be covered or overlapped by another, stitch the underneath piece to the background fabric first. Note that on the appliqué pattern pieces, the area to be overlapped by another piece is indicated with a dotted or dashed line.

Most of the patterns for appliqué pieces in this book are finished size and are printed with only a single line. Draw around these templates on the right side of the fabric, as shown in **Diagram 12,** leaving ½ inch between the pieces. The lines you draw will be your guides for turning under the edges of the appliqué pieces. Then add a scant ¼-inch seam allowance as you cut out the pieces.

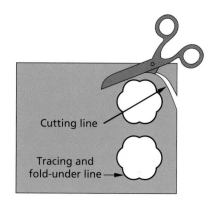

Cutting line

Tracing and fold-under line →

Diagram 12

Freezer Paper Method

With freezer paper appliqué, the freezer paper forms a base around which the fabric is shaped.

1. Trace the templates for the appliqués from the book onto template material and cut out.

2. Using the template, trace the appliqué shape onto the noncoated, or dull, side of the freezer paper and cut out.

3. With a dry iron set at wool, press the coated, or shiny, side of the freezer paper template to the wrong side of the fabric. Be sure to allow ½ inch between shapes for seam allowances, as in **Diagram 12.**

4. Cut out the appliqué shape ⅛ to ¼ inch outside of paper edge for seam allowance. Clip concave curves if necessary to allow you to turn them under more easily, as shown in **Diagram 13.**

Diagram 13

5. Pin the appliqué to the quilt block or top. Appliqué the shape to the quilt with a blind hem stitch, as shown in **Diagram 11,** turning the seam allowance under against the edge of the paper.

6. Remove the freezer paper by one of two methods. One method is to leave a ½-inch opening. Finger press the fabric over the paper. Then slide your needle into this opening to loosen the freezer paper from the appliqué. Gently pull the freezer paper out, and the fold should still be in the fabric. Finish stitching the appliqué in place. Another way to remove the freezer paper is to slit the fabric from the back and remove the paper.

Buttonhole Stitch

You can also use pearl cotton and the buttonhole stitch when doing primitive appliqué. The buttonhole stitch is used to appliqué the flowers onto the top of the Mountain Flower quilt. Use one strand of number 8 pearl cotton for the buttonhole stitch. The end result will be a thicker edging with a bit more sheen than embroidery floss will give. When stitching with pearl cotton, use a needle with a large eye to accommodate the thicker thread.

Buttonhole stitch

Primitive Appliqué

I use this primitive appliqué method in some of my designs. This has been popular because it is more casual and is such a great look used in whimsical designs, such as Sunflower Field.

1. Trace the templates from the book onto template material.

2. Place the appliqué template face down on the paper side of sewable, fusible webbing, such as Trans Web, and trace.

3. Cut out the shapes loosely and place the rough side of the webbing against the wrong side of the fabric. Follow the manufacturer's directions and fuse with a dry iron. Let cool.

4. Cut out the shapes along the drawn lines and peel off the backing.

5. Position the appliqué shapes on the quilt and press in place with a hot, dry iron according to the manufacturer's directions.

6. Using three strands of embroidery floss, stitch around the appliqué shape with the primitive

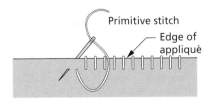

Diagram 14

stitch, as shown in **Diagram 14.** Stitches are about ⅛ inch long and ⅛ inch apart. The primitive stitch is very quick and easy and outlines the shapes nicely.

Needle Turn Method

1. Make finished-size templates. Trace lightly around the templates on the right side of the fabric leaving about ½ inch between shapes.

2. Cut the pieces out, allowing a scant ¼ inch on the outside of the lines for folding under.

3. Pin the appliqué pieces in place and stitch them to the background fabric. Use the tip and shank of your appliqué needle to turn under ½-inch long sections of seam allowance at a time. As you turn under a section, finger-press the fold with your thumb and then stitch it in place.

MACHINE APPLIQUÉ

Machine appliqué can be used for most of the appliqué projects in this book. It's a quick and easy way to add appliqué pieces to projects without spending a lot of time doing the hand stitching. It also stands up well to repeated washings.

You'll need a machine that has a zigzag stitch setting. Set your machine for a medium-width zigzag stitch and a very short stitch length. Test this satin stitch on a scrap of fabric. The stitches should form a band of color and be ⅛ to 3/16 inch wide. If necessary, loosen the top tension slightly so the top thread is just slightly pulled to the wrong side.

The appliqué piece should be either fused, pinned, or basted to the background fabric. (See steps 1 through 4 under "Primitive Appliqué" on page 239 for instructions on using fusible webbing.)

1. Stabilize the background fabric to give you more control and eliminate puckering. You can use a sheet of typing paper or a commercial stabilizer such as Tear-Away. Pin it to the wrong side of the background fabric where you will be stitching.

2. Use the machine satin stitch around the edges of the appliqué pieces, covering the raw edges. Change thread colors as necessary to match the pieces. When stitching is complete, carefully tear away the stabilizer from the wrong side.

If you have a sewing machine with other stitches, you could also use a machine buttonhole stitch or other decorative stitch to stitch down the edges after fusing or stabilizing.

ASSEMBLING THE QUILT TOP

To assemble your quilt top, refer to the quilt diagram, photograph, and other diagrams for each project. Lay out all the blocks, alternate blocks, and corner and side triangles as appropriate for the quilt. Position them right side up as they will be in the completed quilt.

Pin and sew the blocks together in horizontal, vertical, or diagonal rows, as directed in the project instructions. Press seams in opposite directions from row to row. Join the rows, abutting the pressed seam allowances so the intersections will match perfectly.

If you are assembling a large quilt top, you may want to join rows into pairs first and then join the pairs to keep it more manageable.

Squaring Up Blocks

To square up your blocks, first check the seam allowances. This is usually where the problem is, and it is always best to alter within the block rather than trim the outer edges. Next, make sure you have pressed accurately. Sometimes a block can become distorted by overly enthusiastic pressing.

To trim up block edges, I like to use one of the many clear plastic squares available on the market. Determine the center of the block; mark with a pin. Lay the square over the block and align as many perpendicular and horizontal lines as you can to the seams in your block. This will indicate where the block is off. Do not trim all off on one side; this usually results in real distortion of the pieces in the block and the block design. Take a little off all sides until the block is square. When assembling many blocks, it is necessary to make sure *all* are the same.

Press the completed top on the back side first, carefully clipping and removing hanging threads. Then press the front, making sure all seams are flat.

TRIMMING SIDE AND CORNER TRIANGLES

To trim side and corner triangles, use a wide see-through ruler, cutting mat, and rotary cutter.

• Begin at a corner first and line up your ruler ¼ inch beyond the points of the corners of the blocks, as shown in **Diagram 15.** Lightly draw a line along the edge of the ruler. Repeat this along all four sides of the quilt top, lightly marking cutting lines.

• Check all the corners before you do any cutting. Make sure they are 90 degree angles. Adjust the cutting lines as needed to ensure square corners.

• When you are certain that everything is as parallel and perpendicular as it can be, line up your ruler over the quilt top. Using your marked lines as guides, cut away the excess with your rotary cutter, leaving the ¼-inch seam allowance beyond the block corners. See **Diagram 16.**

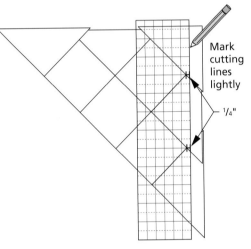

Mark cutting lines lightly

¼"

Diagram 15

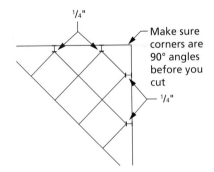

¼"

Make sure corners are 90° angles before you cut

¼"

Diagram 16

BORDER BASICS

For most of the quilts in this book, the borders are straight, not mitered. We cut most of our borders cross-grain. The exceptions are woven plaids and if we need a long length to match or control plaids. We might even have the top and bottom borders cut cross-grain and the sides cut lengthwise. It is generally more cost-efficient to cut crosswise, but if your quilt is very large with large borders, it might not matter. I also may cut a floral fabric lengthwise for better appearance and to get the repeat of the design. I make the borders work for the quilt . . . I don't have a rigid rule.

To piece border strips, use a diagonal seam. This makes it less visible than a straight seam. It works better for quilting, too. The seam won't fall right down the center of the design motif, and it eliminates the possibility of a seam always appearing in any one place of a quilting design. (If you are trying to match plaids or some other fabric, sew border strips together using a straight seam. It is pretty tricky to do it on a diagonal.)

For diagonal piecing, place two border strips together at a 90 degree angle with right sides together, as shown in **Diagram 17.** Each strip should extend ¼ inch beyond the other. Stitch across diagonally, making sure to start and stop your stitching precisely in the V notch of the two strips. Trim off the excess to leave a ¼-inch seam allowance.

HINTS & HELPS

Many of the projects, such as Cottage Flower, Mountain Flower, Birds and Blooms, Sunflower Field, Harbor Town, and Dresden Square, have pieced borders. The pieced borders must fit the quilt top perfectly so that the quilt lies flat. If you find that the pieced border does not fit the quilt, you must adjust the seam allowances, by taking in or letting out a little bit at several seams.

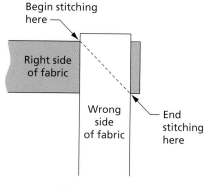

Diagram 17

Follow the border directions for each quilt and read these additional tips, which can help you with any quilt you make.

• Measure your completed quilt top through the vertical and horizontal center rather than along the edges. Use these measurements to determine the exact length of your borders. This will avoid wavy or rippled borders, since the edges may have stretched from handling. It will also help in squaring up your quilt. Measure and mark your borders first, and make necessary adjustments or ease in any fabric that may have stretched along the edge as you pin your borders to the quilt top.

• For borders with corner blocks, use the desired finished measurement and add ½ inch for seams.

• Measure and mark sewing dimensions on the ends of borders before sewing them on, and wait to trim off excess fabric until after sewing.

• To mark the halfway point on border strips, fold the strip in half and press lightly, or use a pin to mark the spot. Align this mark with the center point along the quilt side when pinning on the border.

• Always press border seam allowances away from the quilt center.

Tips for Plaid Borders

When cutting plaids cross-grain, cut along a thread. This will ensure that the plaid stays perpendicular.

(When cutting other cross-grain borders, it is not necessary to cut along a thread.) If the border strips need to be longer than the width of the fabric, I cut them on the lengthwise grain to avoid piecing them. It takes more fabric, but I think it is worth the extra expense to have a continuous plaid design uninterrupted by a seam. Seams are easier to blend when using a fabric with an overall print design.

Cut *all* border strips so they have the same plaid pattern repeat. This usually means using scissors, not a rotary cutter, and actually following the plaid thread line. Also, depending on the plaid, you may have to waste a few inches between border strips to make sure they fall on the same pattern repeat, as shown in **Diagram 18.**

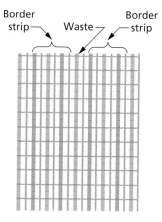

Diagram 18

Next, remember to sew them onto the quilt in the same fashion, paying attention to which part of the plaid should go next to the quilt and which should be on the outside edge. The more complicated the plaid, the more there is to watch. See **Diagram 19** on page 242.

I take a different approach when I'm working with a plaid such as the one shown in **Diagram 20** on page 242, which has a tree in it. I would cut this fabric cross-grain, with scissors, following a thread line so I could have the trees pointing out and away from the center of the quilt.

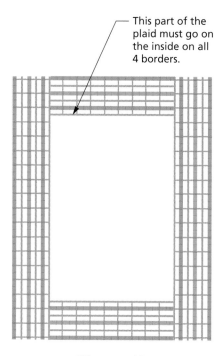

This part of the plaid must go on the inside on all 4 borders.

Diagram 19

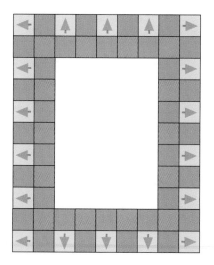

Diagram 20

All of these are guidelines, not steadfast rules. Many quilters like the casual, unplanned look they get by just cutting borders from plaids and not planning the placement. This may actually be more like the antique quilts we love so much!

QUILTING DESIGNS

For each quilt in this book, I have made suggestions for quilting de-

signs in the boxes called "Quilting Ideas." Some quilts lend themselves to very simple quilting patterns, such as outline quilting, while others are beautifully accented by cables, feathers, and floral designs. You can duplicate my design, create your own, or choose from the many quilting stencils available at quilt shops and through mail-order catalogs.

Outline quilting follows the seams of the patchwork. It can be in the ditch, right next to the seam, or ¼ inch away. There's no need to do any marking for in-the-ditch quilting. For ¼-inch outline quilting, you can use ¼-inch-wide masking tape as a guide for stitching or just work by eye. Masking tape in many widths is also helpful in spacing diagonal lines or cross-hatching without marking.

Echo quilting is another type of quilting that needs no marking. You quilt around a shape in concentric rings about ½ inch apart.

Long straight lines and other quilting designs such as cables and floral designs should be marked before the quilt top is layered with batting and backing.

I usually let the size of a piece in the block or a prominent design feature guide my quilting choices. It is a tried-and-true design principle that repetition of a design element is usually pleasing to the eye. For a triangle-pieced square with a 2½-inch diagonal measurement, a 1¼-inch distance between quilting lines is a natural extension of quilting in the ditch along the triangle seam line, as shown in **Diagram 21.**

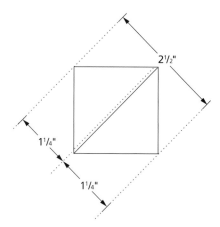

2½"

1¼"

1¼"

Diagram 21

Marking the Quilting Design

When you're ready to mark the quilt top, use a marker that will be visible on the fabric of your quilt and that will wear away or be brushed out once quilting is completed.

Silver quilter's pencils work well on most fabrics. The silvery metallic gray shows up well on both light and dark fabrics, and it washes out easily. An artist's type white pencil or chalk pencil works well to mark dark fabrics. But use a chalk pencil only to mark projects as you go since the markings will disappear or rub off quickly. Chalk pencils and powdered chalk markers are now available in several colors at quilt shops and in catalogs. You may also mark light fabrics with a hard lead 0.5 millimeter pencil, but make sure to *avoid marking heavily* with a pencil. Thin slivers of hand soap also work well for marking dark fabric. (This is actually my favorite little tool for marking dark fabrics. It always comes out easily.)

Quilt Sizes

Don't panic if your quilt top doesn't measure exactly the same as the dimensions we give. There are always slight variations due to individual cutting and piecing techniques that can account for these slight differences.

Cross-Hatching Tips

Cross-hatching is a very old-fashioned quilting technique. I always fall back on it when I want to add quilting but don't want to add another design element. It is particularly nice behind appliquéd motifs, large borders made of a printed fabric that would camouflage other quilting designs, and behind other quilting designs such as a feathered wreath.

To determine cross-hatching lines, first decide how far apart you want your quilting lines to be. I use 2-inch spacing in larger areas and 1-inch spacing in smaller areas. In some small projects, I've actually used ½-inch spacing. Remember, though, the closer together the lines, the more quilting you will have to do!

Once you have determined the spacing you want, look at your quilt and divide it into sections for marking. Make sure the length of your ruler will cover the area. Measure the section and divide it evenly so the lines will be spaced equally apart. For a 10-inch square, for example, you might want to mark a 2-inch crosshatched grid, as shown. Use your ruler and mark the intervals with a fabric marking pencil (the kind you would use for marking a quilt stencil). Lightly connect these lines from one section to the next.

It is a good idea to do some experimenting with several marking tools on scrap fabrics to decide which ones you like before you mark a large area of your quilt. Make sure you make your lines very light, no matter what type of pencil you use.

To mark a quilting design, use a commercially made stencil, make your own stencil, or trace the design from a printed source.

If your marks will stay visible for a long time, mark the entire quilt top before layering. If you are using a powdered chalk marker or a chalk pencil, mark the quilting lines just before quilting them (after you've layered and basted).

QUILT BACKINGS

Many of the quilts in this book are large enough to need pieced backings. There are instructions for doing this in each of the projects. I usually don't put the seam down the center of the quilt. I often put the seam off to one side so that I have a larger piece of leftover fabric.

Cut off all selvage edges from the backing fabric before sewing. Sew the pieces together with a ¼-inch seam allowance and press these seams open. The backing will lie flatter, and it will be easier to quilt through the seam area if the seam is open, rather than pressed to one side, as you do for pieced blocks.

Sometimes I piece quilt backs with a few different fabrics. This way I can use up fun fabrics and it makes the back of the quilt more interesting. If I have extra fabric from the quilt top, I sometimes use it as a center square for the back and put a border of one or two other fabrics around it. This is especially appropriate for machine quilting—the extra seam allowances aren't so difficult to go through. I love finding a surprise or something unexpected on the back of a quilt!

When it is sewn together, the backing should be larger than your completed quilt top so that there is ample space around the edges of your quilt. A 2-inch margin of backing and batting on each side of the quilt will accommodate the natural tendency of these layers to "shrink," or draw up, during the quilting process.

QUILT BATTINGS

There are many wonderful choices when it comes to the middle layer of your quilt. Some battings produce a flat, rather antique look, and others will give your quilt a softly sculpted appearance. Some are perfect for fine hand stitching, and some are especially good for machine quilting. Decide on the type of quilting you will do and the kind of loft (puffiness) you wish to create, and select the batting that will best achieve it.

We use a lightweight batting, such as a polyester light batting when doing hand quilting. It does resemble old quilts, which are soft and floppy. I can get nicer quilting stitches when a thinner batting is used. For machine quilting, we also use polyester light batting. I think cotton batting gets too heavy with all the stitches in it. Whatever batting you use, make sure to take it out of the plastic bag and let it rest for a day or two before layering to let it breathe, get the loft up, and get any wrinkles out. Or you can put it in your drier on the air cycle for 10 or 15 minutes.

Cotton Batting. Cotton has long been a quilter's choice for batting. It is cool in summer and warm in winter with a thickness of approximately $\frac{1}{16}$ to $\frac{1}{8}$ inch. At one time, all-cotton batting had to be quilted at very close intervals (¼ to ½ inch) to prevent lumping and migration of the fibers during washing. Some modern cotton batts can be laundered even when quilting is several inches apart. Cotton batting will shrink when washed—the shrinking batt wrinkles the fabrics around the lines of quilting, instantly creating the look of an antique quilt. If you don't want this look, prewash your batt. A big advantage of cotton is that it will not beard. (Bearding is the migration of fibers through your quilt fabric, creating a fuzzy "bearded" look.)

■ **Cotton/Polyester Blend Batting.** These blends offer all the advantages of cotton without the need to quilt so closely. You can space your stitches as far apart as 3 to 4 inches. These batts are thin (giving the antique effect), very durable, and suited to both hand and machine quilting. They can be prewashed or used without pretreating; just be aware of the shrinkage in a finished quilt.

■ **Polyester Battings.** These are the most common battings on the market. They are generally higher in loft, or thickness, than cotton battings. Polyester batts are selected more often than any other kind, probably because of the wide range of thicknesses available, ease of stitching, durability, and simplicity of laundering. They do beard quite heavily, however. These come in a dark color for quilts with dark or black backgrounds, making the migrating fibers less noticeable.

■ **Wool.** Wool battings are very warm, without being heavy. There is now a wonderful wool batt available at many quilt shops that is easy to use and quilts like butter.

LAYERING AND BASTING

The quilt top, batting, and backing layers must be assembled securely so that the finished quilt will lie flat and smooth. To prepare the quilt "sandwich" for quilting in a hoop or Q-Snap frame, place the pressed backing right-side down and place the batting on top of it, smoothing out any wrinkled spots. To keep the backing taut, use masking tape at the corners, or clamp it to a table with large binder clips.

Place the quilt top over the batting, right side up. Make sure it is centered and smooth out any wrinkles. Remove any loose or hanging threads. The backing and batting should be at least 2 inches larger than the quilt top on all four sides.

Baste these three layers together with white thread so there won't be any residue of color left in your quilt when the thread is removed. Begin in the middle and baste a grid of horizontal and vertical rows that are approximately 4 to 6 inches apart. Use a long darning needle, or even a 3-inch dollmaking needle to make the stitching go faster. Thread a few needles in advance with very long lengths of thread.

For hand quilting on a large floor frame in which the quilt is stretched out to its full dimensions, attach the backing first. Some old frames allow you to use tacks, some require pinning to a muslin sleeve on the frame. Make sure it is nice and taut. Then lay the batting on. Smooth it out and position the quilt top over it. Make sure it is stretched slightly to create some tension for a smooth quilting surface. Tack or pin to the frame.

For machine quilting, use 1-inch-long rust-proof nickel-plated safety pins. Pin from the center out approximately every 3 inches. Be careful not to place the pins where you intend to quilt.

QUILTING

Many of the quilts in this book are hand quilted, but some of the projects are machine quilted. Whether you will be quilting by hand or by machine, the tips that follow can help with your quilting.

Choosing Thread Color for Quilting

Most quilters choose a neutral color thread for their quilting stitches; white and off-white are the most common. You could also choose to do your quilting in a complementary or contrasting color. My preference is to match thread as closely as possible to the general tone of the fabrics in the quilt. I like to see the texture created by quilting, but not necessarily the stitches in a contrasting color. I think this is a matter of personal preference. I change thread colors often to match the fabrics of the quilt tops so that the thread is not obviously a stark contrast in one area and not another—unless that is part of the design. I almost always choose a print for the backing so that the threads will blend in with it. When machine quilting, I use a neutral color for the bobbin and change the top thread to match the fabric of the quilt top. There is a lot of thread laid down

---

Making a Quilting Stencil or Template

To make simple quilting templates such as the reindeer in Fireside Cozy, trace the design onto template plastic or a manila folder as directed in "Making and Using Templates" on page 236. Cut around the outer edge. To make a stencil for the pine sprigs in Fireside Cozy, trace the design onto template plastic or a manila folder and carefully cut out the lines with small sharp scissors. Draw a quilting line onto the fabric through the slits cut for the pine sprigs.

when machine quilting, and if it contrasts, it can affect the overall color of a quilt. The more you match the thread, the less it effects colors in your quilt. It hides any little glitches in your stitching, too.

Hand Quilting

• Use a hoop or frame to keep tension on the quilt as you stitch. To insert the quilt into the hoop, place the quilt over the smaller, inner hoop and then place the larger, outer hoop over the quilt. Adjust the top hoop so that there is even tension on the quilt. Do not keep the tension so tight that it makes stitching difficult.

• Use short quilting needles, called betweens, in size 9 or 10.

• Use 100 percent cotton quilting thread.

• Start with a length of quilting thread about 18 inches long. This is long enough to keep you going for a while, but not long enough to tangle easily.

• With knotted thread, insert the needle through the top and batting about $\frac{1}{2}$ inch away from the place where you will begin your quilting. Bring the needle to the surface in position to make the first stitch. Gently tug on the thread to "pop" the knot through the top and bury it in the batting, as shown in **Diagram 22.**

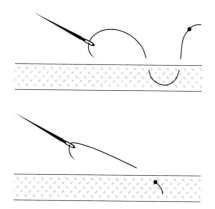

Diagram 22

Primitive Quilting

A running quilting stitch was used on Fireside Cozy and Jingle Socks. When quilting with pearl cotton, knot the thread as you normally do and pull it through the top layer of the fabric. You may need to separate the weave a bit with the tip of your needle to allow the knot to pop through. Keep your quilting stitches large and chunky while using a thimble and a rocking motion. This technique is fun and fast!

• Quilt by making running stitches, about $\frac{1}{16}$ to $\frac{1}{8}$ inch long through all the layers. Use the thimble to push the needle down until you feel the tip of the needle with your finger underneath. Then guide the needle back up through the quilt. As you begin to feel comfortable with this "rocking" technique of quilting, you may like taking more stitches at one time. Try to keep the stitches straight and even. This is more important than tiny stitching.

• To end a thread, place your needle close to your last stitch, parallel to the quilt, and wind the thread around it two or three times. Insert the tip of the needle through the quilt top and batting only, at the correct stitch length, and bring the needle out approximately $\frac{1}{2}$ inch away from the quilting line. Gently tug the thread to "pop" the knot through the quilt top so that it lodges in the batting layer.

• Thread several needles with quilting thread before you begin. Keep them handy while you're working, and you won't have to stop and thread a needle every time you finish a length of thread.

Machine Quilting

Machine quilting takes practice to achieve evenness of stitches and design. We use 100 percent cotton thread for machine quilting or sometimes cotton-wrapped polyester, but never nylon. We use a fairly fine gauge, 12 stitches per inch, that makes the stitches nestle in. When cotton batting is used in machine-

quilted projects it puckers up after washing, and the stitches almost bury themselves.

• Use a walking foot (also called an even feed foot) on your sewing machine for quilting straight lines. Use a darning or machine embroidery foot for free-motion or meander quilting.

• Leave long thread ends at the beginning and ending of a design so that later you can go back with a needle to knot and bury them in the batting layer as you do for hand quilting. Pull the bobbin thread up to the top so that it doesn't get bunched up underneath.

• For free-motion quilting, disengage the feed dogs of your machine so you can manipulate the quilt freely. Choose continuous-line quilting designs so you won't have to lift the needle when quilting the design. Guide the quilt under the needle with both hands, working at an even pace so stitches will be of a consistent length.

MAKING AND ATTACHING THE BINDING

Binding finishes the raw edges of the quilt, giving the edges strength and durability. You can cut binding strips from the cross grain or bias of the fabric. There is some stretch in cross-grain and much greater stretch in bias strips. Straight-grain binding can be used on all quilts, unless there are rounded corners or scalloped edges. Straight-grain binding is quicker and easier to cut than bias

Meander and Stipple Quilting

Both of these machine quilting styles are done freehand. The only difference is the tightness or closeness of the pattern. Meander quilting is much looser and more open, while stipple quilting is very tight and closely spaced. The technique is the same for both.

Disengage the feed dogs of your sewing machine and use a darning foot. Start in a corner, a square, or other designated space of about 8 to 12 inches. Within that area, fill in from one side to another before moving on. You should control the stitching lines and get them to almost appear like a puzzle piece without stitching over other lines of stitching. It's very random and free-flowing. Work in small areas to maintain more control and to keep the meandering more uniform.

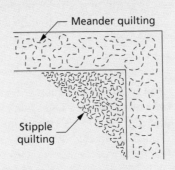

binding, but we find that bias binding is well worth the effort. It can be very decorative and is more durable than a straight-grain binding. Bias binding is essential for quilts that have curved edges, such as Holiday Hearts, Jingle Socks, Tabletop Tree Skirt, and Holly Tree Skirt. Also, if you're using a plaid fabric, cutting on the bias gives you a diagonal effect in the finished binding. We love the look of a plaid binding cut on the bias. If you cut plaid cross-grain, you will end up with relatively boring-looking straight up and down lines of plaid along the quilt edges.

At Thimbleberries, we make French-fold binding (also called double-fold binding) for all our quilts. This binding can be cut straight-grain or on the bias as specified in the individual projects. The binding strip is folded in half, and the raw edges are stitched to the edge of the quilt on the right side. The folded edge is then brought to the back side of the quilt and hand stitched in place.

We have given yardage and cutting directions for a standard binding width, but you may want to vary the width of your binding to accommodate a thicker or thinner batting. Or if you simply prefer a wider or narrower binding, see "Binding Width." Generally, you will need the perimeter of the quilt plus 12 to 20 inches for mitering corners and ending the binding. One yard of fabric is usually enough to make binding for a large quilt. Make and attach the binding as described below, mitering the binding at the corners.

Bias Binding

1. Cut bias strips with your rotary cutter using the 45 degree angle line on your see-through ruler. Straighten the left edge of your fabric, as described on page 235. Align the 45 degree angle line on your ruler with the bottom edge of the fabric, as shown in **Diagram 23A**, and cut along the edge of the ruler to trim off the corner. Move the ruler across the fabric, cutting parallel strips in the needed width, as shown in **Diagram 23B**.

2. Join the strips, as shown in **Diagram 24**. Place strips with right sides together and stitch together using a ¼-inch seam allowance. Be sure to start and end your stitching precisely in the V notch of the two strips. Press the seam allowance open. Continue adding strips until you have the length needed.

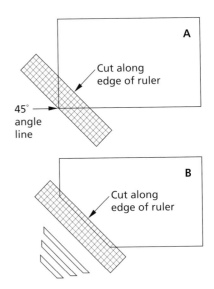

Diagram 23

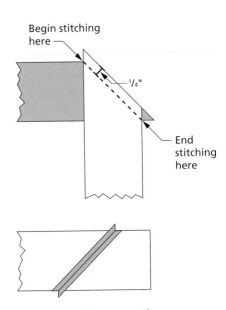

Diagram 24

HINTS & HELPS

When binding a very small circle, as in the Tabletop Tree Skirt, the narrower the binding, the easier it is to make the tight turns.

Straight-Grain Binding

1. Cut the necessary number of strips as specified in the project instructions. Cut straight strips across the width of the fabric rather than along the length. This way they have more stretch and are easier to use.

2. Join the strips using diagonal seams. Place two border strips together at a 90 degree angle with right sides together, as shown in **Diagram 25.** Each strip should extend ¼ inch beyond the other. Stitch across the strips diagonally, making sure to start and end your stitching precisely in the V notch of the two strips.

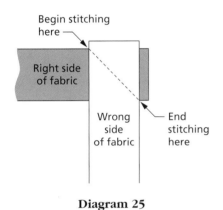

Diagram 25

3. Trim off the excess to leave a ¼-inch seam allowance. Press the seam open.

Preparing a Quilt for Binding

We trim excess batting and backing before adding the binding. It is so nice to eliminate that extra bulk.

1. Use a large see-through ruler or square to square up and trim away the excess batting and backing.

2. Securely hand baste all three layers together a scant ¼ inch from the raw edges. This hand basting keeps the layers from shifting and prevents puckers from forming.

Attaching the Binding

Use a walking foot or an even feed foot, if you have one for your machine, when sewing on binding. It helps to avoid puckers.

1. Once your binding strips are sewn together, fold them in half lengthwise, wrong sides together, and press.

2. Unfold and cut the beginning end at a 45 degree angle. Press the edge under ¼ inch. Refold the strip.

3. Begin attaching the binding along the bottom lower left side. Do not begin binding at a corner.

4. With raw edges of the binding and quilt top even, start stitching about 2 inches from the diagonal cut end, using a ⅜-inch seam allowance. Stop stitching ⅜ inch from the corner.

5. Clip thread and move the quilt out from under the presser foot.

6. Fold the binding strip up and away from the corner of the quilt forming a 45 degree angle, as shown in **Diagram 26A.** Then refold the binding down even with the raw edge of the quilt, as shown in **Diagram 26B.** Begin sewing at the upper edge, as shown. Miter all four corners in this manner.

7. As you approach the point where you started, trim the end of the binding, making sure the end is long enough to tuck inside the be-

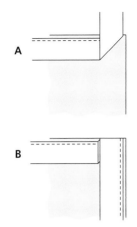

Diagram 26

ginning binding and that the two ends overlap about ⅜ inch. Stitch the remaining binding to the quilt.

8. Turn the folded edge of the binding over to the back side of the quilt covering the stitching line. Hand sew the binding in place, folding in mitered corners as you go. Add several stitches to the folds of the miters on both the front and back to hold them in place, as shown in **Diagram 27** on page 248.

MAKING A HANGING SLEEVE

If you plan to display your quilt, either at home or at a quilt show, you will need to add a hanging sleeve to the back. A rod or dowel can be inserted in the sleeve and supported by nails or hooks on the wall. Follow these instructions to

---

Binding Width

Here's a trick to help you figure out how wide you need to cut your binding. Multiply the desired width of binding by 6. For example, if you want a ½-inch finished binding, multiply ½ by 6, which means you need to cut a 3-inch-wide strip. Remember, if you are using a thicker batting, you may need to add another ¼ to ½ inch. This technique was passed on to me by a fellow quilter. You may need to recalculate yardage requirements if you decide to make a binding wider than the project directions specify. I always cut a sample binding and try it to see if it works—it should cover the edge and fold to the back easily. Sometimes the batting thickness really does affect the width of the binding.

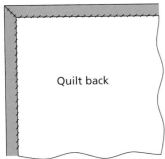

Diagram 27

5. Hand stitch the sleeve in place along the top folded edge and the bottom folded edge, being careful not to sew through to the front of the quilt, as shown in **Diagram 28.**

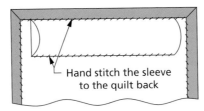

Hand stitch the sleeve to the quilt back

Diagram 28

SIGNING AND DATING YOUR QUILT

Be sure to sign and date your quilt. You can simply sign your name and date with a permanent pen, or make this last step in the quiltmaking process a fun and creative little project in itself. I like to

think of quilt labels as another treat to find tucked away on the back of a quilt.

Some quiltmakers like to embroider their name, the date, and their town on their quilts. Others make delicate labels with short verses, dedications, or the inspiration for the quilt. For Winter Posies, my mother embroidered a poinsettia to the label along with my name and date. I made a label for Windblown Shadows using Pigma pens and copied a sailboat design that was on antique glasses that belonged to my grandmother. If the quilt is a gift, you may want to note the recipient's name and the occasion. You can iron freezer paper onto the wrong side of a piece of fabric to stabilize it for easier writing and drawing on the fabric label. Have fun as you give your quilt the perfect finishing touch.

make a 4-inch-wide hanging sleeve, which can accommodate a 2-inch-diameter dowel or pole. I do not sew hanging sleeves into the binding; this makes it too permanent.

1. Cut a strip of backing fabric or muslin that is 8½ inches wide and 2 inches shorter than the width of the finished quilt. (I like to use the backing fabric so that it looks like it belongs rather than something added on to the quilt.)

2. Machine hem the short ends. Turn under ½ inch on each end, press, and turn under another ½ inch. Stitch next to the pressed fold.

3. Fold and press the strip in half lengthwise, wrong sides together, aligning the two long raw edges. Stitch a ¼-inch seam along the length to make a tube. Press the seam to one side. Place the sleeve against the quilt with the seam side toward the back of the quilt.

4. Position the top of the sleeve so that it abuts the bottom edge of the binding on the back of the quilt, with the seam against the back of the quilt. Pin the sleeve in position.

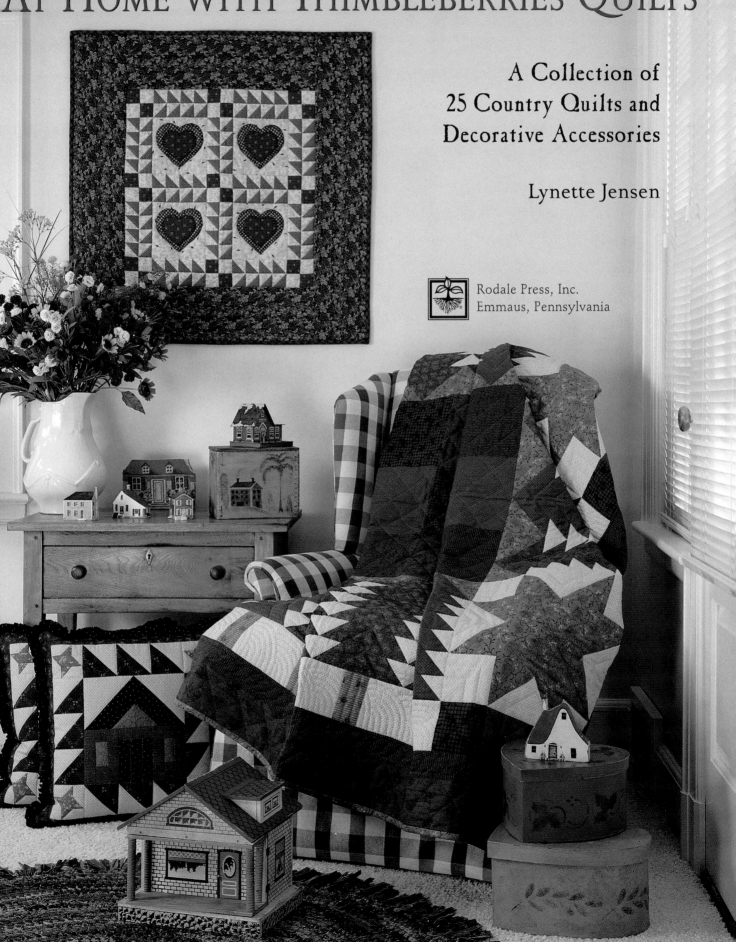

AT HOME WITH THIMBLEBERRIES QUILTS

A Collection of
25 Country Quilts and
Decorative Accessories

Lynette Jensen

Rodale Press, Inc.
Emmaus, Pennsylvania

CONTENTS

ACKNOWLEDGMENTS

The staff at Thimbleberries, Inc., has always been a constant source of energy, talent, and commitment. Their dedication is immeasurable. Deadlines are always met, workmanship is impeccable, and they all have an innate sense of what everyone expects from Thimbleberries. Their lives continue to be demanding and a bit hectic at times, yet they, too, find time to make very special quilts for themselves and others. I think they are a true reflection of today's quilters, who set aside time to enjoy quilting as a form of artistic expression. Even though we work all day with some aspect of quiltmaking, we still take projects home to make during our off hours. Often, I hear parting words like these as we leave the workplace, "I'm going to make this tonight!" My undying gratitude to Sherry Husske, Peggy Christianson, Kathy Lobeck, and Dale Ann Foster and an extra special thank you to Sue Bahr and Lisa Kirchoff for using their exceptional quiltmaking and editorial skills to turn my designs into clear, concise, and well-illustrated instructions.

Also, thank you to the very busy fingers of Leone Rusch, Esther Grischkowsky, and Julie Borg, who are responsible for the extraordinary hand and machine quilting throughout this book. Their talents enhance my designs and truly make them quilts. Julie Jergens, Tracy Schrantz, and Carla Plowman test our patterns, taking care to make sure we have included all the necessary steps to complete each project successfully. Thank you, also, to Christa and Reid for those extra hours after their busy school day. It is all greatly appreciated.

I am ever grateful for my association with Rodale Press, Suzanne Nelson, and her talented staff, who have guided me through the production of my second book. Jane Townswick has been our beacon through this project, and I thank her for her guidance and encouragement. I know that I am blessed by all of these talented people who are dedicated to the growth of Thimbleberries and all that is involved.

Thank You.

INTRODUCTION

Shortly after the photos were taken for my first book, *The Thimbleberries Book of Quilts,* my husband and I had the opportunity to purchase a beautiful old house in a neighborhood filled with homes that reflect the history of our town. Our home sits on the bank of the Crow River, which meanders gently through the middle of our town. Since our children grew up in our other home, we felt considerable nostalgia at leaving, but this was tempered by the excitement we felt at the huge new challenge ahead. I was positive I had one more house renovation in me.

Our "new" old house is a definite style change, and I have really enjoyed the different direction it demanded. Our former house was a delightful example of Prairie-style Arts and Crafts architecture, with lots of dark wood and built-in cabinets. Our new one is a charming 1930s house with arched doorways and painted woodwork, built-in bookcases and corner cupboards, and large paned windows with beautiful views of a wooded lot. Recently, I read through a journal I had kept during the months of renovation. My first entry was, "This house

needs attention, this house needs love, this house needs money!"

We decided to do everything, from top to bottom—replaster, repaint, replace light fixtures, retile, mill woodwork to match the original, and spend endless hours polishing brass knobs, rods, hinges, and door pulls. Throughout the months, my journal records comments like "They started sanding the floors today. What a huge mess, what a huge improvement!" And on another day, "Kerry came home from college today to a 'done' room complete with lots of quilts and fresh flowers. She was surprised and delighted. Her room is so sweet, so light, so fresh, so special."

Our son Matt's room is one of the most inviting hideaways in the house. Its ceiling has all sorts of angles, a dormer that allows sunlight to fill the room, and there is enough space to fill with treasures, collectibles, and quilts. All of these elements make it an inviting, welcome retreat he loves to come home to.

The quilts throughout my house echo my belief that home should always be comfortable and welcoming. When we are at home, we

have an overwhelming sense of well-being that comes from being surrounded by colors and textures, quilts, collectibles, and family pieces, and we strive to pass that same feeling on to all who enter.

Filling the house with my treasures and all the quilts for this book has been like having a blank artist's canvas on which I can apply wonderful colors, patterns, and textures. Just like other quiltmakers, I plan quilts for certain bedrooms, decorating schemes, holiday decorating, gift giving, and special family celebrations. As I wrote this book, I made sure there would be projects to fit all of those occasions.

I hope you will enjoy visiting my home through the pages of this book and that my quilt designs will make you love the wonderful heritage craft of quiltmaking as much as I do.

My Best,

Lynette Jensen

Lynette Jensen

LIVING
with
QUILTS

*A*ll quilts are meant to be enjoyed. I keep mine out where I can enjoy their color, texture, and the warm, cozy feeling they create. Here, Harvest Mix sets the fall theme for my dining room table centerpiece, which includes a cast-iron skillet filled with apples and a candle. In the next few pages, I hope you'll be inspired to find ways to fill your home with the quilts you make.

‹‹‹‹‹‹‹‹‹‹‹‹‹‹‹‹

This simply furnished guest bedroom is the perfect setting for Nine Patch Criss-Cross and Christmas House (draped on the chair in the corner). The antique doll bed holds an assortment of vintage children's books. Adding just the right homespun touch, the crocheted rug picks up the colors in the quilt. Pearl Baysinger, a member of my quilt group, taught me how to crochet rugs from leftover quilt scraps. Pearl's grandmother taught this craft to her, using a hand-carved crochet hook. I must admit that now I'm "hooked" and have filled many rooms in my house with these colorful accents.

My son Matt's room shows how you can create a masculine look with quilts. The dark, rich colors in the quilts set the tone, with Pine Tree Log Cabin casually folded and draped over Pine View (a nice way to think about displaying two bed quilts at the same time). I made the dust ruffle out of a brown and black check fabric to complete the scene. An old parade drum serves as a unique bedside table. The antique quilts on the bucket bench are some of my earliest finds and are what got me hooked on quilt-making.

Tucked in a corner, this reproduction wagon holds a mix of antique quilts and some new Thimbleberries quilts. The small quilt in the background is framed with nonglare glass. To keep it square and flat, I stitched the quilt to a mat board background, working all the way along the outside edges. This is also a good trick for displaying antique quilt blocks.

Banisters make perfect quilt racks. Here, I've folded and draped Raining Cats and Dogs and Sticks and Stones. I change the quilts with the seasons, always picking those I know I can safely launder. Peeking through the arch at the bottom of the stairs, Harvest Mix is draped over the back of the living room couch, another favorite, if unexpected, place where I like to display my quilts.

▶ ▶

Against the neutral background of our master bedroom, the quilts and accessories add a graphic punch without becoming overwhelming. The striped dust ruffle adds a nice contrast to the checkered patterns found in the Home Place quilt on the bed, the framed Cinnamon Hearts on the wall, and the big, chunky check fabric covering the chair. The red pillow on the chair is simply a square of fabric I layered with batting and a muslin backing, then machine quilted in a meander pattern. After the quilting, I sewed the square into a ruffled pillow to add a quick and easy touch of texture to the room.

▶ ▶ ▶ ▶ ▶ ▶ ▶ ▶ ▶ ▶

This dresser-top scene in my daughter's room shows how little finishing touches go a long way in adding colorful accents. In keeping with the light and airy mood of the room, I covered a purchased heart-shaped box with green paper. From leftover fabric scraps, I made yo-yos and glued them to the box lid. Additional yo-yos are stitched together to create a vintage-look doily under a basket of dried flowers.

I used a light touch in Kerry's sun-dappled room, choosing a soft palette of pink, purple, and green. The quilts complement the country-cottage feel of the flower-sprigged wallpaper, without appearing overly matched. In Bloom covers the bed and Wildflower nestles on a green plaid chair. Meadow Lily drapes over the door of the antique wardrobe, one of my favorite impromptu quilt racks. My basic rule for quilt display is this: After one month, I refold, reposition, or move the quilt to an entirely new room.

I love to mix and match and rotate the quilts all through my house. When I put my familiar quilts in a new place, it makes me look at and enjoy them in a fresh way. Here in our family room I tucked Daisy Days over the mantel, with Cinnamon Hearts nestled in a magazine rack in front of the fire. Brown-Eyed Susan is draped over the front door of the TV cabinet. I accordion-folded Pine Ridge and pulled it through the handles of a large basket to create a fuller, softer effect. The big chunky design on the Just Like Home pillow is an eye-catching accent on the couch.

In this corner of our living room, a vintage wicker plant stand holds rolled quilts plus some hooked rugs for texture. Christmas Apple drapes across the front of the stand. Moved from the family room, the Just Like Home pillow adds a fresh punch of color and pattern. Big pillows like this are an inexpensive way to redecorate and create a new look quickly and easily.

We use our screened porch as a relaxing haven from spring through fall. When company comes, I put out a few quilts, like the Christmas Apple and Watermelon Patch draped over the loveseat. I don't leave them out here for long, to avoid sun damage. A few of my favorite collectibles share the space as well, including vintage tin sand pails and shovels and tin lunch pails, plus some vintage watering cans, gardening tools, and seed packets.

One of my lucky finds, this antique planter was made to look like a picket fence with an arbor. I fill it with air-dried flowers from my summer garden. My low-fuss approach is to pick them at their peak, rubber band the stems together, hang them upside-down in a cool, dry, dark place and accept the fact that some will make it and some will not!

My garden also supplies the fixings for these herb bundles. I tie together sprigs of dried herbs and flowers, adding stalks of wheat and twigs for color and interest. Wrapped in squares of plaid or checked tissue paper and tied with raffia, these make delightful hostess gifts, especially when you're invited to a cookout. Placing a bundle on the coals releases a delightful aroma.

▶ ▶

Antique rolling pins and hydrangeas from my garden create an unusual juxtaposition that is sure to catch people's eye. This seemingly unrelated collection of objects, part of an ever-changing display by my back foyer, works together well because the colors and textures complement one another.

Christmas lights twinkle an invitation through the living room archway. With the red and green Cinnamon Hearts setting the stage, I've also gathered my antique dollhouse, a well-loved rocking horse from the 1880s, and my collection of Santas. I love to put up trees in several rooms throughout the house and often leave them unadorned for a couple of days, just to enjoy the simple beauty of their greenery. Next I add the white lights and enjoy just those for a few days, before adding my collection of antique and handmade ornaments.

I love to make my own Christmas boxes for gift giving or just to have stacked around the house for decoration. I purchase papier-mâché boxes from the craft store, then apply a coat of latex paint, sand the surface, add a stencil, then wipe on a layer of stain or graining liquid. A coat of matte acrylic sealer makes them more durable and easier to dust.

Fabric chenille garland is easy to make. Cut 1-inch-wide strips of homespun fabric and sew the short ends together to make a long strip. Zigzag a length of #8 pearl cotton down the center of the strip, gathering it as you sew. Embellish with buttons or red wooden beads.

With Town Square on the wall and Christmas Candy on the coffee table, the basement family room gets dressed up for the holidays. My tip for hanging quilts on plasterboard or wood walls is to use hand-sewing needles as nails. They're so fine they don't leave big holes in the wall or quilt. The black pot is an old vegetable steamer that I stenciled with snowmen and filled with peppermints. Grouping small quilts with items that carry out their theme is an easy decorator touch.

My mother made this dollhouse for me from an apple crate when I was five. I cherish mementos from my childhood and make them part of my home. Sitting atop the Christmas House quilt, I've filled the dollhouse with greens, berries, and pinecones for a holiday scene.

▷▷▷▷▷▷▷▷▷▷▷▷▷▷▷▷▷▷▷▷▷▷▷▷▷▷▷▷▷▷▷▷▷▷

The Yo-Yo Table Topper anchors this Christmas arrangement. An antique doll cradle with original paint holds artificial greens, twigs and berries, papier-mâché stars, and flicker-flame lights. I also use this cradle on the floor for an accent or as the centerpiece on a buffet table. Draping the quilt at an angle adds more interest to the scene.

Terrific gift ideas, these canning jar luminaries are simple to make. Fill canning jars with bells, holiday lights, pinecones, candies... anything goes. Add a votive candle holder to the top and decorate with ribbons as desired.

TEA TIME
Getting Ready

- READ instructions thoroughly before you begin.

- PREWASH and press fabric.

- USE ¼-inch seam allowances throughout unless directions specify otherwise.

- SEAM ALLOWANCES are included in the cutting sizes given.

- PRESS seam allowances in the direction that will create the least bulk, and whenever possible, press toward the darker fabric.

- CUTTING DIRECTIONS for each section of the quilt are given individually. If you like to cut as you go, simply follow the directions as you get to them. If you'd rather cut all your pieces at the same time, skip ahead to find each of the cutting sections and do all the cutting before you begin to sew. 🍃

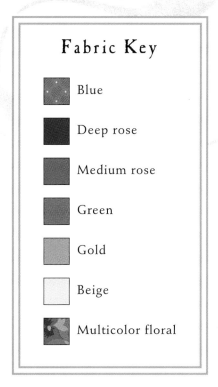

Fabric Key

Blue

Deep rose

Medium rose

Green

Gold

Beige

Multicolor floral

Teapot Blocks
(MAKE 4)

CUTTING

From the beige print fabric:
- Cut four 8½-inch squares
- Cut eight 2½ × 8½-inch rectangles
- Cut one 2⅞ × 7-inch strip

From the multicolor floral fabric:
- Cut thirty-two 2½-inch squares
- Cut one 2⅞ × 7-inch strip

1 Position the fusible web (paper side facing up) over the appliqué shapes on page 29, and trace. NOTE: The shapes are reversed so that when they are fused onto fabric they will appear in the correct position. Trace onto the fusible web four of each of the following shapes: G teapots, A petals, B petals, C petals, D leaves, E stems, and F flower centers. Cut roughly around the shapes.

2 For the G teapot shapes, draw a line approximately ⅜ inch inside the first line you traced, as shown in DIAGRAM 1. Cut away the fusible web on this drawn line, as shown. NOTE: Whenever you are fusing a large shape like the teapot, it is helpful to fuse only the outer edges of the shape. This will keep the teapots from

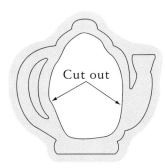

Cut out

DIAGRAM 1

looking stiff and will also make it much easier to buttonhole stitch the flower shapes later.

3 With a hot dry iron, press the coated sides of the fusible web teapot shapes to the wrong side of the fabric chosen for the teapots. Let the fabric cool, and cut out the teapots along the first traced lines. Peel off the paper backing.

4 Place the fusible web flower stem and leaf shapes coated side down on the wrong sides of the fabrics chosen for the flowers. Press with a hot dry iron. Let the fabric cool, and cut out the appliqué shapes. Peel off the paper backing.

5 Referring to DIAGRAM 2 on page 26 as a placement guide, position and fuse the G teapots on the beige print background squares first, followed by the E stems, the A, B, and C petals, the F flower centers, and finally, the D leaves.

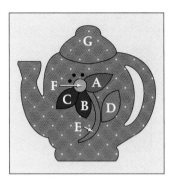

DIAGRAM 2

6 Referring to DIAGRAM 2, use three strands of black embroidery floss to appliqué a teapot and flower onto each block, using the buttonhole stitch. With three strands of floss, stitch French knots above each flower. Outline stitch the bottom of the lid, using three strands of floss. For more information on French knots, outline stitch, and buttonhole stitch, see page 210.

7 With right sides together, position a 2½-inch multicolor floral square on each corner of the Teapot blocks, as shown in DIAGRAM 3. Draw diagonal lines on the floral squares, and stitch on these lines, as shown.

Trim to ¼"

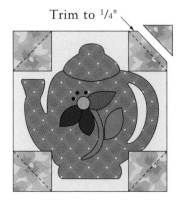

DIAGRAM 3

Trim seam allowances to ¼ inch, as shown. Press.

8 Stitch the four Teapot blocks together, matching seam intersections, as shown in DIAGRAM 4.

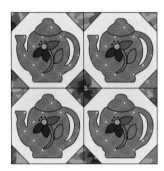

DIAGRAM 4

9 With right sides together, position a 2½-inch multicolor floral square at each end of the eight 2½ × 8½-inch beige pieces, as shown in DIAGRAM 5. Draw a diagonal line on each multicolor floral square, and stitch on these lines, as shown. Trim seam allowances to ¼ inch, as shown. Press.

Trim to ¼"

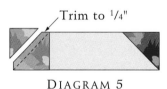

DIAGRAM 5

10 Stitch together eight of the units from Step 9 in pairs, as shown in DIAGRAM 6.

DIAGRAM 6

11 Sew one section from Step 10 to the top of the Teapot blocks and one to the bottom, as shown in DIAGRAM 7. Press.

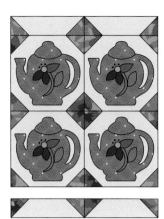

DIAGRAM 7

12 Layer the 2⅞ × 7-inch beige and multicolor floral strips, right sides together, as shown in DIAGRAM 8. Press, but do not sew. Cut the layered strips into two 2⅞-inch squares, as shown.

2⅞"

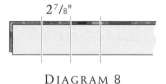

DIAGRAM 8

13 Cut the layered squares in half diagonally, as shown in DIAGRAM 9. Stitch a ¼-inch seam along the diagonal edge, as shown. Press seam allowances toward the multicolor floral fabric.

DIAGRAM 9

14 Stitch the triangle-pieced squares to the ends of the remaining two sections from Step 10, as shown in DIAGRAM 10.

DIAGRAM 10

15 Sew the two rows to the sides of the Teapot blocks, as shown in DIAGRAM 11. Press.

DIAGRAM 11

Borders

C U T T I N G

for Inner Border

NOTE: The yardage given allows for border pieces to be cut cross-grain.

From the deep rose fabric:
• Cut four 1½ × 44-inch strips

Attaching the Inner Border

1 Measure the quilt from left to right through the middle to determine the length of the top and bottom border strips. Cut the deep rose inner border strips to the necessary length. Sew the inner border strips to the top and bottom of the center section of the quilt, as shown in the QUILT ASSEMBLY DIAGRAM. Press seam allowances toward the border strips.

QUILT ASSEMBLY DIAGRAM

2 Measure the quilt from top to bottom through the middle, including the border strips you just added, to determine the length of the side border strips. Cut the deep rose inner border strips to the necessary length, and sew them to the sides of the quilt, as shown. Press seam allowances toward the border strips.

C U T T I N G

for Outer Border

From the blue print fabric:
• Cut four 6½ × 44-inch strips

Attaching the Outer Border

1 Measure the quilt from left to right through the middle to determine the length of the top and bottom outer border strips. Cut two blue print border strips to the necessary length, and sew them to the top and bottom, as shown in the QUILT ASSEMBLY DIAGRAM. Press seam allowances toward the outer borders.

2 Measure the quilt from top to bottom through the middle, including the border strips you just added, to determine the length of the side outer border strips. Cut two blue border strips to the necessary length and sew them to the sides of the quilt. Press seam allowances toward the outer border.

3 Stay stitch ⅛ inch from the raw edges of the outer border strips to stabilize them for the appliqué process.

Appliquéing the Outer Border

1 Prepare the border appliqués in the same manner as for the Teapots. Trace 16 of each of the following shapes: A petals, B petals, C petals, F flower centers, D leaves, and E stems. Fuse each shape to the wrong side of the fabric chosen for the flower appliqués.

2 Referring to the QUILT ASSEMBLY DIAGRAM on page 27 as a placement guide, position and fuse the flower shapes in place on each of the outer border strips.

3 Using three strands of black embroidery floss, buttonhole stitch around each appliqué piece in the same manner as for the Teapots. Using three strands of floss, stitch French knots above the flowers.

Putting It All Together

1 Trim the backing and batting so they are 4 inches larger than the quilt top dimensions.

2 Mark quilting designs on the quilt top.

3 Layer the backing, batting, and quilt top. Baste the layers together and quilt.

4 When quilting is complete, remove basting and trim the excess backing and batting even with the quilt top.

Binding

NOTE: The 2¾-inch binding strips will produce a ⅜-inch-wide binding. If you want a wider or narrower binding,

adjust the width of the strips you cut. (See page 216 for pointers on how to experiment with binding width.) See "Making and Attaching the Binding" on page 215 to complete your quilt.

CUTTING

From the blue print fabric:
• Cut four 2¾ × 44-inch strips for cross-grain binding

Quilting DESIGNS

FOR HAND QUILTING:

🌥 *Keep the quilting in this quilt very simple to serve as background to the appliqué shapes. Quilt lines of cross-hatching spaced at 1¾-inch intervals in the center background areas and in the outer borders.*

🌥 *Quilt around the outlines of each teapot, flower appliqué, square, and narrow border to make them stand out from the cross-hatched areas.*

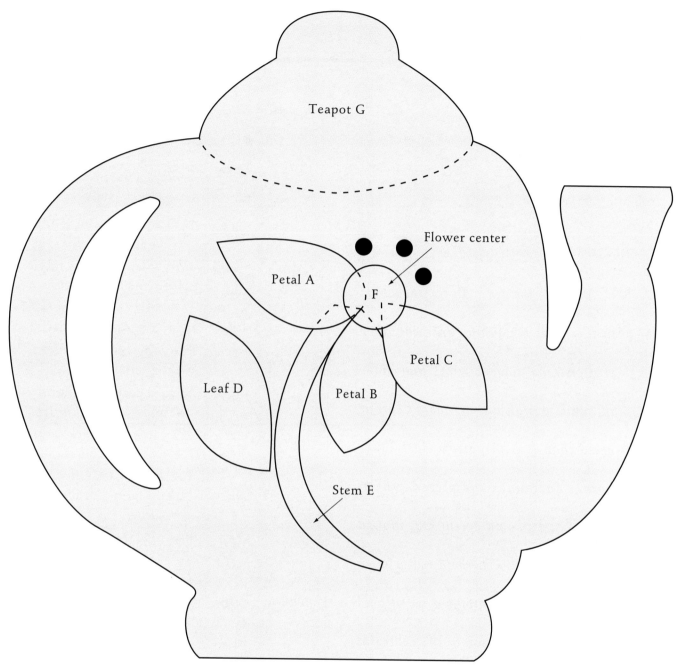

Teapot G

Petal A

Flower center

F

Petal C

Leaf D

Petal B

Stem E

TEAPOT APPLIQUÉ PATTERNS

NINE PATCH
CRISS-CROSS

Because the reds, blues, and golds in this quilt are similar in value, they create strong diagonal lines that make the quilt design appear more complicated than it is. A narrow, dark inner border surrounds the pieced center, functioning like an accent mat around a framed picture. The bold red print in the outer border contains a bit of gold that repeats the color in the center of the quilt. The large cream and black bias binding is an important design element because it echoes the cream tone in the light squares and adds a final flourish to the edges of the quilt.

Size

Bed Quilt: 78 × 96 inches (unquilted)

Finished Block: 6 inches square

Fabrics and Supplies

Yardage is based on 44-inch-wide fabric.

1⅝ yards red print fabric for Nine Patch blocks

1⅓ yards gold print fabric for Nine Patch blocks

1⅓ yards cream print fabric for alternate blocks

1⅝ yards blue print fabric for alternate blocks

⅝ yard dark brown print fabric for inner border

2¼ yards red check fabric for outer border

1¼ yards black and cream plaid fabric for bias binding

6 yards fabric for quilt backing

Quilt batting, at least 82 × 100 inches

Rotary cutter, mat, and see-through ruler with ⅛-inch markings

Getting Ready

- READ instructions thoroughly before you begin.
- PREWASH and press fabric.
- USE ¼-inch seam allowances throughout unless directions specify otherwise.
- SEAM ALLOWANCES are included in the cutting sizes given.
- PRESS seam allowances in the direction that will create the least bulk, and whenever possible, press toward the darker fabric.
- CUTTING DIRECTIONS for each section of the quilt are given individually. If you like to cut as you go, simply follow the directions as you get to them. If you'd rather cut all your pieces at the same time, skip ahead to find each of the cutting sections and do all the cutting before you begin to sew.

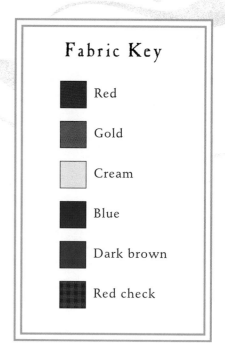

Fabric Key

- Red
- Gold
- Cream
- Blue
- Dark brown
- Red check

Nine Patch Blocks

(MAKE 65)

CUTTING

From the red print fabric:
- Cut sixteen 2½ × 44-inch strips for Strip Set I
- Cut four 2½ × 44-inch strips for Strip Set II

From the gold print fabric:
- Cut eight 2½ × 44-inch strips for Strip Set I
- Cut eight 2½ × 44-inch strips for Strip Set II

Piecing the Nine Patch Blocks

1 To make Strip Set I, sew a 2½ × 44-inch red strip to either side of a 2½ × 44-inch gold strip, as shown in DIAGRAM 1.

Press seam allowances toward the darker fabric. Make eight of Strip Set I. Cut each Strip Set I into one hundred thirty 2½-inch segments, as shown.

2½"

Strip Set I

DIAGRAM 1

2 To make Strip Set II, sew a 2½ × 44-inch gold strip to either side of a 2½ × 44-inch red strip, as shown in DIAGRAM 2. Press seam allowances toward

2½"

Strip Set II

DIAGRAM 2

the darker fabric. Make four of Strip Set II. Cut each Strip Set II into sixty-five 2½-inch segments, as shown.

TO ROTARY CUT segments from a strip set, start by squaring up the end of the strip set so that it is perpendicular to a seam line. Trim away any selvage edges with this first cut. Use the markings on your rotary ruler and cutting mat to continuously line up the strip set. If it begins to look uneven, trim the cut edge again to make sure it stays perpendicular to the seam line. Check often for accuracy as you cut.

TIPS AND TRICKS

3 Sew a Strip Set I segment to opposite sides of a Strip Set II, as shown in DIAGRAM 3. Make 65 of these Nine Patch blocks.

DIAGRAM 3

Alternate Blocks
(MAKE 65)

C U T T I N G

From the cream print fabric:
• Cut eight 4¾ × 44-inch strips; from these strips cut sixty-five 4¾-inch squares.

From the blue print fabric:
• Cut thirteen 3⅞ × 44-inch strips; from these strips, cut one hundred thirty 3⅞-inch squares. Cut the squares in half diagonally to make two hundred sixty triangles.

Piecing the Alternate Blocks

1 Sew blue triangles to opposite sides of each 4¾-inch cream square, as shown in DIAGRAM 4. Press seam allowances toward the triangles.

DIAGRAM 4

2 Sew blue triangles to the remaining sides of the cream squares, as shown in DIAGRAM 5. Make 65 alternate blocks.

DIAGRAM 5

Joining the Blocks

1 Sew five Nine Patch blocks and five alternate blocks together in a row, alternating the blocks, referring to the QUILT ASSEMBLY DIAGRAM on page 34. Make 13 horizontal rows.

2 Referring to the QUILT ASSEMBLY DIAGRAM for block placement, sew the rows together, matching seam intersections.

Borders

C U T T I N G

NOTE: The yardage given allows for the border pieces to be cut cross-grain.

From the dark brown print fabric:
• Cut seven 2½ × 44-inch strips for the inner border

From the red check fabric:
• Cut nine 7½ × 44-inch strips for the outer border

Attaching the Borders

1 Measure the quilt from left to right through the middle to determine the length of the top and bottom border strips. Diagonally piece and cut the dark brown inner border strips to the necessary length, and sew them to the top and bottom of the quilt, referring to the QUILT ASSEMBLY DIAGRAM on page 34.

2 Measure the quilt from top to bottom through the middle, including the border strips you just added, to determine the length of the side border strips. Diagonally piece and cut the dark brown inner border strips to the necessary lengths, and sew them to the sides of the quilt, referring to the QUILT ASSEMBLY DIAGRAM on page 34.

3 For the top and bottom outer border strips, measure as you did for the inner border in Step 1. Diagonally piece the red check outer border strips, trim them to the necessary lengths, and sew them to the top and bottom of the quilt.

4 For the side outer border strips, measure as for the inner border. Diagonally piece the red check outer strips, trim them to the necessary lengths, and sew them to the sides of the quilt.

Putting It All Together

1 Cut the 6-yard length of backing in half crosswise. Remove selvages and sew the two lengths together. Press the seam open. Trim backing and batting to 4 inches larger than quilt top.

2 Mark quilting designs on the quilt top.

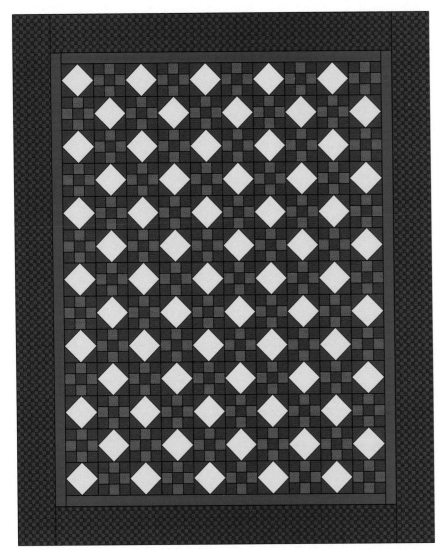

QUILT ASSEMBLY DIAGRAM

3 Layer the backing, batting, and quilt top. Baste these layers together, and quilt.

4 Remove the basting and trim the excess backing and batting even with the quilt top.

Binding

NOTE: The 2¾-inch bias strips will produce a ⅜-inch-wide binding. If you want a wider or narrower binding, adjust the width of the cut strips. (See page 216 for pointers on binding width.) See "Making and Attaching the Binding" on page 215 to complete your quilt.

CUTTING

From the black and cream plaid:
• Cut enough 2¾-inch bias strips to make a 370-inch strip for bias binding

Quilting DESIGNS

FOR HAND QUILTING:

❧ Because of the colors and prints in this quilt, quilting designs will not be highly visible, except in the light blocks. Simple stitch-in-the-ditch quilting will work well to highlight the shapes in the pieced areas.

❧ Choose a purchased quilting stencil with a floral motif to complement the light alternating squares on-point.

❧ You can treat the two borders as one by using a purchased quilting stencil with a large feathered chain design, or choose another large design you like. I find it helpful to keep a variety of large border stencils on hand. That way, I'm prepared with a choice of quilting designs for any border or combination of borders.

FOR MACHINE QUILTING:

❧ An overall pattern of meander quilting will work well for machine quilting the pieced areas of this quilt.

❧ You can machine quilt the light on-point squares and the borders with the very same types of designs listed under hand quilting.

JUST LIKE HOME

I have always loved to give rooms in my home an exciting, fresh look by making some new pillows. I think this is a clever way to introduce a touch of color, brighten up a corner, or just add a bit of handwork to soften the look of a chair or any other piece of furniture. Simply lining up three or four pillows can add a colorful accent that will dramatically change the appearance of a couch or loveseat. The House block in this Just Like Home pillow is big, bold, and graphic. With its narrow ruffle, this pillow makes a fun pictorial accessory for any room.

Size

Pillow without ruffle: 18 inches square (unquilted)

Fabrics and Supplies

Yardage is based on 44-inch-wide fabric.

⅜ yard beige print fabric for backgrounds and sawtooth border

⅛ yard red print #1 fabric for house

⅛ yard dark gold print fabric for inner roof and windows

¾ yard black print fabric for outer roof, door, and ruffle

⅛ yard gold print fabric for stars

¼ yard blue print fabric for sawtooth

¼ yard red print #2 fabric for outer border

⅝ yard muslin for backing for pillow top

⅝ yard dark red print fabric for pillow back

18-inch square pillow form

Rotary cutter, mat, and see-through ruler with ⅛-inch markings

JUST LIKE HOME
Getting Ready

• READ instructions thoroughly before you begin.

• PREWASH and press fabric.

• USE ¼-inch seam allowances throughout unless directions specify otherwise.

• SEAM ALLOWANCES are included in the cutting sizes given.

• PRESS seam allowances in the direction that will create the least bulk, and whenever possible, press toward the darker fabric.

• CUTTING DIRECTIONS for each section of the quilt are given individually. If you like to cut as you go, simply follow the directions as you get to them. If you'd rather cut all your pieces at the same time, skip ahead to find each of the cutting sections and do all the cutting before you begin to sew. 🍂

Fabric Key

☐ Beige

■ Red #1

■ Dark gold

■ Black

■ Gold

■ Blue

■ Red #2

■ Dark red backing

House Block
(MAKE 1)

CUTTING

From the beige print fabric:
• Cut one 5⅜-inch square

From the red print #1 fabric:
• Cut one 1½ × 3½-inch rectangle
• Cut four 1½ × 5-inch rectangles
• Cut two 1½-inch squares
• Cut two 1½ × 2-inch rectangles

From the dark gold print fabric:
• Cut two 1½ × 2½-inch rectangles
• Cut two 2½-inch squares

From the black print fabric:
• Cut one 5⅜-inch square
• Cut one 3½ × 4-inch rectangle

Piecing the House Block

1 Layer the 5⅜-inch beige square and the black square right sides together, as shown in DIAGRAM 1. Cut the layered squares in half diagonally and stitch a ¼-inch seam along each diagonal edge. Press seam allowances toward the black fabric.

DIAGRAM 1

2 Position a 2½-inch dark gold print square on the black corner of the triangle-pieced square, right sides together, as shown in DIAGRAM 2. Draw a diagonal line on the dark gold square, as shown, and stitch on this line. Trim the seam allow-

ances to ¼ inch, and press. Make two of these units.

Trim to ¼"

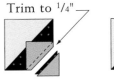

DIAGRAM 2

3 Sew the two pieced units together as shown in DIAGRAM 3, completing the roof unit.

DIAGRAM 3

4 Sew a 1½ × 3½-inch red #1 rectangle to the 3½ × 4-inch black rectangle to make the door

unit, as shown in DIAGRAM 4. Press seam allowances toward the black fabric.

DIAGRAM 4

5 To make a window unit, sew a 1½-inch red square to the top and a 1½ × 2-inch red rectangle to the bottom of a 1½ × 2½-inch dark gold rectangle, as shown in DIAGRAM 5. Press seam allowances toward the red fabric. Repeat to make a second window unit.

DIAGRAM 5

6 Sew a 1½ × 5-inch red rectangle to both sides of the window units, as shown in DIAGRAM 6. Press seam allowances toward the red fabric. Sew the window units to both sides of the door unit, as shown. Press seam allowances toward the black fabric.

DIAGRAM 6

7 Sew the roof and lower house units together to complete the House block, as shown in DIAGRAM 7. At this point, the House block should measure 9½ inches square.

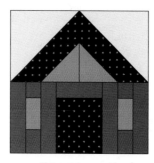

DIAGRAM 7

Star Blocks
(MAKE 4)

CUTTING

From the gold print fabric:
• Cut four 1½ × 3½-inch rectangles
• Cut eight 1½-inch squares

From the beige print fabric:
• Cut eight 1½ × 2½-inch rectangles
• Cut sixteen 1½-inch squares

Piecing the Star Blocks

1 Position a 1½-inch gold print square on the corner of a 1½ × 2½-inch beige print rectangle, as shown in DIAGRAM 8. Draw a diagonal line on the gold print square, and stitch on this line, as shown. Trim seam allowances to ¼ inch. Press seam allowances toward the gold fabric. Sew a 1½-inch beige square to the gold triangle, as shown below. Make a total of eight of these units, as shown.

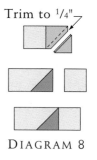

Trim to ¼"

DIAGRAM 8

2 Position a 1½-inch beige square on the corner of a 1½ × 3½-inch gold rectangle, as shown in DIAGRAM 9. Draw a diagonal line on the beige square, as shown, and stitch on this line. Trim seam allowances to ¼ inch. Press seam allowances toward the gold fabric. Repeat at the opposite corner of the gold print rectangle, as shown below. Make a total of four of these units.

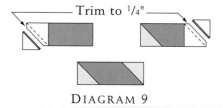

Trim to ¼"

DIAGRAM 9

3 Sew two units from Step 1 to each of the units from Step 2, completing the Star blocks, as shown in DIAGRAM 10. At this point, the Star blocks should measure 3½ inches square.

DIAGRAM 10

Sawtooth Border

C U T T I N G

From the beige print fabric:
• Cut one 3⅞ × 44-inch strip

From the blue print fabric:
• Cut one 3⅞ × 44-inch strip

Piecing
the Sawtooth Border

1 Layer the 3⅞ × 44-inch beige
print and blue print strips
right sides together. Press the
strips together, but do not sew.
Cut the layered strips into six
3⅞-inch squares, as shown in
DIAGRAM 11.

3⅞"

DIAGRAM 11

2 Cut the layered squares in
half diagonally, and stitch a
¼-inch seam along each diagonal
edge, as shown in DIAGRAM 12.
Press seam allowances toward
the darker fabric.

DIAGRAM 12

3 Sew three triangle-pieced
squares together, completing
a sawtooth border, as shown in
DIAGRAM 13. Make four of these
sawtooth borders. Press.

DIAGRAM 13

4 Sew a sawtooth border to
the top and bottom of the
House blocks, as shown in DIA-
GRAM 14. Press.

DIAGRAM 14

5 Sew a Star block to both
ends of the remaining two
sawtooth borders, as shown in
DIAGRAM 15. Sew these borders
to the sides of the House block,
as shown.

DIAGRAM 15

Outer Border

C U T T I N G

From the red print #2 fabric:
• Cut two 2 × 15½-inch strips
• Cut two 2 × 18½-inch strips

Attaching
the Outer Border

1 Sew the 2 × 15½-inch red #2
strips to the top and bottom
of the pillow, as shown in the
PILLOW ASSEMBLY DIAGRAM.
Press seam allowances toward
the borders.

PILLOW ASSEMBLY DIAGRAM

2 Sew the 2 × 18½-inch red #2
strips to the sides of the
pillow, as shown. Press seams allowances toward the borders.

Putting It All Together

1 Trim the muslin backing and batting so they are 4 inches larger than the pillow top dimensions.

2 Layer the muslin backing, batting, and pillow top. Baste the layers together and quilt.

3 When quilting is complete, remove basting and trim the excess backing and batting even with the pillow top.

TO PREPARE the pillow top before attaching the ruffle, I suggest hand basting the edges of all three layers of the pillow top together. This will prevent the edge of the pillow top from rippling when you attach the ruffle.

TIPS AND TRICKS

Pillow Ruffle

CUTTING

From the black print fabric:
• Cut five 2½ × 44-inch strips

GATHERING RUFFLES

🖊 HERE'S ANOTHER quick and easy way to gather a ruffle. Do a wide, long zigzag stitch over two strands of regular-weight sewing thread or a heavier thread positioned ¼ inch in from the raw edges of the ruffle. NOTE: You will need a length of thread at least 2 times the circumference of your pillow. Secure one end of the heavy thread by stitching across it. Then zigzag over the heavy thread all the way around the ruffle, taking care not to sew through it. Pull on the heavy thread to gather up the ruffle to fit the edges of your pillow top.

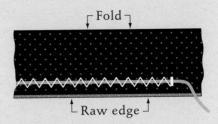

Fold

Raw edge

Attaching the Ruffle

1 Sew the 2½ × 44-inch black strips together with diagonal seams to make a continuous ruffle strip. For more information on diagonal seams, see page 211. Trim seam allowances to ¼ inch. Press seam allowances open.

2 With wrong sides together, fold the continuous ruffle strip in half lengthwise, and run gathering stitches all the way around the strip, ¼ inch from the raw edges, as shown in DIAGRAM 16.

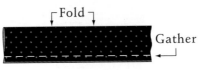

Fold

Gather

DIAGRAM 16

3 Pull up the gathering stitches until the ruffle fits the pillow top, taking care to allow fullness in the rufffle at each corner, as shown in DIAGRAM 17. Sew the ruffle to the pillow top, using a scant ¼-inch seam allowance.

DIAGRAM 17

Pillow Back

C U T T I N G

From the dark red print backing fabric:
• Cut two 18½ × 21-inch pieces

Assembling the Pillow Back

1 Fold the two dark red backing pieces in half, wrong sides together, to form two 10½ × 18½-inch double-thick back pieces. Overlap the two folded edges by 2 inches, as shown in DIAGRAM 18. Baste across the overlapped areas ¼ inch in from each edge to secure them in place, as shown. The doubled layers of fabric will make the pillow back more stable and add a nice finishing touch.

2 Place the pillow back and the pillow top right sides together, as shown in DIAGRAM 19, making sure that the folded edge of the ruffle faces the center of the pillow top. Pin the edges of the pillow front and back together, and stitch around the outside edge, using a ⅜-inch seam allowance.

DIAGRAM 18

DIAGRAM 19

3 Trim the pillow back and corner seam allowances, if needed to reduce bulk, turn the pillow right side out, and fluff up the ruffle. Insert the pillow form through the back opening. If desired, slipstitch the back opening closed.

Quilting DESIGNS

FOR HAND OR MACHINE QUILTING:

Quilt in the ditch around the outside of the house, around each of the windows, and around the stars and the triangles. Quilt two vertical lines inside the door, spacing them an inch in from the sides of the door.

Quilt in the ditch of each of the border seams.

HARVEST MIX

For this quilt, I gathered fabrics in colors that signal the end of summer, when the trees around my home turn to glorious shades of rust, ochre, brown, and gold. I chose a different main color for each of the blocks in the center of the quilt. They all share the same background print, creating a feeling of unity. The mellow, medium-value fabric in the side triangles frames the blocks gently, and two coordinated plaids in the borders add strong visual interest. The tan and red prints in the corner blocks draw the eye outward to the edges of the quilt.

Size
Lap Quilt: 56 × 66 inches
Finished Block: 8 inches square

Fabrics and Supplies
Yardage is based on 44-inch-wide fabric.

⅛ yard *each* of two check fabrics for Triangle-Pieced Square blocks

¼ yard *each* of three rust print fabrics for Nine Patch blocks

1¼ yards beige print fabric for all pieced blocks

⅛ yard *each* of four dark fabrics for Ohio Star points

One 4½-inch square *each* of four plaids for Ohio Star centers

⅛ yard *each* of nine coordinating print fabrics for Sixteen Patch blocks

⅝ yard tan print for side and corner triangles

¼ yard gold print for corner blocks

¼ yard red print for corner blocks

1½ yards chestnut/black check for inner border

2 yards black/rust plaid for outer border

¾ yard brown plaid for binding

3⅓ yards fabric for Option I quilt backing

1½ yards black/tan check fabric for Option II pieced quilt backing

2¼ yards small chestnut/black check fabric for Option II pieced quilt backing

Quilt batting, at least 60 × 70 inches

Rotary cutter, mat, and see-through ruler with ⅛-inch markings

Getting Ready

- READ instructions thoroughly before you begin.
- PREWASH and press fabric.
- USE ¼-inch seam allowances throughout unless directions specify otherwise.
- SEAM ALLOWANCES are included in the cutting sizes given.
- PRESS seam allowances in the direction that will create the least bulk, and whenever possible, press toward the darker fabric.
- CUTTING DIRECTIONS for each section of the quilt are given individually. If you like to cut as you go, simply follow the directions as you get to them. If you'd rather cut all your pieces at the same time, skip ahead to find each of the cutting sections and do all the cutting before you begin to sew. ✎

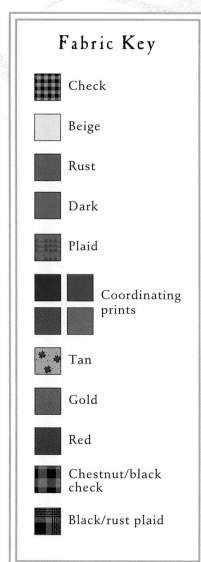

Fabric Key

- Check
- Beige
- Rust
- Dark
- Plaid
- Coordinating prints
- Tan
- Gold
- Red
- Chestnut/black check
- Black/rust plaid

Triangle-Pieced Blocks

(MAKE 2)

CUTTING

for Each Triangle-Pieced Square Block

TRIANGLE-PIECED SQUARE
BLOCK DIAGRAM

From the check fabric:
- Cut one 2⅞ × 26-inch strip

From the beige print fabric:
- Cut one 2⅞ × 26-inch strip

Piecing the Triangle-Pieced Square Blocks

1 With right sides together, layer a check 2⅞ × 26-inch strip and a beige 2⅞ × 26-inch strip. Press together but do not sew. Cut the layered strips into eight 2⅞-inch squares. Repeat.

2 Cut the layered squares in half diagonally, as shown in DIAGRAM 1. Stitch ¼ inch from the diagonal edges. Press seam allowances toward the check fabric. Make a total of 16 triangle-pieced squares for each block.

DIAGRAM 1

3 To piece the blocks, sew four of the triangle-pieced squares together in a row. Repeat to make four rows and sew them together; see DIAGRAM 2. Make two Triangle-Pieced Square blocks, each measuring 8½ inches square.

DIAGRAM 2

Nine Patch Blocks
(MAKE 3)

for Each Nine Patch Block

NINE PATCH
BLOCK DIAGRAM

From one of the rust print fabrics:
• Cut four 2½-inch squares
• Cut one 4½-inch square

From the beige print fabric:
• Cut four 2½ × 4½-inch pieces

Piecing
the Nine Patch Blocks

1 Sew a 2½ × 4½-inch beige piece to the top and bottom of each of the 4½-inch rust squares, as shown in DIAGRAM 3.

DIAGRAM 3

2 Sew a 2½-inch rust square to each end of the remaining 2½ × 4½-inch beige pieces, as shown in DIAGRAM 4.

DIAGRAM 4

3 Sew the units from Step 2 to the sides of each Step 1 unit, as shown in DIAGRAM 5. At this point, the Nine Patch blocks should measure 8½ inches square.

DIAGRAM 5

Ohio Star Blocks
(MAKE 4)

for Each Ohio Star Block

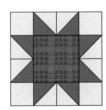

OHIO STAR
BLOCK DIAGRAM

From one of the dark fabrics:
• Cut one 2⅞ × 14-inch strip

From the beige print fabric:
• Cut four 2½-inch squares
• Cut one 2⅞ × 14-inch strip

From one of the plaid fabrics:
• Cut one 4½-inch square

Piecing
the Ohio Star Blocks

1 Layer the 2⅞ × 14-inch dark and beige strips right sides together. Press, but do not sew. Cut the layered strips into four 2⅞-inch squares; see DIAGRAM 6. Cut the squares in half diagonally and stitch a ¼-inch seam along each diagonal edge, for a total of eight triangle-pieced squares. Repeat for each of the remaining blocks.

DIAGRAM 6

2 Sew the triangle-pieced squares together in pairs to make four star-point units for each Ohio Star block. Sew a star-point unit to the top and bottom of each 4½-inch plaid square, as shown in DIAGRAM 7.

DIAGRAM 7

3 Sew a 2½-inch beige square to the remaining star-point units, as shown in DIAGRAM 8. Sew these units to the sides of each Ohio Star block, as shown. At this point, the Ohio Star blocks should measure 8½ inches square.

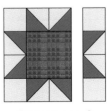

DIAGRAM 8

Sixteen Patch Blocks
(MAKE 9)

for Each Sixteen Patch Block

SIXTEEN PATCH
BLOCK DIAGRAM

From one of the coordinating print fabrics:
• Cut one 2½ × 22-inch strip

From the beige print fabric:
• Cut one 2½ × 22-inch strip

Piecing the Sixteen Patch Blocks

1 With right sides together, sew a 2½ × 22-inch coordinating print fabric strip to a 2½ × 22-inch beige strip. Press seam allowances toward the coordinating print fabric. Crosscut the strip set into eight 2½-inch segments, as shown in DIAGRAM 9. Repeat for each of the remaining Sixteen Patch blocks.

2½"

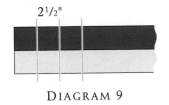

DIAGRAM 9

2 Sew four units together in a row, alternating colors, referring to DIAGRAM 10. Make two of these rows and sew them together for each of the nine Sixteen Patch blocks. At this point, the Sixteen Patch blocks should measure 8½ inches square.

DIAGRAM 10

Quilt Center

From the tan print fabric:
• Cut three 13-inch squares; cut these into quarters diagonally to make 12 side triangles
NOTE: You will use only 10 of the triangles in the quilt.
• Cut two 8-inch squares; cut these in half diagonally to make four corner triangles
NOTE: The side and corner triangles will be larger than necessary and will be trimmed after they have been added to the pieced blocks.

Assembling the Quilt Center

NOTE: When sewing the blocks into rows, press the seam allowances between blocks in the opposite direction from the previous row. This allows for easy matching and sewing at block intersections.

1 Sew the pieced blocks together in diagonal rows, as shown in DIAGRAM 11 on the opposite page, beginning and ending each row with side triangles as needed. Do not attach the corner triangles yet.

2 Sew the diagonal rows together, pinning the block intersections for accuracy. Press all seam allowances between rows in the same direction.

3 Sew the triangles to the corners of the quilt top, referring to DIAGRAM 11.

4 Trim excess fabric from the side and corner triangles, making sure to allow a ¼-inch seam allowance beyond the block corners. Before you trim, be sure to see "Trimming Side and Corner Triangles" on page 211 to be certain you make these cuts accurately.

Borders and Corner Blocks

NOTE: The yardage given allows for border strips to be cut lengthwise.

From the gold and red print fabrics:
• Cut two 7¼-inch squares of each fabric for the corner blocks; cut the squares diagonally into quarters, forming eight triangles

DIAGRAM 11

From the chestnut/black check fabric:
• Cut two 6½ × 38-inch strips for the top and bottom inner borders
• Cut two 6½ × 48-inch strips for the side inner borders

From the black/rust plaid fabric:
• Cut two 5 × 49-inch strips for the top and bottom outer borders
• Cut two 5 × 69-inch strips for the side outer borders

Piecing the Corner Blocks

1 Layer a gold triangle and a red triangle. Sew a ¼-inch seam along one of the bias edges, as shown in DIAGRAM 12, being careful not to stretch the triangles. Also, make sure to sew on the same bias edge for each pair of triangles so that the pieced triangles will all have the red fabric on the same side. Press seam allowances toward the red fabric. Make eight of these units, as shown.

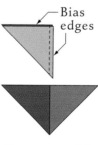

Bias edges

DIAGRAM 12

2 Sew two of these units together to make a corner block measuring 6½ inches square, as shown in DIAGRAM 13. Make a total of four corner blocks.

DIAGRAM 13

Inner Border

1 Measure the quilt through the center from left to right to determine the length for the top and bottom border strips. Trim the two 6½ × 38-inch chestnut/black check strips to this measurement. Sew these borders to the top and bottom of the quilt, referring to the QUILT ASSEMBLY DIAGRAM on page 48. Press seam allowances toward the border.

2 Measure the quilt through the center from top to bottom, including seam allowances but *not* the top and bottom border strips. Cut the 6½ × 48-inch chestnut/black check strips to the length needed. Sew a corner square to each end of these border strips, referring to the QUILT ASSEMBLY DIAGRAM. Sew the side border strips to the quilt, and press seam allowances toward the border.

Outer Border

1 Measure the quilt as in Step 1 of "Inner Border," and include the inner border in this measurement. Cut the 5 × 49-inch black/rust plaid outer border

QUILT ASSEMBLY DIAGRAM

backing and batting to about 4 inches larger than the quilt top.

2 Mark quilting designs on the quilt top.

3 Layer the backing, batting, and quilt top. Baste the layers together, and quilt by hand or machine.

4 When quilting is complete, remove the basting stitches and trim the excess backing and batting even with the quilt top.

strips to this measurement and sew them to the top and bottom of the quilt, referring to the QUILT ASSEMBLY DIAGRAM. Press.

2 Measure the quilt from top to bottom through the middle, including the border strips you just added, to determine the length of the side border strips. Cut the 5 × 69-inch black/rust plaid strips to this measurement and sew them to the sides of the quilt. Press.

Putting It All Together

NOTE: Choose the backing option you like best for your quilt.

Option I Backing

1 Cut the 3⅓-yard length of backing fabric in half crosswise. Remove the selvages and sew the two lengths together. Press this seam open. Trim the

Option II Backing

CUTTING

From the black/tan check fabric:
• Cut one 43 × 53-inch piece

From the small chestnut/black check fabric:
• Cut two 11 × 43-inch strips
• Cut two 11 × 74-inch strips

Assembling the Pieced Back

1 With right sides together, sew the 11 × 43-inch chestnut/black strips to the top and bottom of the 43 × 53-inch black/tan check piece, referring to DIAGRAM 14. Press seam allowances toward the borders.

2 Sew the 11 × 74-inch chestnut/black strips to the sides, referring to DIAGRAM 14. Press seam allowances toward the borders.

Option II backing

DIAGRAM 14

3 Trim the backing and batting so they are about 4 inches larger than the quilt top.

4 Mark quilting designs on the quilt top.

5 Layer the pieced backing and batting. Center the quilt top over the backing and the batting. Baste the three layers together, and then quilt.

Binding

NOTE: The 2¾-inch-wide plaid bias strips will produce a ⅜-inch-wide binding. If you want a wider or narrower binding, adjust the width of the strips you cut. (See page 216 for pointers on how to experiment with binding width.) Refer to "Making and Attaching the Binding" on page 215 to complete your quilt.

CUTTING

From the brown plaid fabric:
• Cut enough 2¾-inch bias strips to make a 260-inch binding strip

Quilting DESIGNS

FOR HAND QUILTING:

🌿 *Try quilting in the ditch around all of the pieces in each block to make the shapes stand out visually from the background as well as from each other. In the side triangles, try quilting angled lines spaced at 1¼-inch intervals, as shown in* QUILTING DIAGRAM 1. *This will echo the shapes of the triangles.*

🌿 *For an easy way to add texture to the inner borders, try filling them with lines of diagonal cross-hatching spaced at 2¾-inch intervals.*

🌿 *I used a purchased quilting stencil with a simple chain design for the outer border, as shown in* QUILTING DIAGRAM 2, *which makes a nice contrast to the straight lines in the inner border.*

FOR MACHINE QUILTING:

🌿 *Quilting similar designs by machine will work nicely. A medium-size pattern of meander quilting stitches can be very effective in the middle border and is easier to machine quilt than long straight lines of cross-hatching.*

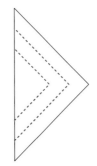

QUILTING DIAGRAM 1

QUILTING DIAGRAM 2

PINE TREE LOG CABIN

Log Cabin quilts, traditional favorites, typically feature lots of colors. They almost call out to us to curl up and get cozy in them. In Pine Tree Log Cabin, I coordinated a variety of reds, greens, chestnusts, and creams to create richness and depth in the pieced "logs." The large Pine Tree blocks in the border corners have beige prints in the background and a green print in the pine trees, which relates them visually to the Log Cabin blocks. As a final touch, I repeated some of the same colors in the border to create a strong frame around the center of the quilt.

Size

Bed Quilt: 64¾ × 90 inches (unquilted)

Finished Block: 8¾ inches square

Fabrics and Supplies

Yardage is based on 44-inch-wide fabric.

2½ yards *total* of a variety of six light fabrics (or, 14 × 44 inches each) for Log Cabin blocks

2½ yards *total* of a variety of six dark fabrics (or, 14 × 44 inches each) for Log Cabin blocks

¼ yard gold print #1 fabric for Log Cabin block center squares

½ yard green print fabric for Tree blocks

⅝ yard beige print fabric for Tree background

1 yard gold print #2 fabric for inner border

½ yard dark green print fabric for middle border

1½ yards dark red print fabric for outer border

1 yard gold print #1 fabric for binding

5½ yards fabric for quilt backing

Quilt batting, at least 69 × 95 inches

Rotary cutter, mat, and see-through ruler with ⅛-inch markings

Getting Ready

- READ instructions thoroughly before you begin.

- PREWASH and press fabric.

- USE ¼-inch seam allowances throughout unless directions specify otherwise.

- SEAM ALLOWANCES are included in the cutting sizes given.

- PRESS seam allowances in the direction that will create the least bulk, and whenever possible, press toward the darker fabric.

- CUTTING DIRECTIONS for each section of the quilt are given individually. If you'd like to cut as you go, simply follow the directions as you get to them. If you'd rather cut all your pieces at the same time, skip ahead to find each of the cutting sections and do all the cutting before you begin to sew. ✍

Fabric Key

Gold #1

Light fabrics

Dark fabrics

Green

Beige

Gold #2

Dark green

Dark red

Log Cabin Blocks
(MAKE 40)

CUTTING

From the variety of light fabrics:
- Cut at least thirty-seven 1¾ × 44-inch strips

From the variety of dark fabrics:
- Cut at least thirty-nine 1¾ × 44-inch strips

From the gold print #1 fabric:
- Cut two 1¾ × 44-inch strips; from these strips, cut forty 1¾-inch center squares

Piecing the Log Cabin Blocks

NOTE: You may vary the position of the light fabrics from block to block, or place them in the same position in each block. The same is true for the dark fabrics. Follow Steps 1 through 3 to piece each of the 40 Log Cabin blocks.

1 With right sides together, stitch a 1¾ × 44-inch light strip to a 1¾-inch gold print square. Press the seam allowance toward the gold strip. Trim the strip even with the edge of the center square, creating a two-piece unit, as shown in DIAGRAM 1.

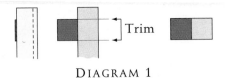

DIAGRAM 1

2 Turn the two-piece unit to the right a quarter turn. Stitch a different 1¾-inch-wide light strip to the two-piece unit. Press and trim the edges of this strip even with the edges of the two-piece unit, as shown in DIAGRAM 2.

DIAGRAM 2

3 Working counter-clockwise around the center square, continue adding alternating light and dark strips to complete the Log Cabin block, referring to DIAGRAM 3 for placement. Press each seam allowance toward the strip just added, and trim each strip before adding the next. Each Log Cabin block should measure 9¼ inches square when completed. Adjust seam allowances if needed.

DIAGRAM 3

4 Sew the five blocks together in eight horizontal rows, referring to the QUILT ASSEMBLY DIAGRAM. Sew the horizontal rows together, matching the intersections of the blocks.

Tree Blocks
(MAKE 4)

C U T T I N G

From the green print fabric:
• Cut two $2\frac{7}{8} \times 44$-inch strips
• Cut one $1\frac{3}{4} \times 44$-inch strip; from this strip, cut four $1\frac{3}{4} \times 9$-inch-long pieces
• Cut four $4\frac{1}{2}$-inch squares for trees

• Cut four $2\frac{1}{2}$-inch squares for tree bases

From the beige print fabric:
• Cut two $2\frac{7}{8} \times 44$-inch strips
• Cut eight $2\frac{1}{2}$-inch squares
• Cut four $6\frac{1}{2}$-inch squares

Piecing the Tree Blocks

1 Layer two $2\frac{7}{8} \times 44$-inch green and beige strips. Press, but do not sew. Layer the remaining $2\frac{7}{8}$-inch-wide strips in the same manner. Cut the layered strips into twenty-eight $2\frac{7}{8}$-inch squares. Cut the layered squares in half diagonally, and stitch a $\frac{1}{4}$-inch seam along the diagonal edges, as shown in DIAGRAM 4. Press. Make 56 triangle-pieced squares.

DIAGRAM 4

2 Draw a diagonal line on each of the $6\frac{1}{2}$-inch beige squares, as shown in DIAGRAM 5. *Do not* cut.

DIAGRAM 5

3 Fold the $1\frac{3}{4} \times 9$-inch green strips in half lengthwise, wrong sides together. Press.

4 Position a green strip on each beige square so that the raw edges are even with the diagonal line. Stitch together with a $\frac{1}{4}$-inch seam, as shown

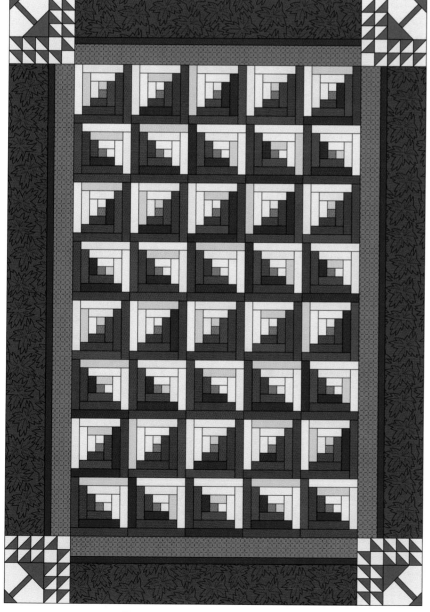

QUILT ASSEMBLY DIAGRAM

in DIAGRAM 6. Fold the green strip over the raw edges and hand stitch in place, as shown.

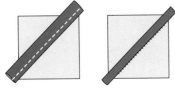

DIAGRAM 6

5 Position a 4½-inch green square on one end of each beige square, as shown in DIAGRAM 7. Position a 2½-inch green square on the opposite end of each beige square. Draw a diagonal line across each of the green squares, and stitch on these lines, as shown. Make four of these tree base units.

DIAGRAM 7

6 Trim away the excess fabric ¼ inch from each seam allowance, creating the tree base units, as shown in DIAGRAM 8. Press.

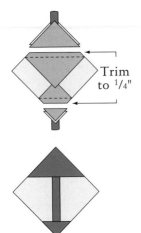

Trim to ¼"

DIAGRAM 8

7 Sew together eight sections of three triangle-pieced squares each, as shown in DIAGRAM 9. Sew two of these sections to each of the four tree base units, as shown.

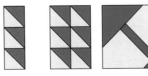

DIAGRAM 9

8 Sew together four triangle-pieced units with a beige square at the end, referring to DIAGRAM 10 for placement. Press. Make four of these sections.

DIAGRAM 10

9 Sew together three triangle-pieced units, a beige square, and another triangle-pieced unit at the end, referring to DIAGRAM 11 for placement. Press. Make four of these sections.

DIAGRAM 11

10 Sew the sections made in Step 8 and 9 to each tree base unit, as shown in DIAGRAM 12, creating the Tree blocks. Press. At this point, the Tree blocks should measure 10½ inches square. Adjust seam allowances if needed.

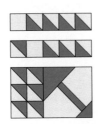

DIAGRAM 12

Borders

NOTE: The three border strips are sewn to the quilt as one unit. The yardage given allows for the border pieces to be cut cross-grain.

From the gold print #2:
• Cut seven 3½ × 44-inch inner border strips

From the dark green print fabric:
• Cut seven 1½ × 44-inch middle border strips

From the dark red print fabric:
• Cut seven 6½ × 44-inch outer border strips

Attaching the Borders

1 Measure the quilt from left to right through the center to determine the length of the top and bottom border strips. Diagonally piece the strips in each color to get the length needed. Cut two 3½-inch-wide gold strips, two 1½-inch-wide dark green strips, and two 6½-inch-wide dark red strips to this measurement. Sew the three border strips together in the order shown in DIAGRAM 13. Add these top and bottom border strips to the quilt, referring to the QUILT ASSEMBLY DIAGRAM on page 53.

DIAGRAM 13

2 For the side border strips, measure the quilt from top to bottom, including the seam allowances but not the top and bottom borders. As in Step 1, diagonally piece strips in each color to get the length needed, and cut them to this measurement. Sew the three border strips together for the side borders, referring to DIAGRAM 13. Sew a Tree corner block to each end of the side borders, referring to the QUILT ASSEMBLY DIAGRAM for placement. Sew the side borders to the quilt.

Putting It All Together

1 Cut the 5½-yard length of backing in half crosswise. Remove the selvages and sew the long edges of the two lengths together. Press this seam open.

TRY PEARL COTTON #12 for hand quilting. It gives quilting stitches a heavier, stronger appearance, which is often a nice addition to a casual, rustic design. Experiment a bit to find a nice small needle that has an eye large enough to hold this slightly larger thread.

Quilting
DESIGNS

FOR HAND OR MACHINE QUILTING:

❧ *The long, straight lines in the Log Cabin blocks make it seem natural to quilt along the seam lines of each "log." Whether you like to quilt by hand or machine, it will be easy to quilt this way, because no marking there is required.*

❧ *Quilt the Pine Tree corner blocks in the same manner as the other blocks.*

❧ *Treat borders as a single unit. Quilt lines at 1¼-inch intervals, from the Log Cabin blocks out to the outer edges of the quilt. This will repeat the lines formed by the "logs" in the Log Cabin blocks.*

Trim the backing and batting so they are about 4 inches larger than the quilt top.

2 Mark quilting designs on the quilt top.

3 Layer the backing, batting, and quilt top. Baste these layers together and quilt.

4 When quilting is complete, remove basting and trim the excess backing and batting even with the quilt top.

Binding

NOTE: This quilt has a narrower binding and requires attaching it with a ¼-inch seam allowance, so that the tips of the pine trees

in the border corner blocks will not be cut off. See "Making and Attaching the Binding" on page 215 to complete your quilt.

CUTTING

From the gold #1 fabric:
• Cut nine 2½ × 44-inch strips for cross-grain binding

GLORIES
from my
GARDEN

*B*eautiful flowers
are like an invitation, with
brilliant colors and gentle
fragrances that capture your
senses, drawing you closer.
From early spring through
late fall, I plant delphiniums,
mums, asters, hollyhocks,
and blue veronicas so lovely
they almost pull you from
the courtyard right up to the
front door of my house. In
my quilts, I try to capture all
the colors and gentle beauty
I see in my garden.

CHECKERBOARD CHERRIES

The deep reds and greens of the small tone-on-tone prints in this quilt make it fit right into my country home, and I like the pleasant picture created by round plump cherries floating on a cream background. Because the checkerboard in itself is such a strong design image, I selected calm fabrics with just enough print to create visual interest and texture. Then I repeated those fabrics in the cherry appliqués to create harmony throughout the quilt. The primitive stitching around the appliqué designs adds surface texture as well as a decorative outline.

Size

Wall Quilt: 15 inches square (unquilted)

Finished Block: 4 inches square

Fabrics and Supplies

Yardage is based on 44-inch-wide fabric.

¼ yard beige print fabric for background

⅜ yard green print fabric for leaves, checkered lattice, border, and binding

¼ yard red print fabric for cherries, checkered lattice, and border

⅛ yard brown print fabric for stems

⅝ yard fabric for quilt backing

Lightweight quilt batting, at least 19 inches square

¼ yard fusible web, 16 inches wide

1 skein black embroidery floss

Rotary cutter, mat, and see-through ruler with ⅛-inch markings

Getting Ready

- READ instructions thoroughly before you begin.

- PREWASH and press fabric.

- USE ¼-inch seam allowances throughout unless directions specify otherwise.

- SEAM ALLOWANCES are included in the cutting sizes given.

- PRESS seam allowances in the direction that will create the least bulk, and whenever possible, press toward the darker fabric.

- CUTTING DIRECTIONS for each section of the quilt are given individually. If you like to cut as you go, simply follow the directions as you get to them. If you'd rather cut all your pieces at the same time, skip ahead to find each of the cutting sections and do all the cutting before you begin to sew.

- INSTRUCTIONS are given for quick cutting and piecing the blocks. Note that for some of the pieces, the quick-cutting method will result in leftover fabric. 🌿

Fabric Key

◻ Beige

◼ Green

◼ Red

◼ Brown

Cherry Blocks
(MAKE 4)

C U T T I N G

From the beige print fabric:
- Cut four 4½-inch squares

1 Position the fusible web (paper side facing up) over the appliqué shapes on page 62. Trace 12 cherries, 12 leaves, and four stems onto the fusible web. Roughly cut around the shapes.

2 Place fusible web shapes, coated side down, on the wrong side of the fabrics chosen for the appliqué shapes. Press with a hot dry iron, following the manufacturer's directions for your brand of fusible web. Let

the fabric cool, cut out on the traced lines, and remove the paper backing.

3 Center the appliqué pieces on each 4½-inch beige square, as shown in the PLACEMENT DIAGRAM. Press in place with a hot dry iron.

4 Appliqué the shapes in place. Shapes may be ironed on and left as they are, machine or hand appliquéd, or stitched with a primitive stitch, using two

strands of black embroidery floss. For more information on the primitive stitch, see page 210.

This is how appliqué shapes should appear when ironed on the background squares

PLACEMENT DIAGRAM

WHEN YOU want to separate six-strand embroidery floss into groups of two or three strands each, pull out one thread at a time. Then put the individual strands together in groups of two or three. This will make the floss fluff up and appear fuller when it is stitched.

TIPS AND TRICKS

Checkered Lattice and Border

CUTTING

From the green print fabric:
- Cut three 1½ × 44-inch strips
- Cut two 1½ inch squares

From the red print fabric:
- Cut three 1½ × 44-inch strips

Piecing the Checkerboard Lattice and Borders

NOTE: To make the checkerboard lattice and borders, you will need to construct a Strip Set I and a Strip Set II.

1 For Strip Set I, sew a red strip to both sides of a green strip, as shown in DIAGRAM 1. Cut into twenty-seven 1½-inch segments, as shown.

1½"

Strip Set I

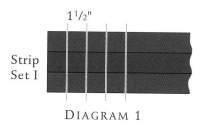

DIAGRAM 1

2 For Strip Set II, sew a green strip to both sides of a red strip, as shown in DIAGRAM 2. Cut into twenty-six 1½-inch segments, as shown.

1½"

Strip Set II

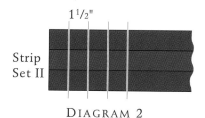

DIAGRAM 2

3 To make the lattice, sew a 1½-inch green square to one Strip Set I segment, as shown in DIAGRAM 3. Repeat to make another unit like this.

DIAGRAM 3

4 Sew a Cherry block to each side of these units, as shown in DIAGRAM 4.

DIAGRAM 4

5 To make the horizontal lattice, sew a Strip Set II segment to both sides of a Strip Set I segment, as shown in DIAGRAM 5.

DIAGRAM 5

6 Join the Cherry blocks to this horizontal lattice strip, as shown in DIAGRAM 6.

DIAGRAM 6

7 To make the top and bottom checkered border strips, sew five Strip Set I segments and four Strip Set II segments together, alternating colors, beginning and ending with a Strip Set I segment, as shown in DIAGRAM 7. Make two of these border strips. Sew the top and bottom border strips to the quilt.

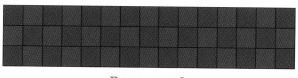

DIAGRAM 7

8 To make the side border strips, sew seven Strip Set I segments and eight Strip Set II segments together, alternating colors, beginning and ending with a Strip Set II segment, as shown in DIAGRAM 8. Make two of these borders strips. Then sew the side border strips to the sides of the quilt, completing the quilt top, as shown in the QUILT ASSEMBLY DIAGRAM on page 62.

DIAGRAM 8

QUILT ASSEMBLY DIAGRAM

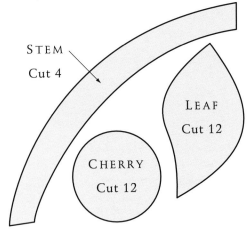

STEM
Cut 4

LEAF
Cut 12

CHERRY
Cut 12

Note: Leaf will appear in the correct position when traced onto fusible web

Putting It All Together

1 Trim the backing and batting so they are 4 inches larger than the quilt top dimensions.

2 Layer the backing, batting, and quilt top. Baste the layers together, and quilt by hand or machine.

3 When quilting is complete, remove basting and trim the excess backing and batting even with the quilt top.

Binding

NOTE: The 2¼-inch strip will make a ¼-inch-wide finished binding. If you want a wider or narrower binding, adjust the width of the strips you cut. (See page 216 for pointers on how to experiment with binding width.) See "Making and Attaching the Binding" on page 215 to complete your quilt.

CUTTING

From the green fabric:
• Cut two 2¼ × 44-inch strips for cross-grain binding

Quilting DESIGNS

Because of the pieced checkerboard squares in this quilt, the only spaces to quilt are in the ditch of each of the checkerboard squares and around the cherry branches, the cherries, and the leaves. The texture created by this subtle quilting is just enough to enhance the pieced design and give the appliqué added visual depth.

TULIP STAND

To define the tulips in this quilt and make them stand out visually, choose a strong floral print for the petals and three coordinating green prints for the stems and leaves. Repeating these tulip and stem fabrics in the quilt center and echoing the border fabric in the checkerboard center squares will help create a feeling of unity throughout your quilt. A mellow maple color in the inner border will separate the center of the quilt from the tulip border, and using that same fabric in your binding will act as a gentle reminder of that same soft shade.

Size

Bed Quilt: 72 × 88 inches (unquilted)

Finished Blocks: 4 and 8 inches square

Fabrics and Supplies

Yardage is based on 44-inch-wide fabric.

2 yards dark red print fabric for Four Patch blocks, tulips, and corner blocks

⅞ yard green check fabric for Four Patch blocks, corner blocks, and stems

2¾ yards medium red print fabric for plain blocks, corner blocks, and outer border

2¾ yards beige print fabric for background

¾ yard maple print fabric for inner border

⅜ yard dark green print fabric for leaves

½ yard light green print fabric for leaves

⅞ yard chestnut print fabric for binding

5½ yards fabric for quilt backing

Quilt batting, at least 76 × 92 inches

Rotary cutter, mat, and see-through ruler with ⅛-inch markings

TULIP STAND
Getting Ready

- READ instructions thoroughly before you begin.

- PREWASH and press fabric.

- USE ¼-inch seam allowances throughout unless directions specify otherwise.

- SEAM ALLOWANCES are included in the cutting sizes given.

- PRESS seam allowances in the direction that will create the least bulk, and whenever possible, press toward the darker fabric.

- CUTTING DIRECTIONS for each section of the quilt are given individually. If you like to cut as you go, simply follow the directions as you get to them. If you'd rather cut all your pieces at the same time, skip ahead to find each of the cutting sections and do all the cutting before you begin to sew. 🍃

Fabric Key

 Dark red

 Green check

 Medium red

 Beige

 Maple

 Dark green

 Light green

---

Four Patch Blocks
(MAKE 24 FULL AND 20 PARTIAL BLOCKS)

From the dark red print fabric:
- Cut five 2½ × 44-inch strips

From the green check fabric:
- Cut five 2½ × 44-inch strips

Piecing the Four Patch Blocks

1 Sew the five 2½ × 44-inch-wide dark red and green check strips together in pairs. Press the seam allowances toward the darker fabric. Crosscut

this strip set into sixty-eight 2½-inch segments, as shown in DIAGRAM 1.

2½"

DIAGRAM 1

2 Sew 48 of the segments together in pairs to make 24 full blocks, as shown in DIAGRAM 2. The remaining units will be the 20 partial blocks, as shown.

Full block   Partial block
DIAGRAM 2

Quilt Center and Corner Squares

From the medium red print fabric:
- Cut five 4½ × 44-inch strips; from these strips, cut thirty-nine 4½-inch squares

From the beige print fabric:
- Cut eight 4½ × 44-inch strips; from these strips, cut fifty-eight 4½-inch squares, twenty-four 2½ × 4½-inch rectangles, and one 4½ × 22-inch strip
- Cut eight 2½ × 4½-inch rectangles

From the dark red print fabric:
- Cut one 2½ × 22-inch strip
- Cut two 2½-inch squares

From the green check fabric:
• Cut one 2½ × 22-inch strip
• Cut two 2½-inch squares

Assembling the Quilt Center and Corner Blocks

NOTE: To assemble the quilt center, use 24 full and 20 partial Four Patch blocks, thirty-five 4½-inch medium red squares, fifty-eight 4½-inch beige squares, twenty-four 2½ × 4½-inch beige rectangles, two 2½-inch dark red squares, and two 2½-inch green check squares.

1 Assemble the quilt center in 11 vertical rows, as shown in DIAGRAM 3. Sew the 11 vertical rows together, as shown. Press.

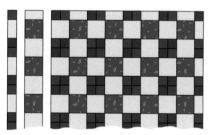

DIAGRAM 3

2 Make the corner blocks; set aside. Sew the 2½ × 22-inch dark red and green check strips to both sides of the 4½ × 22-inch beige strip. Press seams toward the darker fabric. Crosscut the strip set into eight 2½-inch segments, as shown in DIAGRAM 4.

2½"

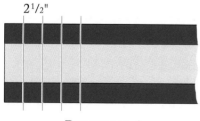

DIAGRAM 4

3 Sew a 2½ × 4½-inch-wide beige rectangle to the top and bottom of the 4½-inch medium red squares, as shown in DIAGRAM 5. Press seam allowances toward the darker fabric.

DIAGRAM 5

4 Sew a unit from Step 2 to the sides of each square, as shown in DIAGRAM 6. Press seam allowances away from each square. The four corner blocks should measure 8½ inches at this point.

DIAGRAM 6

Borders

CUTTING

NOTE: The yardage given allows for the borders to be cut cross-grain.

From the maple print fabric:
• Cut five 2½ × 44-inch strips for the inner border
• Cut eight 2½ × 8½-inch rectangles for the tulip border

From the dark red print fabric:
• Cut twelve 4⅞-inch squares; cut these squares in half

diagonally to form twenty-four triangles for the tulips
• Cut six 5¼-inch squares; cut these squares diagonally into quarters to form twenty-four triangles for the tulips

From the green check fabric:
• Cut three 2 × 44-inch strips for stems

From the dark green print fabric:
• Cut three 2½ × 44-inch strips; from these strips, cut twenty-four 2½ × 4½-inch rectangles for leaves

From the light green print fabric:
• Cut four 2½ × 44-inch strips; from these strips, cut twenty-four 2½ × 6½-inch rectangles for leaves

From the beige print fabric:
• Cut six 5¼-inch squares; cut these squares diagonally into quarters to form twenty-four triangles for the tulip backgrounds
• Cut six 1¾ × 44-inch strips for stem backgrounds
• Cut four 2½ × 44-inch strips; from these strips, cut twenty-four 2½ × 6½-inch rectangles for leaf backgrounds
• Cut three 2½ × 44-inch strips; from these strips, cut twenty-four 2½ × 4½-inch rectangles for leaf backgrounds

From the medium red fabric:
• Cut ten 6½ × 44-inch strips for the outer border

Inner Border

1 Piece the 2½-inch-wide maple print border strips together with diagonal seams, as shown in DIAGRAM 7. Trim seam allowances to ¼ inch and press them open.

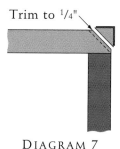

Trim to ¹⁄₄"

DIAGRAM 7

2 Measure the quilt from left to right through the middle to determine the length of the top and bottom borders. Cut two inner border strips to this length

and sew the maple print inner borders to the top and bottom of the quilt, referring to the QUILT ASSEMBLY DIAGRAM.

3 Measure the quilt from top to bottom through the middle, including the borders you just added, to determine the length of the side borders. Cut two inner border strips to the necessary lengths and sew the maple print inner borders to the sides of the quilt, as shown in the QUILT ASSEMBLY DIAGRAM.

Tulip Border

1 With right sides together, sew a 1³⁄₄ × 44-inch beige strip to both sides of a 2 × 44-inch green check strip. Make three strip sets. Press seam allowances toward the darker fabric. Crosscut the strip sets into twenty-four 4¹⁄₂-inch stem units, as shown in DIAGRAM 8.

4¹⁄₂"

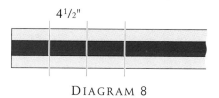

DIAGRAM 8

QUILT ASSEMBLY DIAGRAM

2 With right sides together, position a 2¹⁄₂ × 6¹⁄₂-inch beige rectangle on a 2¹⁄₂ × 4¹⁄₂-inch dark green rectangle, as shown in DIAGRAM 9. Draw a diagonal line on the beige rectangle, as shown, and stitch on the line. Trim seam allowance to ¹⁄₄ inch. Press. Repeat to make 24 left leaf units, as shown.

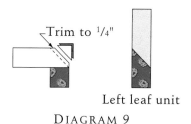

Trim to ¹⁄₄"

Left leaf unit
DIAGRAM 9

3 With right sides together, position a 2¹⁄₂ × 6¹⁄₂-inch light green rectangle on a 2¹⁄₂ × 4¹⁄₂-inch beige piece, as shown in DIAGRAM 10 on page 68. Draw a diagonal line on the light green rectangle, as shown, and stitch on the line. Trim seam allowances to ¹⁄₄ inch. Press. Repeat to make 24 right leaf units, as shown.

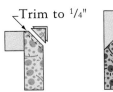

Trim to ¹/₄"

Right leaf unit
DIAGRAM 10

4 To piece the tulip units, sew the smaller dark red triangles to the beige triangles, right sides together, as shown in the left portion of DIAGRAM 11, and sew the larger dark red triangle to these units, as shown.

DIAGRAM 11

5 To assemble a Tulip block, sew a stem unit to the bottom of the tulip unit, as shown in the left portion of DIAGRAM 12. Sew the right and left leaf units to the sides of the tulip unit, as shown in the right part of DIAGRAM 12. At this point, the Tulip block should measure 8½ inches square.

Tulip unit
DIAGRAM 12

6 Sew five Tulip blocks together for the top and bottom borders. Add a 2½ × 8½-inch maple rectangle to each end,

MAKE MATCHING pillow-cases to go with your next quilt, or simply use a small amount of the quilt fabric to edge or trim the hems of purchased pillowcases.

TIPS AND TRICKS

as shown in DIAGRAM 13. Sew these borders to the top and bottom of the quilt, referring to the QUILT ASSEMBLY DIAGRAM on page 67.

7 Sew seven Tulip blocks together for each side border. Add a 2½ × 8½-inch maple rectangle and a corner block to each end, as shown in DIAGRAM 14. Sew these borders to the sides of the quilt, referring to the QUILT ASSEMBLY DIAGRAM on page 67.

Outer Border

1 Piece the 6½-inch-wide medium red border strips together with diagonal seams in the same manner as for the maple inner border. Trim seams to ¼-inch and press open.

2 Measure the quilt from left to right through the middle to determine the length of the top and bottom borders. Cut two outer border strips to this length, and sew the medium red print outer borders to the top and bottom of the quilt, referring to the QUILT ASSEMBLY DIAGRAM on page 67.

3 Measure the quilt from top to bottom through the middle, including the borders you just added, to determine the lengths of the side borders. Cut two outer border strips to this length, and sew the medium red print outer borders to the sides of the quilt, referring to the QUILT ASSEMBLY DIAGRAM on page 67.

Putting It All Together

1 Prepare the backing for the quilt by cutting the 5½-yard length of backing fabric in half crosswise to make two 2¾-yard lengths. Remove the selvages and sew the long edges of the two lengths together. Press seam open. Trim the backing and batting so they are about 4 inches larger than the quilt top.

DIAGRAM 13

DIAGRAM 14

2 Mark quilting designs on the quilt top.

3 Layer the backing, batting, and quilt top. Baste the layers together and quilt.

4 When the quilting is complete, remove the basting stitches and trim the excess backing and batting even with the quilt top.

Binding

NOTE: The 2¾-inch strips will produce a ⅜-inch-wide binding. If you want a wider or narrower binding, adjust the width of the strips you cut. (See page 216 for pointers on how to experiment with binding width.) See "Making and Attaching the Binding" on page 215 to complete your quilt.

C U T T I N G

From the chestnut print fabric:
• Cut nine 2¾ × 44-inch strips for cross-grain binding

Quilting
DESIGNS

FOR MACHINE QUILTING:

The 4-inch blocks in the center of the quilt feature the continuous-line floral quilting design shown in QUILTING DIAGRAM 1.

Choose medium-scale meander quilting for all background areas, as well as behind tulips, leaves, and the feathered chain designs in the outer borders. This meander quilting pattern, as shown in QUILTING DIAGRAM 2, enhances the feathered chain in the outer borders and makes them more visually prominent.

The stems of the tulips are quilted with two vertical lines that divide each stem into three ½-inch sections.

In the 2-inch maple borders, the 1¼-inch chain quilting design shown in QUILTING DIAGRAM 3 effectively separates these borders from the other quilted areas.

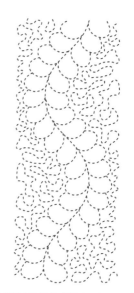

QUILTING DIAGRAM 2

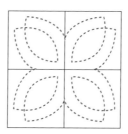

QUILTING DIAGRAM 1

QUILTING DIAGRAM 3

BROWN-EYED SUSAN

Wall Quilt and Bed Quilt

An old-fashioned flower-seed catalog inspired the design for Brown-Eyed Susan. The plaid flower centers create a sense of texture, and the colorful prints surrounding them are bright and beckoning. For the border, I used a dark red print with hints of the same gold tones as the lattice posts and other prints in the quilt center. A mellow background fabric unifies the blocks throughout the quilt, and the bias-cut plaid binding is a subtle hint of color that coordinates the border and corner blocks with the flower centers.

Size

Wall Quilt: 60 inches square (unquilted)

Finished Block: 12 inches square

Fabrics and Supplies

Yardage is based on 44-inch-wide fabric.

3/8 yard *each* of nine coordinating print fabrics for Flower blocks

4½-inch squares of nine coordinating plaid fabrics for flower centers

1¼ yards beige plaid fabric for background

¾ yard blue print fabric for lattice

⅛ yard gold print fabric for lattice posts

1½ yards red print fabric for borders

⅓ yard brown print fabric for corner squares

¾ yard red plaid fabric for bias binding

4 yards fabric for quilt backing

Quilt batting, at least 64 inches square

Rotary cutter, mat, and see-through ruler with ⅛-inch markings

Getting Ready

- READ instructions thoroughly before you begin.

- PREWASH and press fabric.

- USE ¼-inch seam allowances throughout unless directions specify otherwise.

- SEAM ALLOWANCES are included in the cutting sizes given.

- PRESS seam allowances in the direction that will create the least bulk, and whenever possible, press toward the darker fabric.

- CUTTING DIRECTIONS for each section of the quilt are given individually. If you like to cut as you go, simply follow the directions as you get to them. If you'd rather cut all your pieces at the same time, skip ahead to find each of the cutting sections and do all the cutting before you begin to sew.

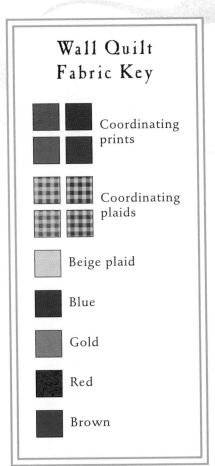

Wall Quilt Fabric Key

Coordinating prints

Coordinating plaids

Beige plaid

Blue

Gold

Red

Brown

Flower Blocks
(MAKE 9)

CUTTING

From each of the nine coordinating print fabrics:
- Cut two 2½ × 4½-inch pieces and two 2½ × 8½-inch pieces
- Cut one 2⅞ × 44-inch strip

From each of the nine coordinating plaid fabrics:
- Cut one 4½-inch square

From the beige plaid fabric:
- Cut thirty-six 2½-inch squares
- Cut nine 2⅞ × 44-inch strips

Piecing the Flower Blocks

1 Using one of the nine coordinating print fabrics, sew two 2½ × 4½-inch pieces to the top and bottom of a coordinating plaid 4½-inch square. Sew the 2½ × 8½-inch pieces to the sides, as shown in DIAGRAM 1. Do the same for each of the remaining Flower blocks.

DIAGRAM 1

2 To make the sawtooth sections, layer one 2⅞ × 44-inch beige plaid strip and one of the print fabric strips right sides together. Press these fabrics together, but do not sew. Cut the layered strips into eight 2⅞-inch squares. Cut the layered squares in half diagonally, and sew a ¼-inch seam allowance along the diagonal edge, as shown in DIAGRAM 2. Make a total of 16 triangle-pieced squares in each of the nine coordinating flower fabrics.

DIAGRAM 2

3 Sew four triangle-pieced squares together, as shown in DIAGRAM 3. Make four of these units in each of the nine flower fabrics.

DIAGRAM 3

4 Sew two of these triangle-pieced units to the top and bottom of each Flower block, as shown in DIAGRAM 4.

DIAGRAM 4

5 Sew a beige plaid 2½-inch square to each of the remaining triangle-pieced units, as shown in DIAGRAM 5.

DIAGRAM 5

6 Sew these units to the sides of each Flower block, as shown in DIAGRAM 6, making sure that the triangle squares match each other in each Flower block. At this point, the Flower blocks should measure 12½ inches square.

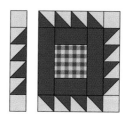

DIAGRAM 6

Quilt Center

From the blue print fabric:
• Cut twenty-four 2½ × 12½-inch lattice strips

From the gold print fabric:
• Cut sixteen 2½-inch squares

Assembling the Quilt Center

1 Sew four blue 2½ × 12½-inch strips and three Flower blocks together in a row, as shown in DIAGRAM 7. Make three of these rows.

2 Sew three blue 2½ × 12½-inch strips and four gold 2½-inch squares together, as shown in DIAGRAM 8. Make four of these strips.

3 Stitch the rows together to make the quilt center, as shown in DIAGRAM 9.

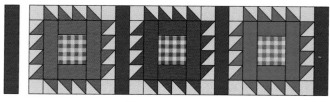

DIAGRAM 7

DIAGRAM 8

DIAGRAM 9

Border

From the red print fabric:
• Cut four 8½ × 46-inch strips on the lengthwise grain

From the brown fabric:
• Cut four 8½-inch squares

Attaching the Border

1 Measure the quilt from left to right through the center.

From the 8½ × 46-inch red strips, cut four borders to the actual length needed for your quilt. Sew two of them to the top and bottom of the quilt.

2 Measure the quilt from top to bottom, not including the border strips you just added, and add ½ inch for seam allowances. Cut two border strips to this length and sew an 8½-inch brown square to each end of the two border strips.

3 Sew the side border strips to the sides of the quilt, as shown in the WALL QUILT AS-SEMBLY DIAGRAM. Press seam allowances toward the borders.

KEEP an old-fashioned mechanical lead pencil handy for marking lines. The lead is always sharp; therefore, the lines you mark will always be thin and crisp.

Putting It All Together

1 Prepare the backing for the quilt by cutting the 4-yard length of backing fabric in half crosswise to make two 2-yard lengths. Remove the selvages and sew the long edges of the two lengths together with one center seam. Press this seam open.

2 Trim the backing and batting so they are 4 inches larger than the quilt top dimensions.

WALL QUILT ASSEMBLY DIAGRAM

3 Mark quilting designs on the quilt top.

4 Layer the backing, batting, and quilt top. Baste the layers together, and quilt.

5 When quilting is complete, remove basting and trim the excess backing and batting even with the quilt top.

Binding

NOTE: The 2¾-inch-wide plaid bias strips will produce a ⅜- to ½-inch-wide finished binding. If you want a wider or narrower binding, adjust the width of the strips you cut. (See page 216 for pointers on how to experiment

with binding width.) Refer to "Making and Attaching the Binding" on page 215 to complete your quilt.

CUTTING

From the red plaid fabric:
• Cut enough 2¾-inch-wide bias strips to make a 255-inch strip

BROWN-EYED SUSAN

Bed Quilt

Size

Bed Quilt: 74 × 88 inches (unquilted)

Finished Block: 12 inches square

Fabrics and Supplies

Yardage is based on 44-inch-wide fabric.

4 yards red print fabric for Flower blocks and lattices

3/8 yard plaid fabric for flower centers

1½ yards beige print fabric for background

¼ yard tan print fabric for lattice posts

2 yards large red plaid fabric for borders

1/3 yard brown print fabric for corner squares

1 yard plaid fabric for bias binding

5¼ yards fabric for quilt backing

Quilt batting, at least 78 × 92 inches

Rotary cutter, mat, and see-through ruler with 1/8-inch markings

Flower Blocks

(MAKE 20)

C U T T I N G

From the red print fabric:
• Cut forty 2½ × 4½-inch pieces and forty 2½ × 8½-inch pieces
• Cut twelve 2⅞ × 44-inch strips

From the plaid fabric:
• Cut twenty 4½-inch squares

From the beige print fabric:
• Cut eighty 2½-inch squares
• Cut twelve 2⅞ × 44-inch strips

Piecing the Flower Blocks

Follow Steps 1 through 5 under "Piecing the Flower Blocks" on page 72. Make 320 triangle-pieced squares for the 20 Flower blocks in the bed quilt.

Quilt Center

C U T T I N G

From the red print fabric:
• Cut forty-nine 2½ × 12½-inch strips

From the tan print fabric:
• Cut thirty 2½-inch squares

Assembling the Quilt Center

NOTE: Refer to Steps 1 and 2 under "Assembling the Quilt Center" on page 73.

Bed Quilt Fabric Key

Red

Beige

Tan

Large red plaid

Brown

1 Sew five red 2½ × 12½-inch strips and four Flower blocks together in a row. Make five rows.

2 Sew four red 2½ × 12½-inch strips and five tan 2½-inch squares together. Make six lattice strips.

3 Stitch the rows together to complete the quilt center, as shown in the BED QUILT AS-SEMBLY DIAGRAM on page 76.

Border

C U T T I N G

NOTE: The yardage given allows for the border pieces to be cut cross-grain.

From the large red plaid:
• Cut eight 8½ × 44-inch strips

From the brown print fabric:
• Cut four 8½-inch squares

BED QUILT ASSEMBLY DIAGRAM

Attaching the Border

1 Piece the 8½ × 44-inch red plaid strips together. Trim seam allowances to ¼ inch, and press them open.

2 Measure the quilt from left to right through the center. From the 8½-inch-wide plaid strip, cut two border strips to the length needed and sew the border strips to the top and bottom edges of the quilt, referring to the BED QUILT ASSEMBLY DIAGRAM.

3 Measure the quilt from top to bottom through the center, not including the border strips you just added. Add ½ inch for seam allowances. From the 8½-inch-wide plaid strip, cut two border strips to this length.

4 Sew the 8½-inch brown corner squares to each end of the side border strips. Sew the border strips to the quilt sides.

Putting It All Together

1 For the backing, cut the 5¼-yard length of backing fabric in half crosswise to make two 2⅝-yard lengths. Remove the selvages and sew the long edges of the two lengths together. Press this seam open.

2 Trim the backing and batting so they are 4 inches larger than the quilt top dimensions.

3 Layer the backing, batting, and quilt top. Mark quilting designs on the quilt top. Baste the layers together, and quilt.

4 When quilting is complete, remove the basting stitches, and trim the excess backing and batting even with the quilt top.

Binding

NOTE: The 2¾-inch-wide plaid bias strips will produce a ⅜- to ½-inch-wide binding. If you want a wider or narrower binding, adjust the width of the strips you cut. (See page 216 for pointers on binding width.) Refer to "Making and Attaching the Binding" on page 215 to complete your quilt.

CUTTING

From the plaid fabric:
• Cut enough 2¾-inch bias strips to make a 340-inch strip

Quilting DESIGNS

FOR HAND QUILTING:

❧ Quilt ½-inch diagonal cross-hatched lines in the flower centers.
❧ Quilt in the ditch around the flower pieces.
❧ Stitch in the ditch of the seams on each side of the lattice strips and lattice posts.
❧ Use a quilting stencil that has a soft, simple curved design for the border.
❧ Quilt the corner blocks with 2-, 3-, and 4-inch concentric circles.

WATERMELON PATCH

For realistic images like the watermelon wedges in this little quilt, I coordinated a group of colors and prints as luscious and tempting as the first thick slices of this fruit in summer. I chose four different green prints, ranging from rich, dark greens to medium shades. For the flesh of the melons, I chose a juicy red print with just enough black to represent the look of the seeds. For the rinds, I used a green check fabric cut on the bias, which creates a pleasing effect in these curved spaces. The wide variety of prints adds visual texture throughout the entire quilt.

Size

Wall Quilt: 44 inches square (unquilted)

Finished Blocks: 9 inches square

Fabrics and Supplies

Yardage is based on 44-inch-wide fabric.

3/8 yard beige print fabric for background

1 yard red print fabric for watermelon, lattice posts, corner squares, and borders

3/4 yard green check fabric for rind, pieced block borders, and lattice strips

1/4 yard green print fabric #1 for pieced block borders

1 1/8 yards dark green print fabric #2 for pieced block borders and outer borders

3/8 yard green print fabric #3 for pieced block borders, lattice, and corner blocks

3/8 yard black print fabric for block border

2 2/3 yards fabric for quilt backing

3/4 yard green check fabric #1 for bias binding

Quilt batting, at least 48 inches square

1 yard fusible web

1 skein black embroidery floss

Rotary cutter, mat, and see-through ruler with 1/8-inch markings

WATERMELON PATCH
G e t t i n g   R e a d y

- READ instructions thoroughly before you begin.

- PREWASH and press fabric.

- USE ¼-inch seam allowances throughout unless directions specify otherwise.

- SEAM ALLOWANCES are included in the cutting sizes given.

- PRESS seam allowances in the direction that will create the least bulk, and whenever possible, press toward the darker fabric.

- CUTTING DIRECTIONS for each section of the quilt are given individually. If you like to cut as you go, simply follow the directions as you get to them. If you'd rather cut all your pieces at the same time, skip ahead to find each of the cutting sections and do all the cutting before you begin to sew. ✍

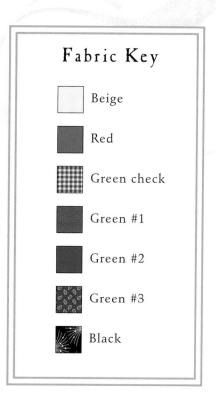

Fabric Key

☐ Beige

■ Red

▦ Green check

■ Green #1

■ Green #2

▨ Green #3

■ Black

Watermelon Units
(MAKE 16)

C U T T I N G

From the beige print fabric:
- Cut sixteen 4½-inch squares

1 Position the fusible web (paper side facing up) over the watermelon shapes on page 83. Trace 16 watermelons and 16 rinds onto the fusible web. Roughly cut around the shapes.

2 Place the fusible web shapes, coated side down, on the wrong side of the red fabric for watermelons and the green check fabric for the rinds. Press with a hot dry iron, following the manufacturer's directions for your brand of fusible web. Let the shapes cool, cut out watermelons and rinds on the tracing lines, and remove the paper backing.

Appliquéing the Watermelon Units

1 Center the appliqué pieces on the 4½-inch beige squares, as shown in DIAGRAM 1, layering the rinds over the watermelons. Press in place with a hot dry iron.

DIAGRAM 1

2 Primitive stitch the shapes in place with two strands of black embroidery floss, as shown in DIAGRAM 2. For more information on the primitive stitch, see page 210. To make the three watermelon seeds on each watermelon, do straight stitches using four strands of black embroidery floss. For more information on the straight stitch, see page 210.

DIAGRAM 2

WHEN DOING *machine buttonhole stitching or feather stitching around appliqué shapes, thread two strands of regular sewing thread through one needle. This will produce a heavier decorative stitch.*

TIPS AND TRICKS

Watermelon Blocks
(MAKE FOUR)

C U T T I N G

From the red print fabric:
• Cut thirty-six 1½-inch squares for the center squares and pieced borders
• Cut four 1½ × 44-inch strips; from these strips, cut sixteen 1½ × 11½-inch borders

From the green check fabric:
• Cut two 1½ × 44-inch strips for the pieced border

From the green print #1 fabric:
• Cut two 1½ × 44-inch strips for the pieced border

From the dark green print #2 fabric:
• Cut two 1½ × 44-inch strips for the pieced border

From the green print #3 fabric:
• Cut two 1½ × 44-inch strips for the pieced border
• Cut sixteen 1½ × 4½-inch lattice strips
• Cut sixteen 2½-inch corner squares

From the black print fabric:
• Cut four 1½ × 44-inch strips; from these strips, cut sixteen 1½ × 11½-inch borders

Assembling the Watermelon Blocks

1 Sew a watermelon unit to each side of a 1½ × 4½-inch green #3 strip, as shown in DIAGRAM 3. Repeat for the remaining watermelon units. Press seam allowances toward the green fabric.

DIAGRAM 3

2 Sew a 1½ × 4½-inch green #3 strip to both sides of four 1½-inch red squares, as shown in DIAGRAM 4. Make four of these lattice strips. Press seam allowances toward the green fabric.

DIAGRAM 4

3 Sew a watermelon unit to both sides of a lattice strip, as shown in DIAGRAM 5. Repeat for the remaining lattice strips to make a total of four watermelon blocks. Press seam allowances toward the green fabric.

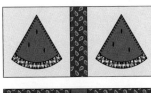

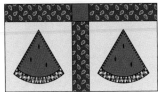

DIAGRAM 5

4 To make the pieced borders for each watermelon block, sew one of each of the 1½ × 44-inch green strips together along the lengthwise edges to form a strip set, as shown in DIAGRAM 6. Make two of these strip sets. Press seam allowances in one direction. Crosscut the strip sets into thirty-two 1½-inch segments, as shown.

1½"

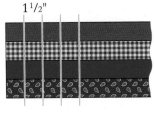

DIAGRAM 6

5 Sew pieced border segments to both sides of sixteen of the 1½-inch red squares, as shown in DIAGRAM 7. Press seam allowances away from the red fabric.

DIAGRAM 7

6 Sew a pieced border segment to the top and bottom of each watermelon block, as shown in DIAGRAM 8. Press seam allowances toward the pieced borders.

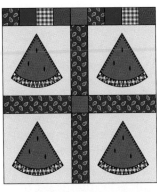

DIAGRAM 8

7 Sew a 1½-inch red square to both ends of the remaining eight pieced border segments, as shown in DIAGRAM 9. Press seam allowances away from the red fabric.

DIAGRAM 9

8 Attach the side pieced borders to the sides of each watermelon block, as shown in DIAGRAM 10. Press seam allowances toward the pieced borders.

DIAGRAM 10

9 Sew a 1½ × 11½-inch black print border strip to each of the sixteen 1½ × 11½-inch red border strips, as shown in DIAGRAM 11. Press seam allowances toward the black fabric.

DIAGRAM 11

10 Sew a pieced border to the top and bottom of each watermelon block, as shown in DIAGRAM 12, making sure the red strip is on the outside.

DIAGRAM 12

11 Add a 2½-inch green #3 corner square to both ends of the remaining eight pieced border units, as shown in DIAGRAM 13. Press seam allowances away from the green fabric.

DIAGRAM 13

12 Attach the pieced side borders to the sides of each watermelon block, as shown in DIAGRAM 14. Press.

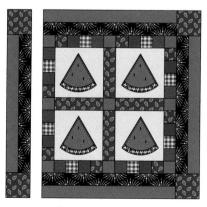

DIAGRAM 14

Lattice Strips, Posts, and Borders

CUTTING

NOTE: The yardage given allows for the border pieces to be cut cross-grain.

From the green check fabric:
• Cut twelve 2½ × 15½-inch lattice strips

From the red fabric:
• Cut nine 2½-inch squares for lattice posts
• Cut four 4½-inch corner squares

From the dark green print #2 fabric:
• Cut four 4½ × 44-inch outer border strips

Attaching the Lattice Strips and Borders

1 Sew a 2½ × 15½-inch green check lattice strip between two watermelon blocks, as shown in DIAGRAM 15 on page 82. Add a green check 2½ × 15½-inch lattice strip to both sides of the row, as shown. Press seam allowances toward the green check fabric. Make two of these rows.

2 Stitch two green check lattice strips and three 2½-inch red lattice posts together in a row, as shown in DIAGRAM 16 on page 82. Press seam allowances toward the green check lattice strips. Make three of these rows.

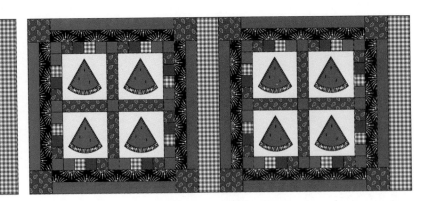

DIAGRAM 15

DIAGRAM 16

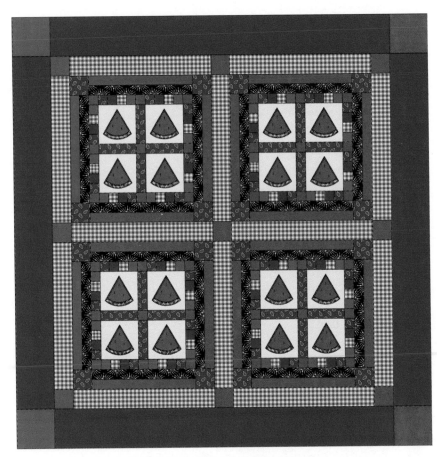

QUILT ASSEMBLY DIAGRAM

length needed. Attach the top and bottom border strips to the quilt, referring to the QUILT ASSEMBLY DIAGRAM. Press seam allowances toward the green check fabric.

5 For the side border strips, measure the quilt from top to bottom. Do *not* include the top and bottom border strips in your measurement. Add ¼ inch on each end for seam allowances, and cut two green #2 strips to this length. Sew a 4½-inch red corner square to each end of the border strips. Attach the side border strips to the quilt, as shown. Press seam allowances toward the green check fabric.

Putting It All Together

1 Prepare the backing for the quilt by cutting the 2⅔-yard length of backing fabric in half crosswise to make two 1⅓-yard lengths. Remove the selvages.

2 Sew the two long edges together. Press seam allowances open. Trim backing and batting so they are 4 inches larger than the quilt top.

3 Mark quilting designs on the quilt top.

4 Layer the backing, batting, and quilt top. Baste the layers together, and quilt.

5 When quilting is complete, remove the basting stitches, and trim the excess backing and batting even with the quilt top.

3 Sew the rows of the quilt together, as shown in the QUILT ASSEMBLY DIAGRAM. Press seam allowances toward the green check fabric.

4 Measure the quilt from left to right, through the center, to determine the length of the top and bottom border strips. Cut two green #2 strips to the

Binding

NOTE: The 2¾-inch bias strips will produce a ⅜-inch-wide binding. If you want a wider or narrower binding, adjust the width of the strips you cut. (See page 216 for pointers on how to experiment with binding width.) See "Making and Attaching the Binding" on page 215 to complete your quilt.

C U T T I N G

From the green check fabric:
• Cut enough 2¾-inch bias strips to make a 200-inch strip

Quilting
DESIGNS

FOR MACHINE QUILTING:

↝ *Use a variety of meander quilting patterns in different sizes. A small pattern of meander quilting in the background of the watermelon blocks will make the melon wedges stand out visually.*

↝ *A single feathered chain design from a purchased quilting stencil is quilted in the outer border, along with a small pattern of meander quilting around the chain.*

↝ *Quilt a medium-size pattern of meander quilting for the rest of the quilt, matching your thread as closely as possible to your fabrics.*

FOR HAND QUILTING:

↝ *Quilt in the ditch around each watermelon slice to enhance the wedge shapes.*

↝ *Select a purchased stencil with a simple quilting motif and a coordinating corner design for the outer borders.*

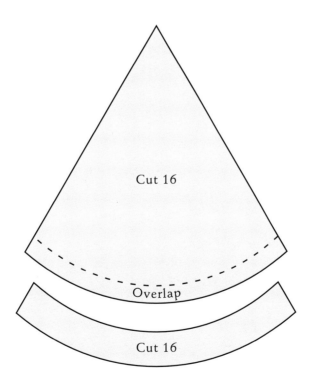

Cut 16

Overlap

Cut 16

APPLIQUÉ PATTERN PIECES

WILDFLOWER

This quilt combines a large variety of print fabrics with a lovely large-scale floral print at the center of each of the pieced Wildflower blocks. If you love to collect fabric, this is a quilt you're sure to enjoy making. Choose a light tone-on-tone print for the alternating blocks to make the pieced blocks more prominent. A variety of greens will give the shaded effect of real leaves. An interesting mix of colorful squares around the edge of the pieced center will add to the appearance of a bed of wildflowers, one that will not fade when winter months arrive.

Size

Bed Quilt: 82 × 95 inches (unquilted)

Block Size: 9 inches square

Fabrics and Supplies

Yardage is based on 44-inch-wide fabric.

½ yard large floral print for block centers

1¾ yards *total* of a variety of medium prints for Wildflower blocks and border squares

2 yards light tan print for Wildflower blocks

⅜ yard *total* of a variety of blue prints for Wildflower blocks

¼ yard *each* of five green prints for Wildflower blocks

3¼ yards beige dot fabric for alternate blocks, side triangles, corner triangles, and the pieced border

2 yards green tone-on-tone print for pieced border and outer border

1 yard green tone-on-tone print for binding

7½ yards fabric for quilt backing

Quilt batting, at least 86 × 99 inches

Rotary cutter, mat, and see-through ruler with ⅛-inch markings

Getting Ready

• READ instructions thoroughly before you begin.

• PREWASH and press fabric.

• USE ¼-inch seam allowances throughout unless directions specify otherwise.

• SEAM ALLOWANCES are included in the cutting sizes given.

• PRESS seam allowances in the direction that will create the least bulk, and whenever possible, press toward the darker fabric.

• CUTTING DIRECTIONS for each section of the quilt are given individually. If you like to cut as you go, simply follow the directions as you get to them. If you'd rather cut all your pieces at rhe same time, skip ahead to find each of the cutting sections and do all the cutting before you begin to sew. ✎

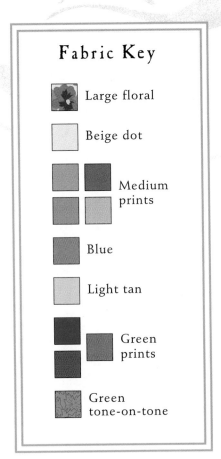

Fabric Key

- Large floral
- Beige dot
- Medium prints
- Blue
- Light tan
- Green prints
- Green tone-on-tone

Wildflower Blocks
(MAKE 30)

C U T T I N G

From the large floral fabric:
• Cut three 3½ × 44-inch strips; from these strips, cut thirty 3½-inch squares for block centers

From the medium print fabrics:
• Cut a total of twenty 1½ × 44-inch strips

From the light tan print fabric:
• Cut forty-two 1½ × 44-inch strips

From the blue print fabrics:
• Cut five 1½ × 44-inch strips

From the five green print fabrics:
• Cut a total of eleven 1½ × 44-inch strips

Piecing
the Wildflower Blocks

1 To make Strip Set I, sew a 1½ × 44-inch light tan strip to both sides of a 1½ × 44-inch green print strip, as shown in DIAGRAM 1. Press seam allowances toward the green fabric. Make 11 of these strip sets, and crosscut them into one hundred twenty 3½-inch segments, as shown.

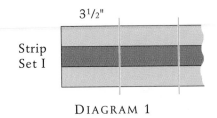

3½"

Strip Set I

DIAGRAM 1

2 To make Strip Set II, sew a 1½ × 44-inch medium print strip to both sides of a 1½ × 44-inch light tan strip, as shown in DIAGRAM 2. Press seam allowances toward the medium fabric. Make ten of these strip sets, and crosscut into two hundred forty 1½-inch segments, as shown.

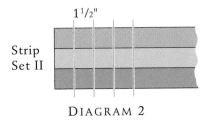

1½"

Strip Set II

DIAGRAM 2

3 To make Strip Set III, sew a 1½ × 44-inch light tan strip to both sides of a 1½ × 44-inch blue print strip, as shown in DIAGRAM 3. Press seam allowances toward the blue fabric. Make five of these strip sets, and crosscut them into one hundred twenty 1½-inch segments, as shown.

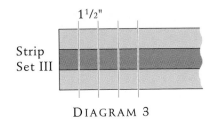

1½"

Strip Set III

DIAGRAM 3

4 Sew a Strip Set II segment to both sides of the Strip Set III segments to make the nine-patch units, as shown in DIAGRAM 4. Press. Make 120 nine-patch units.

DIAGRAM 4

5 To complete each Wildflower block, sew the units from Steps 1 and 4 and a 3½-inch large floral square together in three horizontal rows, as shown in DIAGRAM 5. Press. Sew these horizontal rows together. Press. At this point, the Wildflower blocks should measure 9½ inches square.

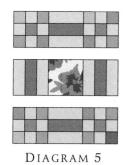

DIAGRAM 5

Quilt Center

CUTTING

From the beige dot fabric:
• Cut twenty 9½-inch squares for the alternate blocks.
• Cut five 14-inch squares. Cut the squares diagonally in both directions to form 20 triangles. You will need only 18 of these for the side triangles. NOTE: Both the side triangles and corner triangles are larger than necessary and will be trimmed after they have been added to the pieced blocks.

• Cut two 10-inch squares. Cut the squares in half diagonally to form four corner triangles.

Assembling the Quilt Center

1 Sew the Wildflower blocks and the 9½-inch alternate blocks together in diagonal rows, as shown in DIAGRAM 6. Begin and end with the side triangles. NOTE: Do not attach the corner triangles at this time. Press seam allowances between blocks in the opposite direction of the previous row for easy matching.

2 Sew all the diagonal rows together, pinning block

intersections for accuracy. Press all seam allowances between rows in the same direction.

3 Sew the corner triangles to the quilt, referring to DIAGRAM 6. Trim the excess fabric from the side and corner triangles, taking care to allow a ¼-inch seam allowance beyond the corners of each block. Before you begin, see "Trimming Side and Corner Triangles" on page 211 to be certain you make these cuts accurately. Use a ruler, cutting mat, and rotary cutter to measure and cut accurate seam allowances beyond the block corners. At this point, the quilt should measure 64¼ × 77 inches. If it doesn't, adjust seam allowances so that the borders will fit.

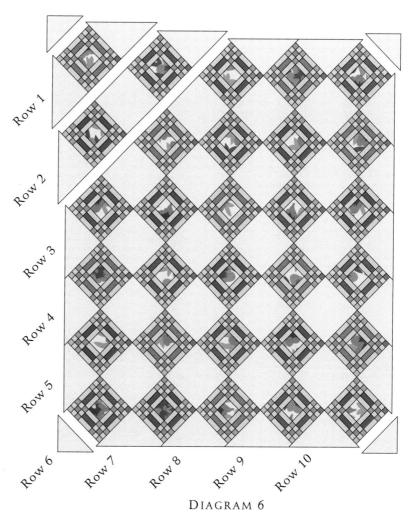

Row 1
Row 2
Row 3
Row 4
Row 5
Row 6 Row 7 Row 8 Row 9 Row 10

DIAGRAM 6

Borders

for Pieced Border

NOTE: The yardage given allows for border pieces to be cut cross-grain.

From the beige dot fabric:
• Cut three 5½ × 44-inch strips. From these strips, cut seventeen 5½-inch squares. Cut these squares in half diagonally in both directions to form 66 side triangles for the pieced border.
• Cut two 3-inch squares. Cut squares in half diagonally to form four corner triangles for the pieced border.

From the green tone-on-tone print fabric:
• Cut three 5½ × 44-inch strips. From these strips, cut seventeen 5½-inch squares. Cut these squares diagonally in both directions to form 66 side triangles for the pieced border.
• Cut six 3-inch squares. Cut the squares in half diagonally to form 12 corner triangles for the pieced border.

From the medium print fabrics:
• Cut seven 3½ × 44-inch strips. From these strips, cut seventy 3½-inch squares for the pieced border.

Assembling the Pieced Border

1 To make the top pieced border strip, sew together 15 medium print squares, 14 green side triangles, 14 beige side triangles, 2 beige corner triangles, and 2 green corner triangles in diagonal rows, as shown in DIAGRAM 7. Note that there will be one beige and one green corner triangle at each end of the border strip. Repeat for the bottom pieced border strip.

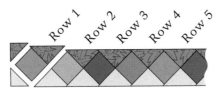

DIAGRAM 7

2 Sew the top and bottom pieced border strips to the quilt, referring to the QUILT ASSEMBLY DIAGRAM. Press.

3 Referring to DIAGRAM 8 and the QUILT ASSEMBLY DIAGRAM, sew the pieced side border strips together in the same manner. Use 20 medium print squares, 19 green side triangles, 19 beige side triangles, and 4 green corner triangles for each border strip. NOTE: All of the corner triangles on the side pieced border strips are green.

DIAGRAM 8

4 Sew the side pieced borders to the sides of the quilt, and press.

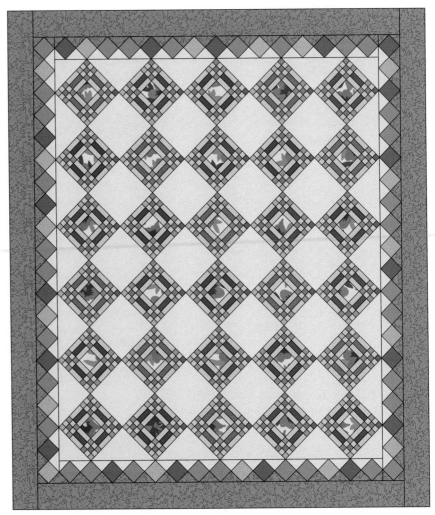

QUILT ASSEMBLY DIAGRAM

CUTTING
for Outer Border

From the green tone-on-tone print fabric:
• Cut nine 5½ × 44-inch strips

Attaching the Outer Border

1 Sew the 5½-inch green border strips together with diagonal seams. Trim seam allowances to ¼ inch, and press seams open. For more information on diagonal seams, see page 211.

2 Measure the quilt from left to right through the middle to determine the length of the top and bottom border strips. Cut the top and bottom outer border strips to the necessary length, sew them to the top and bottom of the quilt, and press.

3 Measure the quilt from top to bottom through the middle, including the border strips you just added, to determine the lengths of the side border strips. Cut the side outer border strips to the necessary length, sew them to the sides of the quilt, and press.

Putting It All Together

1 Prepare the backing for the quilt by cutting the 7½-yard length of backing fabric in thirds crosswise to make three 2½-yard lengths. Remove the selvages,

MARK UNPIECED blocks before assembling the quilt center. It's easier to handle individual blocks than a large quilt top. — TIPS AND TRICKS

and sew the long edges of the three lengths together so that the seams run horizontally. Press seams open.

2 Trim the backing and batting so they are 4 inches larger than the quilt top dimensions.

3 Mark quilting designs on the quilt top.

4 Layer the backing, batting, and quilt top. Baste the layers together, and quilt.

5 When quilting is complete, remove the basting stitches, and trim excess backing and batting even with the quilt top.

Binding

NOTE: The 2¾-inch strips will produce a ⅜-inch-wide binding. If you want a wider or narrower binding, adjust the width of the strips you cut. (See page 216 for pointers on how to experiment with binding width.) See "Making and Attaching the Binding" on page 215 to complete your quilt.

CUTTING

From the green tone-on-tone fabric:
• Cut ten 2¾ × 44-inch strips for cross-grain binding

Quilting DESIGNS

FOR HAND QUILTING:

🍂 Choose a purchased quilting stencil, as shown in QUILTING DIAGRAM 1, for quilting the alternating block.

🍂 Half of that same purchased stencil, turned as shown in QUILTING DIAGRAM 2, will work beautifully when quilted in the half-square triangles at the outer edges of the quilt.

🍂 The pieced blocks are quilted in the ditch of each seam. Cross-hatching adds texture to the outer border and frames the quilt center.

QUILTING DIAGRAM 1

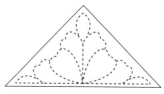

QUILTING DIAGRAM 2

HOME

for the HOLIDAYS

Christmas is a cozy season. In the midst of the cold and snow of a Minnesota winter, I make my home a warm and soothing haven. I love to fill every corner with a mix of holiday collectibles, antique toys, ornaments, and quilts. My holiday memories wouldn't be complete without the deep, rich colors and soft textures of my favorite quilts.

TOWN SQUARE

Tree Skirt and Tablecloth

Town Square makes an outstanding table topper, couch throw, wall quilt, or tree skirt. I chose a very dark green print to give the trees a stately appearance and to help balance them with the chunky red houses. The subtle print in the houses makes the appliqué motifs almost glow in the windows. Strong dark green and dark brown prints create an effective frame around the fence border without distracting from it. And the gold fabric in the center star is echoed by the gold prints in the corner squares of each border.

Size

Tablecloth: 60 inches square (unquilted)

Tree Skirt: 52 inches square

Fabrics and Supplies

Yardage is based on 44-inch-wide fabric.

FOR TABLECLOTH AND TREE SKIRT

⅔ yard small black/brown check fabric for roofs, tree trunks, and windows

⅔ yard red print for houses

⅞ yard beige print for background

⅝ yard green print for trees

Five assorted 4 × 16-inch gold/brown fabric scraps for window appliqués

¾ yard gold print for center star, house corner squares, and center binding

⅞ yard cream print for fence border

¾ yard red print for fence border background

1 skein red embroidery floss

½ yard fusible web, 16 inches wide

Rotary cutter, mat, and see-through ruler with ⅛-inch markings

FOR TABLECLOTH ONLY

¼ yard large black/brown check fabric for fence border corner squares

1½ yards green print for checkerboard border and binding

¾ yard dark brown print for checkerboard border

¼ yard dark gold print for checkerboard border corner squares

Quilt batting, at least 64 inches square

3¾ yards backing fabric

FOR TREE SKIRT ONLY

¼ yard red/brown plaid fabric for fence border corner squares

¾ yard green print binding fabric

3½ yards backing fabric

Quilt batting, at least 56 inches square

G e t t i n g   R e a d y

- READ instructions thoroughly before you begin.

- PREWASH and press fabric.

- USE ¼-inch seam allowances throughout unless directions specify otherwise.

- SEAM ALLOWANCES are included in the cutting sizes given.

- PRESS seam allowances in the direction that will create the least bulk, and whenever possible, press toward the darker fabric.

- CUTTING DIRECTIONS for each section of the quilt are given individually. If you like to cut as you go, simply follow the directions as you get to them. If you'd rather cut all your pieces at the same time, skip ahead to look for each of the cutting sections and do all the cutting before you begin to sew.

- INSTRUCTIONS are given for quick cutting and piecing the blocks. Note that for some of the pieces, the quick-cutting method will result in leftover fabric. ✐

Fabric Key

▪	Red
▪	Small black/brown check
▪	Green
▪	Gold
▪	Dark gold
▫	Beige
▦	Cream
▦	Large black/brown check
▪	Dark brown

House Blocks
(MAKE 4)

C U T T I N G

From the small black/brown check fabric:
- Cut two 8⅞-inch squares; cut the squares in half diagonally
- Cut two 3½ × 44-inch strips

From the red print fabric:
- Cut eight 2 × 12-inch pieces
- Cut four 3 × 12-inch pieces
- Cut eight 3 × 3½-inch pieces
- Cut two 2 × 44-inch strips

From the beige print fabric:
- Cut four 8⅞-inch squares; cut the squares in half diagonally
- Cut four 4⅞-inch squares; cut the squares in half diagonally

From the gold print fabric:
- Cut four 4½-inch squares

Piecing
the House Blocks

1 With right sides together, stitch the 2 × 44-inch red print strip to the 3½ × 44-inch small black/brown check strip. Make two of these strip sets. Cut into sixteen 3½-inch segments. See DIAGRAM 1.

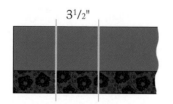

3½"

DIAGRAM 1

2 Sew one of these segments to each side of a 3 × 3½-inch red piece. Make eight of these units, as shown in DIAGRAM 2.

DIAGRAM 2

3 Sew the Step 2 units to both sides of a 3 × 12-inch red strip, as shown in DIAGRAM 3. Make four of these units. Sew a 2 × 12-inch red strip to both sides of this unit, as shown. Make four house units.

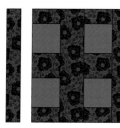

DIAGRAM 3

4 Sew a small beige print triangle to both sides of a 4½-inch gold print square; see DIAGRAM 4. Make four of these units.

DIAGRAM 4

5 Sew the Step 4 units to the bottom edges of the house units, as shown in DIAGRAM 5. Sew the black/brown roof triangles to the house tops, matching center points. Sew the large beige triangles to both sides of the house units, matching center points. At this point the House block should measure 16½ inches square.

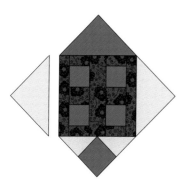

DIAGRAM 5

Window Appliqués
(MAKE 16)

1 Position the fusible web (paper side up) over the appliqué pieces on page 101, and trace. Roughly cut out the shapes.

2 Place the coated side of the fusible web on the wrong side of the fabrics chosen for the window appliqués. NOTE: Use a different fabric for the candle flame than for the candle itself. Press with a hot dry iron, following the manufacturer's directions for your brand of fusible web. Let the fabric and fusible web cool, cut out the pieces on the drawn lines, and remove the paper backing.

3 Center the appliqué pieces in each window. Press in place with a hot dry iron. With three strands of embroidery floss, stitch around the shapes using the primitive stitch or the buttonhole stitch. For more information on the primitive and buttonhole stitches, see page 210.

Tree Blocks
(MAKE 4)

CUTTING

From the green print fabric:
• Cut four 4½ × 8½-inch pieces
• Cut five 2½ × 44-inch strips; from these strips, cut twenty 2½ × 8½-inch pieces

From the beige print fabric:
• Cut three 2½ × 44-inch strips; from these strips, cut forty 2½-inch squares

• Cut two 3½ × 12-inch strips

From the gold print fabric:
• Cut eight 4½-inch squares
• Cut one 8½-inch square for star center

From the black/brown check fabric:
• Cut one 2½ × 12-inch strip

Piecing the Tree Blocks

1 With right sides together, position a 4½-inch gold print square over a 4½ × 8½-inch green piece, as shown in DIAGRAM 6. Draw a diagonal line from corner to corner on the gold square and stitch on the diagonal line, as shown. Trim the seam allowance to ¼ inch and press toward the green fabric.

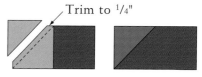

Trim to ¼"

DIAGRAM 6

2 Repeat this procedure for the opposite corner of the green piece, as shown in DIAGRAM 7. Make four of these tree top units.

DIAGRAM 7

3 With right sides together, position a 2½-inch beige square on both corners of a 2½ × 8½-inch green piece, as shown in DIAGRAM 8 on page 96. Draw diagonal lines from corner to corner, stitch on these lines, and

trim seams as in Step 1. Repeat this process to make 20 of these branch units.

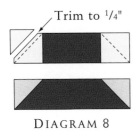

DIAGRAM 8

4 Sew a 3½ × 12-inch beige strip to both sides of the 2½ × 12-inch small black/brown check strip. Cut into four 2½-inch trunk units, as shown in DIAGRAM 9.

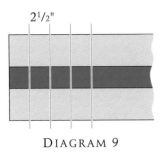

DIAGRAM 9

5 For each tree, sew together five of the units from Step 3. Sew a tree top unit to the top edge and a trunk unit to the bottom edge of each tree, as shown in DIAGRAM 10. At this point, the Tree block should measure 8½ × 16½ inches.

DIAGRAM 10

Quilt Center

1 Stitch a Tree block to opposite sides of the 8½-inch gold print square to make a tree/center star unit, as shown in DIAGRAM 11.

2 Stitch a House block to both sides of the remaining Tree blocks, as shown in DIAGRAM 12.

3 Stitch the house/tree sections to both sides of the tree/center star section, as shown in DIAGRAM 13.

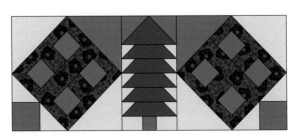

DIAGRAM 11

DIAGRAM 12

DIAGRAM 13

Fence Border

C U T T I N G

From the cream print fabric:
• Cut three 2½ × 44-inch strips
• Cut seven 2½ × 44-inch strips; cut these strips into forty 2½ × 6½-inch pieces

From the red print fabric:
• Cut six 2½ × 44-inch strips
• Cut three 2½ × 44-inch strips;

cut these strips into forty
2½-inch squares

From the black/brown plaid
fabric:
• Cut four 6½-inch squares

Piecing
the Fence Border

1 With right sides together, sew
a 2½ × 44-inch red print strip
to both sides of a 2½ × 44-inch
cream print strip. Make three of
these strip sets. Cut into forty
2½-inch segments, as shown in
DIAGRAM 14.

2½"

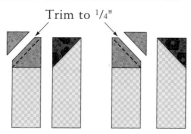

DIAGRAM 14

2 With right sides together, position a 2½-inch red square
on one end of a 2½ × 6½-inch
cream piece. Draw a diagonal line
on the red square from corner to
corner and stitch just a hair to the
outside of the diagonal line. Trim
the seam allowance to ¼ inch
and press toward the cream
fabric, as shown in DIAGRAM 15.
Make 20 of these fence units
with the points on the right,
and reverse the direction of the

Trim to ¼"

DIAGRAM 15

diagonal line on the remaining 20
to create points on the left side,
as shown.

3 To construct each of the four
fence borders, sew ten Step 1
fence sections and ten Step 2
fence sections together, as shown
in DIAGRAM 16. Sew a 6½-inch
large black/brown check square

to each end of two of the fence
border strips, as shown.

4 Stitch two fence sections to
the top and bottom of the
quilt center. Stitch the remaining
fence/corner square sections to
the sides of the quilt, as shown
in the TABLECLOTH ASSEMBLY
DIAGRAM.

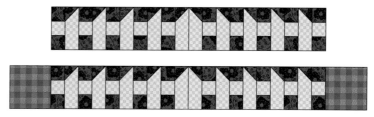

DIAGRAM 16

TABLECLOTH ASSEMBLY DIAGRAM

5 If you are making a tree skirt, skip ahead to Step 5 under "Putting It All Together." If you are making the tablecloth, make the checkerboard border next.

DIAGRAM 18

Checkerboard Border

CUTTING

From the green print fabric:
• Cut three 4½ × 44-inch strips
• Cut four 4½-inch squares

From the dark brown print fabric:
• Cut three 4½ × 44-inch strips

From the dark gold print fabric:
• Cut four 4½-inch squares

Piecing the Checkerboard Border

1 Sew a 4½ × 44-inch green print strip to a 4½ × 44-inch dark brown print strip, as shown in DIAGRAM 17. Make three strip sets in this manner. Cut into twenty-four 4½-inch segments, as shown.

4½"

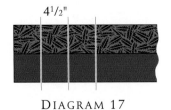

DIAGRAM 17

2 To construct each border section, sew six checkerboard segments together, as shown in DIAGRAM 18. Add a

4½-inch green square to each brown ending square, as shown. Sew a 4½-inch dark gold print square to both ends of two of the four checkerboard border sections, as shown.

3 Stitch two checkerboard sections to the top and bottom of the quilt center, referring to the TABLECLOTH ASSEMBLY DIAGRAM on page 97. Stitch the remaining checkerboard/corner square sections to the sides of the tablecloth.

FOR A QUILT that has a pieced outer border, I like to sew a 2-inch-wide strip of scrap fabric to the outside edges of the border. That way, when I attach the quilt to a quilt frame or insert it into a hoop, the tension will not cause the seams to pull apart.

TIPS AND TRICKS

Putting It All Together

1 For the tablecloth, prepare the backing by cutting the 3¾-yard length of backing fabric in half crosswise to make two 1⅞-yard lengths. Remove the

selvages and sew the long edges of the two lengths together. Press this seam open.

2 Trim the backing and batting so they are 4 inches larger than the quilt top dimensions. Mark quilting designs on the quilt top.

3 Layer the backing, batting, and quilt top. Baste the layers together and quilt.

4 When quilting is complete, remove the basting and trim the excess backing and batting even with the quilt top.

5 For the tree skirt, prepare the backing by cutting the 3½-yard length of backing fabric in half crosswise to make two 1¾-yard lengths. Remove the selvages and sew the long edges of the two lengths of fabric together with one center seam. Press this seam open. Repeat Steps 2 through 4 for the tree skirt.

6 For the tree skirt, use the Center Circle Template on page 101 to draw a 4¾-inch diameter circle at the center of the tree skirt, as shown in DIAGRAM 19. Draw a straight line from the circle to the midpoint of one edge of the tree skirt, as shown. NOTE: This line must go through the center of a tree. Machine stitch ¼ inch outside the circle and ¼ inch away from the

straight line on each side. Cut on the straight line and on the circle.

Tree skirt
DIAGRAM 19

Binding

NOTE: The 2¾-inch-wide bias strips will make a ⅜- to ½-inch-wide binding. If you want a wider or narrower binding, adjust the width of the strips you cut. (See page 216 for pointers on how to experiment with binding width.) See "Making and Attaching the Binding" on page 215 to complete your quilt.

From the green print fabric, for binding the outer edges:
• For the tablecloth, cut six 2¾ × 44-inch cross-grain strips

• For the tree skirt, cut seven 2¾ × 44-inch cross-grain strips

From the gold print fabric, for the tree skirt center:
• Cut enough 2½-inch-wide bias strips to make a 56-inch strip

Attaching the Binding

1 Piece the binding strips together diagonally, trim the seams, and press the seam allowances open.

2 Fold the binding in half lengthwise, wrong sides together, and press.

3 With raw edges even, and using a ⅜-inch-wide seam allowance, stitch the binding to the tablecloth or the tree skirt, mitering corners where necessary. For the tree skirt, begin and end at the opening by the center circle, as shown in DIAGRAM 20. For information on mitering corners, see "Border Basics" on page 211.

4 Turn the binding to the back side of the tablecloth or tree skirt and hand stitch the folded edges in place.

5 Bind the center opening of the tree skirt in the same way, allowing 20 inches of gold bias binding to extend beyond each opening edge to serve as ties, as shown in DIAGRAM 21.

Sew the folded edges of the binding together along the tie extensions, turning in the raw ends.

Tree skirt
DIAGRAM 20

Tree skirt
DIAGRAM 21

Quilting DESIGNS

FOR HAND QUILTING:

✎ *Stitch in the ditch, outlining the houses, the window appliqué shapes, the pine trees, the fence posts, and the checkerboard squares.*

✎ *Inside the pieced pine trees, quilt the triangular shape of each branch, as shown in* QUILTING DIAGRAM 1.

✎ *Inside the house roofs, quilt lines that will echo the triangular shapes, as shown in* QUILTING DIAGRAM 2.

✎ *In the center star, quilt diagonal lines from each point to the opposite point, as shown in* QUILTING DIAGRAM 3.

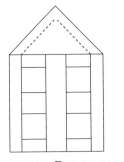

QUILTING DIAGRAM 2

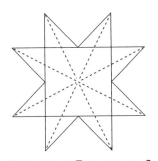

FOR MACHINE QUILTING:

✎ *Quilt curved, swooping lines to represent boughs in the trees and bark in the trunks, as shown in* QUILTING DIAGRAM 4.

✎ *Outline quilt around the houses, the appliqué shapes, the pine trees, the fence posts, and the checkerboard squares. Quilt the fence posts in a "roller coaster" design to emphasize their vertical lines, as shown in* QUILTING DIAGRAM 5.

✎ *Free-motion meander quilting works well for large background areas, such as around the houses and behind the fence posts. Vary the size of your meander quilting in different portions of the quilt to add interesting surface textures.*

QUILTING DIAGRAM 3

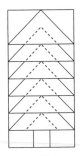

QUILTING DIAGRAM 1

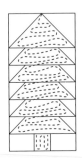

QUILTING DIAGRAM 4

QUILTING DIAGRAM 5

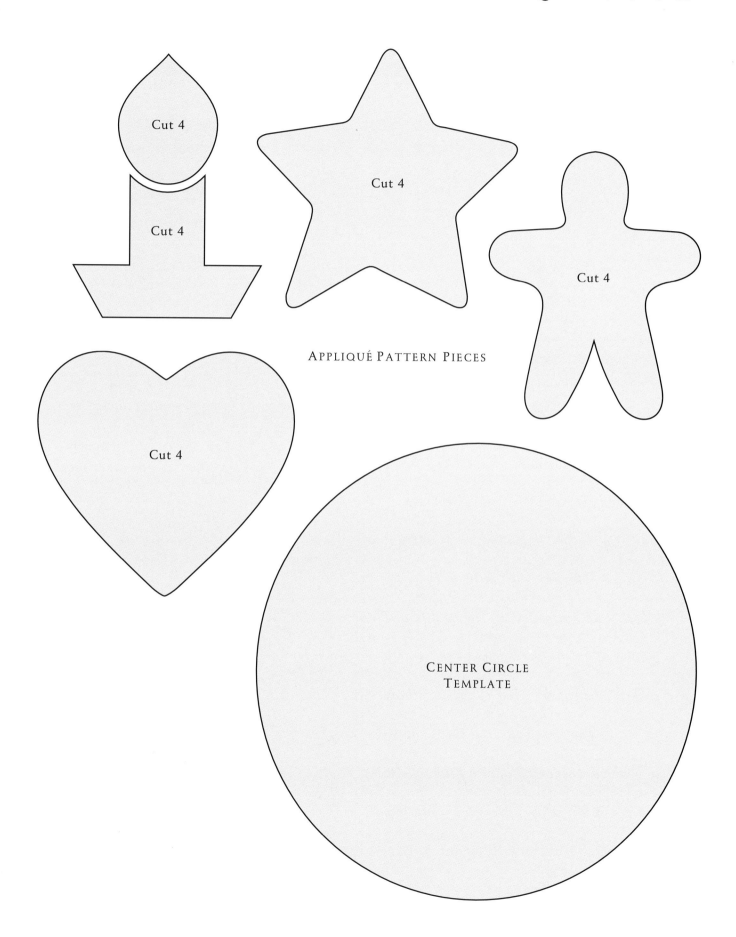

Cut 4

Cut 4

Cut 4

Cut 4

APPLIQUÉ PATTERN PIECES

Cut 4

CENTER CIRCLE
TEMPLATE

YO-YO TABLE TOPPER

An updated version of an old-fashioned favorite, this yo-yo table topper makes a wonderful complement to the wood tones of a country pine table or adds a touch of warmth to any holiday table setting. Cotton homespun plaids in deep reds, greens, and creams in the tree motifs and borders create an overall look that is both country and casual. I like to cut out all my yo-yos at one time and keep them handy, to work on whenever I have a little time to spare—on car trips, whenever I'm waiting for someone or something, or during moments spent relaxing on my porch.

Size

Table Topper: 24 inches square (unquilted)

Fabrics and Supplies

Yardage is based on 44 inch-wide fabric.

⅛ yard black plaid homespun for trunk

1⅔ yards green plaid homespun for tree and outer border

1½ yards beige plaid homespun for tree background

1½ yards red plaid homespun for inner border

Quilting thread to match

G e t t i n g   R e a d y

- READ instructions thoroughly before you begin.
- PREWASH and press fabric.
- TRACE the yo-yo circle onto template material and cut it out. 🍃

Fabric Key

- Black plaid
- Green plaid
- Beige plaid
- Red plaid

CUTTING

NOTE: Trace around the template on the wrong side of the fabric.

From the black plaid homespun:
- Cut 6 circles

From the green plaid homespun:
- Cut 133 circles

From the beige plaid homespun:
- Cut 122 circles

From the red plaid homespun:
- Cut 120 circles

Assembling the Table Topper

1 Turn the edges of each circle under ⅛ inch, gauging this distance by eye. Take care to keep the seam allowances of each circle the same size. Use a single strand of quilting thread to make running stitches close to the fold, taking care to make

these stitches approximately ¼ inch long and ¼ inch apart. Consistency in the length and spacing of your gathering stitches will produce finished yo-yos that are the same size.

2 To form each yo-yo, pull up the gathering thread so that the circle is gathered on the right side, as shown in DIAGRAM 1. The other side of each yo-yo will be flat. Take two stitches through the gathered folds at the center, knot, and clip the thread close to the fabric.

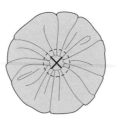

DIAGRAM 1

3 Lay the yo-yos on a flat surface, working on a quarter-section of the design at a time, as shown in DIAGRAM 2.

4 Stitch the yo-yos together with very fine whipstitches at the outer edges, as shown in DIAGRAM 3 on the opposite page. To do so, place yo-yos right sides together and whip-stitch about a ⅛-inch section. Make a secure knot and clip the thread. Continue adding yo-yos in this fashion.

THREAD YOUR needle with the end of the thread that comes off the spool first. It is less likely to fray or tangle.

TIPS AND TRICKS

5 Stitch yo-yos together in rows, butting edges, completing a quarter of the table topper at a time. Sew the four quarters together and add the corner yo-yos, as shown in the TABLE TOPPER ASSEMBLY DIAGRAM.

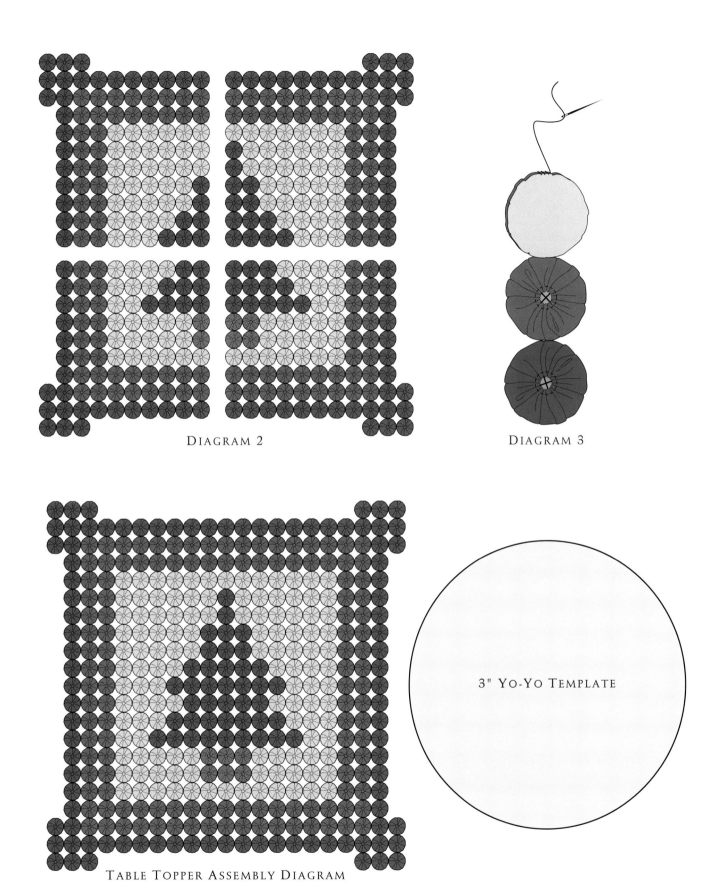

DIAGRAM 2

DIAGRAM 3

TABLE TOPPER ASSEMBLY DIAGRAM

3" YO-YO TEMPLATE

TRIM THE TREE STOCKING

This Christmas stocking, with colorful buttons scattered over a deep green Christmas tree, combines all my favorite things—homespun plaids, ticking, big, bold, chunky shapes, and deep traditional colors. I like to hang several along the stairway for decoration, unfilled, so they're not too heavy.

I tuck in extra bits of batting or scrunched scraps of fabric to fill them out a bit. Twining artificial pine garland gets dressed up with twigs, red berries, and white frosted foliage for a simple finishing touch.

Size

Stocking: 12 × 18 inches (unquilted)

Fabrics and Supplies

Yardage is based on 44-inch-wide fabric.

½ yard cream/black plaid fabric for stocking front and back

¼ yard green print fabric for tree appliqué

⅛ yard red print fabric for heart appliqués and ruffle

¼ yard gold print fabric for star appliqués, ruffle, and binding

3 × 5-inch piece dark brown print fabric for tree base

½ yard muslin for lining

Variety of red, black, and gold print fabric scraps for covered button ornaments

Lightweight quilt batting, at least 14 × 19 inches

¼ yard 16-inch-wide fusible webbing

1 skein black embroidery floss

Thirteen 7/16-inch buttons to be covered

Template material

Rotary cutter, mat, and see-through ruler with ⅛-inch markings

Getting Ready

- READ instructions thoroughly before you begin.

- PREWASH and press fabric.

- USE ¼-inch seam allowances throughout unless directions specify otherwise.

- SEAM ALLOWANCES are included in the cutting sizes given.

- PRESS each seam allowance in the direction that will create the least bulk, and whenever possible, press toward the darker fabric.

- TRACE the tree, heart, star, and tree base templates on pages 112–114 onto template material and cut out the shapes.

- CUTTING DIRECTIONS for each section of the quilt are given individually. If you like to cut as you go, simply follow the directions as you get to them. If you'd rather cut all your pieces at the same time, skip ahead to find each of the cutting sections and do all the cutting before you begin to sew.

Fabric Key

- Cream/black plaid
- Green
- Red
- Gold
- Dark brown

Stocking Front

C U T T I N G

From the cream/black plaid fabric:
- Cut one template A for the stocking front

From the green print fabric:
- Cut one 9 × 12-inch piece for the tree

From the red print fabric:
- Cut one 2 × 9-inch piece for the hearts

From the gold print fabric:
- Cut one 3 × 7-inch piece for the stars

From the dark brown print fabric:
- Cut one 3 × 5-inch piece for the tree base

From the muslin:
- Cut one 14 × 19-inch piece for the lining

From the batting:
- Cut one 14 × 19-inch piece

Appliquéing the Stocking Front

1 Position the fusible web (paper side facing up) over the shapes on pages 112–114. Trace one tree base, one large star, two small stars, and four hearts onto the fusible web. Roughly cut around the shapes.

2 Place fusible web shapes, coated side down, on the wrong side of the fabrics chosen for each shape. Press with a hot dry iron, following the manufacturer's directions for your brand of fusible web. Let the fabrics and fusible web cool, cut out the shapes on the tracing lines, and remove the paper backing.

3 Position the appliqué shapes on the stocking front. Refer to DIAGRAM 1 for placement. Press the shapes in place.

DIAGRAM 1

ANCHORING YOUR BUTTONHOLE STITCHES

🖊 WITH THE PASSAGE OF TIME, I have found that buttonhole stitching can "roll off" the edges of appliqué shapes. If this happens to your buttonhole stitches, you can carefully tack them back in place with matching sewing thread.

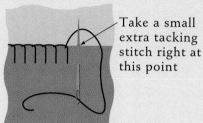

Take a small extra tacking stitch right at this point

🖊 TO PREVENT THIS from happening, take an extra tacking stitch in the same place as you make the buttonhole stitch, as shown. I suggest taking an extra tacking stitch on each buttonhole stitch going around outer curves, corners, and points. For straight edges, I find that taking a tacking stitch every inch is enough.

4 Using three strands of black embroidery floss, appliqué the shapes onto the stocking front with the buttonhole stitch. For more information on the buttonhole stitch, see page 210.

Assembling the Stocking Front

1 Layer the muslin lining, batting, and stocking front facing up, as shown in DIAGRAM 2. Baste the three layers together and quilt.

2 Machine baste around the quilted stocking front, ¼ inch from the edges.

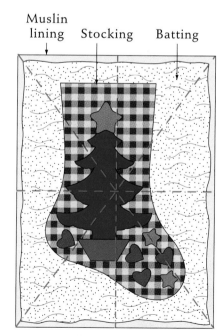

Muslin lining   Stocking   Batting

DIAGRAM 2

3 Trim the muslin lining and batting even with the raw edges of the stocking front.

4 Cover thirteen ⁷⁄₁₆-inch buttons with the red, black, and gold print fabric scraps. Sew the covered buttons to the tree, referring to the photo on page 107 for placement. The thread should go through to the lining side of the stocking front.

Stocking Back

NOTE: Do not cut the stocking shape from the fabrics designated for the stocking back. The technique that follows treats the stocking back as a rectangular unit of layered fabric and batting. This technique is much easier and more accurate than trying to align so many layers and cut edges. Read through the directions carefully before proceeding.

CUTTING

From the cream/black plaid fabric:
• Cut one 14 × 19-inch rectangle for the stocking back

From the muslin:
• Cut one 14 × 19-inch rectangle for the lining

From the batting:
• Cut one 14 × 19-inch rectangle

Assembling the Stocking Back

1 Layer the muslin lining, batting, and plaid stocking back, right side up.

2 Lay the stocking front unit, lining side up, on top of the stocking back unit. Pin the stocking front unit in place with right sides facing each other, as shown in DIAGRAM 3.

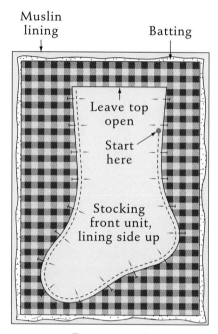

DIAGRAM 3

Labels: Muslin lining, Batting, Leave top open, Start here, Stocking front unit, lining side up

3 Referring to DIAGRAM 3, stitch the front and back units together, starting at the dot and ending at the opposite upper edge. Leave the top edge open.

4 Trim the backing, batting, and lining even with the raw edges of the stocking front.

5 Turn the stocking right side out.

> **DON'T PULL** your quilting thread tight by tugging on the needle. This will eventually fray the thread where it passes through the eye of the needle. Instead, grasp the thread between your thumb and forefinger a few inches behind the needle, and pull the thread.

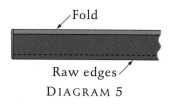

TIPS AND TRICKS

Top Ruffle

CUTTING

From the red print fabric:
• Cut one 2 × 32-inch strip for the inner ruffle

From the gold print fabric:
• Cut one 3 × 32-inch strip for the outer ruffle

Assembling the Top Ruffle

1 Sew the red and gold strips together along one long edge, right sides together. Press seam allowances toward the red fabric, as shown in DIAGRAM 4.

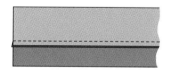

DIAGRAM 4

2 Fold the strip in half lengthwise, wrong sides together. Run a gathering stitch ¼ inch from the raw edges, as shown in DIAGRAM 5. Gently pull up the gathering stitches until the ruffle fits the top edge of the stocking.

DIAGRAM 5

Labels: Fold, Raw edges

3 Pin the ruffle to the stocking top with right sides together and raw edges even. The red side of the ruffle should lie next to the stocking. Baste a scant ¼ inch from the raw edges.

Binding and Hanger

CUTTING

From the gold print fabric:
• Cut one 2 × 17-inch strip for inner binding
• Cut one 1¼ × 10-inch strip for hanger

Attaching the Binding

1 Fold the 2 × 17-inch strip in half lengthwise, with wrong sides together.

2 Pin the binding to the top edge of the stocking, with raw edges even. Stitch through all layers, with a ¼-inch seam allowance, as shown in DIAGRAM 6.

Stitch ¼" from raw edges

DIAGRAM 6

3 Fold the binding to the inside of the stocking and
hand stitch the binding in place.
The ruffle will be standing
straight up.

4 Stitch the the remainder of
the back seam of the stocking closed. Be sure to include
the binding and the raw edges
of the ruffle in this seam as you
stitch it.

Attaching the Hanger

1 Fold the edges of the 1¼ × 10-
inch gold strip in toward each
other so that they will meet at the
center, as shown in DIAGRAM 7.

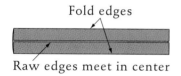

Fold edges

Raw edges meet in center

DIAGRAM 7

2 Fold the strip in half lengthwise once more, and stitch
⅛ inch away from the folded
edges, as shown in DIAGRAM 8.

DIAGRAM 8

3 Fold the hanger strip in half
crosswise into a loop and
sew the hanger strip to the seam
allowance of the ruffle and
stocking with a medium zigzag
stitch. Approximately 2½ inches
of the hanger should extend
above the ruffle, as shown in DI-
AGRAM 9.

DIAGRAM 9

Quilting
DESIGNS

🖎 Very little quilting is
necessary on this stocking
because so much of its
surface is covered by the
large appliqué shapes.
Simply quilt around the
shapes for emphasis.

🖎 The buttons will an-
chor the tree, giving it the
kind of texture you can otherwise accomplish by adding
more quilting stitches.

Align with blue line of Template C

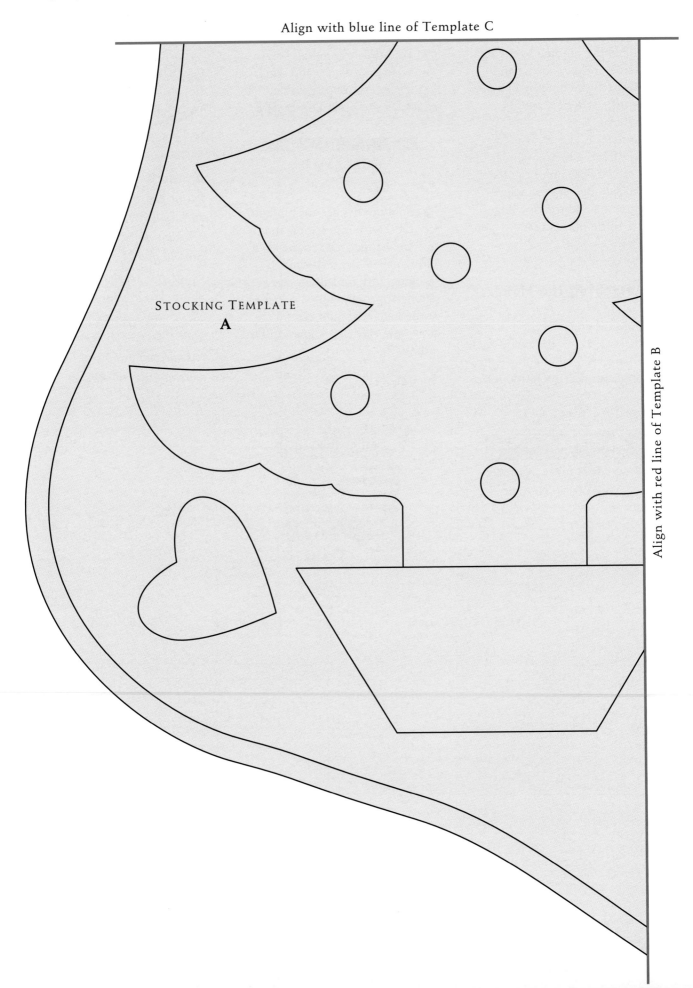

STOCKING TEMPLATE
A

Align with red line of Template B

Align with blue line of Template C

Align with blue line of Template C

STOCKING TEMPLATE
B

Align with red line of Template A

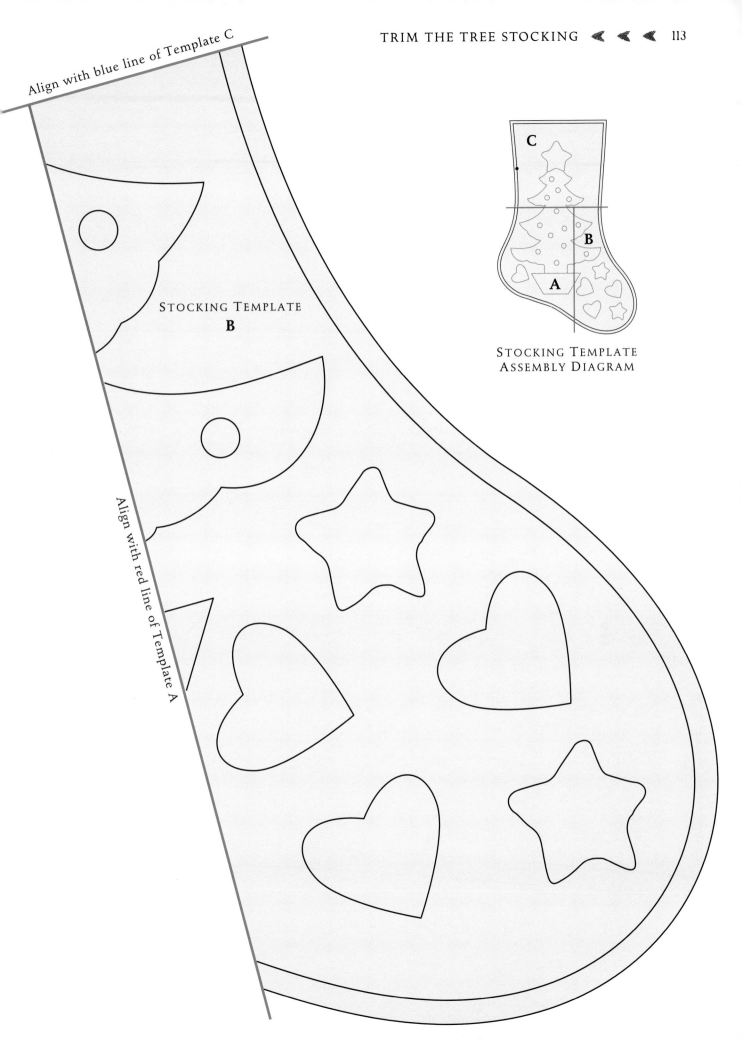

STOCKING TEMPLATE
ASSEMBLY DIAGRAM

STOCKING TEMPLATE
C

Align with blue lines of Templates A and B

CHRISTMAS CANDY

This little wall quilt is as bright and crisp as a jar of peppermints. The two red fabrics are very close in color. I used the darker red print in the border to frame the center of the quilt and the lighter one for highlighting the lattice squares, candy canes, and border pinwheels. A printed tone-on-tone muslin adds a touch of "sugar" to the candy canes, and a soft medium green background print stands out against the darker green lattice and red border strips. The darker green print contains a tiny touch of red and white, which ties the whole top together visually.

Size

Wall Quilt: 15 inches square (unquilted)

Fabrics and Supplies

Yardage is based on 44-inch-wide fabric.

¼ yard light green print fabric for background

¼ yard dark green print fabric for lattice strips and binding

¼ yard red print #1 fabric for candy cane stripes, lattice posts, and pinwheels

⅛ yard beige print fabric for candy canes and pinwheels

¼ yard red print #2 fabric for border

⅝ yard fabric for quilt backing

Lightweight quilt batting, at least 19 inches square

⅜ yard 16-inch-wide fusible web

1 skein black embroidery floss

Rotary cutter, mat, and see-through ruler with ⅛-inch markings

CHRISTMAS CANDY
Getting Ready

- READ instructions thoroughly before you begin.

- PREWASH and press fabric.

- USE ¼-inch seam allowances throughout unless directions specify otherwise.

- SEAM ALLOWANCES are included in the cutting sizes given.

- PRESS seam allowances in the direction that will create the least bulk, and whenever possible, press toward the darker fabric.

- CUTTING DIRECTIONS for each section of the quilt are given individually. If you like to cut as you go, simply follow the directions as you get to them. If you'd rather cut all your pieces at once, skip ahead to find each of the cutting sections and do all the cutting before you begin to sew. 🍃

Fabric Key

- Light green
- Dark green
- Beige
- Red #1
- Red #2

Candy Cane Blocks
(MAKE 4)

CUTTING

From the light green print fabric:
- Cut four 4½-inch squares

1 Position the fusible web (paper side facing up) over the candy cane shapes on page 119. Trace four candy canes onto the fusible web. Then trace the stripes and roughly cut around the shapes.

2 Place fusible web shapes, coated side down, on the wrong side of the fabrics chosen for the candy canes and their stripes. Press with a hot dry iron, following the manufacturer's directions for your brand of fusible

WHEN PLANNING color schemes for your quilts, remember that light, bright, and hot colors come forward visually, while dark, dull, and cool colors recede into the background.

TIPS AND TRICKS

web. Let the fabrics cool, cut out the candy canes on the tracing lines, and remove the paper backing. NOTE: It is better to cut the stripes a tiny bit wider than the candy canes so the stripes will be sure to cover the entire width of the candy canes. Cut out stripes along the *outside* edge of the tracing lines and trim the stripes to fit the candy canes, if necessary. Peel off the paper backing.

Appliquéing the Candy Cane Blocks

1 Center the appliqué pieces on the 4½-inch light green squares and position the stripes on top of the candy canes, as shown in the PLACEMENT DIAGRAM. Press in place with a hot dry iron.

This is how the candy canes should appear when ironed on the background squares

PLACEMENT DIAGRAM

2 Appliqué the shapes in place. Shapes may be ironed on and left as they are, machine appliquéd, or primitive stitched using two strands of black embroidery floss. For more information on the primitive stitch, see page 210.

Quilt Center

CUTTING

From the dark green print fabric:
• Cut twelve 1½ × 4½ inch lattice strips

From the red print #1 fabric:
• Cut nine 1½ inch squares

Assembling the Quilt Center

1 Sew a Candy Cane block to each side of a dark green lattice strip, and sew a lattice strip to the other sides of the blocks, as shown in DIAGRAM 1. Repeat for the two remaining Candy Cane blocks.

DIAGRAM 1

2 Sew a dark green lattice strip to both sides of a 1½-inch red #1 square. Add a red lattice post to the ends, as shown in DIAGRAM 2. Make two more of these lattice strips.

DIAGRAM 2

3 Join the Candy Cane blocks with a lattice strip between them. Sew the remaining lattice strips to the top and bottom of the quilt, as shown in DIAGRAM 3.

DIAGRAM 3

Border and Pinwheel Corner Blocks

CUTTING

NOTE: The yardage given allows for the border pieces to be cut cross-grain.

From the red print #1 fabric:
• Cut one 1⅞ × 44-inch strip

From the beige print fabric:
• Cut one 1⅞ × 44-inch strip

From the red print #2 fabric:
• Cut four 2½ × 11½-inch strips

Piecing the Pinwheels

1 With right sides together, layer the red #1 and beige 1⅞ × 44-inch strips. Press them together, but do not sew. Cut the layered strips into eight 1⅞-inch layered squares. Cut the squares

in half diagonally, as shown in DIAGRAM 4, and stitch a seam ¼ inch from the diagonal edge of each pair of triangles. Press seams toward the red fabric. Make 16 of these triangle-pieced squares.

DIAGRAM 4

2 Sew the triangle-pieced squares together in pairs. Sew the pairs together to form four pinwheels, as shown in DIAGRAM 5.

DIAGRAM 5

Attaching the Border

1 Measure the quilt from left to right through the middle, to determine the length to cut the top and bottom border strips. Cut two 2½-inch-wide red #2 strips this length. Sew these strips to the top and bottom of the quilt.

2 For the side border strips, cut two 2½-inch-wide red #2 strips to the measurement taken in Step 1.

3 Sew the pinwheel blocks to each end of the red #2 side border strips, as shown in DIAGRAM 6.

DIAGRAM 6

4 Sew the border strips to the sides of the quilt, completing the quilt top, as shown in the QUILT ASSEMBLY DIAGRAM.

Putting It All Together

1 Trim the backing and batting so they are 4 inches larger than the quilt top dimensions.

2 Layer the backing, batting, and quilt top. Baste the layers together and quilt.

3 When quilting is complete, remove the basting stitches and trim the excess backing and batting even with the quilt top.

Binding

NOTE: The 2¼-inch-wide strips will make a ¼-inch-wide binding. If you want a wider or narrower binding, adjust the width of the strips you cut. (See page 216 for pointers on how to experiment with binding width.) See "Making and Attaching the Binding" on page 215 to complete your quilt.

From the dark green print fabric:
• Cut two 2¼ × 44-inch strips for cross-grain binding

Quilting DESIGNS

FOR HAND QUILTING:

☁ *This small quilt actually needs very little quilting. Simply stitch in the ditch around the candy cane shapes, the lattice strips, and the pinwheels in the corners of the border.*

☁ *A purchased quilting stencil with a simple chain or rope design will be effective in the border areas.*

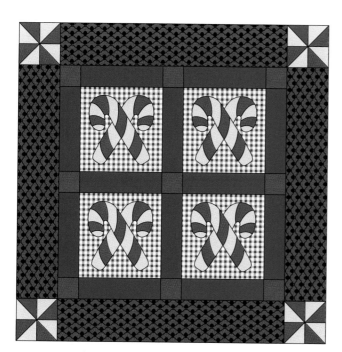

QUILT ASSEMBLY DIAGRAM

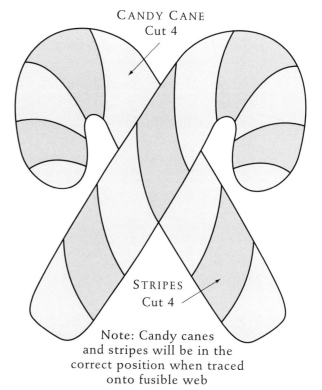

CANDY CANE
Cut 4

STRIPES
Cut 4

Note: Candy canes and stripes will be in the correct position when traced onto fusible web

APPLIQUÉ PATTERNS

CINNAMON HEARTS

Large Quilt and Small Quilt

I wanted these Cinnamon Hearts quilts to look as warm and inviting as their name sounds. I chose warm red fabrics for the hearts and a spicy brown print for the triangles and squares. The two reds contain deeper shades and beige tones that relate to each other, to the background fabric, and to the pieced shapes. Medium green overall prints add visual interest to the unpieced outer borders and draw the eye toward the centers of the quilts. The red bias plaid binding repeats the red colors in the hearts.

Size

Large Quilt: 33 inches square (unquilted)

Fabrics and Supplies

Yardage is based on 44-inch-wide fabric.

¼ yard beige print #1 fabric for heart background

¼ yard red plaid fabric for large heart

⅛ yard small red check fabric for small heart

¼ yard brown print fabric for sawtooth borders

⅛ yard small red check fabric for corner blocks

½ yard beige print #2 fabric for sawtooth borders

¾ yard green print fabric for outer borders

¾ yard red plaid fabric for bias binding

1 yard fabric for quilt backing

Quilt batting, at least 37 inches square

½ yard 16-inch-wide fusible web

1 skein black embroidery floss

Rotary cutter, mat, and see-through ruler with ⅛-inch markings

Getting Ready

- READ instructions thoroughly before you begin.

- PREWASH and press fabric.

- USE ¼-inch seam allowances throughout unless directions specify otherwise.

- SEAM ALLOWANCES are included in the cutting sizes given.

- PRESS seam allowances in the direction that will create the least bulk, and whenever possible, press toward the darker fabric.

- CUTTING DIRECTIONS for each section of the quilt are given individually. If you like to cut as you go, simply follow the directions as you get to them. If you'd rather cut all your pieces at the same time, skip ahead to find each of the cutting sections and do all the cutting before you begin to sew. 🍃

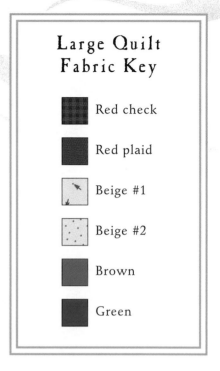

Large Quilt Fabric Key

�	Red check
■	Red plaid
▨	Beige #1
▨	Beige #2
■	Brown
■	Green

Heart Blocks
(MAKE 4)

C U T T I N G

From the beige print #1 fabric:
- Cut four 6½-inch squares

Appliquéing the Heart Blocks

1 Position the fusible web (paper side facing up) over the heart shapes on page 127. Trace four small and four large hearts. Roughly cut around the shapes.

2 Place fusible web shapes, coated side down, on the wrong side of the fabrics chosen for the hearts. Press with a hot

dry iron, following the manufacturer's instructions for your brand of fusible web. Let the fabric and fusible web cool, cut out on tracing lines, and remove the paper backing.

3 Center the large heart shapes on the four 6½-inch beige squares, as shown in DIAGRAM 1, and press in place with a hot dry iron. Center the small hearts on the large hearts, and press.

DIAGRAM 1

4 Referring to DIAGRAM 1, and working with three

strands of black embroidery floss, appliqué the hearts onto the blocks, using the buttonhole stitch. For more information on the buttonhole stitch, see page 210.

Sawtooth Borders

C U T T I N G

From the brown print fabric:
- Cut three 2⅜ × 44-inch strips

From the beige print #2 fabric:
- Cut three 2⅜ × 44-inch strips

Piecing the Sawtooth Borders

1 With right sides together, layer the brown and beige

2⅜ × 44-inch strips and press them together. Cut the layered strips into forty-eight 2⅜-inch squares.

2 Cut the squares in half diagonally, as shown in DIAGRAM 2. Stitch ¼ inch from the diagonal edges. Press seam allowances toward the brown fabric. Repeat to make a total of 96 triangle-pieced squares.

DIAGRAM 2

> **TRIM OFF** *points of patches to within ¼ inch of seam lines to reduce bulk. Press seams before crossing another seam.*
>
> TIPS AND TRICKS

3 Sew 4 triangle-pieced squares together in a row, as shown in DIAGRAM 3. Repeat to make a total of 12 of these units. Make another row with the triangle-pieced squares in the opposite positions, as shown on the right. Make 12 of these units.

DIAGRAM 3

4 Refer to DIAGRAM 4 for placement to assemble the sawtooth borders. Sew the sawtooth border strips together in pairs. Make six of Section A and six of Section B, as shown.

Section A   Section B

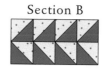

DIAGRAM 4

Corner Blocks
(MAKE 9)

C U T T I N G

From the small red check fabric:
- Cut one 2 × 44-inch strip

From the beige print #2 fabric:
- Cut one 2 × 44-inch strip

Piecing the Corner Blocks

1 Sew the red and beige strips together. Press seam allowances toward the red fabric.

2 Cut this strip set into eighteen 2-inch-wide segments, as shown in DIAGRAM 5.

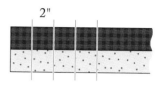

DIAGRAM 5

3 Sew two segments together, alternating colors, as shown in DIAGRAM 6. Repeat to make nine of these Four Patch corner blocks.

DIAGRAM 6

Quilt Center

1 Sew the Section A segments and heart blocks together in two vertical rows, as shown in DIAGRAM 7. Press seam allowances toward the heart blocks.

DIAGRAM 7

2 Sew the Section B segments and corner blocks together in three vertical rows, as shown in DIAGRAM 7 on page 123. Press the seam allowances toward the corner blocks.

3 Referring to DIAGRAM 7, sew the vertical rows together. Press the seam allowances toward the heart blocks.

Outer Border

NOTE: The yardage given allows for cutting the border pieces cross-grain.

From the green print fabric:
• Cut four 6½ × 44-inch strips

LARGE QUILT ASSEMBLY DIAGRAM

1 Measure the quilt from left to right through the middle to determine the length of the top and bottom border strips. Cut the top and bottom border strips to the length needed and sew them to the quilt, referring to the LARGE QUILT ASSEMBLY DIAGRAM. Press seam allowances toward the outer border.

2 Measure the quilt from top to bottom through the middle, including the border strips just added, to determine the length of the side border strips. Cut the side border strips to the length needed and sew them to the quilt, as shown. Press seam allowances toward the outer border.

Putting It All Together

1 Trim the backing and batting so they are 4 inches larger than the quilt top dimensions.

2 Mark quilting designs on the quilt top.

3 Layer the backing, batting, and quilt top. Baste the layers together and quilt.

4 When quilting is complete, remove basting and trim the excess backing and batting even with the quilt top.

Binding

NOTE: The 2¾-inch strips will make a ⅜- to ½-inch-wide finished binding. If you want a wider or narrower binding, adjust the width of the strips you cut. (See page 216 for pointers on how to experiment with binding width.) See "Making and Attaching the Binding" on page 215 to complete your quilt.

From the red plaid fabric:
• Cut enough 2¾-inch bias strips to make a 147-inch strip

CINNAMON HEARTS

Small Quilt

Size

Small Quilt: 18 inches square (unquilted)

Fabrics and Supplies

Yardage is based on 44-inch-wide fabric.

7-inch square of beige print #1 fabric for heart background

5-inch square of red print fabric for small heart

7-inch square of red plaid fabric for large heart

¼ yard chestnut print fabric for sawtooth borders

¼ yard beige print #2 fabric for sawtooth borders

⅛ yard red stripe fabric for corner blocks

½ yard green print fabric for border

⅜ yard red print fabric for binding

⅝ yard fabric for quilt backing

Quilt batting, at least 22 inches square

¼ yard fusible webbing

1 skein black embroidery floss

Rotary cutter, mat, and see-through ruler with ⅛-inch markings

Heart Block
(MAKE 1)

CUTTING

From the beige print #1 fabric:
• Cut one 6½-inch square

Appliquéing the Heart Block

Refer to "Appliquéing the Heart Blocks," Steps 1 through 4, in the Cinnamon Hearts large quilt, and appliqué the heart block for the small quilt in the same manner.

Sawtooth Borders

CUTTING

From the chestnut print fabric:
• Cut one 2⅜ × 44-inch strip

From the beige print #2 fabric:
• Cut one 2⅜ × 44-inch strip

Piecing the Sawtooth Borders

Refer to "Piecing the Sawtooth Borders," Steps 1 through 4, in the Cinnamon Hearts large quilt, and piece the sawtooth borders for the small quilt in the same manner. Make two of Section A and two of Section B.

Small Quilt Fabric Key

☐ Beige #1

▢ Beige #2

■ Chestnut

▩ Red plaid

■ Red

■ Green

Corner Blocks
(MAKE 4)

CUTTING

From the red stripe fabric:
• Cut one 2 × 18-inch strip

From the beige print #2 fabric:
• Cut one 2 × 18-inch strip

Referring to "Corner Blocks," Steps 1 through 3, in the Cinnamon Hearts large quilt, and "Cutting" above, make a strip set for the corner blocks for the small quilt. Cut this strip set into eight 2-inch segments. Make a total of four corner blocks.

Quilt Center

1 Sew the Section A strips to the top and bottom of the heart block, as shown in DIAGRAM 8.

DIAGRAM 8

2 Sew the corner blocks to the ends of the Section B strips, and sew these rows to the sides of the heart block, as shown in DIAGRAM 8.

Outer Border

C U T T I N G

NOTE: The yardage given allows for the border pieces to be cut cross-grain.

From the green fabric:
• Cut two 3½ × 44-inch strips

Attaching the Outer Border

1 Measure the quilt from left to right through the middle to determine the length of the top and bottom border strips. Cut the

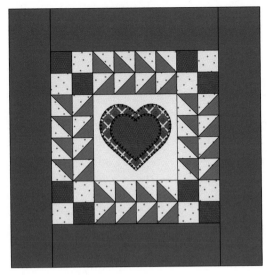

SMALL QUILT ASSEMBLY DIAGRAM

top and bottom border strips to the length needed, and sew them to the quilt, referring to the SMALL QUILT ASSEMBLY DIAGRAM.

2 Measure the quilt from top to bottom through the middle, including the border strips just added, to determine the length of the side border strips. Cut the side border strips to the length needed and sew them to the quilt, referring to the SMALL QUILT ASSEMBLY DIAGRAM.

Putting It All Together

1 Trim the backing and batting so they are 4 inches larger than the quilt top dimensions.

2 Mark quilting designs on the quilt top.

3 Layer the backing, batting, and quilt top. Baste the layers together and quilt.

4 When quilting is complete, remove the basting stitches, and trim the excess backing and batting even with the quilt top.

Binding

NOTE: The 2¾-inch strips will make a ⅜- to ½-inch-wide binding. If you want a wider or narrower binding, adjust the width of the strips you cut. (See page 216 for pointers on how to experiment with binding width.) See "Making and Attaching the Binding" on page 215 to complete your quilt.

C U T T I N G

From the red print fabric:
• Cut two 2¾ × 44-inch strips for cross-grain binding

Quilting
D E S I G N S

FOR HAND QUILTING:

❧ *Quilt around the pieced shapes and appliqué hearts in both the large and small quilts to make them stand out from the background fabrics and appear to be slightly stuffed.*

❧ *Choose a feathered cable design, as shown in* QUILTING DIAGRAM 1, *for quilting the wide, solid borders in the small quilt.*

❧ *I find it a real joy to hand quilt where there are no seam allowances. There are also fewer restrictions in the types of designs you can choose for solid borders, so select any design that will fit the quilt borders. For the large quilt, you can choose a feather and swag design, as shown in* QUILTING DIAGRAM 2.

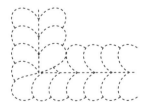

QUILTING DIAGRAM 1

QUILTING DIAGRAM 2

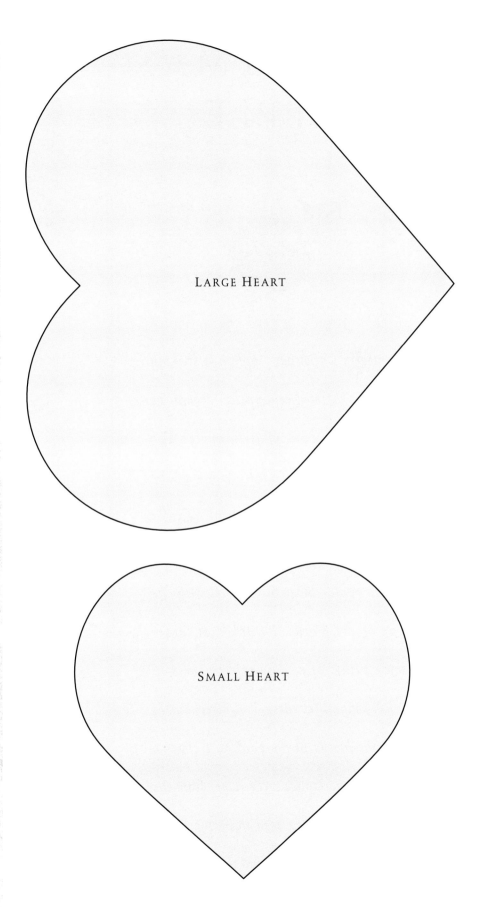

LARGE HEART

SMALL HEART

CHRISTMAS APPLE

The graphic pieced checkerboard pattern in Christmas Apple is a striking place for a floral centerpiece, decorative candles, or a bowl of fresh apples. The pine trees in small-scale, tone-on-tone green prints re-create the depth of color in real trees. The small-scale red fabric in the apples harmonizes well with the size of the blocks; I think that large-scale prints often lose effectiveness in small shapes like these. For the centers of the star blocks in the borders, I chose a plaid that combines three colors from the other prints. I also used the same fabric in the inner red border and the binding.

Size

Table Runner: 24 × 42 inches (unquilted)

Fabrics and Supplies

Yardage is based on 44-inch-wide fabric.

¼ yard blue print fabric for center squares

¼ yard brown plaid fabric for center squares

¼ yard dark red print fabric for inner border

¼ yard red check fabric for apples

⅛ yard dark green print fabric for leaves

¾ yard beige print fabric for background

⅛ yard *each* of four coordinating green print fabrics for trees

⅛ yard brown check fabric for tree trunks

⅛ yard gold plaid fabric for star center

⅛ yard gold print fabric for star

1¼ yards fabric for quilt backing

⅜ yard red print fabric for binding

Quilt batting, at least 28 × 46 inches

Rotary cutter, mat, and wide see-through ruler with ⅛-inch markings

Getting Ready

- READ instructions thoroughly before you begin.
- PREWASH and press fabric.
- USE ¼-inch seam allowances throughout unless directions specify otherwise.
- SEAM ALLOWANCES are included in the cutting sizes given.
- PRESS seam allowances in the direction that will create the least bulk, and whenever possible, press toward the darker fabric.
- CUTTING DIRECTIONS for each section of the quilt are given individually. If you like to cut as you go, simply follow the directions as you get to them. If you'd rather cut all your pieces at the same time, skip ahead to find each of the cutting sections and do all the cutting before you begin to sew. 🍃

Fabric Key

⬛	Blue
▦	Brown plaid
⬛	Dark red
▦	Red check
⬛	Dark green
⬜	Beige
⬛	Green #1
⬛	Green #2
⬛	Green #3
⬛	Green #4
⬛	Brown check
▦	Gold plaid
⬜	Gold

Patchwork Center

CUTTING

From the blue print fabric:
- Cut two 3½ × 20-inch strips
- Cut one 3½ × 17-inch strip

From the brown plaid fabric:
- Cut two 3½ × 17-inch strips
- Cut one 3½ × 20-inch strip

Piecing the Patchwork Center

1 To make Strip Set I, sew a 3½ × 20-inch blue strip to each side of a 3½ × 20-inch brown plaid strip, as shown in DIAGRAM 1. Press the seam allowances toward the brown fabric. Crosscut the strip set into five 3½-inch segments.

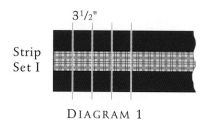

3½"

Strip Set I

DIAGRAM 1

2 To make Strip Set II, sew a 3½ × 17-inch brown plaid strip to each side of a 3½ × 17-inch blue strip, as shown in DIAGRAM 2. Press seam allowances toward the brown fabric. Crosscut the strip set into four 3½-inch segments.

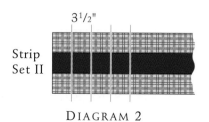

3½"

Strip Set II

DIAGRAM 2

3 Sew the Strip Set I and Strip Set II segments together, alternating colors, as shown in DIAGRAM 3. Begin and end with a Strip Set I segment. At this time, the piece should measure 9½ × 27½ inches.

DIAGRAM 3

Inner Border

From the dark red print fabric:
• Cut two 2 × 9½-inch strips
• Cut two 2 × 30½-inch strips

Attaching the Inner Border

1 Sew the 9½-inch-long dark red print border strips to the short edges of the runner center, as shown in DIAGRAM 4. Press seam allowances toward the border.

2 Sew the 30½-inch-long border strips to the long edges of the runner center, as shown in DIAGRAM 4. Press seam allowances toward the border.

DIAGRAM 4

Apple Blocks
(MAKE 12)

From the red check fabric:
• Cut one 3½ × 44-inch strip; from this strip, cut twelve 3½-inch squares

From the dark green print fabric:
• Cut two 2 × 44-inch strips;

from these strips, cut twenty-four 2-inch squares

From the beige print fabric:
• Cut two 2 × 44-inch strips; from these strips, cut twenty-four 2 × 3½-inch pieces
• Cut two 1¼ × 44-inch strips; from these strips, cut forty-eight 1¼-inch squares

Piecing the Apple Blocks

1 With right sides together, position a 2-inch dark green square on the corner of a 2 × 3½-inch beige piece. Stitch diagonally from corner to corner on the green square, as shown in DIAGRAM 5. Trim away excess fabric, leaving a ¼-inch seam allowance. Press seam allowances toward the dark green fabric. Repeat for the opposite corner, as shown. Repeat to make a total of 12 leaf units.

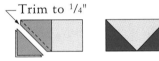

DIAGRAM 5

2 With right sides together, position four 1¼-inch beige squares at each corner of a 3½-inch red check square, as shown in DIAGRAM 6.

DIAGRAM 6

3 Stitch diagonally from corner to corner, as shown in DIAGRAM 7. Trim away the excess fabric from each corner, leaving ¼-inch seam allowances.

Press seam allowances toward the red fabric. Repeat Steps 2 and 3 for each of the 12 apple units.

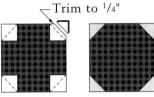

DIAGRAM 7

4 Sew a leaf unit to the top of each apple unit, as shown in DIAGRAM 8. Sew a 2 × 3½-inch beige piece to the bottom of each apple unit, as shown. Press seam allowances toward the apples. At this point, the Apple block should each measure 3½ × 6½ inches.

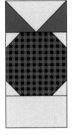

DIAGRAM 8

Tree Blocks
(MAKE 8)

From each of the four green print fabrics:
• Cut one 2⅜ × 44-inch strip. Cut a total of sixty-six 2⅜-inch squares from these four strips. Cut the squares in half diagonally to form 132 triangles. This will allow you extra triangles so you can mix them if you wish.

From the brown check fabric:
• Cut one 1½ × 18-inch strip.

From the beige print fabric:
• Cut two 3 × 18-inch strips.
• Cut two 2⅜ × 44-inch strips; from these strips, cut twenty-four 2⅜-inch squares. Cut the squares in half diagonally to form forty-eight triangles.
• Cut sixteen 2-inch squares.

Piecing the Tree Blocks

NOTE: Mix colors and patterns to give the trees depth; to make all trees identical, see DIAGRAM 9.

1 Sew the green and beige triangles and squares in three horizontal rows, referring to DIAGRAM 9 for color placement. Press seam allowances in each row in one direction, alternating the direction with each row. Join the rows, as shown. Repeat for each tree unit.

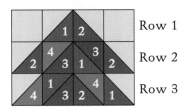

Row 1
Row 2
Row 3

DIAGRAM 9

2 To make Strip Set III for the trunk unit, sew a 3 × 18-inch beige strip to each side of the 1½ × 18-inch brown strip, as shown in DIAGRAM 10. Press seam allowances toward the brown fabric. Crosscut this strip set into eight 2-inch segments, as shown.

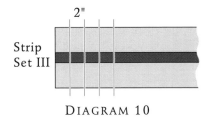

2"

Strip Set III

DIAGRAM 10

3 Sew the trunk units to the trees. At this point, the Tree block should measure 6½ inches square.

Star Blocks
(MAKE 4)

CUTTING

From the gold plaid fabric:
• Cut four 3½-inch squares

From the gold print fabric:
• Cut two 2 × 44-inch strips; from these strips, cut thirty-two 2-inch squares

From the beige print fabric:
• Cut two 2 × 44-inch strips; from these strips, cut sixteen 2 × 3½-inch pieces
• Cut sixteen 2-inch squares

Piecing the Star Blocks

1 With right sides together, position a 2-inch gold print square on a 2 × 3½-inch beige piece, as shown in DIAGRAM 11. Stitch diagonally from corner to corner on the gold square, as shown. Trim away excess fabric, leaving a ¼-inch seam allowance. Press seam allowances toward the gold fabric. Repeat for the opposite corner. Make a total of sixteen star point units.

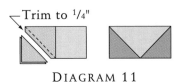

Trim to ¼"

DIAGRAM 11

2 Sew a star point unit to the top and bottom edge of each 3½-inch gold plaid square, as shown in DIAGRAM 12.

DIAGRAM 12

3 Sew a 2-inch beige square to each end of the remaining star point units, as shown in DIAGRAM 13.

DIAGRAM 13

4 Sew one of these units to each side of the Star blocks, as shown in DIAGRAM 14. At this point, the Star block should measure 6½ inches square.

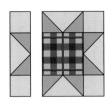

DIAGRAM 14

WHEN JOINING *two pieced sections together, here's an easy way to match seams. Before you sew, place a pin directly through both seam lines, making sure that the seam allowance of the top section faces away from you and the seam allowance of the underlying section faces toward you. This will eliminate bulk and produce perfectly aligned seams.*

TIPS AND TRICKS

Pieced Border

1 For each of the two short border strips, sew an Apple block to each side of a Tree block, as shown in DIAGRAM 15.

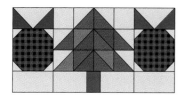

DIAGRAM 15

2 For each of the two long border strips, sew three Tree blocks and four Apple blocks together, alternating blocks, as shown in DIAGRAM 16. Sew a Star block to each end of the border strips, as shown.

Assembling the Table Runner

1 Sew the short pieced border strips to the short edges of the runner top, as shown in the TABLE RUNNER ASSEMBLY DIAGRAM.

2 Sew the long pieced border strips to the long edges of the runner top, as shown.

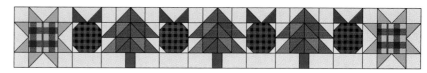

DIAGRAM 16

Putting It All Together

1 Trim the backing and batting so they measure approximately 4 inches larger than the table runner top.

2 Mark quilting designs on the quilt top.

3 Layer the backing, batting, and quilt top. Baste or pin these layers together and quilt.

4 When quilting is complete, remove the basting stitches, and trim the excess backing and batting even with the quilt top.

Binding

NOTE: The 2¼-inch binding strips will produce a ¼-inch-wide binding. If you want a wider or narrower binding, adjust the width of the strips you cut. (See page 216 for pointers on how to experiment with binding width.) See "Making and Attaching the Binding" on page 215 to complete your quilt.

C U T T I N G

From the red print binding fabric:
• Cut four 2¼ × 44-inch strips for cross-grain binding

Quilting DESIGNS

FOR HAND OR MACHINE QUILTING:

❧ *Quilt in the ditch of each seam. Also quilt diagonally from corner to corner in the squares at the center of the quilt to create a secondary geometric pattern.*

❧ *Quilt the squares in the corner Star blocks in the same manner as the center squares. Repeating the same type of quilting design in more than one area of a quilt helps to create visual unity throughout the quilt.*

❧ *Quilt in the ditch around the apples, stars, and trees to add texture and highlight the pieced triangles.*

TABLE RUNNER ASSEMBLY DIAGRAM

CHRISTMAS HOUSE

Christmas House is filled with many of my favorite country motifs—stars, pine trees, hearts, and a house with a picket fence. When I choose fabrics for a quilt like this, I like to look for prints, plaids, and checks that feature many of the same colors, in order to unify a variety of different design elements. Here, I decided to use a neutral background that would visually tie the individual blocks together, and I selected small-scale, simple prints and plaids to stay in keeping with the whimsical country style of the quilt.

Fabrics and Supplies

Yardage is based on 44-inch-wide fabric.

⅛ yard red dot fabric for house

⅛ yard black check fabric for windows, chimney, and door

⅛ yard black plaid fabric for roof

¾ yard beige print fabric for background

⅓ yard red check fabric for Nine Patch and hearts

⅛ yard dark green print fabric for trees

⅛ yard brown check fabric for trunks

¼ yard gold print fabric for stars

¼ yard cream print fabric for fence

¼ yard green print fabric for fence background

⅛ yard red plaid fabric for pieced border

⅛ yard tan print for fabric pieced border

⅓ yard black print fabric for narrow inner border and corner squares

½ yard gold/black plaid fabric for outer border

½ yard red dot fabric for binding

1⅓ yards fabric for quilt backing

Quilt batting, at least 35 × 38 inches

Rotary cutter, mat, and see-through ruler with ⅛-inch markings

Getting Ready

- READ instructions thoroughly before you begin.
- PREWASH and press fabric.
- USE ¼-inch seam allowances throughout unless directions specify otherwise.
- SEAM ALLOWANCES are included in the cutting sizes given.
- PRESS seam allowances in the direction that will create the least bulk, and whenever possible, press toward the darker fabric.
- CUTTING DIRECTIONS for each section of the quilt are given individually. If you like to cut as you go, simply follow the directions as you get to them. If you'd rather cut all your pieces at the same time, skip ahead to find each of the cutting sections and do all the cutting before you begin to sew. ✄

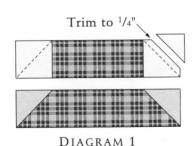

Fabric Key

■	Red dot
■	Black check
▦	Black plaid
▦	Beige
▦	Red check
■	Green
▦	Brown
■	Gold
▦	Cream
■	Dark green
■	Red plaid
▦	Tan
■	Black print
▦	Gold/black plaid

House Block
(MAKE 1)

CUTTING

From the red dot fabric:
- Cut three 1½ × 6½-inch pieces for the house
- Cut five 1½ × 2½-inch pieces for the house

From the black check fabric:
- Cut one 2½ × 3½-inch piece for the door
- Cut two 1½ × 2½-inch pieces for the small windows
- Cut one 2½-inch square for the large window
- Cut two 1½-inch squares for the chimneys

From the black plaid fabric:
- Cut one 2½ × 9½-inch strip for the roof

From the beige print fabric:
- Cut two 1½ × 6½-inch pieces for the house background
- Cut one 1½ × 3½-inch piece for the chimney background
- Cut two 1½ × 2½-inch pieces for the chimney background
- Cut two 2½-inch squares for the roof background

Piecing
the House Blocks

1 To make the roof unit, position the 2½-inch beige squares on the corners of the 2½ × 9½-inch black plaid piece. Stitch diagonally on the beige squares, as shown in DIAGRAM 1. Trim away excess fabric, leaving a ¼-inch seam allowance, as shown. Press seam allowances toward the plaid fabric.

Trim to ¼"

DIAGRAM 1

2 Sew a 1½-inch black check square to each side of the 1½ × 3½-inch beige piece, as shown in DIAGRAM 2. Sew a 1½ × 2½-inch beige piece to each side, creating the chimney unit, as shown.

DIAGRAM 2

3 To make Unit A, sew a 1½ × 2½-inch red dot piece to each side of a 1½ × 2½-inch black check piece, as shown in DIAGRAM 3. Sew the 2½ × 3½-inch black check piece to the bottom of this unit, as shown.

Unit A

DIAGRAM 3

4 To make Unit B, sew a 1½ × 2½-inch red dot piece to each side of a 1½ × 2½-inch black check piece, as shown in DIAGRAM 4. Sew a 2½-inch black check square to the bottom of this unit, and add a 1½ × 2½-inch red dot piece below the black check square, as shown.

Unit B

DIAGRAM 4

5 Sew two each of the 1½ × 6½-inch beige and red dot strips together, as shown in DIAGRAM 5. Sew one of these units to the left side of Unit A and one to the right side of Unit B. Sew Units A and B to each side of the remaining 1½ × 6½-inch red dot strip to make the house unit, as shown.

Unit A   Unit B

DIAGRAM 5

6 Sew together the chimney, roof, and house base units from Steps 1 through 5, as shown in DIAGRAM 6. At this point, the House block should measure 9½ inches square.

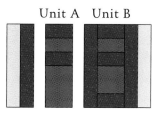

DIAGRAM 6

Nine Patch Blocks
(M A K E 8)

C U T T I N G

From the red check fabric:
• Cut two 1½ × 26-inch strips
• Cut one 1½ × 15-inch strip

From the beige print fabric:
• Cut one 1½ × 26-inch strip
• Cut two 1½ × 15-inch strip

Piecing the Nine Patch Blocks

1 To make Strip Set I, sew a 1½ × 26-inch red check strip to both sides of a 1½ × 26-inch beige strip, as shown in DIAGRAM 7. Press seam allowances toward the red fabric. Crosscut the strip set into sixteen 1½-inch segments, as shown.

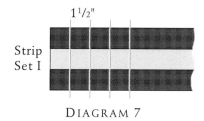

1½"

Strip Set I

DIAGRAM 7

2 To make Strip Set II, sew a 1½ × 15-inch beige strip to both sides of a 1½ × 15-inch red check strip, as shown in DIAGRAM 8. Press seam allowances toward the red fabric. Crosscut the strip set into eight 1½-inch segments, as shown.

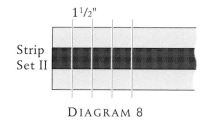

1½"

Strip Set II

DIAGRAM 8

3 Sew a Strip Set I segment to each side of a Strip Set II segment to make each of the Nine Patch blocks, as shown in DIAGRAM 9 on page 138. At this point, the Nine Patch Blocks should measure 3½ inches square.

DIAGRAM 9

Tree Blocks
(MAKE 8)

CUTTING

From the dark green print fabric:
• Cut eight Template A triangles for trees; mark notches on each piece

From the beige print fabric:
• Cut eight Template B triangles; mark a notch on each piece
• Cut eight Template B reversed triangles; mark a notch on each piece
• Cut two 1½ × 12-inch strips for trunk background

From the brown check fabric:
• Cut one 1½ × 12-inch strip for trunks

Piecing the Tree Blocks

1 Referring to DIAGRAM 10, sew a beige B and B reverse piece to the sides of each dark green A triangle, matching notches. Press seam allowances toward the green fabric.

DIAGRAM 10

2 To make tree trunks, sew a 1½ × 12-inch beige strip to either side of the 1½ × 12-inch brown check strip. Press seam allowances toward the brown fabric. Crosscut this strip set into eight 1¼-inch segments, as shown in DIAGRAM 11.

1¼"

DIAGRAM 11

3 Sew a tree trunk unit to the bottom of each tree unit, as shown in DIAGRAM 12. At this point, the Tree blocks should measure 3½ inches square.

DIAGRAM 12

Quilt Center

1 Referring to DIAGRAM 13, sew a horizontal row consisting of two Tree blocks and one Nine Patch block. Make two of these rows and sew them to the top and bottom of the house block, as shown.

2 Referring to DIAGRAM 13, sew a vertical row consisting of three Nine Patch blocks and two Tree blocks. Make two of these rows and sew them to the sides of the house block, as shown.

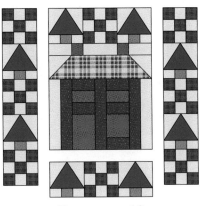

DIAGRAM 13

Star Blocks
(MAKE 5)

CUTTING

From the gold print fabric:
• Cut five 1½-inch squares
• Cut one 1⅞ × 22-inch strip

From the beige print fabric:
• Cut twenty 1½-inch squares
• Cut one 1⅞ × 22-inch strip

Piecing the Star Blocks

1 With right sides together, layer a 1⅞ × 22-inch gold strip and a 1⅞ × 22-inch beige strip. Press the strips together. Cut the layered strips into ten 1⅞-inch squares. Cut the squares in half diagonally, and stitch ¼ inch from the diagonal edges, as shown in DIAGRAM 14. Press seam allowances toward the gold fabric to make twenty 1½-inch triangle-pieced squares.

DIAGRAM 14

2 To make Unit A, sew a 1½-inch beige square to each side of ten of the 1½-inch triangle-pieced squares, as shown in DIAGRAM 15.

Unit A

DIAGRAM 15

3 To make Unit B, sew a 1½-inch triangle-pieced square to each side of the five 1½-inch gold squares, as shown in DIAGRAM 16.

Unit B

DIAGRAM 16

4 Sew a Unit A to each side of a Unit B to make each Star block, as shown in DIAGRAM 17. At this point, the Star blocks should measure 3½ inches square.

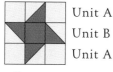 Unit A
Unit B
Unit A

DIAGRAM 17

5 Stitch the five Star blocks together in a row and add this row to the top of the quilt center, referring to the QUILT ASSEMBLY DIAGRAM.

Pieced Border

CUTTING

From the tan print fabric:
• Cut nine 3½ × 4½-inch pieces

From the red plaid fabric:
• Cut eight 3½ × 4½-inch pieces

Assembling the Pieced Borders

1 To make side border strips, sew together three red plaid pieces and three tan pieces, as shown in DIAGRAM 18. Sew

these border strips to the sides of the quilt center, referring to the QUILT ASSEMBLY DIAGRAM.

DIAGRAM 18

QUILT ASSEMBLY DIAGRAM

2 To make the top border strip, sew together two red plaid pieces and three tan pieces, as shown in DIAGRAM 19. Do *not* sew the top border strip to the quilt center at this time.

DIAGRAM 19

Heart Blocks
(MAKE 2)

From the red check fabric:
• Cut four 1½ × 2½-inch pieces
• Cut two 3½ × 4½-inch pieces

From the beige print fabric:
• Cut eight 1½-inch squares
• Cut four 2½-inch squares

Piecing the Heart Blocks

1 With right sides together, position a 1½-inch beige square on one corner of a 1½ × 2½-inch red check piece, as shown in DIAGRAM 20. Stitch diagonally on the beige square and trim away excess fabric, leaving a ¼-inch seam allowance, as shown. Repeat at the other corner. Press seam allowances toward the red fabric. Make two of these units.

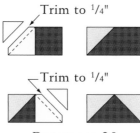

Trim to ¼"

Trim to ¼"

DIAGRAM 20

2 Sew two of the Step 1 units together, creating a heart top unit, as shown in DIAGRAM 21. Make two of these heart top units.

DIAGRAM 21

3 With right sides together, position a 2½-inch beige square on the corner of a 3½ × 4½-inch red check piece, as shown in DIAGRAM 22. Stitch diagonally on the beige square. Trim away excess fabric, leaving a ¼-inch seam allowance, as shown. Press seam allowances toward the red fabric. Repeat for the opposite corner, as shown. Make two of these heart base units.

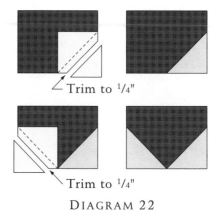

Trim to ¼"

Trim to ¼"

DIAGRAM 22

4 Sew each heart top unit to a heart base unit, as shown in DIAGRAM 23.

DIAGRAM 23

5 Sew the Heart blocks to the sides of the top pieced border, referring to the QUILT ASSEMBLY DIAGRAM on page 139. Sew this pieced border to the top of the quilt center.

Fence Border

From the cream print fabric:
• Cut one 1½ × 20-inch strip
• Cut twelve 1½ × 4½-inch pieces

From the green print fabric:
• Cut one 1½ × 20-inch strip
• Cut twelve 1½-inch squares
• Cut one 2½ × 20-inch strip

Piecing the Fence Border

1 To make the fence background units, sew the 1½ × 20-inch green and cream print strips together, as shown in DIAGRAM 24 on the opposite page. Sew the 2½ × 20-inch green strip to the other side of the beige strip, and crosscut the strip set into eleven 1½-inch segments, as shown.

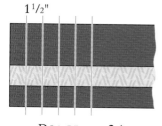

1½"

DIAGRAM 24

2 To make the 12 fence post units, position a 1½-inch green square on the corner of a 1½ × 4½-inch cream piece, as shown in DIAGRAM 25. Stitch diagonally on the green square. Trim away excess fabric, leaving a ¼-inch seam allowance, as shown. Press seam allowances toward the beige fabric.

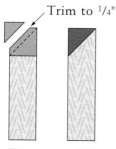

Trim to ¼"

DIAGRAM 25

3 Sew the fence post units and the fence background units together, as shown in DIAGRAM 26. Sew this border strip to the bottom of the quilt center, referring to the QUILT ASSEMBLY DIAGRAM on page 139.

Outer Borders

CUTTING

NOTE: The yardage given allows for the border pieces to be cut cross-grain.

From the black print fabric:
• Cut four 1½ × 44-inch strips for the inner border
• Cut four 3½-inch corner squares

From the gold/black plaid fabric:
• Cut four 3½ × 44-inch strips for the outer border

Attaching the Outer Borders

1 Measure the quilt from left to right through the middle to determine the length of the top and bottom narrow border strips. Cut two black print inner border strips to the necessary length and sew them to the top and bottom of the quilt, referring to the QUILT ASSEMBLY DIAGRAM on page 139.

2 Measure the quilt from top to bottom through the middle, including the border strips you just added, to determine the length of the inner side border strips. Cut two black print inner border strips to the

necessary length and sew them to the sides of the quilt, as shown. Press.

3 For the top and bottom outer border strips, measure as in Step 1 for the inner border. Cut the gold/black plaid fabric to the necessary length, and sew the border strips to the top and bottom of the quilt, as shown. Press.

4 For the wide side outer border strips, use the measurement taken in Step 2. Cut the gold/black plaid fabric to the necessary length. Sew the 3½-inch black print squares to the ends of these border strips and sew the wide border strips to the sides of the quilt, as shown in the QUILT ASSEMBLY DIAGRAM on page 139. Press.

Putting It All Together

1 Trim the backing and batting so they are about 4 inches larger than the quilt top.

2 Mark quilting designs on the quilt top.

3 Layer the backing, batting, and quilt top. Baste the layers together and quilt.

4 When quilting is complete, remove the basting stitches, and trim the excess backing and batting even with the quilt top.

DIAGRAM 26

Binding

NOTE: The 2¾-inch binding strips will produce a ⅜-inch-wide binding. If you want a wider or narrower binding, adjust the width of the strips you cut. (See page 216 for pointers on how to experiment with binding width.) See "Making and Attaching the Binding" on page 215 to complete your quilt.

C U T T I N G

From the red dot fabric:
• Cut four 2¾ × 44-inch strips for cross-grain binding

FOR AN UNUSUAL, fun binding, piece together approximately 18- to 24-inch lengths of a variety of the fabrics in your quilt. If your quilt is a small one, simply cut your strips a shorter length.

TIPS AND TRICKS

Quilting
D E S I G N S

FOR HAND QUILTING:

✿ *Outline quilt around each of the patchwork motifs in the quilt to make them stand out from the background.*

✿ *In the 3 × 4-inch blocks at both the top and sides of the house, quilt vertical lines, spacing them at 1-inch intervals.*

✿ *Choose a purchased quilting stencil with a rope* design, *as shown in the* QUILTING DIAGRAM, *for the outer border. The soft diagonal lines of the rope make a nice contrast to the plaid fabric in the border.*

QUILTING DIAGRAM

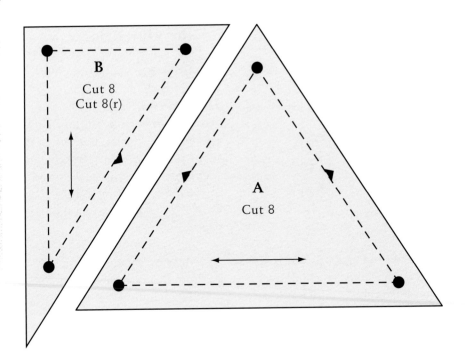

B
Cut 8
Cut 8(r)

A
Cut 8

PINE RIDGE

My fascination with antique woven wool coverlets led me to design this bold, simple, yet striking Pine Ridge quilt. I started with squares and surrounded them with repeating motifs and large Star blocks at the corners to stay in keeping with the tradition of woven coverlets. To create a rich dark center for the quilt, I used deep shades of red and green and subtle prints. The weight of the towering giant pines helps to balance the dark center blocks, and selecting dark greens for the trees adds even more visual strength to the quilt design. This quilt will shield you from chilly temperatures and add a warm glow to any room.

Size

Twin Quilt: 76 × 84 inches
  (unquilted)

Fabrics and Supplies

*Yardage is based on
44-inch-wide fabric.*

1¼ yards green print #1
  fabric for trees

¾ yard green print #2 fabric
  for trees

¾ yard green print #3 fabric
  for trees

¼ yard brown print fabric
  for trunks

1½ yards gold print fabric
  for stars and quilt center
  points

2⅜ yards beige print fabric
  for background

¾ yard red print #1 fabric
  for patchwork center and
  pieced corner sections

1½ yards red print #2 fabric
  for patchwork center and
  outer border

1 yard dark green print
  fabric for patchwork
  center and inner border

⅞ yard green plaid fabric for
  patchwork center and
  pieced corner sections

1 yard gold print fabric for
  binding

5⅓ yards fabric for quilt
  backing

Quilt batting, at least
  80 × 88 inches

Rotary cutter, mat, and
  see-through ruler with
  ⅛-inch markings

PINE RIDGE
Getting Ready

- READ instructions thoroughly before you begin.
- PREWASH and press fabric.
- USE ¼-inch seam allowances throughout unless directions specify otherwise.
- SEAM ALLOWANCES are included in the cutting sizes given.
- PRESS seam allowances in the direction that will create the least bulk, and whenever possible, press toward the darker fabric.
- CUTTING DIRECTIONS for each section of the quilt are given individually. If you like to cut as you go, simply follow the directions as you get to them. If you'd rather cut all your pieces at the same time, skip ahead to find the cutting sections and do all the cutting before you begin to sew. ✎

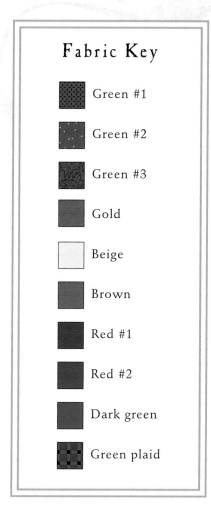

Fabric Key

- Green #1
- Green #2
- Green #3
- Gold
- Beige
- Brown
- Red #1
- Red #2
- Dark green
- Green plaid

Tree Blocks
(MAKE 14)

C U T T I N G

From the green print #1 fabric:
- Cut six 4½ × 8½-inch pieces
- Cut thirty-six 2½ × 8½-inch pieces

From the green print #2 fabric:
- Cut four 4½ × 8½-inch pieces
- Cut twenty-four 2½ × 8½-inch pieces

From the green print #3 fabric:
- Cut four 4½ × 8½-inch pieces
- Cut twenty-four 2½ × 8½-inch pieces

From the gold print fabric:
- Cut twenty-eight 4½-inch squares for center points

From the beige print fabric:
- Cut one hundred sixty-eight 2½-inch squares for background
- Cut four 3½ × 44-inch strips for background

From the brown print fabric:
- Cut two 2½ × 44-inch strips for trunks

Piecing the Tree Blocks

1 With right sides together, position a 4½-inch gold square on the corner of a 4½ × 8½-inch green piece, as shown in the top portion of DIAGRAM 1. Stitch diagonally on the gold square. Trim away excess fabric, leaving a ¼-inch seam allowance, as shown. Press seam allowances toward the green fabric. Repeat for the opposite corner, creating a tree top unit, as shown. Repeat for the remaining 4½ × 8½-inch green #1, green #2, and green #3 pieces.

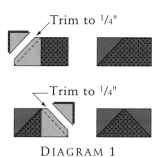

Trim to ¼"

Trim to ¼"

DIAGRAM 1

2 With right sides together, position a 2½-inch beige print square on each corner of a 2½ × 8½-inch green piece to make a tree branch unit, as shown in DIAGRAM 2 on page 146. Stitch diagonally on the beige square. Trim away excess fabric, leaving a ¼-inch seam allowance, as shown. Press seam allowances toward the green

fabric. Repeat for the remaining 2½ × 8½-inch green #1, green #2, and green #3 pieces.

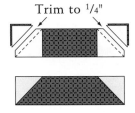

Trim to ¼"

DIAGRAM 2

3 Sew a 3½ × 44-inch beige strip to each side of a 2½ × 44-inch brown strip, as shown in **DIAGRAM 3**. Repeat to make two strip sets. Crosscut the strip sets into fourteen 4½-inch trunk units, as shown.

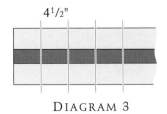

4½"

DIAGRAM 3

4 For each tree block, sew six tree branch units together. Add a matching tree top and a trunk unit, as shown in **DIAGRAM 4**. Press seam allowances toward the tree fabrics. At this point, the tree blocks should measure 8½ × 20½ inches.

NOTE: Make six green #1 tree blocks. Make four green #2 tree blocks. Make four green #3 tree blocks.

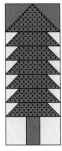

DIAGRAM 4

5 Sew four tree blocks together in a row, referring to **DIAGRAM 5** for color placement. Repeat.

6 Sew three tree blocks together in a row, referring to **DIAGRAM 5** for color placement. Repeat.

Star Blocks
(MAKE 4)

C U T T I N G

From the gold print fabric:
• Cut four 8½-inch squares for Star blocks
• Cut thirty-two 4½-inch squares for Star blocks

From the beige print fabric:
• Cut sixteen 4½-inch squares for background
• Cut sixteen 4½ × 8½-inch pieces for background

From the red print #1 fabric:
• Cut two 4½ × 44-inch strips for corner sections

From the green plaid fabric:
• Cut two 4½ × 44-inch strips for corner sections
• Cut four 4½-inch squares for corner sections

Piecing the Star Blocks

1 With right sides together, position a 4½-inch gold square on the corner of a 4½ × 8½-inch

DIAGRAM 5

beige piece, as shown in DIA-GRAM 6. Stitch diagonally from corner to corner on the gold square. Trim away excess fabric, leaving a ¼-inch seam allowance, as shown. Press seam allowances toward the gold fabric. Repeat for the opposite corner. Repeat for each of the 4½-inch gold squares and 4½ × 8½-inch beige pieces.

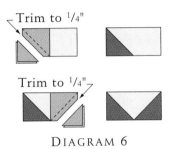

DIAGRAM 6

2 Sew one of these star point units to the top and one to the bottom of each 8½-inch gold square, as shown in DIAGRAM 7.

DIAGRAM 7

3 Sew a 4½-inch beige square to each end of the remaining star point units, as shown in DIAGRAM 8.

DIAGRAM 8

4 Sew a star point to each side of the Star blocks, as shown in DIAGRAM 9. At this time, the

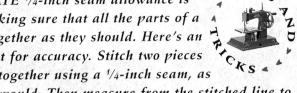

Star blocks should measure 16½ inches square.

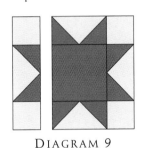

DIAGRAM 9

5 Sew the 4½ × 44-inch red #1 and green plaid strips together, alternating colors, as shown below in DIAGRAM 10. Crosscut this strip set into eight 4½-inch segments, as shown in DIAGRAM 10.

4½"

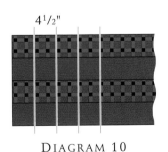

DIAGRAM 10

6 Sew one of these segments to each Star block, as shown in DIAGRAM 11. Add a 4½-inch

green square to the remaining units, and sew these units to the Star blocks.

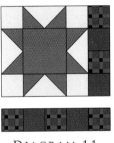

DIAGRAM 11

Patchwork Center

CUTTING

From the red print #1 fabric:
• Cut three 8½-inch squares

From the red print #2 fabric:
• Cut three 8½-inch squares

From the green plaid fabric:
• Cut three 8½-inch squares

From the dark green print fabric:
• Cut three 8½-inch squares

Piecing the Patchwork Center

1 Sew the 8½-inch squares together in horizontal rows, as shown in DIAGRAM 12. Sew the rows together to form the patchwork center, and press.

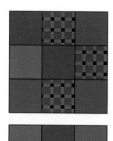

DIAGRAM 12

2 Sew the three tree-block rows to the top and bottom of the quilt center, as shown in DIAGRAM 5 on page 146. Sew a Star block to both sides of the remaining tree units, as shown, and sew these units to the sides of the quilt center.

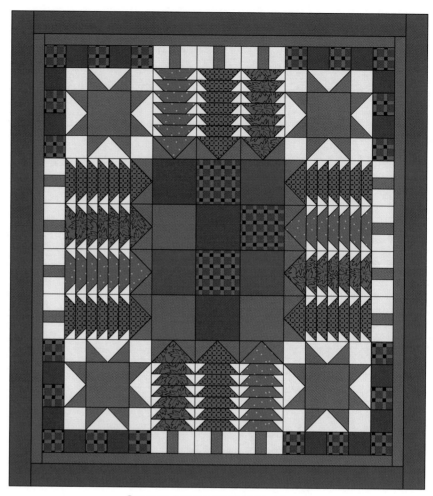

QUILT ASSEMBLY DIAGRAM

Borders

CUTTING

Note: The yardage given allows for the border pieces to be cut cross-grain.

From the dark green print fabric:
• Cut seven 2½ × 44-inch strips for the inner border

From the red print #2 fabric:
• Cut eight 4½ × 44-inch strips for the outer border

Attaching the Borders

1 Measure the quilt from left to right through the middle to determine the length of the top and bottom border strips. Diagonally piece and cut the dark green inner border strips to this length. Sew to the top and bottom of the quilt, as shown in the QUILT ASSEMBLY DIAGRAM, and press.

2 Measure the quilt from top to bottom through the middle to determine the length of the side border strips. Diagonally piece and cut the dark green inner border strips to this length. Sew them to the sides of the quilt, as shown, and press.

3 For the top and bottom outer border, measure as for the inner border in Step 1. Diagonally piece and trim the red #2 fabric to the necessary lengths and sew to the top and bottom of the quilt, and press.

4 For the side outer border strips, measure as you did for the inner border in Step 2. Sew the border strips to the sides of the quilt, and press.

Putting It All Together

1 Cut the 5⅓-yard length of backing fabric in half crosswise. Remove the selvages and sew the long edges of the two lengths together. Press this seam open. Trim the backing and batting so they are about 4 inches larger than the quilt top.

2 Mark quilting designs on the quilt top.

3 Layer the backing, batting, and quilt top. Baste these layers together and quilt.

4 When quilting is complete, remove the basting stitches and trim the excess backing and batting even with the quilt top.

Binding

NOTE: The 2¾-inch bias strips will produce a ⅜-inch-wide binding. If you want a wider or narrower binding, adjust the width of the strips you cut. (See page 216 for pointers on how to experiment with binding width.) See "Making and Attaching the Binding" on page 215 to complete your quilt.

From the gold print fabric:
• Cut nine 2¾ × 44-inch strips for cross-grain binding

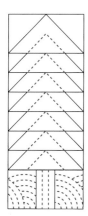

Quilting DESIGNS

FOR HAND QUILTING:

🌀 The center blocks and outer borders are crosshatched at 2-inch intervals, which creates an old-fashioned overall design.

🌀 Quilt the triangles in the tops of the trees, as shown in QUILTING DIAGRAM 1.

🌀 Quilt in the ditch around the edges of the trees to make them prominent, and stitch diagonal lines 1 inch inside the edges of each piece, referring to QUILTING DIAGRAM 1.

🌀 Quilt two vertical lines inside each tree trunk, as shown in QUILTING DIAGRAM 1, and quilt curved arcs to create the illusion of snow mounds beside the trunks.

🌀 Quilt the stars from point to point, as shown in QUILTING DIAGRAM 2, and quilt the background squares and triangles behind the stars with two lines spaced at 1-inch intervals, following each shape.

🌀 Choose a commercial stencil with a small rope design, as shown in QUILTING DIAGRAM 3, for the 2-inch dark green borders, because the soft curves are a pleasing contrast to the other straight-line designs.

QUILTING DIAGRAM 1

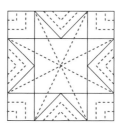

QUILTING DIAGRAM 2

QUILTING DIAGRAM 3

PLACES
in the
HEART

Quilts speak softly to those we love. Stitch by stitch, we make memories for the people who occupy special places in our hearts. Birthdays and anniversaries, holidays and graduations—quilts help us celebrate these special moments. I made this quilt for my daughter, Kerry, in her favorite colors to make her bedroom a special place where she can surround herself with lovely memories and mementos from her childhood days.

DAISY DAYS

The striking potted flower motifs in Daisy Days gain visual strength from repetition. The rectangular shape of this charming quilt makes it a perfect choice to display over a mantelpiece or above the headboard of a bed or a jelly cupboard. A beige background print effectively camouflages the seams of the flower pots and the leaves, making them almost seem to float on top of the fabric. Oversize double circles at the center of each flower lend a bold look, and the triangles in the sawtooth borders repeat the shapes of the flower petals, creating a dramatic frame for the quilt center.

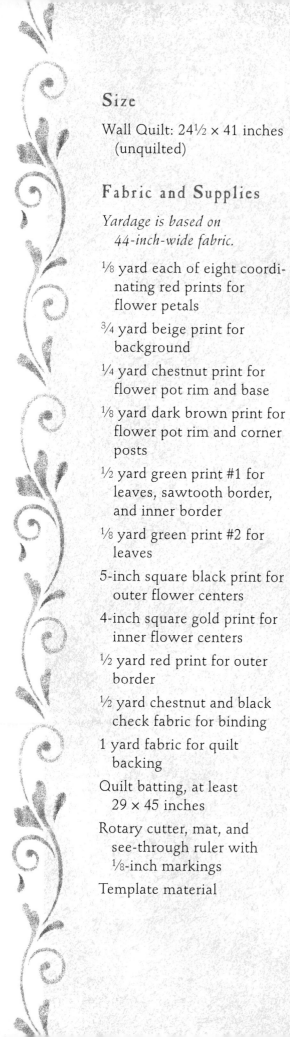

Size

Wall Quilt: 24½ × 41 inches (unquilted)

Fabric and Supplies

Yardage is based on 44-inch-wide fabric.

⅛ yard each of eight coordinating red prints for flower petals

¾ yard beige print for background

¼ yard chestnut print for flower pot rim and base

⅛ yard dark brown print for flower pot rim and corner posts

½ yard green print #1 for leaves, sawtooth border, and inner border

⅛ yard green print #2 for leaves

5-inch square black print for outer flower centers

4-inch square gold print for inner flower centers

½ yard red print for outer border

½ yard chestnut and black check fabric for binding

1 yard fabric for quilt backing

Quilt batting, at least 29 × 45 inches

Rotary cutter, mat, and see-through ruler with ⅛-inch markings

Template material

Getting Ready

- READ instructions thoroughly before you begin.

- PREWASH and press fabric.

- USE ¼-inch seam allowances throughout unless directions specify otherwise.

- SEAM ALLOWANCES are included in the cutting sizes given.

- PRESS seam allowances in the direction that will create the least bulk, and whenever possible, toward the darker fabric.

- TRACE templates A, B, and C from page 159 onto template material and cut them out.

- CUTTING DIRECTIONS for each section of the quilt are given individually. If you like to cut as you go, simply follow the directions as you get to them. If you'd rather cut all your pieces at the same time, skip ahead to find each of the cutting sections and do all the cutting before you begin to sew. 🍂

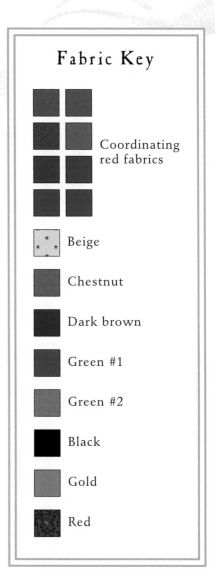

Fabric Key

Coordinating red fabrics

Beige

Chestnut

Dark brown

Green #1

Green #2

Black

Gold

Red

Flower Pot
(MAKE 3)

CUTTING

From the chestnut print fabric:
- Cut three 3½ × 8-inch rectangles
- Cut six 2-inch squares

From the dark brown print fabric:
- Cut nine 2-inch squares

From the beige print fabric:
- Cut six 3½-inch squares

Piecing the Flower Pot

1 With right sides together, position a 3½-inch beige square at each end of a 3½ × 8-inch chestnut rectangle, as shown in DIAGRAM 1. Draw a diagonal line on the beige squares, and stitch on these lines. Trim seam allowances to ¼ inch, as shown. Press seam allowances toward the darker fabric. Make three of these units, as shown.

Trim to ¼"

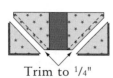

DIAGRAM 1

2 Sew three 2-inch dark brown squares and two 2-inch chestnut squares together, alternating colors, as shown in DIAGRAM 2. Press. Make three of these units.

DIAGRAM 2

3 Sew a unit from Step 1 and a unit from Step 2 together to form each flower pot, as shown

TIPS AND TRICKS

EVEN AFTER prewashing, very dark fabrics may still bleed color. To test for this, sew a piece of the fabric in question to a piece of light fabric and place them in a bowl of cool water. Soak, squeeze out the water, dry, and press the fabrics. If there is no trace of color on the lighter fabric, you should be safe. The peace of mind you'll gain from this process is worth spending the extra time to do this test.

in DIAGRAM 3. At this point, each flower pot should measure 5 × 8 inches.

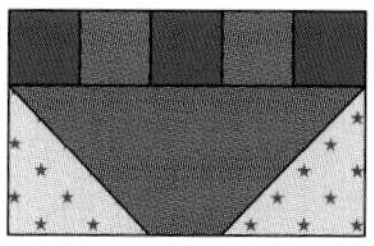

DIAGRAM 3

Leaves

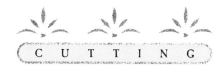

CUTTING

From the green print #1 fabric:
- Cut one 2⅜ × 10-inch strip
- Cut one 2⅜ × 18-inch strip
- Cut three 2 × 3½-inch rectangles

From the green print #2 fabric:
- Cut two 2⅜ × 10-inch strips

From the beige print fabric:
- Cut one 2⅜ × 18-inch strip
- Cut one 2⅜ × 10-inch strip

Piecing the Leaves

1 With right sides together, layer the 2⅜ × 18-inch green #1 strip with the 2⅜ × 18-inch beige strip. Press, but do not sew. Cut the layered strips into six 2⅜-inch squares, as shown in DIAGRAM 4.

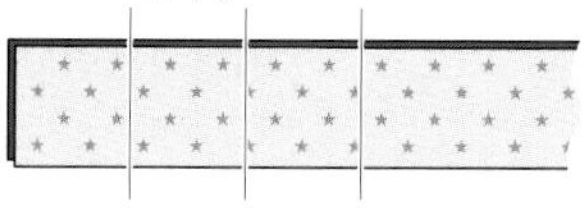

DIAGRAM 4

2 Cut the squares in half diagonally and stitch ¼ inch from the diagonal edges, as shown in DIAGRAM 5. Press seam allowances toward the green #1 fabric to form twelve 2-inch triangle-pieced squares, as shown.

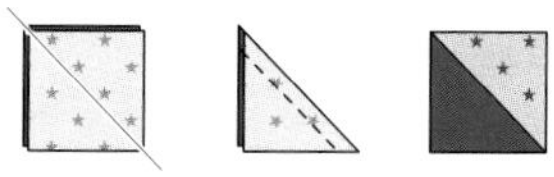

DIAGRAM 5

3 In the same manner, layer the 2⅜ × 10-inch green #2 strip with the 2⅜ × 10-inch beige strip. Cut these layered strips into three 2⅜-inch squares. Cut the squares in half diagonally and stitch ¼ inch from each diagonal edge, as shown in DIAGRAM 6. Press to form six 2-inch triangle-pieced squares.

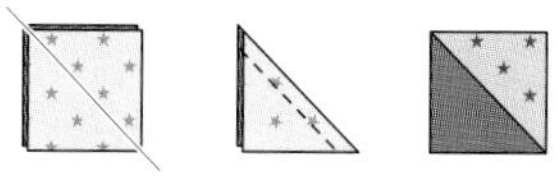

DIAGRAM 6

4 In the same manner, layer the 2⅜ × 10-inch green #1 and green #2 strips. Cut the layered strips into three 2⅜-inch squares. Cut the squares in half diagonally and stitch ¼ inch from each diagonal edge. Press to form six 2-inch triangle-pieced squares, as shown in DIAGRAM 7.

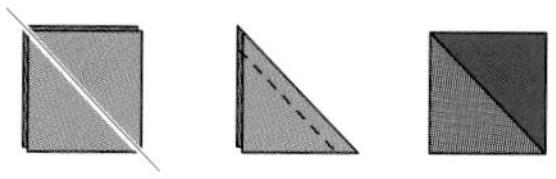

DIAGRAM 7

5 To make a left leaf unit, sew together two triangle-pieced squares from Step 2, one from Step 3, and one from Step 4, as shown in DIAGRAM 8. To make a right leaf unit, reverse the order of the triangle squares, as shown in the diagram. Make three left and three right leaf units.

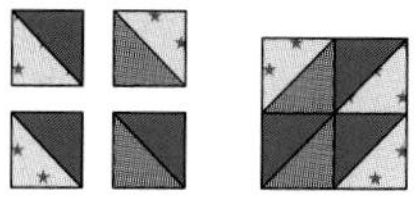

DIAGRAM 8

6 Sew these units to both sides of each 2 × 3½-inch green #1 rectangle, as shown in DIAGRAM 9. Press. Make three of these leaf sections. At this point, each leaf section should measure 3½ × 8 inches.

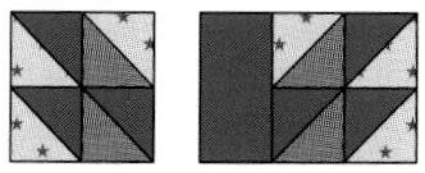

DIAGRAM 9

Quilt Center

C U T T I N G

From the beige print fabric:
• Cut four 2 × 8-inch rectangles
• Cut one 5 × 29-inch strip

Assembling the Quilt Center

1 Sew each of the leaf and flower pot sections together, as shown in DIAGRAM 10.

DIAGRAM 10

2 Sew the four 2 × 8-inch beige rectangles and the leaf/pot sections together, as shown in DIAGRAM 11. Press. Add the 5 × 29-inch beige strip to the top of this unit, as shown. At this point, the quilt center should measure 12½ × 29 inches.

Flowers
(MAKE 3)

C U T T I N G

From the eight coordinating red print fabrics for flower petals:
• Cut a total of 24 of template A.

From the black print fabric:
• Cut three of template B, positioning the template on the wrong side of the black print fabric. Trace around template B, leaving ½ inch between each circle. Cut out the fabric circles, adding ¼-inch seam allowances.

From the gold print fabric:
• Cut three of template C in the same manner as for template B.

Piecing the Flowers

1 Fold the red print A pieces in half lengthwise, right sides together, as shown in DIAGRAM 12. Sew a ¼-inch seam along the top edge, and trim away the excess seam allowance at the point, as shown.

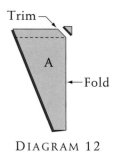

DIAGRAM 12

2 Turn each A petal right side out, and push the tips out with a blunt pencil. Press, making sure the seam lines are centered on the wrong side and both sides are symmetrical, as shown in DIAGRAM 13.

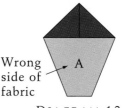

DIAGRAM 13

3 Sew eight petals together for each flower, as shown in DIAGRAM 14. Press all seam allowances in the same direction.

DIAGRAM 14

4 Referring to the QUILT ASSEMBLY DIAGRAM, position the flowers on the quilt center so that the flower petals overlap the stems and just touch the leaf units. Using matching thread, slip stitch the flowers in place.

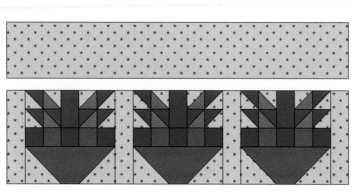

DIAGRAM 11

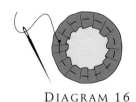

QUILT ASSEMBLY DIAGRAM

5 To create smooth, well-rounded center circles for the flowers, run a line of basting stitches around each of the black B and gold C circles, placing these stitches halfway between the drawn line and the cut edge of each circle, as shown in DIAGRAM 15. After basting each circle, keep the needle and thread attached for Step 6.

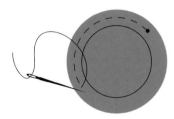

DIAGRAM 15

6 Place the template on the wrong side of each fabric circle and pull on your basting stitches, gathering the fabric over the template, as shown in DIAGRAM 16. When the fabric is tight, space the gathers evenly, and make a backstitch or knot to secure the thread, as shown. Clip the thread, press the circle, and remove the paper template.

DIAGRAM 16

7 Appliqué the gold print C circles to the center of each black print B circle, referring to the QUILT ASSEMBLY DIAGRAM.

8 Appliqué the layered flower centers to the flowers, referring to the QUILT ASSEMBLY DIAGRAM.

Borders

C U T T I N G

NOTE: The yardage given allows for border pieces to be cut cross-grain.

From the green print #1 fabric:
• Cut two 2 × 29-inch strips for the inner border
• Cut two 2 × 12½-inch strips for the inner border
• Cut two 2⅜ × 44-inch strips for the sawtooth border

From the dark brown print fabric:
• Cut four 2-inch squares for the corner posts

From the beige print fabric:
• Cut two 2⅜ × 44-inch strips for the sawtooth border
• Cut four 2-inch squares for the sawtooth border

From the red print fabric:
• Cut two 3½ × 35-inch strips for the outer border
• Cut two 3½ × 24½-inch strips for the outer border

Attaching the Inner Border

1 Sew the 2 × 29-inch green #1 border strips to the top and bottom of the quilt, referring to the QUILT ASSEMBLY DIAGRAM on page 157. Press seam allowances toward the border.

2 Sew a 2-inch brown square to each end of the 2 × 12½-inch green border strips, referring to the QUILT ASSEMBLY DIAGRAM on page 157. Press. Sew these border strips to the sides of the quilt. Press seam allowances toward the border.

Piecing the Sawtooth Border

1 Layer a 2⅜ × 44-inch green #1 strip and a 2⅜ × 44-inch beige strip, right sides together, as you did for the leaf sections. Press, do not sew. Repeat with the remaining green #1 and beige strips. Cut the layered strips into thirty-one 2⅜-inch squares.

2 Cut the squares in half diagonally, and stitch ¼-inch from the diagonal edges, in the same manner as for the leaf sections. Press seam allowances toward the green fabric. Make 62 of these triangle-pieced squares.

DIAGRAM 17

3 Referring to DIAGRAM 17, sew 21 of the triangle-pieced squares together for each of the top and bottom sawtooth border strips. Sew these border strips to the top and bottom of the quilt, referring to the QUILT ASSEMBLY DIAGRAM on page 157. Press seam allowances toward the inner border.

4 Sew ten of the triangle-pieced squares together for each of the side border strips, as shown in DIAGRAM 18. Sew a 2-inch beige square to each end of the side sawtooth border strips, as shown. Press. Sew these border strips to the sides of the quilt, referring to the QUILT ASSEMBLY DIAGRAM on page 157. Press seam allowances toward the inner border.

DIAGRAM 18

Attaching the Outer Border

1 Sew the 3½ × 35-inch red print strips to the top and bottom of the quilt, referring to the QUILT ASSEMBLY DIAGRAM on page 157. Press the seam allowances toward the outer border.

2 Sew the 3½ × 24½-inch red print strips to the sides of the quilt, as shown in the QUILT

ASSEMBLY DIAGRAM on page 157. Press seam allowances toward the outer border.

Putting It All Together

1 Trim the backing and batting so they are 4 inches larger than the quilt top dimensions.

2 Mark quilting designs on the quilt top.

3 Layer the backing, batting, and quilt top. Baste the layers together and quilt.

Binding

NOTE: The 2¾-inch binding strips will produce a ⅜-inch-wide binding. If you want a wider or narrower binding, adjust the width of the strips you cut. (See page 216 for pointers on how to experiment with binding width.) See "Making and Attaching the Binding" on page 215 to complete your quilt.

CUTTING

From the chestnut and black check binding fabric:
• Cut enough 2¾-inch bias strips to make 150 inches of bias binding

Quilting
DESIGNS

FOR HAND QUILTING:

🌸 *Quilting in the ditch around the shapes in this quilt will help to accentuate the flower pots and make them almost "pop" off the background fabric.*

🌸 *Quilt the entire background in a grid of horizontal and vertical lines that are spaced 1½ inches apart. Notice that these grid lines are spaced at the same intervals as the triangle-pieced squares in the leaves and the squares in the flower pot rims. This grid will make the flower pots appear almost to float on top of the background fabric.*

🌸 *Quilting in the ditch in the sawtooth border will emphasize the strong design.*

🌸 *Quilt the outer border in a pattern of straight lines that continue outward from the seam lines in the sawtooth border.*

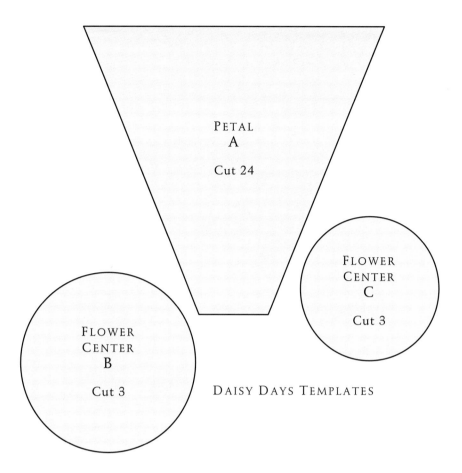

PETAL
A

Cut 24

FLOWER
CENTER
C

Cut 3

FLOWER
CENTER
B

Cut 3

DAISY DAYS TEMPLATES

MEADOW LILY

Meadow Lily has a simple block arrangement that looks more complicated than it is. I chose a creamy beige tone-on-tone print for the background and the borders to enhance the effect of the flower blocks and the single Irish Chains. The flower blocks in the borders echo the colors in the quilt center. When choosing fabrics for your own Meadow Lily quilt, you can create a pleasing color mix by selecting fabrics that share common colors and varying the scale of the prints. Bind your quilt with the border fabric to keep the focus on the colors in the center of your quilt.

Size

Bed Quilt: 72 × 92 inches (unquilted)

Finished Block: 10 inches square

Fabrics and Supplies

Yardage is based on 44-inch-wide fabric.

2 yards purple print fabric for Meadow Lily blocks and middle border

¾ yard maple print fabric for Meadow Lily block centers and inner border

4½ yards beige print fabric for background and outer borders

¾ yard light green print fabric for leaves

¾ yard dark green print fabric for leaves

1 yard purple floral print fabric for Meadow Lily block centers and Nine Patch blocks

1 yard beige print fabric for binding

5½ yards fabric for quilt backing

Quilt batting, at least 76 × 96 inches

Rotary cutter, mat, and see-through ruler with ⅛-inch markings

Getting Ready

- READ instructions thoroughly before you begin.
- PREWASH and press fabric.
- USE ¼-inch seam allowances throughout unless directions specify otherwise.
- SEAM ALLOWANCES are included in the cutting sizes given.
- PRESS seam allowances in the direction that will create the least bulk, and whenever possible, press toward the darker fabric.
- CUTTING DIRECTIONS for each section of the quilt are given individually. If you like to cut as you go, simply follow the directions as you get to them. If you'd rather cut all your pieces at the same time, skip ahead to find each of the cutting sections and do all the cutting before you begin to sew. ✍

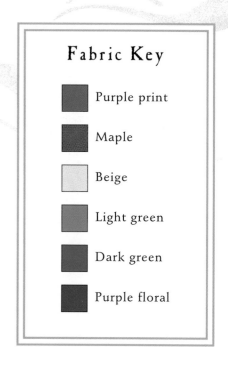

Fabric Key

- Purple print
- Maple
- Beige
- Light green
- Dark green
- Purple floral

Meadow Lily Blocks
(MAKE 18 FULL, 4 HALF, AND 4 QUARTER BLOCKS)

C U T T I N G

From the purple print fabric:
- Cut six 2½ × 44-inch strips; from these strips, cut eighty-four 2½-inch squares
- Cut seven 2⅞ × 44-inch strips

From the maple print fabric:
- Cut four 1½ × 44-inch strips

From the beige print fabric:
- Cut seven 2⅞ × 44-inch strips
- Cut four 1½ × 44-inch strips
- Cut six 1½ × 44-inch strips; from these strips, cut eighty-four 1½ × 2½-inch rectangles

Piecing the Lily Units

1 With right sides together, layer a 2⅞ × 44-inch purple print strip and a 2⅞ × 44-inch beige strip. Layer the remaining purple and beige 2⅞-inch strips in the same manner. Press the strips together, but do not sew.

2 Cut the layered strips into eighty-four 2⅞-inch squares, as shown in DIAGRAM 1.

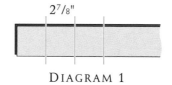

2⅞"

DIAGRAM 1

3 Cut the squares in half, as shown in DIAGRAM 2. Stitch ¼ inch from the diagonal edges, as shown. Press seam allowances toward the darker fabric to make a 2½-inch triangle-pieced square, as shown. Repeat for the remaining squares.

DIAGRAM 2

4 Sew each 1½ × 44-inch maple strip to a 1½ × 44-inch beige strip, as shown in DIAGRAM 3. Press seam allowances toward the maple fabric. Cut these strip sets into eighty-four 1½-inch segments, as shown.

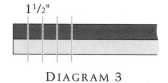

1½"

DIAGRAM 3

5 Sew a 1½ × 2½-inch beige rectangle to each of the segments from Step 4, as shown in DIAGRAM 4.

DIAGRAM 4

WHEN PLANNING a quilt, it is a good idea to make a sample block to test the accuracy of the pattern, as well as to decide how you like the positions of your fabrics in the block.

6 For each lily unit, sew together two triangle-pieced squares, one unit from Step 5, and one 2½-inch purple print square, as shown in DIAGRAM 5. Make 84 lily units.

DIAGRAM 5

Leaf Units

From the light green print fabric:
• Cut ten 1½ × 44-inch strips; from these strips, cut eighty-four 1½ × 4½-inch rectangles

From the dark green print fabric:
• Cut ten 1½ × 44-inch strips; from these strips, cut eighty-four 1½ × 4½-inch rectangles

From the beige print fabric:
• Cut seven 1½ × 44-inch strips; from these strips, cut one hundred sixty-eight 1½-inch squares

From the purple floral print fabric:
• Cut two 2½ × 44-inch strips; from these strips, cut eighteen 2½-inch squares
• Cut four 1½ × 2½-inch rectangles
• Cut four 1½-inch squares

Piecing the Leaf Units

1 With right sides together, layer a 1½-inch beige square on one end of a light green 1½ × 4½-inch rectangle, as shown in DIAGRAM 6. Draw a diagonal line from corner to corner on the beige square. Stitch on this line, and trim the seam allowance to ¼ inch, as shown. Press the seam allowance toward the darker fabric. Make 84 light green leaf units, as shown.

Trim to ¼"

DIAGRAM 6

2 Repeat Step 1, using the 1½ × 4½-inch dark green rectangles and the 1½-inch beige squares, as shown in DIAGRAM 7. Make sure that the diagonal line is drawn in the *opposite* direction from the lines drawn in Step 1. Make 84 dark green leaf units, as shown.

Trim to ¼"

DIAGRAM 7

3 Sew the light green and dark green leaf units together to make 76 pairs, as shown in DIAGRAM 8.

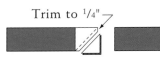
DIAGRAM 8

4 Sew a leaf unit from Step 3 to both sides of a 2½-inch purple print square, as shown in DIAGRAM 9. Make 18 of these units to be used in the full Meadow Lily blocks.

DIAGRAM 9

5 Sew a light green and a dark green leaf unit to both sides of a 1½ × 2½-inch purple print rectangle, as shown in DIAGRAM 10. Make four of these units to be used in the half–Meadow Lily blocks.

DIAGRAM 10

Assembling the Meadow Lily Blocks

1 Sew together four lily units, two leaf units, and one unit from Step 4, as shown in DIAGRAM 11. Make 18 Meadow Lily blocks, as shown. At this point, the Meadow Lily blocks should measure 10½ inches square.

DIAGRAM 11

2 Sew together two lily units, one leaf unit, and one unit from Step 5, as shown in DIAGRAM 12. Make four half–Meadow Lily blocks, as shown. Set these blocks aside to be used for the pieced border.

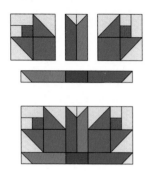

DIAGRAM 12

3 Sew together one lily unit and two leaf units, as shown in DIAGRAM 13. Make four quarter–Meadow Lily blocks, as shown. Set these blocks aside to be used for the pieced border.

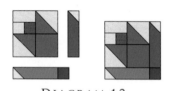

DIAGRAM 13

Nine Patch Blocks
(MAKE 17)

CUTTING

From the purple floral print fabric:
• Cut nine 2½ × 44-inch strips

From the beige print fabric:
• Cut four 2½ × 44-inch strips
• Cut four 6½ × 44-inch strips; from two of these strips, cut thirty-four 2½ × 6½-inch rectangles

Piecing the Nine Patch Blocks

1 To make Strip Set I, sew a 2½ × 44-inch purple floral strip to each side of a 2½ × 44-inch beige strip, as shown in DIAGRAM 14. Make another Strip Set I. Press seam allowances toward the darker fabric. Cut these strip sets into a total of thirty-four 2½-inch segments. NOTE: You may need to make an extra Strip Set I if your fabric is not wide enough.

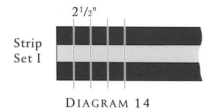

2½"

Strip Set I

DIAGRAM 14

2 To make Strip Set II, sew a 2½ × 44-inch beige strip to each side of a 2½ × 44-inch purple floral strip, as shown in DIAGRAM 15. Press seam allowances toward the darker fabric. Cut this strip set into seventeen 2½-inch segments, as shown. NOTE: You may need to make an extra Strip Set II if your fabric is not wide enough.

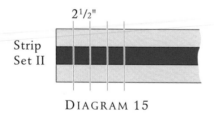

2½"

Strip Set II

DIAGRAM 15

3 Sew two Strip Set I segments and one Strip Set II segment together, matching block intersections, as shown in DIAGRAM 16. Make 17 of these nine-patch units, as shown.

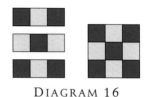

DIAGRAM 16

4 Sew a 2½ × 6½-inch beige rectangle to both sides of each nine-patch unit, as shown in DIAGRAM 17.

DIAGRAM 17

5 To make Strip Set III, sew a 2½ × 44-inch purple floral strip to both sides of a 6½ × 44-inch beige strip, as shown in DIAGRAM 18. Press seam allowances toward the darker fabric. Make two of these strip sets and cut them into thirty-four 2½-inch-wide segments, as shown.

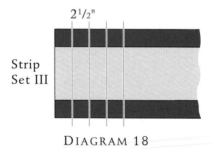

2½"

Strip Set III

DIAGRAM 18

6 Sew one segment from Step 5 to the top and one to the bottom of each nine-patch unit, as shown in DIAGRAM 19.

DIAGRAM 19

Quilt Center

1 Sew the blocks into rows, alternating Meadow Lily blocks and Nine Patch blocks, referring to the QUILT ASSEMBLY DIAGRAM. Press seam allowances toward the Nine Patch blocks.

2 Join the seven horizontal rows to make the quilt center, as shown. The quilt top should measure 50½ × 70½ inches at this time. Adjust seam allowances if necessary.

Borders

C U T T I N G

NOTE: The yardage given allows for the borders to be cut cross-grain. Press seam allowances toward the borders.

From the maple print fabric:
• Cut seven 1½ × 44-inch strips for the inner border

From the purple print fabric:
• Cut eight 2½ × 44-inch strips for the middle border

From the beige print fabric:
• Cut seven 5½ × 44-inch strips for the outer border
• Cut nine 3½ × 44-inch strips for the outer border

1 Measure the quilt from left to right through the middle to determine the length for the top and bottom inner border strips. Sew the maple inner border strips together with diagonal seams, as shown in DIAGRAM 20. Trim

QUILT ASSEMBLY DIAGRAM

seam allowances to ¼ inch, as shown. Cut two strips to the necessary length.

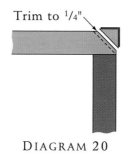

Trim to ¼"

DIAGRAM 20

2 Sew a maple inner border strip to the top and bottom edges of the quilt, referring to the QUILT ASSEMBLY DIAGRAM.

3 Measure the quilt from top to bottom through the middle, including the border strips just added, to determine the length for the side inner border strips. Cut two maple inner border strips to the necessary length, and sew them to the sides of the quilt.

Middle Border

1 Measure the quilt from left to right through the middle to determine the length of the top and bottom middle border strips. Sew the purple middle border strips together with diagonal seams in the same manner as for the maple inner borders. Trim seam allowances to ¼ inch and cut two strips to the necessary length.

2 Sew the top and bottom purple print middle border strips to the quilt.

3 Measure the quilt from top to bottom through the middle, including the border strips just added, to determine the length for the side middle border strips. Cut two purple middle border strips to the necessary length and sew them to the sides of the quilt.

Pieced Border

1 Measure the quilt from left to right through the middle. Subtract 10 inches from this measurement to allow for a quarter–Meadow Lily block at each end. Sew the 5½-inch beige border strips together with diagonal seams, trim seam allowances to ¼ inch, and press. Cut two strips to the necessary length.

2 Sew a quarter–Meadow Lily block to each end of these two beige border strips, as shown in DIAGRAM 21.

3 Sew the beige pieced border strips to the top and bottom edges of the quilt, referring to the QUILT ASSEMBLY DIAGRAM on page 165.

4 Measure the quilt from top to bottom through the middle, including the borders just added. Subtract 20 inches from this measurement to allow for a half–Meadow Lily block at each end. Cut two 5½-inch border strips to the necessary length.

5 Sew a half–Meadow Lily block to each end of these border strips, as shown in DIAGRAM 22.

6 Sew the beige pieced side borders to the quilt.

Outer Border

1 Measure the quilt from left to right through the middle to determine the length for the top and bottom outer borders. Sew the 3½-inch beige outer border strips together with diagonal seams, as before, and trim the seam allowances to ¼ inch, and press. Cut two strips to the necessary length.

2 Sew the top and bottom beige outer borders to the quilt, referring to the QUILT ASSEMBLY DIAGRAM on page 165.

3 Measure the quilt from top to bottom through the middle, including the borders just added, to determine the length for the side outer borders. Cut two strips to the necessary length, and sew the beige side outer borders to the quilt.

Putting It All Together

1 Prepare the backing for the quilt by cutting the 5½-yard length of backing fabric in half crosswise to make two 2¾-yard lengths. Remove the selvages.

2 Sew the long edges of the two lengths together with one center seam. Press the seam open. Trim the backing and batting so they are about 4 inches larger than the quilt top.

DIAGRAM 21

DIAGRAM 22

3 Mark quilting designs on the quilt top.

4 Layer the backing, batting, and quilt top. Baste the layers together and quilt.

5 When quilting is complete, remove the basting stitches, and trim the excess backing and batting even with the quilt top.

Binding

NOTE: The 2¾-inch binding strips will produce a ⅜-inch binding. If you want a wider or narrower binding, adjust the width of the strips you cut. (See page 216 for pointers on how to experiment with binding width.) Refer to "Making and Attaching the Binding" on page 215 to complete your quilt.

C U T T I N G

From the beige print fabric:
• Cut nine 2¾ × 44-inch strips for cross-grain binding

Quilting
D E S I G N S

FOR HAND QUILTING:

To decide on quilting designs that I want to use, I like to think about what should be most visually prominent in the finished quilt. For this project, I wanted the squares and clusters of flowers to advance, so I decided to emphasize each element by stitching along the seams of these pieces. Another benefit of this kind of quilting is that no marking is required.

Quilt the purple border and the maple border as one unit, using a commercial stencil that features a 2½-inch floral motif, as shown in the QUILTING DIAGRAM at right.

Cross-hatching at 2-inch intervals finishes off the border and works nicely behind the clusters of lilies at the corners.

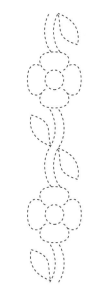

QUILTING DIAGRAM

In Bloom

The magic of In Bloom lies in the simplicity of its design and the repeat of the motif as it changes direction in alternating rows. Using fabrics in similar colors will impart a feeling of uniformity throughout the quilt, and a variety of two-color and tone-on-tone prints will hold the viewer's interest. Muslin for the background and borders allows the flowers and the grid latticework to remain the focal features. Because the pieces of this quilt are large and the construction is uncomplicated, you can piece the blocks very quickly and soon have a bed-size quilt ready for the quilt frame.

Size

Bed quilt: 90 × 102 inches (unquilted)

Finished Block: 9 inches square

Fabrics and Supplies

Yardage is based on 44-inch-wide fabric.

¾ yard *each* of assorted gold print, purple print, and pink print fabrics for flowers

1⅝ yards dark green print fabric for leaves

7 yards muslin for background

2 yards medium green print fabric for lattice

1 yard fabric for binding

8 yards fabric for quilt backing

Quilt batting, at least 94 × 106 inches

Rotary cutter, mat, and see-through ruler with ⅛-inch markings

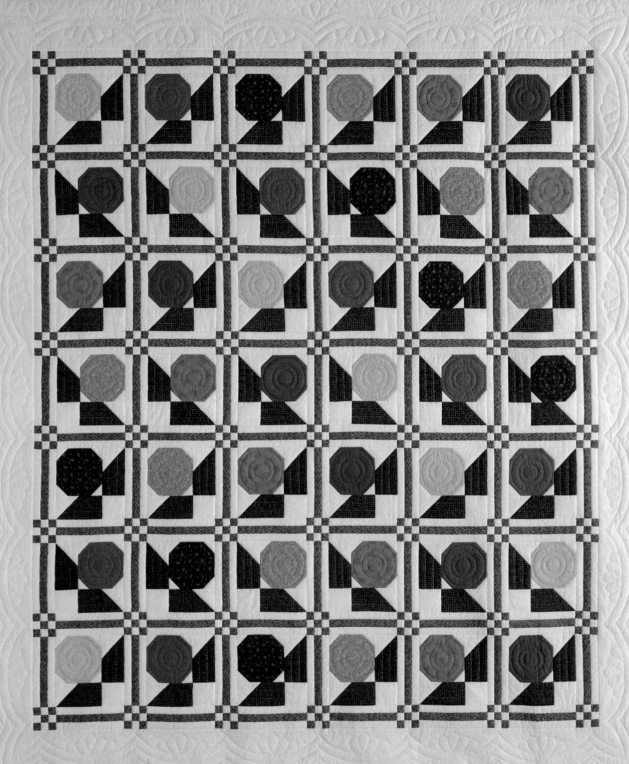

Getting Ready

- READ instructions thoroughly before you begin.

- PREWASH and press fabric.

- USE ¼-inch seam allowances throughout unless directions specify otherwise.

- SEAM ALLOWANCES are included in the cutting sizes given.

- PRESS seam allowances in the direction that will create the least bulk, and whenever possible, press toward the darker fabric.

- CUTTING DIRECTIONS for each section of the quilt are given individually. If you like to cut as you go, simply follow the directions as you get to them. If you'd rather cut all your pieces at the same time, skip ahead to find each of the cutting sections and do all the cutting before you begin to sew. 🍃

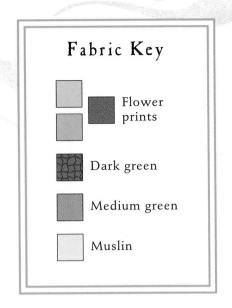

Fabric Key

Flower prints

Dark green

Medium green

Muslin

Flower Blocks

(MAKE 42 TOTAL—14
FROM EACH COLOR
OF FABRIC)

CUTTING

From the pink print fabrics:
- Cut a total of three 6½ × 44-inch strips; from these strips, cut fourteen 6½-inch squares

From the purple print fabrics:
- Cut a total of three 6½ × 44-inch strips; from these strips, cut fourteen 6½-inch squares

From the gold print fabrics:
- Cut a total of three 6½ × 44-inch strips; from these strips, cut fourteen 6½-inch squares

From the dark green print fabric:
- Cut fourteen 3½ × 44-inch strips; from these strips, cut eighty-four 3½ × 6½-inch rectangles

From the muslin:
- Cut nine 2 × 44-inch strips; from these strips, cut one hundred sixty-eight 2-inch squares
- Cut eleven 3½ × 44-inch strips; from these strips, cut one hundred twenty-six 3½-inch squares

Piecing the Flower Blocks

1 With right sides together, position a 2-inch muslin square at each corner of a 6½-inch pink square, as shown in DIAGRAM 1. Draw a diagonal line from corner to corner on each muslin square, and stitch on these lines. Trim seam allowances to ¼ -inch, as shown, and press seam allowances toward the pink fabric. Referring to DIAGRAM 1, make 14 of these units using gold squares, 14 using purple squares, and 14 using pink squares.

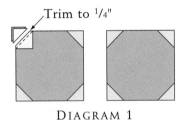

Trim to ¼"

DIAGRAM 1

2 With right sides together, position a 3½-inch muslin square on the corner of a 3½ × 6½-inch dark green rectangle, as shown in DIAGRAM 2. Draw a diagonal line from corner to corner on the muslin square, as shown, and stitch on this line. Trim seam allowances to ¼-inch, as shown, and press toward the dark green fabric. Repeat to make 42 of these left leaf units.

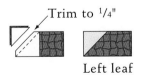

Trim to ¼"

Left leaf

DIAGRAM 2

3 Repeat Step 2, this time reversing the direction of the seam, as shown in DIAGRAM 3. Make 42 of these right leaf units.

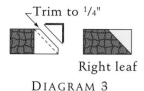

Trim to ¼"

Right leaf

DIAGRAM 3

4 Sew a left leaf unit to a flower unit, as shown in DIAGRAM 4. Press seam allowances toward the leaf unit. Repeat for all 42 flower units.

DIAGRAM 4

5 Sew a 3½-inch muslin square to each of the right leaf units, as shown in DIAGRAM 5. Press seam allowances toward the leaf units.

DIAGRAM 5

6 Sew a right leaf unit created in Step 5 to each of the 42 flower units, as shown in DIAGRAM 6. At this point, the Flower blocks should measure 9½ inches square.

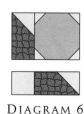

DIAGRAM 6

Lattice Strips

C U T T I N G

From the medium green print fabric:
• Cut twenty-five 1½ × 44-inch strips

From the muslin:
• Cut fifty 1½ × 44-inch strips

Piecing the Lattice Strips

Sew a 1½ × 44-inch muslin strip to both sides of a 1½ × 44-inch medium green strip, as shown in DIAGRAM 7. Press seam allowances toward the green strip. Sew the remaining medium green and muslin strips together in the same manner to make 25 strip sets. Crosscut the strip sets into a total of 97 segments, each 9½ inches wide, as shown.

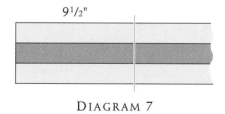

9½"

DIAGRAM 7

Nine-Patch Lattice Posts

C U T T I N G

From the medium green print fabric:
• Cut ten 1½ × 44-inch strips

From the muslin:
• Cut eight 1½ × 44-inch strips

Piecing the Nine-Patch Lattice Posts

1 To make Strip Set I, sew a 1½ × 44-inch medium green strip to both sides of a 1½ × 44-inch muslin strip, as shown in DIAGRAM 8. Press seam allowances toward the green strip. Make a total of four of Strip Set I, and crosscut them into a total of 112 segments, each 1½ inches wide, as shown.

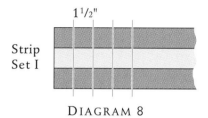

1½"

Strip Set I

DIAGRAM 8

2 To make Strip Set II, sew a 1½ × 44-inch muslin strip to both sides of a 1½ × 44-inch medium green print strip, as shown in DIAGRAM 9. Press seam allowances toward the green strip. Make two of Strip Set II, and crosscut them into 56 segments, each 1½ inches wide, as shown.

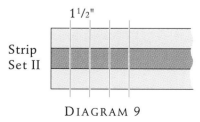

1½"

Strip Set II

DIAGRAM 9

3 Sew a Strip Set I segment to both sides of a Strip Set II segment, as shown in DIAGRAM 10. Press. Make 56 nine-patch lattice posts, as shown.

DIAGRAM 10

Quilt Center

1 Referring to the QUILT ASSEMBLY DIAGRAM for color placement, sew together a horizontal row of six Flower blocks alternating with seven lattice strip segments. Refer to the QUILT ASSEMBLY DIAGRAM to determine which direction the Flower blocks should face within each row. Make seven of these horizontal rows. Press seam allowances toward the Flower blocks.

2 To make the lattice strips between the rows of Flower blocks, sew together a horizontal row of seven nine-patch lattice posts and six lattice segments, referring to the QUILT ASSEMBLY DIAGRAM. Make eight of these horizontal lattice strips. Press seam allowances toward the nine-patch lattice posts.

3 Referring to the QUILT ASSEMBLY DIAGRAM, sew the horizontal flower rows and horizontal lattice strips together to form the quilt center. Press.

Border

C U T T I N G

NOTE: The yardage given allows for the border pieces to be cut cross-grain.

From the muslin:
• Cut twelve 8 × 44-inch strips

Attaching the Border

1 Measure the quilt from left to right through the middle to determine the length of the top and bottom border strips. For

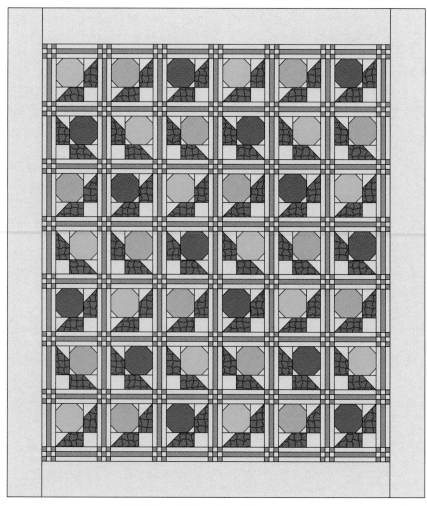

QUILT ASSEMBLY DIAGRAM

each of the top and bottom
border strips, piece together
three muslin border strips with
diagonal seams, and cut them to
the necessary length. For more
information on diagonal seams,
see page "Border Basics" on page
211. Sew these border strips to
the top and bottom of the quilt.
Press seam allowances toward
the border.

2 Measure the quilt from top
to bottom through the
middle, including the borders
you just added, to determine the
length of the side border strips.
For each of the side border strips,
piece together three muslin strips
with diagonal seams, and cut
them to the necessary length.
Sew these border strips to the
sides of the quilt. Press seam allowances toward the border.

Putting It All Together

1 Cut the 8-yard length of
backing fabric in thirds crosswise to make three 2⅔-yard
pieces. Remove the selvages and
sew the long edges of the lengths
together. Press these seams open.
Trim the backing and batting so

they are about 4 inches larger
than the quilt top dimensions.

2 Mark quilting designs on the
quilt top.

3 Layer the backing, batting,
and quilt top. Baste the
layers together and quilt.

4 When quilting is complete,
remove the basting stitches,
and trim the excess backing and
batting even with the quilt top.

Binding

NOTE: The 2¾-inch binding
strips will produce a ⅜-inch-
wide binding. If you want a
wider or narrower binding, adjust the width of the strips you
cut. (See page 216 for pointers on
how to experiment with binding
width.) See "Making and Attaching the Binding" on page 215
to complete your quilt.

CUTTING

From the binding fabric:
• Cut ten 2¾ × 44-inch strips for
cross-grain binding

Quilting DESIGNS

FOR HAND QUILTING:

Choose quilting de-
signs that will enhance the
shapes of the flowers in this
quilt. Notice how the concentric circles make the
snowball blocks appear
rounder than they are.

Channel quilting
in the leaves accentuates
the straight lines and acts
as a welcome contrast to
the circular motion of the
blooms in the Flower blocks.

Quilting in the ditch
beside the green pieces in
the lattice gridwork makes
those green pieces seem
more visually prominent.

Cross-hatching in
the borders expresses the
same feeling of simplicity
as in the design of this quilt.

STICKS AND STONES

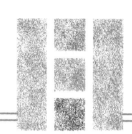

Sticks and Stones has a cheerful, warm childlike quality, and it makes a great "get it done in a hurry" project. All it takes are six coordinating fabrics; one of these should be much lighter than the other five, to be used for the background of the Stones blocks. Notice that the stones fabric in the center of these blocks is echoed in the border. This repetition helps to guide the eye outward from the center to the edges of the quilt. The diagonally striped border travels around the quilt, adding visual movement without the need for complicated piecing.

Size

Bed Quilt: 78 × 90 inches (unquilted)

Finished Block: 6 inches square

Fabrics and Supplies

Yardage is based on 44-inch-wide fabric.

1 yard *each* of three coordinating print fabrics for Sticks blocks

2¾ yards gold print fabric for Stones blocks and corner squares

1½ yards blue print fabric for Stones block centers and outer border

1¼ yards red print fabric for outer border

⅞ yard red print fabric for binding

5½ yards fabric for quilt backing

Quilt batting, at least 82 × 94 inches

Rotary cutter, mat, and see-through ruler with ⅛-inch markings

Getting Ready

- READ instructions thoroughly before you begin.
- PREWASH and press fabric.
- USE ¼-inch seam allowances throughout unless directions specify otherwise.
- SEAM ALLOWANCES are included in the cutting sizes given.
- PRESS seam allowances in the direction that will create the least bulk, and whenever possible, press toward the darker fabric.
- CUTTING DIRECTIONS for each section of the quilt are given individually. If you like to cut as you go, simply follow the directions as you get to them. If you'd rather cut all your pieces at the same time, skip ahead to find each of the cutting sections and do all the cutting before you begin to sew. ✎

Fabric Key

- Coordinating fabrics
- Gold
- Blue
- Red

Sticks Blocks
(MAKE 72)

CUTTING

From each of the three coordinating print fabrics:
- Cut twelve 2½ × 44-inch strips

Piecing the Sticks Blocks

Sew three 2½ × 44-inch coordinating print strips together to make a strip set, as shown in DIAGRAM 1. Make 12 of these strip sets. Press all seam allowances in the same direction. Crosscut the strip sets into seventy-two 6-½-inch segments, creating the Sticks blocks. Check

IF YOU are a beginner, avoid being tempted by a project that is too advanced and complicated. Rather, try to select a smaller project or one that has just a few design elements, which will allow you to gain confidence. Sticks and Stones is a perfect project for a beginning quilter.

TIPS AND TRICKS

to make sure that each block is 6½ inches square.

6½"

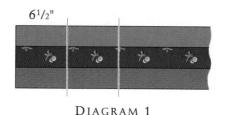

DIAGRAM 1

Stones Blocks
(MAKE 71)

CUTTING

From the gold print fabric:
- Cut thirty-four 2½ × 44 strips; from 24 of these strips, cut 142 rectangles, each 2½ × 6½ inches

From the blue print fabric:
- Cut five 2½ × 44-inch strips

Piecing the Stones Blocks

1 With right sides together, sew a 2½ × 44-inch gold strip to both sides of a 2½ × 44-inch blue print strip, as shown in DIAGRAM 2. Make five of these strip sets. Press seam allowances

toward the blue fabric. Crosscut the strip sets into seventy-one 2½-inch segments, as shown.

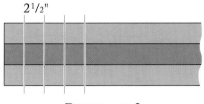

2½"

DIAGRAM 2

2 With right sides together, sew a 2½ × 6½-inch gold rectangle to both sides of the segments made in Step 1, creating the Stones blocks, as shown in DIAGRAM 3. Press seam allowances toward the gold fabric. At this point, the Stones blocks should measure 6½ inches square.

DIAGRAM 3

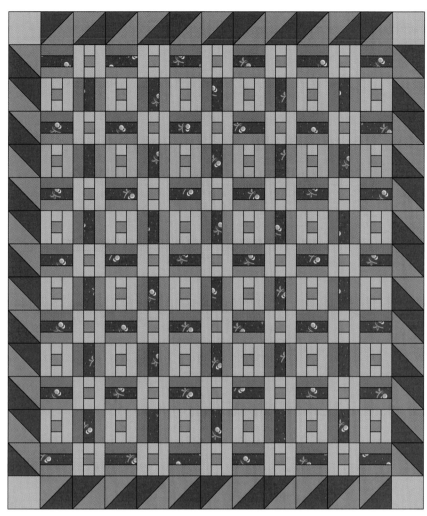

QUILT ASSEMBLY DIAGRAM

Quilt Center

1 Sew the blocks into 13 horizontal rows of 11 blocks each. Alternate the Sticks blocks and Stones blocks in each row, as shown in the QUILT ASSEMBLY DIAGRAM. Press seam allowances toward the Stones blocks.

2 Sew the 13 horizontal rows together. The quilt center should measure 66½ × 78½ inches. If necessary, trim seam allowances so that the pieced border will fit.

Border

CUTTING

NOTE: The yardage given allows for border pieces to be cut cross-grain.

From the red print fabric:
• Cut five 6⅞ × 44-inch strips

From the blue print fabric:
• Cut five 6⅞ × 44-inch strips

From the gold print fabric:
• Cut four 6½-inch squares

Piecing the Border

1 With right sides together, layer the 6⅞ × 44-inch red strips and the 6⅞ × 44-inch blue strips. Press together, but do not sew. Layer the remaining strips in the same manner.

2 Cut the layered strips into twenty-four 6⅞-inch squares. Cut the squares in half diagonally, as shown in DIAGRAM 4 on page 178. Sew a ¼-inch seam along the diagonal edge to form 48 triangle-pieced squares, as shown.

DIAGRAM 4

3 Sew 11 triangle-pieced squares together for the top border strip and 11 for the bottom border strip, referring to the QUILT ASSEMBLY DIAGRAM on page 177. Sew the top and bottom border strips to the quilt, and press.

4 Sew 13 triangle-pieced squares together for each side border. Add a 6½-inch gold print corner square to both ends of the side border strips, referring to the QUILT ASSEMBLY DIAGRAM on page 177. Sew the side border strips to the quilt, and press.

Putting It All Together

1 Prepare the backing for the quilt by cutting the 5½-yard length of backing in half crosswise to make two 2¾-yard lengths. Remove the selvages.

2 Sew the long edges of the two lengths together. Press this seam allowance open. Trim

backing and batting so they are about 4 inches larger than the quilt top.

3 Mark quilting designs on the quilt top.

4 Layer the backing, batting, and quilt top. Baste the layers together and quilt.

5 When quilting is complete, remove the basting stitches, and trim the excess backing and batting even with the quilt top.

Binding

NOTE: The 2¾-inch binding strips will produce a ⅜-inch-wide binding. If you want a wider or narrower binding, adjust the width of the strips you cut. (See page 216 for pointers on how to experiment with binding width.) See "Making and Attaching the Binding" on page 215 to complete your quilt.

CUTTING

From the red print fabric:
• Cut nine 2¾ × 44-inch strips for cross-grain binding

Quilting DESIGNS

FOR MACHINE QUILTING:

✿ *Use a large pattern of meander quilting over the entire surface of this quilt to enhance the simple patchwork blocks and to allow you to finish it quickly.*

FOR HAND QUILTING:

✿ *Another option is to quilt in the ditch of the patchwork blocks to accentuate the individual "sticks" and "stones." If you elect this option, quilting in the ditch of the diagonal border seams will also be very effective.*

✿ *In the corner border blocks, quilt a square shape in the center to echo the "stones" in the pieced blocks, or simply quilt diagonal lines from corner to corner in both directions.*

RAINING CATS AND DOGS

The colors in Raining Cats and Dogs are youthful, happy, and more vivid than pastels, yet with a soft and comforting feel. I often think of them as "Dick and Jane" colors because it's so easy for many of us to visualize the colorful pages of those books. The cats' and dogs' heads are actually adaptations from a pair of pot holders that originally belonged to my grandmother. I decided to set them against a plaid background fabric that contributes to a whimsical country look without competing with the other prints in the quilt.

Size

Crib Quilt: 48 × 58 inches (unquilted)

Fabrics and Supplies

Yardage is based on 44-inch-wide fabric.

1 yard red floral print fabric for inner blocks and corner squares

1 yard blue print fabric for lattice strips

⅔ yard gold print #1 fabric for lattice posts and cat heads

¾ yard green print fabric for inner border and corner squares

1¼ yards gold check fabric for background squares

⅜ yard red print #1 fabric for cat bows

¼ yard gold print #2 fabric for dog noses

⅜ yard red print #2 fabric for dog ears/eyes

⅓ yard green floral print fabric for dog bows

⅛ yard black fabric for dog and cat eyes/noses

⅝ yard green print fabric for binding

3 yards fabric for quilt backing

Quilt batting, at least 52 × 62 inches

1 skein black embroidery floss

Freezer paper

Rotary cutter, mat, and see-through ruler with ⅛-inch markings

RAINING CATS AND DOGS

Getting Ready

- READ instructions thoroughly before you begin.

- PREWASH and press fabric.

- USE ¼-inch seam allowances throughout unless directions specify otherwise.

- SEAM ALLOWANCES are included in the cutting sizes given.

- PRESS seam allowances in the direction that will create the least bulk, and whenever possible, press toward the darker fabric.

- TRACE the templates on pages 186–189 onto freezer paper. For more information on the freezer paper appliqué method of hand appliqué, see page 209.

- CUTTING DIRECTIONS for each section of the quilt are given individually. If you like to cut as you go, simply follow the directions as you get to them. If you'd rather cut all your pieces at the same time, skip ahead to find each of the cutting sections and do all the cutting before you begin to sew. ✍

Fabric Key

Red floral

Blue

Gold #1

Gold #2

Green print

Gold check

Red #1

Red #2

Green floral

Black

Quilt Center

C U T T I N G

From the red floral print fabric:
- Cut four 6½-inch squares
- Cut two 8½ × 44-inch strips; from these strips, cut two 8½-inch squares and six 6½ × 8½-inch pieces

From the blue print fabric:
- Cut four 2½ × 44-inch strips; from these strips, cut seven 2½ × 8½-inch pieces and ten 2½ × 6½-inch pieces

From the gold print #1 fabric:
- Cut six 2½-inch squares

Assembling the Quilt Center

1 With right sides together, sew a 2½ × 6½-inch blue lattice strip to both sides of a 6½ × 8½-inch red floral piece, as shown in DIAGRAM 1. Sew a 6½-inch red floral square to both sides of the blue lattice strips, as shown. Make two of these units.

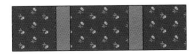

DIAGRAM 1

2 With right sides together, sew a 2½ × 8½-inch blue lattice strip to both sides of a 8½-inch red floral square, as shown in DIAGRAM 2. Then sew a 6½ × 8½ red floral piece to both sides of the blue lattice strips, as shown. Make two of these units.

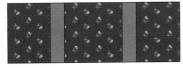

DIAGRAM 2

3 To construct the horizontal lattices, sew a 2½-inch gold #1 square to each side of a 2½ × 8½-inch blue lattice strip, as shown in DIAGRAM 3 on page 182. Sew a 2½ × 6½-inch blue lattice strip to the outer side of the gold squares, as shown. Make three of these horizontal lattices.

DIAGRAM 3

4 Sew the block strips and horizontal lattices together to form the quilt center, referring to the QUILT ASSEMBLY DIAGRAM. At this point, the quilt top should measure 24½ × 34½ inches.

IF YOU have extra blocks left over from a project or extra fabric cut for additional blocks, save them and add other leftover blocks to them to create your very own sampler.

QUILT ASSEMBLY DIAGRAM

Inner Border

CUTTING

From the green print fabric:
• Cut four 4½ × 44-inch strips

Attaching the Inner Border

1 Measure the quilt from left to right through the center to determine the length of the top and bottom border strips. Cut the green print inner border strips to this length and sew them to the top and bottom of the quilt, referring to the QUILT ASSEMBLY DIAGRAM.

2 Measure the quilt from top to bottom through the middle, including the border strips just added, to determine the length of the side border strips. Cut the two remaining green print inner border strips to this length and sew them to the sides of the quilt, referring to the QUILT ASSEMBLY DIAGRAM.

Outer Border

CUTTING

NOTE: Templates for the cat and dog heads are found on pages 186–189. Read appliqué instructions before cutting the pieces.

From the gold check fabric:
• Cut fourteen 8½-inch squares

From the gold print #1 fabric:
• Cut seven cat heads

From the red print #1 fabric:
• Cut seven cat bows

From the gold print #2 fabric:
• Cut seven dog nose sections

From the red print #2 fabric:
• Cut seven dog ears/eyes sections for the right side of each dog head and seven for the left side of each dog head

From the green floral print fabric:
• Cut seven dog bows

From the blue print fabric:
• Cut eighteen 2½ × 8½-inch strips

From the red floral print fabric:
• Cut one 4½ × 44-inch strip

From the green print fabric:
• Cut one 4½ × 44-inch strip

From the black fabric:
• Cut seven right eyes, seven left eyes, and seven noses for the cats
• Cut seven right eyes, seven left eyes, and seven noses for the dogs

Appliquéing the Cat and Dog Blocks

1 Using the freezer paper method for hand appliqué, prepare the appliqué pattern pieces. For more information on the freezer paper method, see page 209.

2 Transfer the head and bow shapes for the cats and dogs on pages 186–189 onto the 8½-inch gold check background squares by positioning each square over one of the tracing diagrams on pages 186–189. Make sure the cat or dog shape is centered and at least ¼ inch away from the raw edges of the fabric to allow for seam allowances. Lightly trace the cat and dog shapes onto the fabric. If you cannot see the lines of the tracing diagram through your fabric, photocopy the tracing diagram. Then place both the background square and tracing diagram over a light box or tape them on a window, and trace the shapes. Trace seven cat heads and seven dog heads onto the background squares.

3 To appliqué a cat block, position and pin a gold #1 cat head on a background square, aligning it with the traced lines. With matching thread, appliqué the cat head by hand with small slip stitches. If you are using the

freezer paper method, needle turn the seam allowance under the edge of the paper. The only exception to this technique is in any area that will be overlapped by another fabric, such as the lower edge of the cat head. Clip curves as needed and remove the freezer paper. For more information on removing the freezer paper, see "Freezer Paper Method" on page 209.

4 Position and pin the red #1 bow on the background square, aligning it with the traced lines, and appliqué it in place in the same manner. Remove the freezer paper.

5 Repeat Steps 3 and 4 for the remaining six cat blocks.

6 To appliqué a dog block, position and pin a gold #2 dog nose section to a background square, aligning it with the traced lines. Appliqué the top edge only. The remaining edges will be overlapped by the ears/eyes and bow. Remove the freezer paper.

7 Place a green floral bow on the background square, aligning it with the traced lines, and appliqué with small slip stitches. Remove the freezer paper.

8 Place the left and right red #2 ears/eyes sections on the background squares, aligning them with the traced lines, and appliqué. Remove the freezer paper.

9 To trace the cat and dog eyes, nose, and embroidery lines from pages 186–189 onto the faces, turn each block over

and carefully trim away the back layer of fabric to approximately ¼ inch inside your stitching lines. When the background fabric is trimmed away, it will be easy to lightly trace the facial features onto each face.

10 Appliqué the eyes and noses in place on each dog and cat head. With two strands of black embroidery floss, stitch around the cat and dog eyes, noses, bows, and heads by hand with the outline stitch. For more information on the outline stitch, see page 210.

Assembling the Outer Border

1 For the top and bottom outer border strips, sew together three appliqué blocks and four 2½ × 8½-inch blue pieces, alternating the position of the cat and dog heads, as shown in DIAGRAM 4. Sew these border strips to the top and bottom of the quilt.

Top border

Bottom border
DIAGRAM 4

2 For the side outer border strips, sew four appliqué blocks and five 2½ × 8½-inch blue pieces together, as shown in DIAGRAM 5 on page 184.

Side borders
DIAGRAM 5

3 To make the corner squares, sew a 4½ × 44-inch red floral strip and a 4½ × 44-inch green print strip together, and cut into eight 4½-inch segments, as shown in DIAGRAM 6.

4 Sew the segments together in pairs to make four corner squares, as shown in DIAGRAM 7.

5 Sew the corner squares to the ends of the side borders, as shown in DIAGRAM 8, and sew the side border strips to the quilt.

Putting It All Together

1 Cut the 3-yard length of backing fabric in half crosswise. Remove the selvages and sew the long edges of the two lengths together. Press this seam open. Trim the backing and batting so they are about 4 inches larger than the quilt top.

2 Mark quilting designs on the quilt top.

3 Layer the backing, batting, and quilt top. Baste the layers together and quilt.

4 When quilting is complete, remove the basting stitches and trim the excess backing and batting even with the quilt top.

Binding

NOTE: The 2¾-inch strips will produce a ⅜-inch-wide binding. If you want a wider or narrower binding, adjust the width of the strips you cut. (See page 216 for pointers on how to experiment with binding width.) See "Making and Attaching the Binding" on page 215 to complete your quilt.

C U T T I N G

From the green print fabric:
• Cut six 2¾ × 44-inch strips for cross-grain binding

Quilting DESIGNS

FOR HAND QUILTING:

❧ The quilting designs selected for Raining Cats and Dogs reflect the design of the quilt top, which helps to maintain a feeling of sweet simplicity in the quilt.

❧ Quilt the plain center blocks in a 2-inch straight grid, echoing the overall design of the center squares.

❧ Quilt the lattice strips in the ditch of the seams.

❧ Choose a very simple 3-inch floral quilting stencil for the green inner border.

❧ Outline quilt around the appliqués and inside the stitched details to make the dogs and cats stand out from the background fabric and give them greater visual dimension and personality.

4½"

DIAGRAM 6

DIAGRAM 7

DIAGRAM 8

OPTIONAL MACHINE APPLIQUÉ

🖋 MACHINE APPLIQUÉ is a quick and easy way to add the appliqué pieces to this quilt. It also stands up well to repeated washings. You will need a machine that has a buttonhole or zigzag stitch.

1 LAY THE FUSIBLE WEB over the appliqué pattern pieces on pages 186–189 with the paper side up, and trace the shapes. Cut roughly ½ inch outside the traced lines, as shown in Step 1.

2 ON EACH SHAPE, draw a line about ⅜ inch inside the first line you traced, as shown in Step 2.

3 WHEN FUSING A LARGE SHAPE, it is a good idea to fuse only the edges so that the large shape will not look stiff in your finished quilt. To make this easier, cut away the fusible web on this second line to leave the center of each shape open, as shown in Step 3.

4 WITH A HOT DRY IRON, following the manufacturer's directions for your brand of fusible web, press the coated side of each fusible web shape to the wrong side of its fabric, as shown in Step 4, and let the shapes cool.

5 CUT OUT EACH SHAPE along the first line you traced, except at any area where there will be another shape overlapping it. At these areas, leave about ¼ inch of extra fabric outside the turning line, as shown in Step 5, so that the appliqué shape can be layered underneath another shape. Peel off the paper backing from each appliqué shape.

6 POSITION THE APPLIQUÉ shape on the block. Fuse the remaining shapes, then layer, and press.

7 SET YOUR MACHINE to the buttonhole or zigzag/satin stitch. You may need to place a paper towel under the background block to stabilize it before machine appliquéing. It is a good idea to stitch a sample to make sure you're getting the results you want. After you have finished appliquéing, tear away the paper towel.

8 MACHINE APPLIQUÉ the eyes and nose in place.

9 USING TWO STRANDS of black embroidery floss, stitch the cats' and dogs' ears, mouths, whiskers, and bow knot details by hand with the outline stitch.

STEP 1

Trace second
line here

STEP 2

Cut fusible
web away

STEP 3

STEP 4

Overlapping area
STEP 5

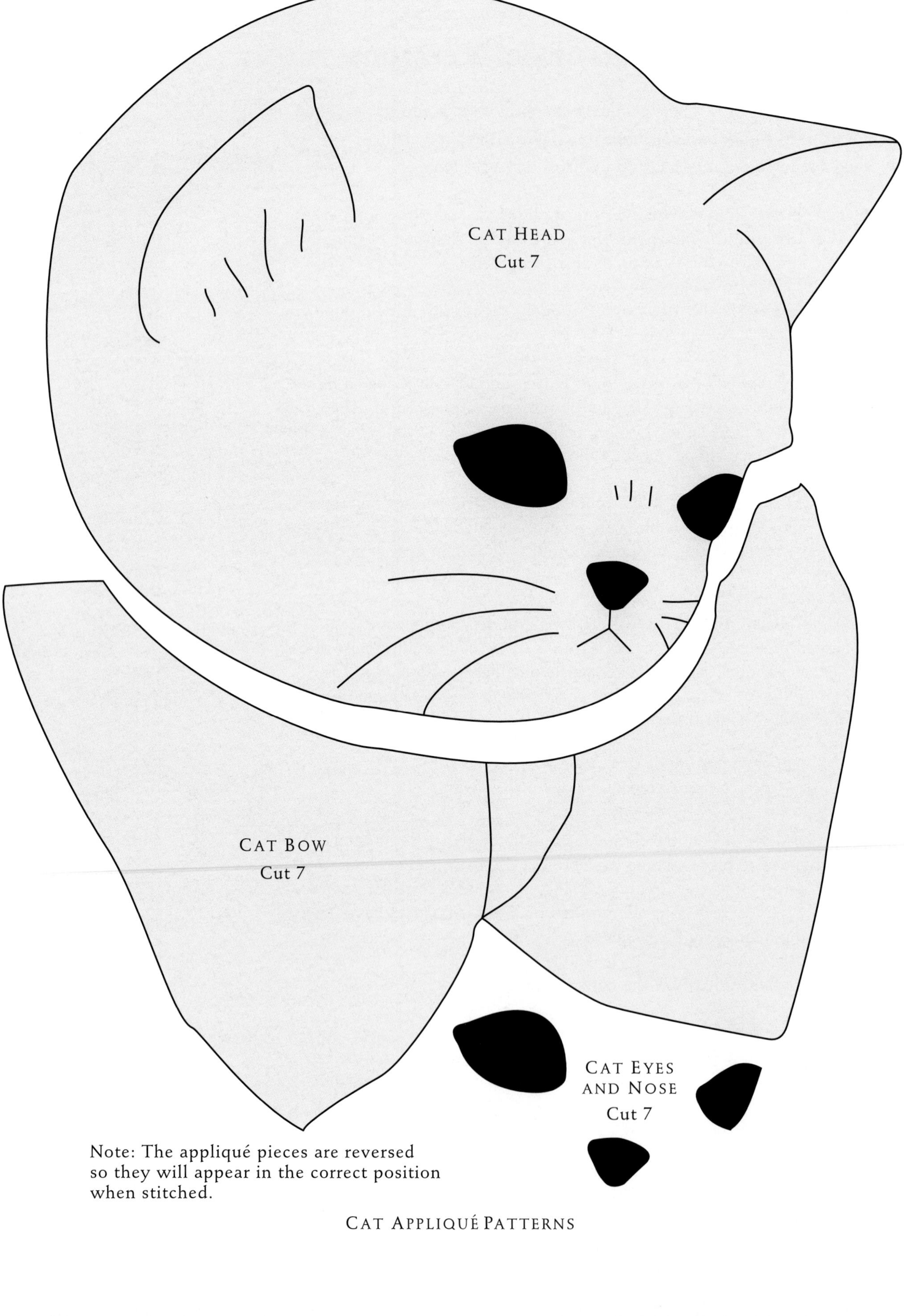

CAT HEAD
Cut 7

CAT BOW
Cut 7

CAT EYES
AND NOSE
Cut 7

Note: The appliqué pieces are reversed
so they will appear in the correct position
when stitched.

CAT APPLIQUÉ PATTERNS

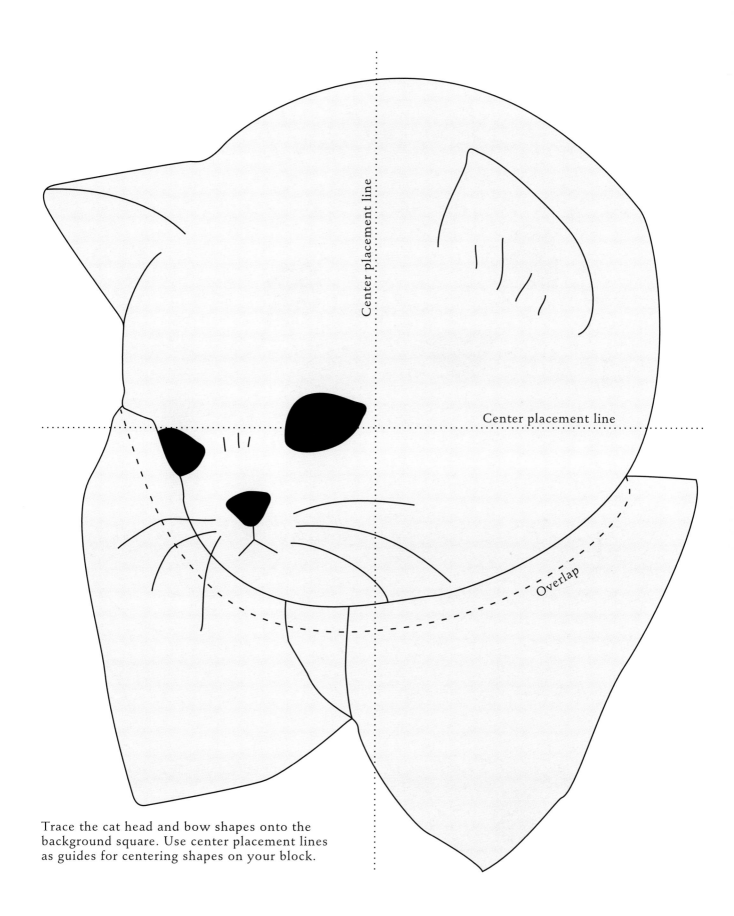

Trace the cat head and bow shapes onto the background square. Use center placement lines as guides for centering shapes on your block.

CAT TRACING DIAGRAM

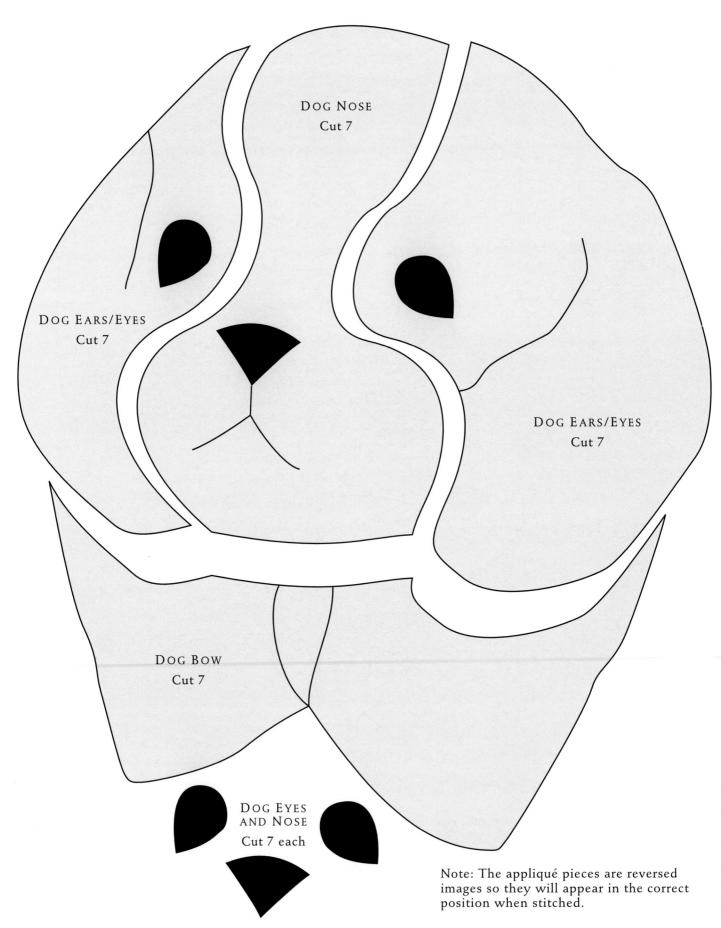

DOG NOSE
Cut 7

DOG EARS/EYES
Cut 7

DOG EARS/EYES
Cut 7

DOG BOW
Cut 7

DOG EYES
AND NOSE
Cut 7 each

Note: The appliqué pieces are reversed
images so they will appear in the correct
position when stitched.

DOG APPLIQUÉ PATTERNS

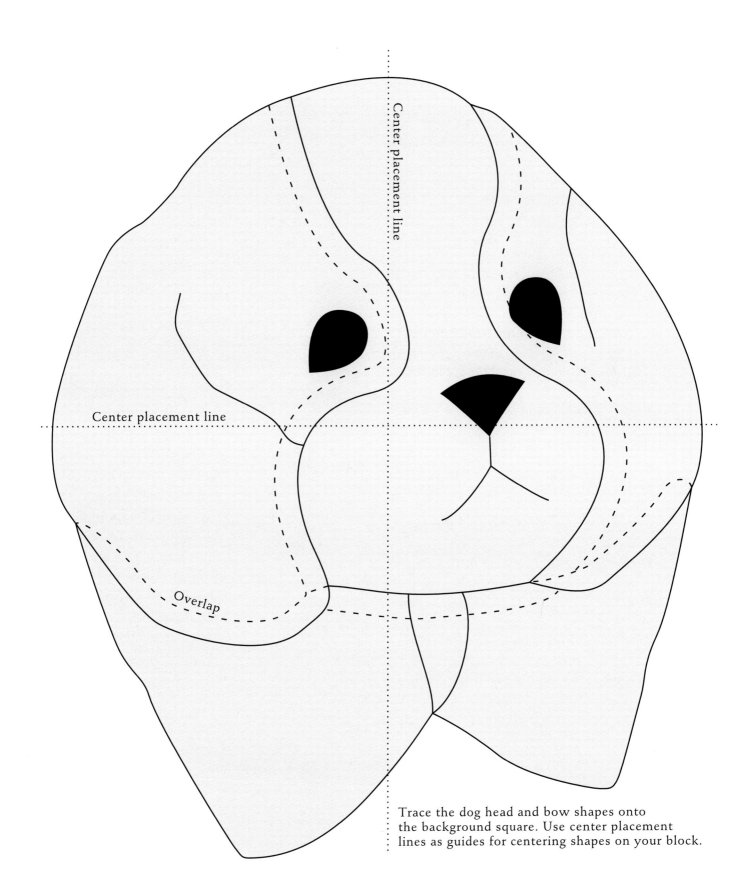

Center placement line

Center placement line

Overlap

Trace the dog head and bow shapes onto
the background square. Use center placement
lines as guides for centering shapes on your block.

DOG TRACING DIAGRAM

HOME PLACE

There are some quilts that are just right for setting the mood of a country-style bedroom, complete with a warm, inviting atmosphere. Home Place is one of those designs. The quiet, restful greens and overall pattern of the Nine Patch squares and vertical lattice strips create a calm quilt that will add color to a room. This design is also subtle enough to harmonize well with other home decorating elements, such as striped or floral wallpaper, patterned upholstery, or decorative artwork. This quilt is meant to be loved and enjoyed every day.

Size

Bed Quilt: 90 × 108 inches (unquilted)

Finished Nine Patch Block: 4½ inches square

Fabrics and Supplies

Yardage is based on 44-inch-wide fabric.

4¼ yards dark green print fabric for Nine Patch blocks, alternate blocks, and outer border

3⅞ yards beige print fabric for background

2½ yards green floral print fabric for lattice strips

¾ yard chestnut print fabric for inner border

1 yard dark green print fabric for binding

8¼ yards fabric for quilt backing

Quilt batting, at least 94 × 112 inches

Rotary cutter, mat, and see-through ruler with ⅛-inch markings

Getting Ready

Fabric Key

- Dark green
- Beige
- Green floral
- Chestnut

- READ instructions thoroughly before you begin.

- PREWASH and press fabric.

- USE ¼-inch seam allowances throughout unless directions specify otherwise.

- SEAM ALLOWANCES are included in the cutting sizes given.

- PRESS seam allowances in the direction that will create the least bulk, and whenever possible, press toward the darker fabric.

- CUTTING DIRECTIONS for each section of the quilt are given individually. If you like to cut as you go, simply follow the directions as you get to them. If you'd rather cut all your pieces at the same time, skip ahead to find each of the cutting sections and do all the cutting before you begin to sew. ✎

Nine Patch Blocks

(MAKE 88)

CUTTING

From the dark green print fabric:
- Cut twenty-three 2 × 44-inch strips

From the beige print fabric:
- Cut nineteen 2 × 44-inch strips

Piecing the Nine Patch Blocks

1 To construct Strip Set I, sew a 2 × 44-inch dark green strip to both sides of a 2 × 44-inch beige strip, as shown in DIAGRAM 1. Press seam allowances toward the darker fabric. Make nine of Strip Set I and crosscut

them into a total of 176 segments, each 2 inches wide, as shown.

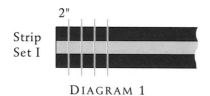

Strip Set I

2"

DIAGRAM 1

2 To construct Strip Set II, sew a 2 × 44-inch beige strip to both sides of a 2 × 44-inch dark green strip, as shown in DIAGRAM 2. Press seam allowances toward the darker fabric. Make five of Strip Set II and crosscut them into a total of 88 segments, each 2 inches wide, as shown.

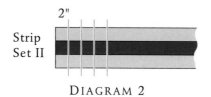

Strip Set II

2"

DIAGRAM 2

3 Sew a Strip Set I segment to both sides of a Strip Set II segment, as shown in DIAGRAM 3, creating a Nine Patch block. Make a total of 88 Nine Patch blocks, as shown. At this point, the Nine Patch blocks should measure 5 inches square.

DIAGRAM 3

Quilt Center

CUTTING

From the beige print fabric:
- Cut six 5 × 44-inch strips; from these strips, cut forty-four 5-inch squares

• Cut twelve 5 × 44-inch strips for Strip Set III

From the dark green print fabric:
• Cut six 5 × 44-inch strips for Strip Set III

From the green floral print fabric:
• Cut fifteen 5 × 44-inch strips for the lattice strips

Assembling the Quilt Center

1 To construct Strip Set III, sew a 5 × 44-inch beige strip to both sides of a 5 × 44-inch dark green strip, as shown in DIA-GRAM 4. Press seam allowances toward the lighter fabric. Make six of Strip Set III and crosscut them into a total of 40 segments, each 5 inches wide, as shown.

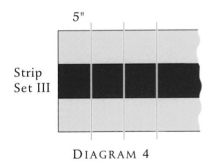

5"

Strip Set III

DIAGRAM 4

2 Sew a Nine Patch block to both sides of a 5-inch beige square, as shown in DIAGRAM 5. Press seam allowances toward the lighter fabric. Make 44 of these units, as shown.

DIAGRAM 5

3 Sew together a vertical row of 11 units from Step 2 and 10 Strip Set III segments from

---

PRESSING FOR STRIP-CUTTING ACCURACY

✎ WHEN SEWING strips of fabric together for strip sets, it is important to press the seam allowances nice and flat, usually toward the darker fabric. Be very careful not to stretch the fabric while you are pressing. This can cause a curved "rainbow" effect in your strip set and affect the accuracy and shapes of the segments you cut from it.

✎ I LIKE to press the wrong side of a strip set first, with the strips placed perpendicular to the length of my ironing board. Then I turn the strip set over and press again on the right side. This prevents little pleats from forming at the seams. Avoid laying the strip set lengthwise on the ironing board, which seems to encourage the kind of rainbow effect shown here.

Step 1, as shown in the QUILT ASSEMBLY DIAGRAM on page 194. Make four of these vertical rows, as shown. Press.

4 To make a lattice strip, sew together three 5 × 44-inch green floral strips with diagonal seams. For more information on diagonal seams, see "Border Basics" on page 211. Make five of these lattice strips. Trim each of the five pieced strips to the same length as your vertical rows.

5 Pin and sew the vertical rows and lattice strips together, creating the quilt center, as shown in the QUILT ASSEMBLY DIAGRAM on page 194. Press seam allowances toward the lattice strips.

Borders

C U T T I N G

NOTE: The yardage given allows for the border pieces to be cut cross-grain.

From the chestnut print fabric:
• Cut ten 2 × 44-inch strips for the inner border

From the dark green print fabric:
• Cut eleven 5½ × 44-inch strips for the outer border

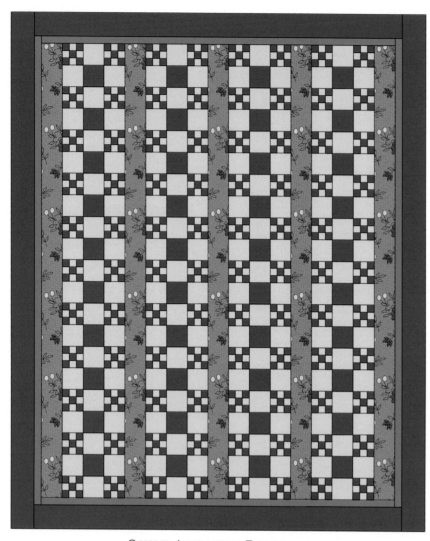

QUILT ASSEMBLY DIAGRAM

4 Measure the quilt from top to bottom through the middle, including the borders you just added, to determine the length for the outer side borders. Trim two 5½-inch dark green border strips to this length, sew them to the sides of the quilt, and press.

Putting It All Together

1 Prepare the backing for the quilt by cutting the 8¼-yard length of backing fabric in thirds crosswise to form three equal lengths that measure about 2¾ yards each. Remove the selvages and sew the long edges of the three lengths together so that the seams run horizontally. Press.

2 Trim the backing and batting so they are 4 inches larger than the quilt top dimensions.

3 Mark quilting designs on the quilt top.

Attaching the Borders

1 Sew the 2 × 44-inch chestnut inner border strips together with diagonal seams. For more information on diagonal seams, see page 211. Measure the quilt from left to right through the middle to determine the length of the top and bottom inner borders. Cut two chestnut strips to this length and sew them to the top and bottom of the quilt. Press seam allowances toward the border.

2 Measure the quilt from top to bottom through the middle, including the borders you just added, to determine the length for the inner side borders. Trim two chestnut strips to this length, sew them to the sides of the quilt, and press.

3 Sew the 5½ × 44-inch dark green strips together with diagonal seams. Measure the quilt from left to right through the middle to determine the length of the top and bottom outer borders. Trim two strips to this length, sew them to the top and bottom of the quilt, and press.

A SLIVER of hard bar soap like Dial is ideal for marking medium to dark fabrics. It rubs off very easily, and it's always simple to create a clean, sharp edge on the soap by breaking off a small piece. Avoid facial soaps with ingredients like oatmeal.

4 Layer the backing, batting, and quilt top. Baste the layers together and quilt.

5 When quilting is complete, remove the basting stitches, and trim the excess backing and batting even with the quilt top.

Binding

NOTE: The 2¾-inch strips will produce a ⅜-inch-wide binding. If you want a wider or narrower binding, adjust the width of the strips you cut. (See page 216 for pointers on how to experiment with binding width.) See "Making and Attaching the Binding" on page 215 to complete your quilt.

C U T T I N G

From the dark green print binding fabric:
• Cut eleven 2¾ × 44-inch strips for cross-grain binding

Quilting
DESIGNS

FOR HAND OR MACHINE QUILTING:

❧ *The alternating green unpieced blocks are the perfect place for a small, continous-line floral design like the one in* QUILTING DIAGRAM 1.

❧ *All of the background areas contain meander quilting, with no quilting in the green sections of the Nine Patches. This makes the Nine Patch blocks stand out more.*

❧ *A simple trailing vine design like the one shown in* QUILTING DIAGRAM 2 *accentuates the vertical lines in the quilt and offers a nice contrast to the other quilting motifs.*

❧ *The feathered quilting design in* QUILTING DIAGRAM 3 *covers both the narrow brown borders and the green outer borders.*

QUILTING DIAGRAM 2

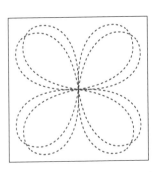

QUILTING DIAGRAM 1

QUILTING DIAGRAM 3

THE
Thimbleberries
LOOK

*T*he look that is identified with Thimbleberries quilts is a direct reflection of my personal taste and lifestyle. Over the years, I have realized that I want my home, quilts, and quilted accessories to be warm and inviting, and the dark rich colors and "unfussy" designs of my quilts convey that. These projects have a casual, traditional style that you can blend comfortably with antiques and the best of country-style decor. These are quilts you can treasure for years to come.

Thimbleberries
STYLE

My Color Palette

Color has become the most identifiable element of the Thimbleberries style. Many years ago, I discovered that there was no color I did not like as long as I could use darker shades of it. Virtually all colors will work together, and even those usually considered clashing can be compatible if they are dark enough. The colors on these pages show how I like to work with color in designing quilts and also make handy color guides for choosing fabrics for your own quilts.

MEDIUM SHADES

The lighter colors in my quilts tend to be darker in value than typical pastels. Medium shades are richer, have more depth of color, and give a quilt a more antique look.

DARKER COLORS

Dark values of red, green, blue, and brown, along with a touch of black, feature prominently in my quilts. These colors create bold contrast and contribute to a strong quilt design.

MELLOW TONES

Incorporating a range of deep, mellow gold fabrics helps to impart the same feeling of warmth I see in old quilts. These colors also enhance the other colors in my palette.

NEUTRAL BACKGROUNDS

Beige and cream shades make effective backgrounds for the rich, dark colors I use. These neutral tones soften a quilt without being as sharp or vibrant as "white-whites." This is the same effect that can be seen in antique furniture, textiles, and artwork, where whites have aged to gentle creams over time, and vibrant, clear colors are faded and soft.

Fabric Types

One of the connections all quiltmakers have to each other is their love of fabric. As a young child, my mother would often point out to me the good characteristics of a piece of fabric she was considering buying, so I learned early on to take note of things like quality, scale of print, and how fabrics would be used in a quilt. On these pages, I have gathered some fabrics from my sewing studio to help illustrate important elements to consider when selecting fabrics for any quilt project.

PRINTED PLAINS

"Printed plain" is a term I use to refer to any print that I treat as a solid color in a quilt. These fabrics are usually tone-on-tone color combinations with subtle allover meandering prints. They lend visual texture to a quilt and have a softening effect on the design.

LOW-CONTRAST PLAINS

These fabrics offer color, design, and texture without a lot of differences in color values. They are interesting to look at without being so visually demanding that they take over a quilt design. Low-contrast prints are also great blenders, which help to coordinate colors throughout a quilt.

LARGE-SCALE PRINTS

I use large-scale prints quite sparingly, usually no more than one per quilt, and in combination with many other prints and plaids. Effective places to use large-scale prints are outside borders and large patches, where the full print is easily visible without being distorted by lots of seams.

PLAIDS AND CHECKS

Both plaids and
checks are staples in my
fabric repertoire. In some
cases, the grainline of a
plaid or check is important
to me, while other times it is not
a concern. For example, when I am
cutting plaids or checks into many small
pieces that will be placed every which direction in a quilt, I cut them without regard to grainline. If I am cutting out big, bold plaid borders, I
take care to use a pair of scissors, so that I can
follow lines of the plaid perfectly to make the
quilt appear straight and square.

STRONG GRAPHIC PRINTS

It takes just a little bit of a
graphic print to add spark to a
quilt. These fabrics are prints that
stand out because of bold images
or strong color definition, so I use
them sparingly, because they can
sometimes interfere with and
distract from a pieced design.
It can be fun to use graphic,
strong prints in places like narrow borders, lattice strips, or
bindings.

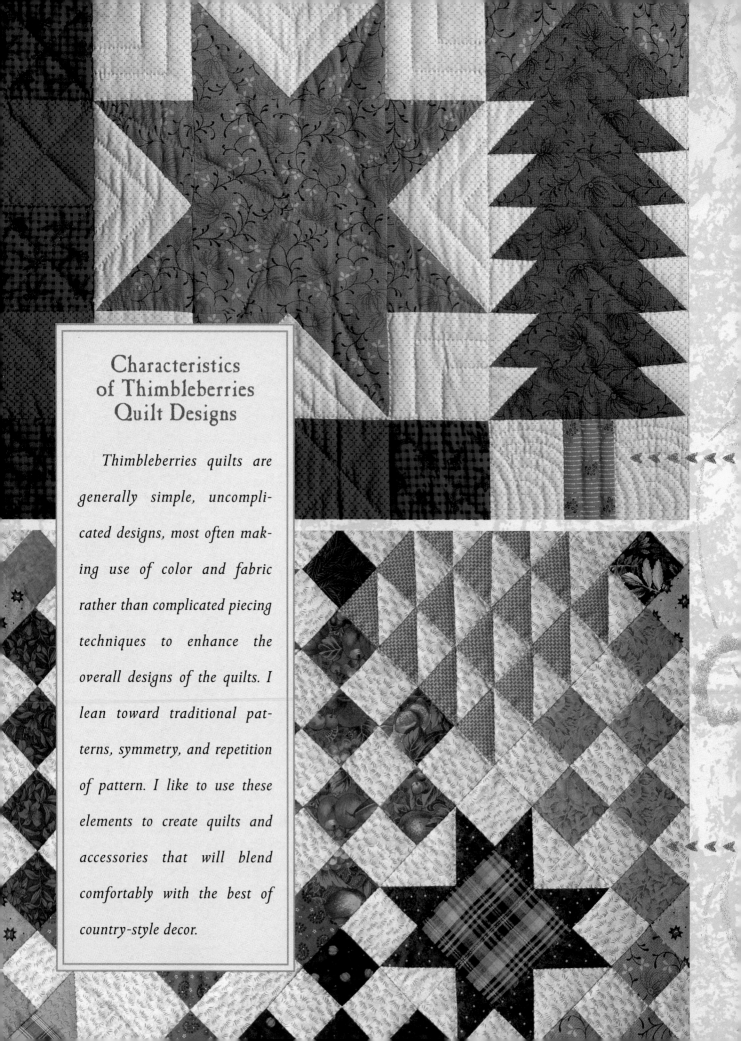

Characteristics of Thimbleberries Quilt Designs

Thimbleberries quilts are generally simple, uncomplicated designs, most often making use of color and fabric rather than complicated piecing techniques to enhance the overall designs of the quilts. I lean toward traditional patterns, symmetry, and repetition of pattern. I like to use these elements to create quilts and accessories that will blend comfortably with the best of country-style decor.

PRINTED BACKS ►►►►►►►

I often use large-scale prints or piece coordinating fabrics together to create an interesting quilt back. I always use really large pieces of fabric, perhaps three different prints that are the same length as the quilt, or a large piece of fabric that is bordered by compatible prints. This will keep the number of seams to a minimum, which you'll appreciate during the quilting process.

TRADITIONAL, CASUAL, CLASSIC, CLEAN LINES

My quilt designs are like many of the antique classics that I refer to as "prairie patchwork." These quilts have straight lines, simple bold shapes, and pattern repeats that all add up to what I consider everyday quilts. They are great for adding color, texture, and warmth to a room and provide handcrafted goodness.

ADDED EMBELLISHMENTS

A bit of embroidery, a few French knots, or buttonhole stitching can do wonders for a quilt. These extra stitches lend dimension and color, as well as definition, to any quilt design. Whether you like working by hand or machine, try out the various effects you can create with embroidery stitches.

MANY PRINTS IN COMBINATION

The combination of a large number of fabrics is a wonderful treat for the eye. Even if the pattern of the blocks is the same throughout a quilt, subtle changes in color and print can create lovely visual effects. I think using lots of fabrics together is reminiscent of old-fashioned country scrap quilts.

Fabric Shopping Tips

A good piece of fabric is always the beginning of my creativity. To choose fabrics for getting the Thimbleberries look in your quilts, visit your local quilt shop with this book in hand, and use the following tips for finding fabrics you'll love.

🌿 USE THE THIMBLEBERRIES PALETTE: A good way to start is to gather fabrics that match the shades you like on pages 198–199. Remember to look for color first, then for print or pattern.

🌿 LOOK FOR COMPATIBLE FABRIC DESIGNS: You will probably discover that you already have strong personal preferences in fabric design. When I shop, my own preference is for fabrics that have a similar feel. For example, sophisticated prints do not mix well with fabrics that have obvious primitive motifs, nor do country novelties blend well with Victorian florals.

🌿 PLAN FOR VARIETY: Try varying the fabric combinations you put together; for example, group some prints that have geometric figures with some small florals, or mix stripes with small dots and, of course, plaids with checks.

🌿 BRING YOUR OWN FABRIC VIEWER: Cut a 2-inch square out of the center of a piece of typing paper and take it with you when you shop for fabric. Place the paper over any fabric you are considering, and let it show through the hole. This will help put the print into perspective. It can be amazing how different fabric looks when viewed in small pieces. Sometimes a whole bolt can be overwhelming.

🌿 STEP BACK: Always view your fabric selections from a distance of about 15 feet, the same distance at which you will be likely to view a finished quilt across a room. This will tell you a lot about how the scale of each fabric will appear from a distance and help you decide whether you will like the look of the fabrics in the finished quilt.

🌿 TRY OUT DIFFERENT COMBINATIONS: Unfold a bolt length of a fabric you're considering for a background fabric, and then arrange fabrics you're considering for the borders along the sides of the first bolt. Then add several more fabrics you like to these, folding each fabric into smaller pieces and lining them up as they may occur in a finished quilt. This will give you a realistic overview of the color and print combinations you've grouped together. Taking time to play and experiment with fabrics before you purchase them will help you determine which combinations you really like.

🌿 MY BUYING FORMULA: I haven't changed my buying formula for years because it has it has served me well. My own rule of thumb is to buy a 1-yard piece when I like a fabric and think the color and print are good and workable for many of the quilts I make. If I really like a fabric, I always buy 3 yards of it, knowing that I will probably use it in more than one project or feature it prominently in a large quilt. Often, I even go so far as to purchase 6 yards of fabric when I know it will make a great backing or it is a print I know I will want to keep around for a while.

Thimbleberries
GUIDE TO QUILTMAKING

Fabric Facts

For best results, stick with 100 percent cotton broadcloth or dress-weight fabrics. Cotton is easy to press because its "memory" allows it to retain a crease for some time. The soft and lightweight quality of cotton makes it easy to quilt through three layers of a quilt sandwich. Cotton can be manipulated to match tricky points, and it is flexible enough to ease around curves. The quilts in this book are all made of 100 percent cotton fabrics.

Selecting Fabrics

The yardages given for the quilts and projects in this book are based on 44-inch-wide fabric, but to allow for slight variations and possible shrinkage, we use a width of 40 inches as the guideline for calculating required yardage for the projects. These yardages are adequate for each project, allowing up to ¼ yard extra as a margin for error, so you'll always have enough in case there's a cutting error or some other mishap. The extra fabric is there if you need it, and if you don't, you can add it to your scrap bag for future projects. The yardages have been double-checked for accuracy, but you may want to buy extra fabric, just to be safe. Even the most experienced quilters sometimes make mistakes. Check the fabric widths before you buy—the fabric may be narrower than 44 inches. You may also lose some yardage in the prewashing and preshrinking process.

Pretreating Fabrics

Always prewash, dry, and press your fabrics. Prewashing shrinks fabric slightly and removes any finishes and sizing, making the cloth softer and easier to handle. Washing will also let the fabrics bleed—something you want to happen *before* you stitch the fabric into your quilt. Wash fabrics in an automatic washer with warm water and a mild detergent or a soap sold specifically for washing quilts. Dry fabrics in the dryer on a medium setting. I usually recommend pretreating fabric the same way you plan to treat it in the completed quilt.

Rotary Cutting

The directions for most of the quilts in this book have been written for rotary cutting, which is faster and more accurate than the traditional method of making templates and using scissors to cut individual pieces. Use the following general guidelines to ensure both safety and accuracy when rotary cutting.

Always:

• Keep rotary cutters out of the reach of children. The blades are extremely sharp!
• Be sure to slide the blade guard into place *whenever* you stop cutting.
• Cut *away* from yourself.
• Square off the left end of your fabric before measuring and cutting pieces, as shown in

A LARGE cutting mat (23 × 35 inches) makes rotary cutting easier and more accurate. Less folding and handling of the fabric is needed when using a larger cutting mat.
WHEN CUTTING multiple fabric layers, try the large-size rotary cutter with 2½-inch blades. Larger blades slice through several layers more easily and efficiently than medium-size blades. And always remember safety precautions.

TIPS AND TRICKS

DIAGRAM 1. Line up the selvages and place a ruled square on the fold. Place a 6 × 24-inch ruler against the side of the square to get a 90 degree angle. Hold the ruler in place, remove the square, and cut along the edge of the ruler. If you are left-handed, work from the other end of the fabric.

6" × 24" ruler

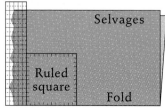

DIAGRAM 1

Cutting Strips, Squares, and Rectangles

Cut strips on the crosswise grain, as shown in DIAGRAM 2, unless instructed otherwise. Strips can then be cut into squares or rectangles, as needed.

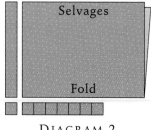

DIAGRAM 2

Check often to make sure that your fabric is square and the strips are straight rather than angled, as shown in DIAGRAM 3. If necessary, refold the fabric, square off the edge, and begin cutting again.

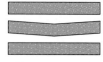

DIAGRAM 3

Cutting Triangles from Squares

The cutting instructions often direct you to cut strips, then squares, and then triangles, as in Brown-Eyed Susan, Harvest Mix, and many others. This method is simple and accurate. The size of the square given in the project will be ⅞ inch larger than the desired finished size of the triangle-pieced square.

For example, for a 2-inch finished triangle-pieced square, each square would be $2\frac{7}{8} \times 2\frac{7}{8}$ inches. Cut a $2\frac{7}{8}$-inch-wide strip of both colors. Layer these strips right sides together and press. Cut the layered strips into $2\frac{7}{8}$-inch squares. You will get two triangle-pieced squares for each pair of squares you cut. Cut the layered squares in half diagonally to make perfect triangles. Sew the triangles together ¼ inch from the diagonal edge, as shown in DIAGRAM 4, and press the seam allowances toward the darker of the two fabrics.

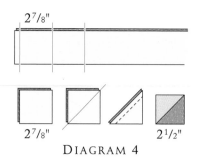

DIAGRAM 4

Cutting Side and Corner Triangles

For projects with side and corner triangles, the instructions will indicate to cut them larger than necessary. This will allow you to truly square up the quilt, and it also eliminates the frustration of

ending up with precut side and corner triangles that do not match your pieced blocks. Refer to "Trimming Side and Corner Triangles" on page 211.

To cut triangles, start by cutting squares. The project directions will tell you what size to make the squares and whether to cut them in half diagonally to make two triangles, as shown in DIAGRAM 5A, or to cut them in quarters diagonally to make four triangles, as shown in DIAGRAM 5B. This cutting method will produce side and corner triangles with the straight of grain running along the outside edges of the quilt.

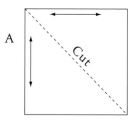

Arrows indicate straight grain

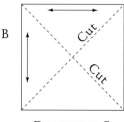

DIAGRAM 5

Making and Using Templates

The template patterns in this book are full-size, so no enlarging or drafting is necessary.

Fine-point or extra-fine-point permanent felt-tip pens are excellent for marking templates. The lines don't smear and the fine points help ensure accuracy. Regular lead pencils also work well, but you may find that the lines are not as easy to see.

At Thimbleberries, we use posterboard or manila folders for making our templates. To do this, place a sheet of tracing paper over the book page and trace the pattern. Glue the tracing paper to the cardboard or manila folder and cut out your templates. Take care to cut off the marking lines as you go. If you cut beyond to the outside edge, you will be adding size to the template when you trace the shape onto fabric. Copy all identification labels, grain lines, and other necessary information onto your templates. Check them against the printed pattern for accuracy.

Thin semitransparent template plastic also makes excellent, durable templates. You can lay the plastic over the book page and carefully trace the patterns directly onto the plastic. Then cut out each shape with scissors. Take care to be as accurate as possible when tracing and cutting templates. Accurate templates are critical for precise piecing.

The patchwork patterns in this book include seam allowances. They are printed with a solid outer line, which is the cutting line, and a dashed inner line, which is the sewing line. We've included dots at the seam intersections, as shown in DIAGRAM 6, to help in matching up and pinning the pieces together for accurate placement. If you wish to mark the seam intersec-

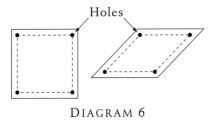

Holes

DIAGRAM 6

tions on your fabric, make holes in your templates at the dots with a heavy needle or a 1/8-inch paper-hole punch.

The holes need to be large enough to accommodate the point of a pencil or marker. Draw around the templates on the wrong side of the fabric, as shown in DIAGRAM 7. This line is the cutting line.

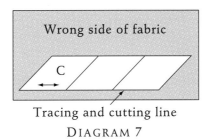

Wrong side of fabric

C

Tracing and cutting line

DIAGRAM 7

Piecing Precisely

An exact 1/4-inch seam allowance is extremely important in quiltmaking. A difference of as little as 1/16 inch on several pattern pieces can alter the dimensions of your quilt by as much as an inch or more.

Some sewing machines have a presser foot that measures exactly 1/4 inch from the point where the needle goes into the fabric to the edge of the presser foot. Measure to determine whether this is true for your machine. If you cannot use your presser foot as a reliable seam guide, you may wish to mark an exact 1/4-inch line on your machine. Lift the presser foot and measure over precisely 1/4 inch from the needle. Lay a piece of 1/4-inch masking tape at that point to help you guide your fabric.

Before sewing a block, sew a test seam to make sure you are taking accurate 1/4-inch seams.

Adjust your machine to sew 10 to 12 stitches per inch. Select a neutral-color thread that blends well with the fabrics you are using. It is a good practice always to cut and piece a sample block before you cut all your fabrics. This will allow you to make certain your color choices work well together and you are cutting the pieces accurately.

Press patchwork seams to one side, toward the darker fabric whenever possible, to prevent them from shadowing through lighter fabrics. Since seams will be stitched down when crossed with another seam, you will need to think about the direction in which you want them to lie.

Chain Piecing

Chain piecing, or assembly-line piecing, can help speed up the process of stitching many of the same-size or -shape pieces together. Referring to DIAGRAM 8, run pairs of pieces or units through the sewing machine one after another without cutting the thread. Once all the units are

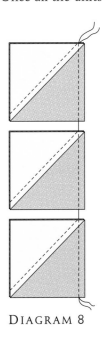

DIAGRAM 8

sewn, snip them apart and press. You can continue to add on more pieces to these units in the same assembly-line fashion until the sections are complete.

Strip Piecing

When squares and rectangles are combined in a repeated pattern, you can simplify assembly by using strip piecing. With strip piecing, you sew together a series of horizontal strips into a strip set. The strip set is then cut into segments. A rotary cutter, used with a see-through ruler with ⅛-inch markings, is ideal for this kind of straight-line cutting. Strips from the strip set are cut ½ inch wider than the finished size of the patch to allow for ¼-inch seam allowances.

When sewing strips of fabric together for strip sets, it is important to press the seam allowances, usually toward the darker fabric. Be very careful not to stretch as you press, causing the "rainbow effect" shown in DIAGRAM 9. This will affect the accuracy and shape of the pieces cut from the strip set. I like to press the wrong side first, with the strips perpendicular to the ironing board. Then I flip the piece over and press on the right side, to prevent little pleats from forming at the seams. Laying the strip set lengthwise on the ironing board seems to encourage the rainbow effect.

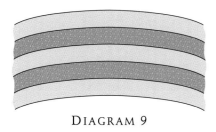

DIAGRAM 9

Pressing Pointers

Pressing is an important step during piecing and assembling a quilt top. Some quilters prefer a dry iron, but I use a steam iron to press pieces. Experiment to see which works best for you. Press by bringing the iron down gently and firmly onto the fabric from above. Ironing your pieces by sliding the iron back and forth across the fabric may stretch them out of shape. Here are some other tips to help you press properly.

• Press a seam before crossing it with another seam.
• Press seam allowances to one side, not open.
• Whenever possible, press seams toward darker fabrics.
• Press seams of adjacent rows of blocks, or rows within blocks, in opposite directions so the pressed seams will abut as the rows are joined (see DIAGRAM 10).
• Press appliqués very gently from the wrong side of the background fabric. They are prettiest when slightly puffed.

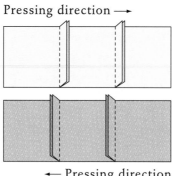

Pressing direction →

← Pressing direction
DIAGRAM 10

Hand Appliqué

Some of the quilts in this book include appliqué, often in combination with patchwork. I use the

needle turn, or freezer paper method, which is especially effective for larger appliqué pieces.

Choose thread to match the appliqué pieces and stitch each appliqué to the background fabric with a blind hem or appliqué stitch, as shown in DIAGRAM 11. The stitches should be a snug ⅛ inch apart, or closer. Use a long thin needle—called a sharp—in size number 11 or 12.

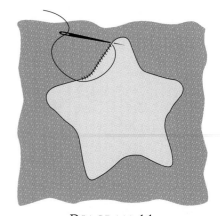

DIAGRAM 11

When making appliqué blocks, always work from the background to the foreground. When one appliqué piece will overlap or cover another, stitch the underneath piece to the background fabric first. Note that on the appliqué pattern pieces, the area to be overlapped by another piece is indicated with a dotted or dashed line.

The patterns for appliqué pieces in this book are finished-size and are printed with only a single line. Draw around these templates on the right side of the fabric, as shown in DIAGRAM 12, leaving ½ inch between the pieces. The lines you draw will be your guides for turning under the edges of the appliqué pieces. Then add a scant ¼-inch seam allowance as you cut out the pieces.

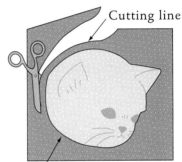

Cutting line

Tracing and fold-under line

DIAGRAM 12

Freezer Paper Method

With the freezer paper method, the freezer paper forms a base around which the fabric is shaped.

1 Trace the posterboard templates for the appliqués from the book onto template material and cut them out.

2 Using the posterboard template, trace the appliqué shape onto the noncoated, or dull, side of the freezer paper and cut out the shape.

3 With a dry iron set at wool, press the coated, or shiny, side of the freezer paper template to the wrong side of the fabric. Be sure to allow ½ inch between shapes for seam allowances, as in DIAGRAM 12.

4 Cut out the appliqué shape ⅛ to ¼ inch outside of the paper edge to allow for seam allowance. Clip concave curves, if necessary, to allow you to turn them under more easily, as shown in DIAGRAM 13.

DIAGRAM 13

5 Pin the appliqué shape to the quilt block or top. Appliqué the shape to the quilt with a blind hem stitch as shown in DIAGRAM 11 on the opposite page, turning the seam allowance under against the edge of the paper.

6 Remove the freezer paper by one of two methods. One method is to leave ½ inch of

the appliqué shape unstitched. Finger press the fabric over the paper. Then slide your needle into this opening to loosen the freezer paper from the appliqué. Gently pull the freezer paper out, and the fold should still be in the fabric. Finish stitching the appliqué in place. Another way to remove the freezer paper is to slit the fabric from the wrong side and remove the paper.

Primitive Appliqué

Primitive appliqué, in which shapes are fused onto the background fabric and then enhanced by embroidery stitches, is a popular look for whimsical designs, such as Checkerboard Cherries and Christmas Candy.

1 Trace appliqué pattern pieces from the book onto template material.

2 Place the appliqué templates face down on the paper side of the fusible web, and trace.

ADDING EMBROIDERY STITCHES

🖊 YOU CAN use pearl cotton or embroidery floss to add other decorative embroidery stitches to your quilts, like the outline stitch, French knot, and the buttonhole stitch, as shown here. The outline stitch is used on the cats' and dogs' heads in Raining Cats and Dogs, and Teatime features buttonhole stitching, outline stitching, and French knots.

French knot

Buttonhole stitch

Outline stitch

EMBROIDERY STITCH DIAGRAM

with a dry iron. Let the fabric and the web cool.

4 Cut out the shapes along the drawn lines and peel off the backing.

5 Position the appliqué shapes on the quilt and press in place with a hot dry iron according to the manufacturer's directions.

6 Using three strands of embroidery floss, stitch around the appliqué shape with the primitive stitch, as shown in DIAGRAM 14. Stitches are about ⅛ inch long and ⅛ inch apart. The primitive stitch is very quick and easy and outlines the shapes nicely.

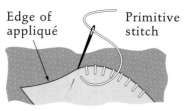

Edge of appliqué   Primitive stitch

DIAGRAM 14

Machine Appliqué

Machine appliqué is a quick and easy way to add appliqué pieces to projects without spending a lot of time doing hand stitching. Machine appliqué also stands up well to repeated washings.

You'll need a sewing machine that has a zigzag stitch setting. Set your machine to a medium-width zigzag stitch and a very short stitch length. Test this satin stitch on a scrap of fabric. Your stitches should form a band of color and they should be ⅛ to ³⁄₁₆ inch wide. If necessary, loosen the top tension slightly so the top thread is just slightly pulled to the wrong side.

The appliqué piece should be either fused, pinned, or basted to the background fabric. See Steps 1 through 4 under "Primitive Appliqué" on page 209 for instructions on using fusible web.

1 Stabilize the background fabric to give more control and eliminate puckering. You can use a sheet of typing paper or a commercial stabilizer such as Tear-Away. Pin it to the wrong side of the background fabric where you will be stitching.

2 Machine satin stitch around the edges of the appliqué pieces, covering the raw edges. Change thread colors as necessary to match the pieces. When stitching is complete, carefully tear away the stabilizer from the wrong side. You can also use a machine buttonhole stitch or other decorative stitch to stitch down the edges after fusing or stabilizing.

Squaring up Blocks

To square up your blocks, first check the seam allowances. This is usually where the problem occurs, and it is always best to alter within the block rather than trim the outer edges. Next, make sure you have pressed accurately. Sometimes a block can become distorted by overly enthusiastic pressing.

To trim up block edges, I like to use one of the many clear plastic squares available on the market. Determine the center of the block; mark it with a pin. Lay the square over the block and align as many perpendicular and horizontal lines as you can to the seams in your block. This will

3 Cut out the shapes loosely and place the rough side of the web against the wrong side of the fabric. Follow the manufacturer's directions and fuse

indicate where the block is off. Do not trim off all the excess on one side; this usually results in real distortion of the pieces in the block and the block design. Take a little off all sides until the block is square. When assembling many blocks, make sure all blocks are the same size.

Pin and sew blocks together in horizontal, vertical, or diagonal rows as directed in the instructions. Press seams between blocks in opposite directions from row to row. Join the rows, abutting the pressed seam allowances so the intersections will match perfectly.

If you are assembling a large quilt top, join rows into pairs first and then join the pairs to keep it more manageable.

Press the completed top on the wrong side first, carefully clipping and removing hanging threads. Then press the front, making sure all seams are flat.

Assembling a Quilt Top

To assemble your quilt top, refer to the QUILT ASSEMBLY DIAGRAM, the quilt photograph, and the step-by-step diagrams in each project. Lay out all the blocks, alternate blocks, and corner and side triangles as appropriate for the quilt. Position them right side up as they will be in the completed quilt.

Trimming Side and Corner Triangles

To trim oversize side and corner triangles before adding borders to a quilt, use a wide acrylic ruler, cutting mat, and rotary cutter.

• Begin at a corner first and line up your ruler ¼ inch beyond the points of the corners of the blocks, as shown in DIAGRAM 15. Lightly draw a line along the edge of the ruler. Repeat this along all four sides of the quilt top, lightly marking cutting lines.

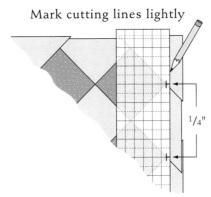

Mark cutting lines lightly

1/4"

DIAGRAM 15

• Check all the corners before you do any cutting. Make sure they are 90 degree angles. Adjust the cutting lines as needed to ensure square corners.
• When you are certain that everything is as parallel and perpendicular as it can be, line up your ruler over the quilt top. Using your marked lines as guides, cut away the excess fabric with your rotary cutter, leaving the ¼-inch seam allowance beyond the block corners (see DIAGRAM 16).

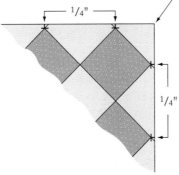

Make sure corners are 90° angles before you cut

1/4"

1/4"

DIAGRAM 16

Border Basics

For most of the quilts in this book, the borders are straight rather than mitered. At Thimbleberries, we cut most of our borders cross-grain. The exceptions are when we need a long strip of fabric to match plaids. It is generally more cost-efficient to cut crosswise, but if your quilt is very large, it may not matter. We sometimes cut the top and bottom borders cross-grain and cut the sides lengthwise. I may also cut a floral print border on the lengthwise grain to preserve the repeat of the design. My goal is to make the borders work for each individual quilt. I don't have a rigid rule.

To piece border strips, I like to use diagonal seams, which are less visible in the finished quilt than straight seams. I think diagonal seams work better for quilting, too, because they eliminate the possibility of a seam always appearing in any one spot in a quilting design. The exception to this is when I am trying to match plaids or some other printed or directional fabric which would look better with straight seams.

To sew two border strips together diagonally, place them together at a 90 degree angle with right sides together, as shown in DIAGRAM 17 on page 212. Each strip should extend ¼ inch beyond the other. Sew the strips together, taking care to start and stop your stitching precisely at the V-shaped notch where the two strips meet, as shown. Trim away the excess fabric, leaving a ¼-inch seam allowance.

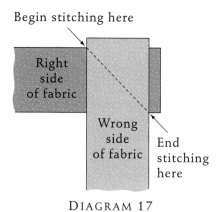

Begin stitching here

Right side of fabric

Wrong side of fabric

End stitching here

DIAGRAM 17

Tips for Plaid Borders

When cutting woven plaids cross-grain, cut along a thread. This will ensure that the plaid stays perpendicular. (When cutting other cross-grain borders, it is not necessary to cut along a thread.) If the border strips need to be longer than the width of the fabric, cut them on the lengthwise grain to avoid piecing. I think it is worth the extra expense to have a continuous plaid design uninterrupted by a seam. Seams are easier to blend when using a fabric with an overall print design.

Cut *all* border strips so they have the same plaid pattern repeat. This usually means using scissors, not a rotary cutter, and actually following the plaid thread line. Also, depending on the plaid, you may have to waste a few inches between border strips to make sure they fall on the same pattern repeat, as shown in DIAGRAM 18.

Next, remember to sew them onto the quilt in the same fashion, paying attention to which part of the plaid should go next to the quilt and which should be on the outside edge. The more complicated the plaid, the more there is to watch, as shown in DIAGRAM 19.

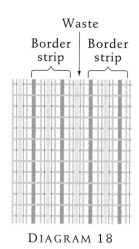

Waste

Border strip   Border strip

DIAGRAM 18

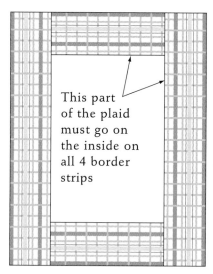

This part of the plaid must go on the inside on all 4 border strips

DIAGRAM 19

I like to take a different approach when I'm working with a plaid fabric such as the one shown in DIAGRAM 20, which has hearts in it. I would cut this fabric cross-grain with scissors, following a thread line, so I could have the hearts pointing outward and away from the center of the quilt.

All of these are guidelines rather than steadfast rules. Many quilters like the casual, unplanned look they get by cutting borders from plaids without planning the placement. This may actually be more like the antique quilts we love so much.

DIAGRAM 20

Quilting Designs

For each quilt in this book, I have made suggestions for quilting designs in the boxes called "Quilting Designs." Some projects lend themselves to very simple quilting patterns, such as outline quilting, while others are beautifully accented by cables, feathers, and floral designs. You can duplicate my designs, create your own, or choose from quilting stencils available at quilt shops or mail-order catalogs.

Marking the Quilting Design

When you're ready to mark the quilt top, choose one of the following markers. They will be visible on the fabric of your quilt and can be brushed out or will wear away after the quilting is completed. Make sure you make your lines very light, no matter what type of pencil you use.

• Quilter's silver pencils
• An artist's white pencil
• Chalk pencils and powdered chalk markers

- Hard lead 0.5 millimeter pencil
- Thin slivers of hand soap

To mark a quilting design, use a commercially made stencil, make your own stencil, or trace the design from a printed source.

If your marks will stay visible for a long time, mark the entire quilt top before layering. If you are using a powdered chalk marker or a chalk pencil, you will need to mark the quilting lines just before quilting them (after you've layered and basted).

Quilt Backings

Many of the quilts in this book are large enough to need pieced backings. There are instructions for the quilt back in each of the projects. I usually don't put the seam down the center of the quilt. I often put the seam off to one side so that I have a larger piece of leftover fabric.

Cut off all selvage edges from the backing fabric before sewing. Sew the pieces together with a ¼-inch seam allowance, and press these seams open. The

backing will lie flatter, and it will be easier to quilt through the seam area if the seam is open rather than pressed to one side.

When it is sewn together, the backing should be larger than your completed quilt top so that there is a 2-inch margin of backing and batting on each side of the quilt. This will accommodate the natural tendency of these layers to "shrink," or draw up, during the quilting process.

Quilt Battings

There are many wonderful choices when it comes to the middle layer of your quilt. We use a lightweight batting, such as a polyester light batting, for hand quilting. It resembles soft, old quilts, and I can get nicer quilting stitches with a light polyester batting. For machine quilting, we also use polyester light batting.

Whatever batting you use, make sure to take it out of the plastic bag and let it rest for a day or two before layering, to let it breathe, get the loft up, and get any wrinkles out. Or you can put it in your dryer on the air-only cycle for 10 to 15 minutes.

Layering and Basting

The quilt top, batting, and backing layers must be anchored securely so that the finished quilt will lie flat and smooth. To prepare the quilt sandwich for quilting in a hoop, place the pressed backing right side down, and position the batting on top of it, smoothing out any wrinkled spots. To keep the backing taut, use masking tape at the corners or clamp it to a table with large binder clips.

Place the quilt top over the batting, right side up. Make sure it is centered, and smooth out any wrinkles. Remove any loose or hanging threads. The backing and batting should be at least 2 inches larger than the quilt top on all four sides.

Baste these three layers together with white thread so there won't be any residue of color left in your quilt when the thread is removed. Begin in the middle of the quilt and baste a grid of horizontal and vertical rows that are approximately 4 to 6 inches apart. Use a long darning needle or even a 3-inch dollmaking needle to make the stitching go faster. Thread a few needles in advance with very long lengths of thread.

To use a large floor frame in which the quilt is stretched out to its full dimensions, attach the backing first. Some old frames allow you to use tacks, while some require pinning to a muslin sleeve on the frame. Make sure the batting is nice and taut. Then lay the batting on. Smooth it out and position the quilt top over it. Make sure it is stretched slightly to create some tension for a smooth quilting surface. Tack or pin to the frame.

For machine quilting, use 1-inch-long rustproof, nickel-plated safety pins to baste a quilt sandwich together. Pin from the center outward, approximately every 3 inches, taking care not to place the pins where you intend to quilt.

Quilting

Under "Quilting Designs" in each project, you'll see whether each project is suitable for hand quilting, machine quilting, or both. However you decide to quilt your projects, the tips that follow will be helpful.

Choosing Thread Color for Quilting

Most quilters choose a neutral color thread; white and off-white are the most common, but complementary or contrasting threads are also effective. My preference is to match thread as closely as possible to the general tone of the fabrics in the quilt, because I like to see the texture created by quilting, rather than the color of a contrasting thread. I often change thread colors to match the fabrics in a quilt top so that the thread is not such a stark contrast between one area and another. For machine quilting, I like to use a neutral color in the bobbin and change the top thread to match the fabric of the quilt top. There is a lot of thread laid down in machine quilting, and a contrasting color can affect the overall color of a quilt. The more you match the thread, the less it affects the colors of your quilt. It hides little glitches in your stitching, too.

Hand Quilting

• Use a hoop or frame to keep tension on the quilt as you stitch. To insert the quilt into the hoop, place the quilt over the smaller, inner hoop and then place the larger, outer hoop over the quilt. Adjust the top hoop so that there is even tension on the quilt. Do not keep the tension so tight that it makes stitching difficult.
• Use short quilting needles, called betweens, in size 9 or 10.
• Use 100 percent cotton or cotton-covered polyester quilting thread.
• Start with an 18-inch length of quilting thread. This will be long enough to keep you going for a while but not long enough to tangle easily.
• With knotted thread, insert the needle through the top and batting about ½ inch away from the place where you will begin your quilting. Bring the needle to the surface in position to make the first stitch. Gently tug on the thread to "pop" the knot through the top and bury it in the batting, as shown in DIAGRAM 21.

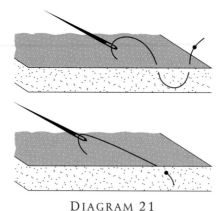

DIAGRAM 21

• Quilt by making running stitches about ¹⁄₁₆ to ⅛ inch long through all the layers. Use a thimble to push the needle down until you feel the tip of the needle with your

finger underneath. Then guide the needle back up through the quilt. As you begin to feel comfortable with this "rocking" technique, you may like taking more stitches at one time. Try to keep the stitches straight and even. This is more important than tiny stitches.
• To end a thread, place your needle close to your last stitch, parallel to the quilt, and wind the thread around it two or three times. Insert the tip of the needle through the quilt top and batting only, at the correct stitch length, and bring the needle out approximately ½ inch away from the quilting line. Gently tug the thread to "pop" the knot through the quilt top so that it lodges in the batting layer, and clip it close to the quilt top.

Machine Quilting

We use 100 percent cotton thread for machine quilting, or sometimes cotton-wrapped polyester, but not nylon. We use a stitch length of 12 stitches per inch, which makes the quilting stitches nestle into the quilt sandwich. When cotton batting is used in machine quilted projects, it puckers up after washing, and the stitches seem almost buried.

• Use a walking foot or an even feed foot on your sewing machine for quilting straight lines. Use a darning or machine embroidery foot for free-motion or meander quilting.

• Leave long thread ends at the beginning and ending of a design so that later you can go back with a needle to knot and bury them in the batting layer. Pull the bobbin thread up to the top so that it doesn't get bunched up underneath.

• For free-motion quilting, disengage the feed dogs of your machine so you can manipulate the quilt freely. Choose continuous-line quilting designs so you won't have to lift the needle when quilting the design. Guide the quilt under the needle with both hands, working at an even pace so your stitches will be consistent in length.

Binding

Binding finishes the raw edges of the quilt, giving the edges strength and durability. The bindings are cut either cross-grain or on the bias, as specified in the each project. There is some stretch in cross-grain binding and much greater stretch in bias binding. Although bias binding will work for any quilt, it is essential for projects that have curved edges, such as Town Square Tree Skirt. Also, if you're using a plaid fabric, cutting binding strips on the bias will create a diagonal effect in the finished binding. If you cut plaid binding strips on the cross grain, you will end up with relatively boring-looking straight lines of plaid along the quilt edges.

At Thimbleberries, we make French-fold, or double-fold,

binding for all our quilts. This binding can be cut straight-grain or on the bias. Straight-grain binding can be used on all quilts except those with rounded corners or curved or scalloped edges.

We have given yardage and cutting directions for a standard binding width, but you may want to vary the width of your binding to accommodate a thicker or thinner batting. Or if you simply prefer a wider or narrower binding, see "Binding Width" on page 216. Generally, you will need the perimeter of the quilt plus 12 to 20 inches for mitering corners and ending the binding. One yard of fabric is usually enough to make binding for a large quilt. Follow the instructions below for straight-grain or bias binding. Attach the binding to the quilt as described below, mitering it at the corners.

Bias Binding

1 Cut bias strips with a rotary cutter, using the 45 degree angle on your ruler. Straighten the left edge of your fabric, as described on page 206. Align the 45 degree line on your ruler with the bottom edge of the fabric, as shown in DIAGRAM 22A, and cut along the edge of the ruler to trim off the corner. Move the ruler across the fabric, cutting parallel strips in the needed width, as shown in DIAGRAM 22B.

2 Join the strips, right sides together, as shown in DIAGRAM 23, and stitch, using a ¼-inch seam allowance. Start and stop exactly at the V notch of the two strips. Press the seam open. Continue adding strips as needed.

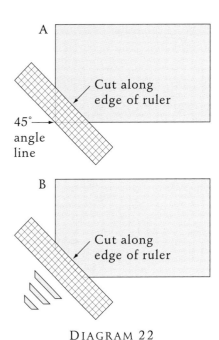

DIAGRAM 22

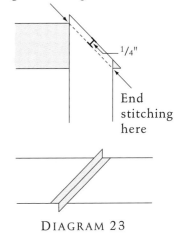

DIAGRAM 23

Straight-Grain Binding

1 Cut the needed number of strips as specified in the project instructions. Cut straight strips across the fabric width.

2 Join the strips using diagonal seams. Place two border strips together at a 90 degree angle with right sides together, as shown in DIAGRAM 24. Each strip should extend ¼ inch

beyond the other. Stitch across diagonally, making sure to start and end your stitching precisely at the V notch of the two strips.

3 Trim off the excess to leave a ¼-inch seam allowance. Press the seam open.

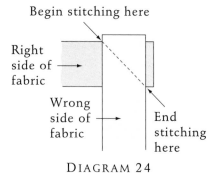

DIAGRAM 24

Binding Width

To figure out how wide to cut your binding, multiply the desired width of the binding by 6. For example, for a ½-inch finished binding, multiply ½ by 6, which means you need to cut a 3-inch-wide strip. If you are using a thicker batting, you may need to add another ¼ to ½ inch. Recalculate yardage requirements if you decide to make a binding wider than the project directions specify. I always cut a sample binding and try it to see if it works—it should cover the edge and fold to the back easily. Sometimes the batting thickness really does affect the width of the binding.

Preparing a Quilt for Binding

1 Use a large see-through ruler or square to square up and trim away the excess batting and backing even with the quilt top.

2 Securely hand baste all three layers together a scant ¼ inch from the raw edges to keep the layers from shifting and prevent puckers from forming.

Attaching the Binding

1 After the binding strips are sewn together, fold them in half lengthwise, wrong sides together, and press.

2 Unfold and cut the beginning end at a 45 degree angle. Press the edge under ¼ inch. Refold the strip.

3 Begin attaching the binding along the bottom lower left side. Do not begin binding at a corner.

4 With raw edges of the binding and quilt top even, start stitching about 2 inches from the diagonal cut end, using a ⅜-inch seam allowance. Stop stitching ⅜ inch from the corner.

5 Clip the thread and remove the quilt from under the presser foot.

6 Fold the binding strip up and away from the corner of the quilt, forming a 45 degree angle, as shown in DIAGRAM 25A. Then refold the binding down even with the raw edge of the quilt, as shown in DIAGRAM 25B. Begin sewing at the upper edge, as shown. Miter all four corners in this manner.

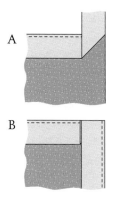

DIAGRAM 25

7 As you approach the point where you started, trim the end of the binding, making sure the end is long enough to tuck inside the beginning of the binding and that the two ends overlap about ⅜ inch. Stitch the remaining binding to the quilt.

8 Turn the folded edge of the binding over to the back side of the quilt, covering the stitching line. Hand sew the binding in place, folding in the mitered corners as you go. Add several stitches to the folds of the miters on both the front and back to hold them in place, as shown in DIAGRAM 26.

DIAGRAM 26

INDEX

METRIC EQUIVALENCY CHART

mm=millimeters
cm=centimeters

Yards to Meters

YARDS	METERS	YARDS	METERS	YARDS	METERS	YARDS	METERS	YARDS	METERS
1/8	0.11	2 1/8	1.94	4 1/8	3.77	6 1/8	5.60	8 1/8	7.43
1/4	0.23	2 1/4	2.06	4 1/4	3.89	6 1/4	5.72	8 1/4	7.54
3/8	0.34	2 3/8	2.17	4 3/8	4.00	6 3/8	5.83	8 3/8	7.66
1/2	0.46	2 1/2	2.29	4 1/2	4.11	6 1/2	5.94	8 1/2	7.77
5/8	0.57	2 5/8	2.40	4 5/8	4.23	6 5/8	6.06	8 5/8	7.89
3/4	0.69	2 3/4	2.51	4 3/4	4.34	6 3/4	6.17	8 3/4	8.00
7/8	0.80	2 7/8	2.63	4 7/8	4.46	6 7/8	6.29	8 7/8	8.12
1	0.91	3	2.74	5	4.57	7	6.40	9	8.23
1 1/8	1.03	3 1/8	2.86	5 1/8	4.69	7 1/8	6.52	9 1/8	8.34
1 1/4	1.14	3 1/4	2.97	5 1/4	4.80	7 1/4	6.63	9 1/4	8.46
1 3/8	1.26	3 3/8	3.09	5 3/8	4.91	7 3/8	6.74	9 3/8	8.57
1 1/2	1.37	3 1/2	3.20	5 1/2	5.03	7 1/2	6.86	9 1/2	8.69
1 5/8	1.49	3 5/8	3.31	5 5/8	5.14	7 5/8	6.97	9 5/8	8.80
1 3/4	1.60	3 3/4	3.43	5 3/4	5.26	7 3/4	7.09	9 3/4	8.92
1 7/8	1.71	3 7/8	3.54	5 7/8	5.37	7 7/8	7.20	9 7/8	9.03
2	1.83	4	3.66	6	5.49	8	7.32	10	9.14

Inches to Millimeters and Centimeters

INCHES	MM	CM	INCHES	CM	INCHES	CM
1/8	3	0.3	9	22.9	30	76.2
1/4	6	0.6	10	25.4	31	78.7
3/8	10	1.0	11	27.9	32	81.3
1/2	13	1.3	12	30.5	33	83.8
5/8	16	1.6	13	33.0	34	86.4
3/4	19	1.9	14	35.6	35	88.9
7/8	22	2.2	15	38.1	36	91.4
1	25	2.5	16	40.6	37	94.0
1 1/4	32	3.2	17	43.2	38	96.5
1 1/2	38	3.8	18	45.7	39	99.1
1 3/4	44	4.4	19	48.3	40	101.6
2	51	5.1	20	50.8	41	104.1
2 1/2	64	6.4	21	53.3	42	106.7
3	76	7.6	22	55.9	43	109.2
3 1/2	89	8.9	23	58.4	44	111.8
4	102	10.2	24	61.0	45	114.3
4 1/2	114	11.4	25	63.5	46	116.8
5	127	12.7	26	66.0	47	119.4
6	152	15.2	27	68.6	48	121.9
7	178	17.8	28	71.1	49	124.5
8	203	20.3	29	73.7	50	127.0